...For Dummies
BESTSELLING BOOK SERIES

Australian & New Zealand
Wine For Dummies

CW00384341

Famous Varieties from the Major Wine Regions

Country	Grape Variety	Wine Region
Australia	Botrytised Semillon	Riverina (Chapter 8)
	Cabernet Sauvignon	Coonawarra (Chapter 19)
		Margaret River (Chapter 22)
		Yarra Valley (Chapter 10)
	Chardonnay	Margaret River (Chapter 22)
		Mornington Peninsula (Chapter 13)
		Yarra Valley (Chapter 10)
	Marsanne	Goulburn Valley (Chapter 11)
	Pinot Noir	Bellarine Peninsula (Chapter 13)
		Tasmania (Chapter 15)
		Yarra Valley (Chapter 10)
	Riesling	Clare Valley (Chapter 18)
		Great Southern (Chapter 23)
		Tasmania (Chapter 15)
	Semillon	Hunter Valley (Chapter 5)
	Shiraz	Barossa Valley (Chapter 18)
		Goulburn Valley (Chapter 11)
		Heathcote (Chapter 11)
		Hunter Valley (Chapter 5)
		McLaren Vale (Chapter 16)
	Viognier	Goulburn Valley (Chapter 11)
New Zealand	Cabernet Sauvignon	Auckland (Chapter 24)
	Chardonnay	Auckland (Chapter 24)
		Hawke's Bay (Chapter 24)
	Merlot	Auckland (Chapter 24)
		Hawke's Bay (Chapter 24)
	Pinot Noir	Marlborough (Chapter 25)
		Otago (Chapter 25)
		Wairarapa (Chapter 24)
	Sauvignon Blanc	Marlborough (Chapter 25)

For Dummies®: Bestselling Book Series for Beginners

FOR DUMMIES®

BESTSELLING
BOOK SERIES

Australian & New Zealand
Wine For Dummies®

Describing Wine Styles

Australia

✔ **Cabernet Sauvignon:** From cool to mild climates, expect some leaf character, blackberry and cassis along with savoury nutty flavours. From warmer areas, the wines are fruity with lots of mulberry and blackberry flavours; full-bodied wines.

✔ **Chardonnay:** From cool regions, flavours are citrus and peaches with a good acidity; potential to age. From warm regions, expect rounded texture, pineapple and stone fruit, some honey; drink young.

✔ **Fortified Muscats and Tokays:** The specialty of the Rutherglen wine region, these luscious dessert wines show loads of tea leaf, caramel and chocolate flavours — a sheer indulgence.

✔ **Merlot:** Usually part of a blend with Cabernet Sauvignon, expect blueberry and mulberry flavours and soft tannins; medium-bodied wines.

✔ **Pinot Noir:** Soft and savoury with black cherries and dark plums, and sometimes a little mushroom; medium-bodied wines.

✔ **Riesling:** Mineral, lime and lemon, acid when young; develops texture, and honey and toast with five years or so in the bottle.

✔ **Sauvignon Blanc:** Tropical fruits; from cool regions, expect some herbal flavours; good lively acidity; drink young.

✔ **Semillon:** From the Hunter Valley, expect acid and lemon; almost bland when young but develops into a rounded toasty and honeyed wine with age; can age well for 20 years. From warm regions, Semillon is riper with stone fruit and pineapple flavours; drink young.

✔ **Shiraz:** From warm regions, expect blackberries, chocolate and liquorice with loads of alcohol (usually more than 14.5 per cent). From cool regions, Shiraz is spicy, black pepper-like and has good potential to age; full- to very full-bodied wines.

✔ **Sparkling red:** An oddity in the Australian wine scene, this red is made using the sparkling winemaking techniques used in sparkling white (Champagne method) — usually from Shiraz but, occasionally Cabernet Franc or Cabernet Sauvignon; very fruity with loads of flavours, occasionally a bit sweet and with the added difference of the bubbles.

New Zealand

✔ **Chardonnay:** Toasty and peachy with an oatmeal character, quite textural and with reasonable acid to lift the finish of the flavour; can age well, up to six or so years.

✔ **Pinot Noir:** Fruit dominant, dark and red cherries, black plums, occasionally some stewed beetroot; medium- to almost full-bodied, such is the ripeness sometimes in the Otago and Wairarapa wine regions.

✔ **Riesling:** Citrus with lemon. Lime and orange being dominant, reasonable acidity, refreshing; usually best when young but can age to around five years.

✔ **Sauvignon Blanc:** Herbal, sometimes grassy, Chinese gooseberries, refreshing, high acidity; extremely popular the world wide; drink young.

Copyright © 2004 Wiley Publishing Australia Pty Ltd. All rights reserved.
For more information about Wiley Publishing Australia Pty Ltd, email: dummies@johnwiley.com.au
Wiley, the Wiley logo, For Dummies, the For Dummies Best Selling Book series and design, and related
trade dress are trademarks or registered trademarks of John Wiley & Sons, Inc. and/or its affiliates in the United States and other countries.
All other trademarks are the property of their respective owners.

For Dummies®: Bestselling Book Series for Beginners

Australian & New Zealand
Wine
FOR
DUMMIES®

Australian & New Zealand Wine

FOR DUMMIES®

By Maryann Egan

WILEY

Wiley Publishing Australia Pty Ltd

Australian & New Zealand Wine For Dummies®

Published 2004 by
Wiley Publishing Australia Pty Ltd
33 Park Road
Milton, Qld 4064
www.dummies.com.au

Offices also in Sydney and Melbourne

Copyright © 2004 Wiley Publishing Australia Pty Ltd

National Library of Australia

Cataloguing-in-Publication data

Egan, Maryann.
   Australian & New Zealand Wine for Dummies.

   Australian and N.Z. ed.

   Includes index.

   ISBN 1 74031 008 X.

   1. Wine and winemaking – Australia. 2. Wine and winemaking – New Zealand.

   I. Title. (Series: For Dummies).

641.22

All rights reserved. No part of this book, including interior design, cover design and icons, may be reproduced or transmitted in any form, by any means (electronic, photocopying, recording or otherwise) without the prior written permission of the Publisher. Requests to the Publisher for permission should be addressed to the Legal Department, Wiley Publishing, Inc., 10475 Crosspoint Blvd., Indianapolis, Indiana, 46256, United States, 317-572-3447, fax 317-572-4447, or email brandreview@wiley.com.

Front cover images: © Corbis Corporation (vineyard); © PhotoDisc, Inc. (wine glass)

Printed in Australia by
McPherson's Printing Group
10 9 8 7 6 5 4 3 2 1

Limit of Liability/Disclaimer of Warranty: THE PUBLISHER AND AUTHORS HAVE USED THEIR BEST EFFORTS IN PREPARING THIS BOOK. THE PUBLISHER AND AUTHORS MAKE NO REPRESENTATIONS OR WARRANTIES WITH RESPECT TO THE ACCURACY OR COMPLETENESS OF THE CONTENTS OF THIS BOOK AND SPECIFICALLY DISCLAIM ANY IMPLIED WARRANTIES OF MERCHANTABILITY OR FITNESS FOR A PARTICULAR PURPOSE. THERE ARE NO WARRANTIES WHICH EXTEND BEYOND THE DESCRIPTIONS CONTAINED IN THIS PARAGRAPH. NO WARRANTY MAY BE CREATED OR EXTENDED BY SALES REPRESENTATIVES OR WRITTEN SALES MATERIALS. THE ACCURACY AND COMPLETENESS OF THE INFORMATION PROVIDED HEREIN AND THE OPINIONS STATED HEREIN ARE NOT GUARANTEED OR WARRANTED TO PRODUCE ANY PARTICULAR RESULTS, AND THE ADVICE AND STRATEGIES CONTAINED HEREIN MAY NOT BE SUITABLE FOR EVERY INDIVIDUAL. NEITHER THE PUBLISHER NOR AUTHORS SHALL BE LIABLE FOR ANY LOSS OF PROFIT OR ANY OTHER COMMERCIAL DAMAGES, INCLUDING BUT NOT LIMITED TO SPECIAL, INCIDENTAL, CONSEQUENTIAL OR OTHER DAMAGES.

Trademarks: Wiley, the Wiley logo, For Dummies, the Dummies Man logo, A Reference for the Rest of Us!, and related trade dress are trademarks or registered trademarks of John Wiley & Sons, Inc. and/or its affiliates in the United States and other countries, and may not be used without written permission. All other trademarks are the property of their respective owners. Wiley Publishing Australia Pty Ltd is not associated with any product or vendor mentioned in this book.

About the Author

Maryann Egan is the wine writer for *donna hay magazine*, a leading food magazine in Australia. Also, she lectured in the wine appraisal course for the Charles Sturt Oenology Degree.

For Maryann, life began among the vines and wine when, in 1963, her father established Wantirna Estate vineyard in the Yarra Valley, Victoria, Australia. Growing up with a wine-mad family (traipsing through the vineyards of Europe for holidays) prepared her for a life in the wine business. Wantirna is now her main focus.

Wantirna Estate is tiny in comparison with some of the huge Australian wine businesses but size doesn't have to count. Her father primarily looks after the vines, Maryann looks after the wines and her mother looks after the computer stuff.

The winery makes four wines, each proudly named after a granddaughter — Isabella Chardonnay, Lily Pinot Noir, Amelia Cabernet Merlot and Hannah Cabernet Franc. The family aims to make the absolute best wine possible and, in doing so, spends a lot of time in the vineyard maximising the potential quality of the fruit.

Maryann's work experience in the wine industry began after completing a physical education degree. Backpacking on a trip to Europe, she worked a vintage in Burgundy with Sophie Confuron at Jean Jacques Confuron in Premauz-Prissey, France. A year in Paris learning French followed.

On returning to Australia, she traded physical education for a degree in oenology (more commonly known as wine science), at Charles Sturt University in Wagga Wagga, New South Wales.

Maryann then worked for a few years at the family winery, interspersed with vintages in the NSW Hunter Valley winery, Tyrrell's Wines, and in Bordeaux, France, in the Médoc wine region.

She returned to Australia to take up a winemaking position with Domaine Chandon in the Yarra Valley, where she remained for almost six years as a winemaker before leaving to have her first daughter.

Maryann became a regular contributor to the *Australian Gourmet Traveller Wine* magazine and was a member of the magazine's main tasting panel. As part of this role, she was a judge for the prestigious 'The *Wine Magazine* Winemaker of the Year' award.

During 1998 and 2000, tapping into her extensive wine industry knowledge, Maryann worked as a presenter for the SBS production, 'The Wine Lovers' Guide to Australia'. The first series won the bronze award for the best wine television program/segment at the 1999 World Food Media Awards. Covering the diversity of people within the wine industry, she shared fascinating stories about the migrant families, their reasons for making particular styles of wine and how the wine industry evolved. The program also focused on all the main wine regions of Australia and New Zealand.

Maryann Egan is married to Justin Robison. They have two children, Amelia and Hannah. When not making wine you can find Maryann and her family working on their half-renovated house, on the slopes of whatever mountain has a big pile of fresh snow or taking surfing lessons from her young nieces!

Author's Acknowledgments

Wine is one of my main loves in life. A night without wine seems incomplete, although I do try for a night a week when I don't open a bottle. And so many people have encouraged this love. Obviously, my parents were the ones to start this passion and the countryside of Europe has much credit to take, too. Just wandering through the vineyards and the divine French villages of Burgundy and Champagne, the Duoro Valley and, well, really everywhere in Europe, is enough to make you want to find a career in winemaking.

I wish to thank my friends and colleagues in the wine industry: Billa Donaldson for gently pushing me into making that first move into wine writing and Peter Forrestal, the first editor to publish me; Donna Hay, whose magazine I continue to write for; and Wayne Donaldson and Tony Jordan, whom I worked with in the early, hectic days of Domaine Chandon Australia. All have had a part in my wine career.

A special thanks to all the wineries of Australia and New Zealand that were generous with their time and wine, and were great company to share a glass or two with.

And in terms of writing *Australian & New Zealand Wine For Dummies*, thank you to Kristen Hammond who patiently demystified the *For Dummies* style of writing, Lesley Beaumont who was always there to take a phone call, and both Nicole McKenzie and Robi van Nooten for being my ever-cheerful editors.

And, finally, a very important big thank you to all those people who constantly stepped in to pick up my children from school, ferry them to all those after-school activities and feed them while I was 'doing it hard' wandering around wine regions tasting wine — my sister Elizabeth Egan, Patti Lowrey and my parents.

Dedication

This book is dedicated to my parents, Reg and Bertina Egan, who raised me on a vineyard. They took me to Europe (many times) where the world of wine and food infused into me. Also, my ever-supportive husband Justin Robison and my winemakers-to-be daughters, Amelia and Hannah.

Publisher's Acknowledgments

We're proud of this book; please register your comments through our Online Registration Form located at www.dummies.com.

Some of the people who helped bring this book to market include the following:

Acquisitions, Development and Editorial

Project Editors: Robi van Nooten, On-Track Editorial Services

Acquisitions Editor: Lesley Beaumont

Developmental Editors: Liz Goodman, Kristen Hammond, Nicole McKenzie, Robi van Nooten

Managing Editor: Peter Storer

Proofreader: Jenny Scepanovic

Indexer: Jo Rudd

Production

Layout: Wiley Production Team

Map art: Margaret Hastie, Ikon Computergraphics

Cartoons: Alan Moir, www.moir.com.au

Contents at a Glance

Table of Contents

Introduction

E ven as little as ten years ago, people around the world were just coming to terms with the thought of Australia and New Zealand being serious wine-producing countries. Probably parts of the world are still surprised by the sheer enormity of hectares that are planted to vines across the agricultural parts of both countries. The fact is, Australia is now the sixth biggest wine-producing country in the world.

Added to the size of the industries is the fact that the quality of the wine is extremely high, and this parameter continues to have its limits pushed. Each year the wines get better; the wines at the low price-point end of the market continue to surprise the critics with terrific value for money offerings and, in the higher-price end, the wines just get more complex, subtle and alluring. In both countries wine drinkers recognise the importance of the regions. No longer do the wines simply come from Australia or New Zealand. Instead, wine buyers celebrate the regional differences. For example, when choosing a bottle of Pinot Noir, wine drinkers are likely to specify the region when asking for a Pinot Noir from say the Yarra Valley in Australia or Central Otago in New Zealand.

The world of wine in both countries is very fluid, with new and exciting developments all the time. So-called new varieties are embraced, with the current passion being for Italian varietals such as Sangiovese and Nebbiolo. This passion is likely to soon spread into the Spanish Tempranillo and a Portugese varietal or two will no doubt pop up as well. And, if you're a wine tourist, then you and these countries are a match made in heaven. The landscape is scattered with winery cellar doors (see the maps throughout) where you can sip away, restaurants where you can dine and sip and hotels where you can dine, sip and sleep the day and night away. Definitely an appealing pastime.

About This Book

When I started writing this book, my thought was to give you a brief overview of the wine regions across these beautiful countries. The diversity across the countries, however, meant that the quick overview turned into something more comprehensive and I found myself researching the regions, by foot. Well, someone had to do it and as I hadn't actually visited all the wine regions, now was a good time. So I spent a few glorious autumn days in the Clare Valley, a few wintery days up in the Canberra and Hilltops region and I extended my skiing break to include the Alpine and King Valleys. I also revisited and updated my favourite places, like Margaret River, the Adelaide Hills and my closer-to-home Victorian regions of the Grampians, Yarra and Mornington and Bellarine Peninsulas. Then of course I took the trip over to New Zealand, where the landscape is breathtaking and the wines are wonderful!

By setting out this book region by region, I hope to inspire you to visit a few wine regions — new ones and your old favs. You can plan any holidays easily or you can go on a tasting tour via your wine shop, picking and choosing wines from a region, and assessing the characteristics that a Chardonnay, for example, may have when produced in the Yarra Valley versus a Chardonnay produced in Margaret River. And, given the enormity of the countries and the breadth across which vineyards are planted, this approach works sensibly, too.

Each section gives a bit of local knowledge and then slips into the climatic conditions of the region and the how, why and what the climate means to the varieties and wines made in the area.

I mention many wineries and, of course, many are omitted because of the sheer number of each country's wine industries. Out of the featured wineries, many different labels come from a single wine company and, again, covering them all would be impossible. Added to the sheer number is the ever-changing range of wines. Only yesterday I received wine samples from three different wine companies that have added yet another new brand to their portfolios. So, even for a 'wine' person, being right up to date with the comings and goings within the industry is tricky. I hope you understand that if your favourite wine didn't make a listing, or if its listing is brief. As much as possible, I offer wines both from the big companies and the small 'boutique' companies, as well as everything in between.

How to Use This Book

Know very little about Australian or New Zealand wines? If you choose to read *Australian & New Zealand Wine For Dummies* from the beginning (which you certainly don't have to do), you'll find all the basics you need to increase your wine knowledge laid out in a logical and clear way.

Or, if you want just the highlights — the pick of the crop from a particular region, for example — you can turn to the part that covers your immediate interest. You can use the maps to find the location of wineries with cellar doors for that weekend away or that longer vacation to a wine region in another state. You can also scan the table of contents or check the index if you have a specific topic in mind.

Certain conventions make using this book easier for you, as well. For example, every time I use a new term or an important phrase, I put the term in *italics* and then immediately tell you what it means.

(For basic information about wine such as how it's made or how to taste it, pick up a copy of *Wine For Dummies*, 3rd Edition, published by Wiley Inc.)

Foolish Assumptions

Feeling intimidated about your current knowledge of wines? Don't be. In this book, I assume that you know basically nothing about wine or that you want to add some top drops to your cellar, and I'm here to help you along the way.

Here are just some of the questions I assume you may want answers for:

- ✔ Why does a particular wine region grow mostly Chardonnay?
- ✔ What does the information on the label mean, especially the little gold medal stickers?
- ✔ Why do I like this wine and not that one, and why does my tongue instantly react to this red but not that one?
- ✔ How can I get a hold of that wine if I live in another state or country?
- ✔ What do all those curious descriptions about a wine's 'nose' mean anyway?

As you thumb through *Australian & New Zealand Wine For Dummies,* you're sure to find the answers to these questions and so many more.

How This Book Is Organised

This book is organised into six parts and an appendix. The following sections describe the type of information in each part.

Part I: The Big Wine Picture Down in Australia and New Zealand

In these four chapters I give a great overview of the current play in the wine industries of both New Zealand and Australia. You find out about the major grapes varieties, where they're planted and what those blurbs and words on the labels actually mean. You find out all about the ways and means to buy and try the wines of Australia and New Zealand.

Part II: Heading to North Oz for the Wine: New South Wales and Queensland

This part looks at the regions of New South Wales and Queensland. I cover the wines of the most famous region in New South Wales — the Hunter Valley. I take you to Mudgee where the reds dominate, and the lesser-known regions of Orange, Cowra, Hilltops and Canberra. I discuss the home of the famous, intense-flavoured, dessert-style wines of Griffith and then take you to the lesser known and smaller wine industry of Queensland.

Part III: Victoria and Tasmania: Something Devilish about Those Wines

My home state of Victoria is a part of this section, with my home in the Yarra Valley. The winegrowing regions in the Central Victoria zone are featured — Heathcote, the Goulburn Valley and the Pyrenees — where you find reference to the full-bodied Shiraz. A discussion on wines from the Northern Victoria wine zone includes the Rutherglen region, which is home to those super-delicious Muscats and Tokays, and the King and Alpine regions, which are forging ahead with the Italian varietals. And the vineyards up on the Murray River reveal lots of grapes grown on irrigated vineyards.

I cover two small regions that are close to the city of Melbourne — Sunbury and Macedon — and the seaside vineyards of the Mornington and Bellarine Peninsulas, and Gippsland with their maritime climate wines.

Then, the small but incredibly beautiful Tasmanian wine scene, where the Pinot Noirs are worth looking out for, rounds out this part.

Part IV: The Wine Regions of South Australia and Western Australia

Out of all the wines that you come across in the bottle shop, the greatest percentage is grown in South Australia. Think of the famous regions of McLaren Vale, Barossa Valley and Coonawarra. But also remember that the Riverland region, up on the Murray River, is a part of South Australia. Although the other regions might be known for their wines of high quality and with high prices to match, the Riverland produces an awful lot of grapes that go into making the backbone of many an inexpensive Australian wine.

Small vineyards dominate the Western Australian wine industry — the antithesis of the Riverland — where the average price per bottle is a whole lot more expensive than those wines from the Riverland.

Part V: New Zealand Wines

All you need to know about the wonderful wine regions of New Zealand is in this section. A tour of the North Island includes the vineyards that are planted on an island near Auckland, the large region of Gisborne and the wonderful wines of Wairarapa (or 'Martinborough' as so many of us know this region by). I move to the cooler South Island and the ever-increasing size and prestige region of Marlborough, the small but high quality Nelson and Canterbury regions and the extremely highly regarded Central Otago region, where Pinot Noir is the reigning variety.

Part VI: The Part of Tens

The fun part of all *For Dummies* books, this part gives you quick access to my top-ten lists. In the age of computers, technology and the Internet, I give you my ten favourite Web sites — all favourites for quite different reasons. This diversity flows through into my selection of my ten favourite cellar doors — some are big and glitzy, others small and charming. And my final indulgence features ten wines that I think are terrific, again for different reasons.

Appendix

The appendix features a collection of useful bits and pieces. You can check out where to find the weekly news from the wine people. You also find a guide to some of the glossy magazines that have wine columns, and if you'd like a guide or two to give you wine ratings I give you a hint to some of the best in Australia and New Zealand.

Icons Used in This Book

To help you with your wine-discovery journey through this book, the following list explains what each icon (the little pictures that sit in the margins) means.

A bit of advice that's worth knowing (such as how long to cellar a wine), so that you can enjoy the wines and the wine regions even more.

This icon reiterates some fundamental information that's important in understanding the world of wine. By using this icon I want to remind you that the subject matter has an effect on the wines and vineyards. I'm not simply repeating myself because I have a bad memory!

Well, I'm a winemaker, so sometimes I wander off into technical explanations. Where you see this icon, feel free to skip over the technical information that follows (the wine will still taste just as delicious) or, if you aspire to wine-geek status, these bits are for you.

You don't see this icon very often, but take notice when it does appear because the Warning icon helps you to avoid confusion or avoid a common mistake.

This clever icon points you in the direction of a handy Web site of interest.

You see this icon whenever I think that a wine is fantastic quality and, although hard to find, worth searching around the traps to find a bottle. You also see this icon whenever a wine represents really good value for the money.

Part I

The Big Wine Picture Down in Australia and New Zealand

www.moir.com.au   *Alan Moir*

In this part . . .

Established winemaking countries such as Australia and New Zealand are now almost sinking under the weight of the new vineyards being planted every year at a furious rate. So, not surprisingly, you now see more and more wines from Australia and New Zealand on the bottle shop shelves. As the world of wine seems to expand at a fierce rate, keeping tabs may seem tricky.

In this part, I begin to unwrap the puzzle of the wine story and take you through the wine regions, explain the varying grape varieties, take you for a quick buying spree and help you work out what the labels really mean.

Chapter 1

Australian and New Zealand Wines: A Success Story

*1*f you travelled overseas ten or fifteen years ago and asked the locals what they knew about Australia and New Zealand, you no doubt got the 'Three *S*' response — sun, surf and sheep. You can probably track this response back to the first *Crocodile Dundee* film, which projected the image of a nation of beer drinkers propping up the bar in outback pubs.

Australia and Australians are, of course, nothing like they're portrayed in the film. And New Zealand is far more than just sheep, hobbits and spectacular scenery. As for drinking beer . . . while a great deal of the amber fluid is still consumed, Australians and New Zealanders drink a lot more wine than beer. Not only are they great at drinking the stuff, but they're also great at making it. Australia and New Zealand have thriving wine industries that meet the demands of not only a thirsty local market but also a booming market overseas. In fact, both Australia and New Zealand export millions of litres of wine annually.

In a 2004 AC Nielsen survey of the 'Top Ten' most popular wines in the United Kingdom, no fewer than six of the wines were Australian. And it's not just the Brits who love Australian wine. Although sales to the United Kingdom reached AUD$72.7 million, North America retained its position as Australia's biggest overseas market by buying wine to the value of AUD$75.6 million.

A brief history of two wine industries

While the first grapevines were planted in Australia in Sydney in 1788, the first record of wine-making is 1796. The first vineyards in New Zealand date back to 1836. Due to economic depression and a preference for fortified wines around the time of the Second World War, neither country had what could be called a wine industry until the 1960s.

Until the 1970s, wine production in New Zealand was almost totally dominated by fortified wines such as Sherry and Port. Then tastes changed, and between the 1970s and the mid-1980s, the demand for fortified wines had all but been replaced by demand for table wines. However, the early table wines were predominantly sweet white wines, far removed from the huge range of sophisticated red and white wines that you can buy today. If we keep moving through this brief history, we find that it wasn't until the mid- to late-1980s that the wine industry in New Zealand found some stability. Instead of falling victim again to a boom-and-bust cycle, winemakers took advantage of firm economic conditions to build their businesses and succeeded so well that New Zealand now has an outstandingly successful wine industry.

Australia has a not dissimilar story. The warm wine regions such as the South Australian river regions and north-east Victoria were the centres of grape growing, and fortified wine dominated the wine industry until the 1950s. Gradually, diversification began in the cooler wine regions. Vines were first planted in Coonawarra around 1890 and in the Yarra in the 1850s. Coonawarra didn't expand until the 1950s, while the Yarra's early vines were pulled up early in the 1900s in favour of dairy cattle, until the Yarra began to be replanted in the late 1960s. By the mid-1970s, the phenomenon known as the 'boutique winery' had begun, as professionals — mainly doctors and lawyers — looking for a weekend escape with a difference established their own small vineyards. Today, the growth in both plantings and people wanting to make wine continues across Australia and New Zealand.

In both Australia and New Zealand, the traditional wine regions are expanding in order to meet the increased demand, and they're being joined by an ever-increasing list of emerging wine regions. More and more people in both countries are becoming winemakers and vines are being planted in increasingly diverse regions. As a result, wine drinkers all over the world are becoming fans of such outstanding wines as Australian Shiraz and Chardonnay, and New Zealand Sauvignon Blanc and Pinot Noir.

In this chapter, I introduce you to the wine styles of Australia and New Zealand, show you where the wine regions are, and draw a picture of what is happening on the wine scene in both countries. (See the sidebar 'A brief history of two wine industries' for the early story about Australian and New Zealand wines.)

Getting Acclimatised in Australia and in New Zealand

A quick look at an atlas tells you that the islands of Australia and New Zealand take up a fair amount of space on this planet. Australia occupies over seven and a half million square kilometres (the United States is over nine and a half million) and the two main islands of New Zealand together are nearly 270 square kilometres in area (larger than the United Kingdom but not quite as large as Italy). Significant variations in the weather also exist.

Australia's climate ranges from the tropical (such as the far north of Queensland) to the temperate (the island of Tasmania) so don't expect me to make sweeping comments about 'the Australian climate'. Grapes are grown in vineyards inland of Brisbane in the northern part of Australia to around Hobart on the south coast of Tasmania; the distance between the two is 1,790 kilometres. Taking an east–west perspective, you find vines very close to Sydney on the east coast and also 3,300 kilometres away in Perth on the west coast, which is home to some of the finest wine regions in the Southern Hemisphere. Between the two coasts is a lot of desert. Some wine regions are coastal, others are inland; some are very hot, some fairly cold; some are at a high altitude and some on low plains. And so on.

New Zealand is no different in its climate variations. The northern-most wine region is Northland and the southern-most is Central Otago. The distance between the two regions is over 1,000 kilometres of diverse landscape, from coastal plains to soaring snowcapped mountains. No generalisations can exist here, either. You find vineyards in sheltered maritime locations and nestling on the slopes of mountain ranges.

Meeting Growing Demand with Diverse Wines

With such diversity in both climate and landscape, not surprisingly, the wines and vines from Australia and New Zealand are also many and varied. The variety in wine production caters for almost all palates and, importantly, most pockets. The choice of what to grow also comes with no strings attached. That is, you can grow whatever grapes you like, wherever you like, with no appellation system such as the ones in Europe to prevent you from doing so. The only thing that can stop you in your winemaking tracks is making bad wine. Do that and no-one will ever buy your label again. Make wines of a consistently high quality, however, and your winery can go from strength to strength.

Statistics show what winemakers are focusing on in order to meet the growing demand worldwide. In Australia in 2003, red grapes reigned supreme in terms of the quantities grown, making up 58 per cent of the total harvest. Of this, Shiraz led the pack with 41 per cent of all red grapes grown. Next was Cabernet Sauvignon at 29 per cent. Of the white varieties, Chardonnay held top spot with 43 per cent, with Semillon in second place at 13 per cent. Broadly speaking, these are the best known Australian varieties, although there is also strong demand for Pinot Noir, Sauvignon Blanc, Merlot and Riesling, as well as a number of other varieties. In fact, the most fashionable thing happening in the wine industry in Australia at the moment is the enthusiastic reception given to varieties such as Pinot Gris, Sangiovese and Viognier.

Over in New Zealand the industry is dominated by white wine varieties, with over 67 per cent of the grapes grown in 2002 being white. The internationally famous Sauvignon Blanc was the most planted, followed by Chardonnay. Of the red varieties grown in New Zealand, the star performer in terms of quantity — and, in my view, overall consistency of quality — is Pinot Noir, which makes up 45 per cent of all the red grapes grown on the two islands. New Zealand Merlot is the second most successful red grape.

See Chapter 2 for lots of information about varieties grown in Australia and New Zealand.

From not much to quite a lot

Here are a few facts and figures to put the wine industries of Australia and New Zealand into a global perspective.

In 2002, the amount of wine that was exported from Australia was 471 million litres, and Australian consumers drank a further 397 million litres of Australian-made wine. Such high exports and local consumption explain the expansion in vineyards in Australia.

In 2003, Australia became the sixth largest wine producer in the world, producing over 1.1 million, million litres, and is the fourth largest exporter of wine. Over 45 per cent of Australian wine exports goes to the United Kingdom and 25 per cent goes to the United States.

The trend in New Zealand is also upward, albeit on a slightly smaller scale. In 2002, 89 million litres of wine were produced, up from 53.3 million in 2001 (due to a bad season of crops, 2003 was a lean year and around 65 million litres was expected).

Wine exports from New Zealand continue to climb. In 2003, exports were up 18 per cent on previous years with the United Kingdom being the biggest customer, followed by the United States. While the vast majority of wine imported into New Zealand comes from Australia, Australia returns the favour by being the third biggest importer of New Zealand wines.

The big players in Australia and New Zealand

As with most industries, the wine industry in both Australia and New Zealand is mostly in the hands of just a few major players. At the time this book went to press, five wine companies dominated the Australian wine industry. However, due to the mergers and acquisitions that take place on a regular basis, that figure may have changed. The companies involved are Southcorp Wines, the Hardy Wine Company (formerly known as BRL Hardy before the merger with the US-based Constellation Brands), Orlando Wyndham, Beringer Blass and McGuigan Simeon Wines.

Of the rest of the 1,625 listed wineries in Australia, 30 per cent produce twenty tonnes or less of grapes annually, which is fewer than 1,350 dozen bottles a year. By comparison, the Penfolds brand, owned by the Southcorp Wines group, alone produces around 1.4 million cases annually.

The scene in New Zealand is similar, albeit on a smaller scale. In total, 386 wineries are in operation. Montana Wines is the largest company, processing over 10,000 tonnes of fruit annually, which translates into rather more than 700,000 cases of wine (exact figures aren't available). Thirty-seven per cent of wineries are small boutique-style operations producing less than 20 tonnes of fruit a year.

Top of the pops: Our favourite wines

Obviously, a correlation exists between the grapes that are grown and the wine that's drunk. After all, the wine industry is like any other industry in that it responds to demand trends for its products. So just which Australian and New Zealand wines are the most popular both in their countries of origin and overseas?

In the United Kingdom, the six Australian labels that made the 'Top Ten' in the 2004 A C Nielsen survey were Nottage Hill, Jacob's Creek, Lindemans, Banrock Station, Rosemount and Wolf Blass.

Obtaining the wine you want

How you buy your wine often depends on where you live. In Europe you find wine and other alcoholic beverages sitting next to the washing powder in the supermarket. In Australia and New Zealand, you can purchase wine in a variety of ways.

For example, you can buy wine from

- A specialist wine shop or what is called a bottle shop, which can be a stand-alone business or next to a supermarket in a quite separate part of the supermarket building.
- The winery itself, either from the cellar door or via the winery's mailing list.
- The Internet, where you can buy direct from a retailer or direct from the winery and have the wine home delivered.
- A wine club where, for a monthly payment, a mixed dozen of red and white wines are delivered to your home. The agonising over which wine to choose has been taken away and you receive a dozen bottles selected by a panel of wine experts.

You keenly search for the wines of your choice (or just fortuitously bid for them at an auction raising funds for your kids' school), perhaps cellar them for a while and then decide to bring them out on show at a twenty-first-birthday bash. Perhaps you bypass the chase-and-save routine altogether, and either get advice or reach for the label information. Whichever style you fit into, I cover the tasting aspects of wine drinking in Chapter 2 and all you need to know about decoding wine labels in Chapter 3.

Getting to know the regions

As you try different wines from across Australia and New Zealand, you get to know the various wine regions. At last count, Australia has 29 wine zones. Depending on the zone, zones are then broken down into regions and, on occasion, into sub-regions. For example, six wine zones occur in the state of Victoria in Australia. One of these zones is called the Central Victoria zone and it consists of five regions. One of these regions is the Goulburn Valley region and it has a sub-region known as the Nagambie Lakes. Conversely, the island state of Tasmania has just one wine zone, although in the future I imagine the island will be broken into at least two regions.

New Zealand has ten wine regions across the two islands but as of this writing, no official delineation of sub-regions.

The rationale for regionalisation or Geographical Indications (GIs) is that because of the diversity of soil, climate and other growing conditions between the areas where grapes are grown, the wines from each region acquire their own regional style and characteristics. See Chapter 3 for more on GIs.

Getting gripped by the grape

If you've never visited Australia or New Zealand, you may be surprised to learn that most people in both countries are city dwellers. For example, a great number of Australia's 20 million people live in the cities on the narrow coastal strip down the east coast. Like city dwellers everywhere, most look for a weekend escape — perhaps an overnight stay in the country or a day trip.

The wine industry has capitalised on this desire for escape from the city, and both in Australia and in New Zealand you have the opportunity to visit wineries at what is known as the *cellar door*. Here you can taste the wine made at that vineyard, maybe meet the winemaker and if you like, purchase some bottles, too.

For many people, this may be the first time you've visited a winery and the experience sparks a heightened interest in wine. Many a wine cellar and a passion for collecting wine results from a visit to a winery. The weekend away in a wine region has very much become part of the Australian and New Zealand psyche. Consequently, the wine regions not only offer the visitor wineries and cellar doors but excellent restaurants and comfortable guesthouses.

With the increase in restaurants and places to stay, more wineries have decided to open a cellar door . . . which attracts more visitors who all need restaurants and places to stay, and so it goes. Not surprisingly then, out of the 1,625 wine producers In Australia, 1,292 have cellar doors. The state of Victoria has the greatest number with 391 cellar doors; of the 81 wine producers in Queensland, 91 per cent have a cellar door. The situation in New Zealand isn't much different; in that country, 258 of the 386 wine producers offer a cellar door.

Competing for Wine Honours in Australia

Although wheat, sheep and cattle still underpin agriculture in Australia, the ever-expanding wine industry is evident in nearly all parts of the country; even Alice Springs has a winery, though more as a novelty factor than anything else.

Most countries are divided into areas — whether they're called states, regions, counties or zones — and a certain amount of rivalry inevitably springs up between the areas. This rivalry isn't confined to football or cricket teams. Winemakers like to think that their region or zone makes the greatest wine in the country (or the world, for that matter). So, being that I come from the state of Victoria in Australia, I'm not even going to enter into a discussion on where the best wines come from. Clearly, the best wines are made in Victoria!

Having said that, I set aside my friendly bias in this section and give a brief outline of the different wine regions in Australia (see Figure 1-1 for the wine zones) . . . just don't miss the bit on the truly fantastic wines that come from Victoria.

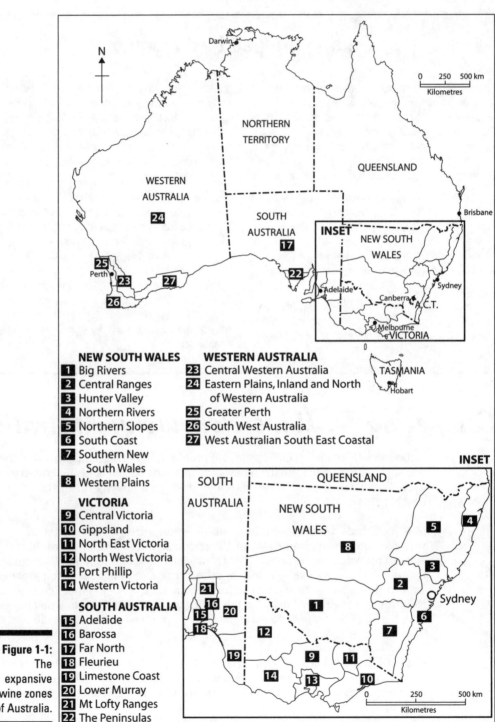

NEW SOUTH WALES
1 Big Rivers
2 Central Ranges
3 Hunter Valley
4 Northern Rivers
5 Northern Slopes
6 South Coast
7 Southern New South Wales
8 Western Plains

VICTORIA
9 Central Victoria
10 Gippsland
11 North East Victoria
12 North West Victoria
13 Port Phillip
14 Western Victoria

SOUTH AUSTRALIA
15 Adelaide
16 Barossa
17 Far North
18 Fleurieu
19 Limestone Coast
20 Lower Murray
21 Mt Lofty Ranges
22 The Peninsulas

WESTERN AUSTRALIA
23 Central Western Australia
24 Eastern Plains, Inland and North of Western Australia
25 Greater Perth
26 South West Australia
27 West Australian South East Coastal

Figure 1-1:
The expansive wine zones of Australia.

New South Wales and a little bit of Queensland

The diversity of climate and landscape in these two states is immense. The Hunter Valley region to the north of Sydney in New South Wales can be humid, dry and hot (I describe the Hunter Valley in Chapter 5). Moving west from the Hunter Valley across the Great Dividing Range brings you inland to where you find cooler nights and the thriving vineyards that surround the Mudgee region (see Chapter 6).

Head south from Mudgee and you arrive in Orange, a delightful country town with a growing and successful wine industry. I describe Orange in Chapter 7 and also discuss other, smaller wine regions such as Tumbarumba in the foothills of the Snowy Mountains, Cowra and Canberra, where the winter is bitterly cold yet the summer has long dry days. In south-west New South Wales you find the Big Rivers Zone — a Little Italy in Australia with the excellent wines you would expect (see Chapter 8).

Queensland has two main grape-growing regions, the best known being the Granite Belt region, which is a relatively cool area due to its high altitude, and the South Burnett region, inland from the Sunshine Coast. You can read about the wines of Queensland in Chapter 9.

Victoria and the emerald isle of Tasmania

From the heat of Rutherglen in the north — home to some famous and fabulous fortified wines — to the cool maritime region of the Mornington Peninsula, Victoria is quite a diverse state. Among the coolest places in the state are the Macedon Ranges, the Strathbogie Ranges and the Whitlands regions. Slightly warmer regions are the Yarra Valley and the Central Victorian High Country.

You find a huge diversity of varieties and styles of wine in Victoria, from the fortified wines and dense Durif of Rutherglen, to the top Pinot Noirs of the Yarra Valley and the rich Shiraz of Heathcote, to name just a few.

I cover the Yarra Valley region in Chapter 10, and Central Victoria, including the Heathcote, Strathbogie and the mountain regions in Chapter 11. Rutherglen, the Alpine Valley and the King Valley are just three of the wine regions I cover in Chapter 12. I describe the Mornington Peninsula and other maritime wine regions, as well as Gippsland, in Chapter 13.

In Chapter 14, we don't have to travel far from Melbourne, the capital of Victoria, to find some excellent wines. The Sunbury wine region is almost on the city fringes and Macedon is only a little further away — very handy for the weekend escape!

Then we travel across Bass Strait to the island of Tasmania where the climate is universally cool. If you enjoy Pinot Noir, aromatic whites such as Riesling and Gewürztraminer, and flavoursome Chardonnay, you should turn to Chapter 15!

The states of South and Western Australia

South Australia is responsible for nearly 50 per cent of the grapes grown in Australia, and is easily the most prolific grapegrowing state. Not surprisingly, when you're in the state, you can drive long distances where nothing but vineyards stretch away on either side.

South Australia was one of the pioneer wine regions and has some of Australia's highest temperatures. The most famous South Australian regions are McLaren Vale (Chapter 16), the Barossa Valley (Chapter 18) and the Coonawarra (Chapter 19).

Without a doubt, South Australia's famous grape is Shiraz, a red grape that enjoys the conditions in that state, with Cabernet Sauvignon from the Coonawarra a close contender for the title of 'best grape'. Of the white wines from South Australia, Riesling from the Clare and Eden Valleys are the best known (see Chapter 18). South Australia is also home to the Riverland, the huge, flat expanse of land where grapes are grown for the mass market (I describe the Riverland in Chapter 20).

Many of the great vineyards of Western Australia are close to the beach, some even have views of the surf. While only 3 per cent of Australia's wine is produced in Western Australia, that wine is mostly at the premium end of the market and has a large following overseas.

Residents of Perth, the capital city of Western Australia, don't have to travel far to visit a winery. Some of the oldest vines can be found in the Swan Valley on the city's doorstep (see Chapter 21) and in the hills behind Perth you can find newer vineyards and wineries. Also close enough for a day trip are the vineyards south of Perth. A bit further on, you come to what is probably the best known wine region in Western Australia, Margaret River. Famous for its Cabernet Sauvignon and Chardonnay, you can read about this wine region and others in Chapter 22. The wines of the diverse Great Southern region are also making their mark (see Chapter 23).

Growing from Strength to Strength in New Zealand

New Zealand's wine boom may have started later than Australia's, but boom and grow it does to catch up with the neighbours. Both islands of New Zealand have experienced amazing growth over the past ten years or so. In 1992, the country had as few as 160 wine producers; ten years later that figure had grown to 373. In terms of the amount of land now dedicated to vineyards: in 1992, around 6,000 hectares were planted to vines, which, by the end of 2002, had grown to nearly 16,000.

Marlborough, at the northern part of the South Island, is New Zealand's largest grape-growing region. Hawke's Bay and Gisborne, both on the North Island of New Zealand, are the second and third largest regions respectively.

You can't go past the Sauvignon Blanc produced in New Zealand, though you would be well advised to take note of the Pinot Noir, which is getting more and more attention. Grapegrowing conditions across the country are so diverse that the harvest time of the same grape variety can vary by almost two months, depending on where the variety is grown.

Exploring the North Island

Six of the ten regions in New Zealand are in the North Island, where they start in the north with the appropriately named Northland region and reach right down to the south of the island and Wairarapa region. The famous Hawke's Bay region, roughly in the middle of the island on the east coast, is the largest region. I take you on a tour of the North Island in Chapter 24.

White wines such as Chardonnay dominate the regions of the North Island. However, you can find some excellent Merlot around the warmer parts of Hawke's Bay. If Pinot Noir is a favourite, you can do no better than visit the Wairarapa region.

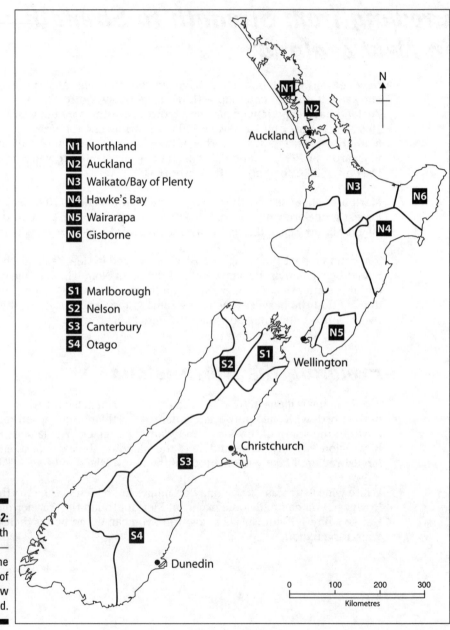

N1 Northland
N2 Auckland
N3 Waikato/Bay of Plenty
N4 Hawke's Bay
N5 Wairarapa
N6 Gisborne

S1 Marlborough
S2 Nelson
S3 Canterbury
S4 Otago

Figure 1-2: From North to South — the wine regions of New Zealand.

Tasting stunning wines in the spectacular South Island

The Marlborough region lies at the north end of the South Island and Otago is the southernmost region. In between the two is some very diverse winemaking. Especially when you realise that the vineyards of Central Otago are in the southernmost winegrowing region in the world. If you live in the Northern Hemisphere, don't forget that the next landfall south of Otago is Antarctica.

The stunning scenery of the South Island is backdrop to numerous vineyards. Marlborough is home to vast tracts of land planted largely to Sauvignon Blanc, while Pinot Noir and Chardonnay are carving out a niche for themselves in Central Otago and Canterbury. You can find all the information you want about the South Island in Chapter 25.

Tuning In to the Top of the Wine World

In today's world of technology, what would information about wine be without giving you a list of Web sites that offer more information on Australian and New Zealand wines (see Chapter 26). You also find information on how to buy wine online. Thinking that you may be interested in some of the best wines in Australia and New Zealand, I really step out and state which, in my opinion, are the ten best wines you'll find — ones that set a very high benchmark of quality and are also representative of the wines of both countries (check out Chapter 27). Chapter 28 is a kind of natural progression from Chapter 27: I recommend some of the best cellar doors in Australia and New Zealand, where you can sample some of the best wines in some of the most spectacular settings.

Tucked away near the end of this book you find an appendix, which directs you to the best newspapers, magazines and books for widening your knowledge about Australian and New Zealand wines.

Throughout this book, I recommend a number of wines — wines that are outstanding for either their quality or reasonable price, or both. Such wines are, of course, much in demand and inevitably, from time to time, demand outstrips supply. If you find that the wine of your choice is no longer available, well, the bare shelf means that you're a discriminating wine drinker! In such a case, you can contact the company that makes the wine to find out when the next vintage is due for release. You can often find the Web address of the wine company on the label; alternatively, you can usually find it through an Internet search engine by keying in the name of the company.

Chapter 2

Uncorking Australian and New Zealand Wines

*H*ere in the Antipodes we really haven't been in the winemaking game for all that long, especially if you compare our history to that of Europe. While grapevines have been planted sporadically over the years in both Australia and New Zealand, it wasn't until the 1970s that grapes really started to become a modern-day serious agricultural pursuit. Unlike in other parts of the world, wine wasn't a feature on the nightly dinner table.

Now wine in New Zealand and Australia has thrown off the image of being a drink only for celebrations and the odd exclusive restaurant. Winemakers and marketers alike are trying to involve everyone in the grip of the grape, and today wine is far more accessible to Mr and Mrs Average than it was 20 years ago. Remember, a glass of wine a day keeps the doctor away (the saying goes something like that . . . I think!).

In this chapter, I introduce you to the varieties of grapes going into the wines from these two great countries, and detail the ways you can get your hands on them — from cellar door to cyberspace and everywhere in between.

Going Grape Downunder

If you're wondering which varieties of grape are grown for Australia's and New Zealand's reds, whites, sparkling and fortified wines, you find that information in this section. I've also detailed those grapes that are growing in popularity — useful information if you want to jump on the bandwagon.

Relishing the reds

Australia makes many a fine red wine and it does so with a wide variety of grapes. But, funnily enough, Australia's most planted grape, and the most recognised one in international wine circles, is the gutsy, high-alcohol Shiraz. 'Why is that funny?' you may be thinking. Well, as recently as 1987, vineyard owners were paid to pull out their Shiraz vines. Too much wine was being made at the time and the Shiraz (and other unwanted vines) were targeted to go.

How things have changed! Those who didn't take the payout are now sitting back chuckling to themselves, because old vines are now thought to be de rigueur for high-quality Shiraz. Whack 'old vines' on a Shiraz label and it sends seasoned Shiraz drinkers, as well as many exclusive wine stores worldwide, price crazy. (The truth is that while the grapes from old vines can produce incredibly intense fruit-flavoured wines, they don't guarantee that the wine will be extraordinary. The grapes still have to be carefully managed by the winemaker to turn the wonderful fruit into great wine, and plenty of important winemaking steps exist between the vineyard and the bottle.) You can read more about labelling in Chapter 3.

Today, Shiraz is the number one planted red grape variety in Australia, and also makes up 24 per cent of the total grapes crushed across Australia — something few would have predicted as the bulldozers ran over many hectares of vines less than 20 years ago.

Cabernet Sauvignon comes in as the second most planted grape variety, with its frequent blending partner, Merlot, in third place. (See Chapter 10 and Chapter 22 for more information on the blending of these two varieties.) Pinot Noir is planted in smaller yet still significant amounts and makes up a larger proportion of the top-price end of the market.

Varieties such as Cabernet Franc and, to a lesser degree, Petit Verdot and Malbec, take up a small percentage of Australia's vineyards. Along with Cabernet Sauvignon and Merlot, these varieties make up what is known as the classic Bordeaux blend, and a move towards this style of wine is the main reason these varieties are being planted. Added to these varieties is an Italian flavour that has been slipping into our varietal mix, through Sangiovese and Barbera.

Some of the less common varieties include Ruby Cabernet, which is slowly disappearing from the vineyards, as well as others that are just beginning to find a place in Australia like Tarrango and Dolcetto and the French variety of Durif (known in the United States as Petite Sirah). Table 2-1 illustrates the extent of planting of each variety of red grape in more detail.

Table 2-1	The Main Red Grape Varieties in Australia by Number of Hectares Planted in 2004	
Variety	*Number of Hectares*	*Percentage of Total*
Shiraz	37,106	39.0%
Cabernet Sauvignon	28,171	29.5%
Merlot	10,352	11.0%
Pinot Noir	4,270	4.5%
Grenache	2,322	2.4%
Petit Verdot	1,337	1.4%
Cabernet Franc	834	0.9%
Sangiovese and Barbera	798	0.8%
Other reds	10,301	11.0%
Total red grapes	95,491	–

Source: Compiled from ABS data.

In New Zealand, only around 34 per cent of the wine produced is from red grapes — and Pinot Noir dominates (see Table 2-2). You can find some Merlot, Cabernet Sauvignon and Shiraz grapes planted but only in the warmer parts of the North Island like Hawke's Bay. (For more information on New Zealand's red wines, see Chapter 23.)

Wowing 'em with whites

New Zealand shines with its white wines, and its Sauvignon Blanc in particular is exemplary. While other countries have been making this variety for some time, New Zealand burst onto the scene with the **1985 Cloudy Bay Sauvignon Blanc** — the Cloudy Bay winery's first release of this type — and really set the scene for the country's white wines. Although much of the wine world had never even heard of New Zealand wines before this time, the 1985 Cloudy Bay beat over 60 French Sauvignon Blancs in a highly regarded tasting held in London.

White varieties make up 66 per cent of the grapes planted in New Zealand and, although Chardonnay has been the most planted variety, Sauvignon Blanc now reigns supreme, as shown in Table 2-2.

Table 2-2	The Main Red and White Grape Varieties in New Zealand by Number of Hectares Planted in 2003	
Variety	**Number of Hectares**	**Percentage of Total**
Sauvignon Blanc	4,085	28.0%
Chardonnay	3,643	24.0%
Pinot Noir	2,431	17.0%
Merlot	1,152	7.8%
Cabernet Sauvignon	800	5.4%
Riesling	606	4.0%
Pinot Gris	291	2.0%
Other varieties	1,794	12.0%

Source: Compiled from NZ Winegrowers Annual Survey data.

Much of Australia and New Zealand's early wine success in the export markets of the United Kingdom and the United States has been through their well-priced whites. Labels such as the **Montana Sauvignon Blanc** from New Zealand and **Lindemans Bin 65 Chardonnay** from Australia really began the introduction of wines from the Antipodes to the rest of the world, and the rest is history. Australia now ranks sixth in the world in terms of volume of wine production, even though it makes up only a mere 3.8 per cent. Unfortunately, New Zealand doesn't make the statistics — yet.

If you're wondering, the top four wine producers in the world are France (20.2 per cent), Italy (18.8 per cent), Spain (11.5 per cent) and the United States (7.3 per cent).

In Australia, Chardonnay continues to dominate, which is primarily due to its versatility. No other grape variety seems to handle so many different growing conditions and reflect each in a variety of flavours. Way behind in actual numbers of tonnes harvested in Australia are Semillon, Riesling and Sauvignon Blanc. These grapes are often bottled as 100 per cent pure, but you do see blends such as Semillon *and* Sauvignon Blanc.

Also produced is a mixed bag of varieties that are mostly used for blending and are at the lower end of the price market, such as Colombard, Chenin Blanc and Sultana (or *Thompson's Seedless*, the name for the grape in the United States). Yes, the humble Sultana grape is the backbone of many a cask wine (known as *jug wine* in the United States). And while the number of hectares of sultana grapes grown is decreasing every year, sultana grapes still take up significant space in the vineyards, as you see in Table 2-3.

Making gains in areas already planted are the glamour grape varieties — the so-called new varieties that have been grown in Europe for decades. These grapes fall into the 'Other white varieties' shown in Table 2.3, and include

✔ **Pinot Gris.** Also known as Pinot Grigio in Italy, this variety is related to Pinot Noir and originates in France. In Australia and New Zealand, both terms are used. Pinot Gris is grown mostly in cool areas such as in Victoria's Mornington Peninsula and New Zealand's Marlborough region. (For more information on these regions, see Chapter 12 and Chapter 24, respectively.)

✔ **Viognier.** A little-known variety that made its name in the Rhone Valley in Southern France, Viognier is found in some of the warmer areas of Australia, such as South Australia's McLaren Vale. Viognier is used as a 100 per cent varietal or blended with Shiraz, as is becoming increasingly fashionable.

✔ **Roussanne and Marsanne.** Also grown in warm areas, such as Nagambie in Victoria, are these two other Rhone white varieties.

Table 2-3	The Main White Grape Varieties in Australia by Number of Hectares Planted in 2003	
Variety	*Number of Hectares*	*Percentage of Total*
Chardonnay	24,138	39.0%
Sultana*	9,685	16.0%
Semillon	6,283	10.0%
Riesling	3,987	6.4%
Sauvignon Blanc	2,953	4.8%
Muscat Gordo Blanco*	2,479	4.0%
Verdelho	1,612	2.6%
Other white varieties	10,914	17.5%
Total white grapes	62,051	—

* These varieties aren't for premium quality wines and are never listed on labels. They're also used for dried fruit.

Source: Compiled from ABS data.

Shining with the sparkling wines

Wines that fizz are an exciting part of the NZ and Australian wine portfolio. Though a reasonable bottle of bubbly was being produced beforehand, the arrival of the big French companies in 1985 — Moët et Chandon, Louis Roederer and Deutz — encouraged improvement in the quality of sparkling wines being produced, particularly Domaine Chandon in Australia, and Deutz in Australia and New Zealand. Consequently, today both countries have some of that *je ne sais quoi* influence of the French, as well as many a winemaker with a much better understanding of what it takes to make a special bottle of sparkle.

Before the mid-1980s, pretty well any grape was used to make a sparkling wine — including the lowly regarded Sultana and Colombard, and even surplus red wine that had been decolourised! An ever-maturing local wine industry, combined with the influx of French wine companies, encouraged more winegrowers to use the classic grape varieties of the French region, Champagne, which are Pinot Noir, Chardonnay and Pinot Meunier.

This shift, combined with the adoption of the classic methods of making such wines, meant that a turnaround was achieved and today's sparkling wines from Australia and New Zealand are top quality. The best come from the cool to almost cold regions such as Tasmania, the Adelaide Hills, Yarra Valley and the Macedon Ranges in Victoria, and the South Island of New Zealand. (For a detailed description of the method involved in making sparkling wines, see *Wine For Dummies, 3rd Edition,* by Ed McCarthy and Mary Ewing-Mulligan, published by Wiley Publishing, Inc.)

Feeling good with fortifieds

Fortified wine is one type of wine that Australia produces and New Zealand doesn't to any degree. The most well known fortified wines in Australia are Port, Muscat and Tokay. The grape variety used to make Tokay is Muscadelle, and the variety called Muscat Blanc à Petit Grains, known as Brown Muscat in Australia, is used to make Muscat.

Tokay and Muscat are made in a similar way. Firstly, the grapes are allowed to mature until they're very ripe, which is about another third more than normal wine grapes — or in figures that are used in the wine industry, *18 Baumé* compared to the normal ripeness of wine grapes, which is *13 Baumé*. Then they're crushed and left for a few days so the juice soaks with the skins and a small amount of fermentation occurs. After this time, alcohol spirit is added, which is usually Brandy spirit, to make the wine about 16 to 18 per cent alcohol. This process is called *fortification* and its purpose is to stop the fermentation of grape sugars to alcohol. (For standard winemaking procedure see *Wine For Dummies,* 3rd Edition, by Ed McCarthy and Mary Ewing-Mulligan, published by Wiley Publishing, Inc.)

By stopping the fermentation at this point, nearly all the natural sugar from the grapes is retained rather than being fermented into alcohol, as is the usual process with winemaking. By using this method the wines stay luscious and sweet, because all the sweetness of very ripe grapes has been captured due to the fortification. The wines are then aged for many years in a barrel so that they gradually become even more concentrated and luscious.

Port is made in a similar way except that the fermentation is allowed to proceed further before the wine is fortified. By doing so, more than half of the natural grape sugars are turned to alcohol, making the final wine less sweet. Like Tokay and Muscat, the wine is then fortified up to around 18 per cent alcohol.

Port is made all over the warmer parts of Australia, predominantly in the north-east of Victoria and in the warm parts of South Australia, such as the Barossa Valley and McLaren Vale. Sometimes wineries that are too cold to grow grapes suitable for Port will buy Port in bulk and then age it in their winery before selling it as part of their cellar door range.

Rutherglen, in north-east Victoria, is without doubt the international capital of Tokay and Muscat. (I discuss this region in Chapter 11.) The weather is warm and dry, allowing the vines to ripen the fruit to the levels needed, and the result is a sweet, full-flavoured wine that may be hard to stop drinking if you have a sweet tooth!

The good news is that because of the way fortified wines are made — they are slowly and deliberately oxidised during production, making any further exposure to oxygen unharmful — you can open the bottle, pour only one or two glasses from it and re-stop it with the cork. Fortified wines such as these don't need to be finished in one night and they can rest in your pantry as a perfect alternative to eating dessert one evening. (From the time you cork it, a normal table wine is really only best for the next 24 hours, because of the exposure to oxygen that affects the flavours of the wine, making them less fruity and less fresh.)

Prized investment wines

For whatever reason — marketing, scarcity of product or just high quality — some wines are able to demand high prices on the secondary market. The most collectable Australian wine is **Penfolds Bin 95 Grange Shiraz** from South Australia. Some others that are in demand — sometimes not even for drinking but for resale — include:

- **Henschke Hill of Grace Shiraz**; Keyneton, South Australia

- **Leeuwin Estate 'Art Series' Chardonnay**; Margaret River, Western Australia

- **Mount Mary 'Quintet' Cabernets**; Yarra Valley, Victoria

- **Moss Wood Cabernet Sauvignon**; Margaret River, Western Australia

- **Penfolds Bin 707 Cabernet Sauvignon**; South Australia

- **Wendouree Shiraz**; Clare Valley, South Australia

Tantalising Your Tastebuds

You may feel overwhelmed by the number of bottles on your wine shop shelves — after a quick count of the number of Australian brands on the market I came up with over 2,400 different labels! New Zealand has around 500 brands and these, too, are expanding rapidly. Now that really is some choice! And taking into account the number of new wineries established daily, along with the steady increase of additional brands from the big companies, this number can only be assumed to be a conservative estimate. So I'm not surprised if you're suffering from wine variety overload. But hold on to your cork! In this section, I detail how you can taste your way through the marketplace and build up your own list of favourites.

Attending a shop tasting

Shop tastings are great for building up your wine memory and finding out what you like. You discover new varieties and wines from emerging regions to taste. And since tastings are seen as wine promotion, they're nearly always free!

Unfortunately, wine companies offer their wines in tiny plastic goblets, which means you can't smell or swirl the wine, and the rim of the cup may scratch your lips — all of which can distract from the quality of the wine.

The key is in the swirl and the sniff

You may believe swirling and sniffing wine before tasting is the domain of the wine snob but it's not. From the time the wine is bottled it's cooped up in a closed environment, so when you swirl it in your glass, you provide some air for it to 'breathe' and revive its aroma and flavours.

The best way to get the knack of swirling, without throwing the wine all over your new white shirt, is to place the glass on a table or other flat surface. Then, hold the glass by the stem with your thumb and middle finger and gently start to turn the glass in a circular motion so that the wine begins to swirl. As soon as

you've got this trick worked out, try swirling the wine while moving the glass slowly up to your nose for a sniff. If you want to go pro, try swirling clockwise and anti-clockwise, which isn't an easy task.

Smelling wine is also important as the aroma can provide you with an idea of how it may taste. So, if the aroma is blackberry, the wine should taste as such. As you gain more experience, the aroma can also alert you to any faults that the wine may have — the scent of wet cardboard or a mouldy aroma, for example, is a sign of a faulty cork.

Ask for a glass or take your own when you go for a tasting. You may feel a little pretentious but at least you're able to really appreciate the wine. And maybe the wine companies will get the hint and prepare tastings properly!

No matter how or where you do a wine tasting, the best way to build up your memory as to the wines that you love or hate is by taking notes. Write down the name of the wine, the vintage year, the variety, what it was that you liked about it, the price and where you can buy it — as much as you can so that you can refer to them later. If you don't want to jot your notes in public, keep a little book in the car so that you can dash out and write down your thoughts straight away.

Visiting the cellar door

If you have a free weekend, plan a day among the vines. Most larger Australian and New Zealand cities have wineries close enough to make a day of it. When you visit a cellar door, you not only begin to feel part of a vineyard, you're also able to taste the wines made at that winery. Alternatively, if you have more time, explore those wine regions that are further afield. Try journeying out from Perth for a couple of days to visit Margaret River (Chapter 22), or wander from Canberra into Orange and Tumbarumba (Chapter 7).

Coming to terms with taxing times

Don't be put off when you see a little sign telling you that the tastings cost. The reason wineries charge is to recoup some money to pay the tax that the government charges on wine, and that includes wine given away as samples. Just imagine how much wine is tasted in a cellar door in one weekend. With the current tax rate for cellar door sales hovering anywhere between 27 per cent and 42 per cent, depending on how big the winery is, that can mean quite a dent into the weekend sales. Most wineries redeem this charge against any purchases that you may make.

Before you go, decide what you want to achieve and make a plan. Do you want to visit a variety of different-sized wineries, those that you have never heard of, or those that are familiar to you? Most wine regions have pretty comprehensive tourist signs to direct you, such as the brown road signs in Australia.

Some of the smaller wineries have a cellar door operated by the family who owns the vineyard, which certainly makes the knowledge that you glean first-hand. Larger wineries have trained cellar door staff who can still give you a good insight into the wines and the philosophies of the winemaking.

If you discover wines that you want to buy but don't want to carry around, most wineries can arrange home delivery. Also, consider putting your name on their newsletter mailing list — a good way to find out about upcoming wine functions or new wine releases.

If you decide to buy a few bottles when you're out (see Chapter 4), make sure you have an esky, cooler or chilly bin in your car to store it. A summer's day in Australia can easily reach over 30 degrees Celsius, and the temperature of your car boot can climb way above this and the wine can literally cook. If the temperature gets too hot in your car, your wine can expand in the bottle and push the cork out. If you don't have a cooler, have the wine couriered home.

Chapter 3

Decoding Aussie and Kiwi Wine Labels

● ●

In this Chapter

▶ Understanding the name game

▶ Keeping within the long arms of the law

▶ Getting to know what GI really means

▶ Sussing out back label basics

▶ Determining the benefit of awards

● ●

*W*hat a wine bottle looks like is really important, because not only does it play a big part in the consumer's buying decision, it also reveals some essential information that can improve your understanding of the wine.

A new Australian winery opens every 61 hours, and produces anywhere from one to six new labels. On top of that, the old-faithful and all-so-recognisable labels are forever getting facelifts. So for you, as the consumer, this means a lot of labels to look at and assess.

What information should you look out for? And what does all the information mean? In this chapter, I peel off all of the crucial elements of a wine label for you one by one — from the basics to the legal must-haves — so that purchasing wine isn't such a terrifying experience.

What's in a Name?

The name of the wine is usually the most recognisable thing on the label. In the case of small vineyards, the brand name and the name of the company are usually the same thing.

With the big wine producers, the name of the winery is often different from those of the wines, given that their range is much larger. Take the producer Beringer Blass. In Australia its portfolio of wines contains household names such as Yellowglen, Wolf Blass and Saltram, along with smaller labels such as St Hubert's and Yarra Ridge. Likewise in New Zealand, the producer Montana owns the winery known as Montana, but also produces brands such as Stoneleigh Vineyards, Corbans and Lindauer.

Basically, winemakers can call their wine anything they like — as long as that name isn't already being used, and somewhere on the bottle the company that produced the wine is listed. Wines are often named after

- **People:** 'Mr Riggs' is named after owner Ben Riggs from McLaren Vale in South Australia. 'Margan Family' wines are made by Andrew Margan in the Hunter Valley.

- **Places:** Dromana Estate is named after — you guessed it! — Dromana, on the Mornington Peninsula in Victoria.

- **Local landmarks:** Jim Barry's Clare Valley wine is called 'The Armagh', after an historical landmark in the region.

A number of wineries produce a range of wines to cater for the various price points, from the budget purchasers to the high end of the market. They use various names to differentiate these wines. For example, the winery Chard Farm in New Zealand's Otago region has various names for the different types of Pinot Noir it produces. The cheapest is called 'Chard Farm River Run', and the most expensive 'Chard Farm Bragato'.

Beware, brown wine!

Have you ever noticed that after you cut open an apple the exposed flesh soon goes brown? In technical terms, the apple has *oxidised*, and the same thing can occur with wine if problems occur during any of the winemaking processes. For example, if an incorrect method is used when pumping the wine between barrels, or the barrel isn't completely full during ageing, the wine — whether white or red — can oxidise. Oxidisation is visible by a browning of the wine's colour, and is therefore more obvious in white wine due to its colour.

TECHNICAL STUFF

Getting it (the name, that is) right!

In the early days of the Australian and New Zealand wine industry, most white wines were called White Burgundy and most reds Claret or Hermitage — none of which had anything to do with grape varieties. White Burgundy was made either from Chenin Blanc, Colombard or Riesling, Claret possibly from Cabernet Sauvignon and Shiraz, while Hermitage was usually straight Shiraz. Not only were these poor descriptions of what was in the bottle, but also they've since become illegal.

Take the term *champagne*. Champagne is a specific region in France and, to call your wine 'champagne', the grapes must be grown in a very strictly governed area in France and comply with strict rules of production as well as wine-making techniques. The French argue that they have made the wine called 'champagne' famous, and for other countries to call their 'wine with bubbles' champagne is unfair. Consequently, in most of the world, naming a sparkling wine champagne is now illegal. (I was personally relieved when this was made law in Australia to parallel New Zealand.) Unfortunately, the United States didn't sign the universal wine agreement, so you may find some American champagnes.

Along with champagne, terms such as 'white burgundy', 'red burgundy' and 'sauterne' have thankfully largely disappeared, and now the actual varieties of grapes that make up the wine take top billing on the label.

No alternative term has come about, yet, for the sparkling wines. In speech, people are beginning to drop the term champagne and use 'sparkling wine' as the description. Producers are relying on the bottle design to reflect the contents. A bottle of sparkling wine looks a little different to other wines: A long foil capsule on the neck of the bottle covers the wire, which is called the *muselet*, holding in the cork, and is often finished off with a neck label.

Examining the Front Line

Every piece of information on a wine label must be accurate. Like any product, federal and state legislation covers the labelling of wine in Australia and New Zealand. The mandatory items include

- ✔ **The name and address of the wine company:** This information is legally more important than the winery's name, trademark or brand name! The address must not be a post office address.

- ✔ **The country of origin:** The label must state which country the wine comes from. And, in the unusual yet occasional situation when some wine from another country is blended in with an Australian wine, this mix of origin must be stated on the label as a percentage, for example, 75 per cent Australian wine plus 25 per cent Chilean.

✔ **The volume of wine:** The volume of wine must be on the *front label*; that is, the label that is the main face and that is exposed to the consumer. This information must also be in a font that is greater than 3.3 mm high.

✔ **Any additives or processing aids:** From 2003, all Australian wine labels must state all products used in the winemaking process. The reason behind this is to warn anyone who has an allergic reaction to any of these products. Consequently, you may find reference to egg products (egg whites), beef tissue (gelatin) or fish tissue (isinglass) on a wine label. These processing aids are sometimes used to clarify the wine and, although it is very unlikely that any of these products remain after the wine has been racked, filtered and bottled, they must be listed on the label if any trace is likely to remain.

Other additives sometimes used include

• **Sulfur dioxide:** Used in both reds and whites, sulfur dioxide, otherwise known as *preservative 220*, is used to prevent oxidation and microbial growth. Yeast also produces it as a by-product during the fermentation process, so the preservative is, to a degree, a part of every wine — even organic ones.

• **Ascorbic acid:** Some white wines include ascorbic acid, or *preservative 300*, which is used as an aid to preventing oxidation. It isn't used in red wine, however, because it can react with some of the red colour pigments and cause a nasty spoilage character.

If the label states that a wine is *preservative free*, as some organic wine labels do, the wine must have less than 10 mg/L of sulfur dioxide.

✔ **The variety:** If the label says Cabernet Sauvignon then the wine must be between 85 per cent and 100 per cent from that variety of grape. Any added variety doesn't have to be declared. If more than one variety is listed on the label then the one used in the biggest proportion is listed first. So in a Grenache, Shiraz and Mourvèdre blend, Grenache makes up the largest portion, Shiraz the second, and so on. The actual proportions don't have to be listed, although you may sometimes find this as part of the back label blurb.

✔ **A description of the wine:** Listing the variety or varieties of grape in the wine isn't mandatory. However, a description of the wine must be included if the variety isn't listed. So, instead of listing the blend — for example Shiraz, Cabernet, Durif and Malbec — you can state that it is a 'dry red wine'.

✔ **The percentage of alcohol and the number of standard drinks per bottle:** Australia has a law that states that the label of any alcoholic beverage must convey the number of 'standard drinks' per bottle. Basically, this information is to save you doing the calculations for yourself by giving you some idea as to how much alcohol you've drunk, thereby guiding you as to whether you're under the legal limit to drive or operate machinery, for example.

A *standard drink* is any drink that contains 10 grams of alcohol. So you can safely assume that wine with 13 per cent alcohol contains approximately 7.7 standard drinks per 750 mL bottle. If the wine has less alcohol, say 11 per cent, a standard drink would be larger and if it has more, say 14.5 per cent, a standard drink would be smaller.

For wine sold solely in New Zealand or Australia, items such as alcohol content and any additives can go either on the front or the optional back label (see later in the chapter in the section 'Bringing Up the Rear . . . Label, That Is!'). The only stipulation is that the alcohol, additives and volume must all be in the same field of vision. Figure 3-1 illustrates some of these items commonly located on the front label.

Figure 3-1: Some of the elements of a typical wine front label.

Source: Label courtesy of McWilliam's Wines, Chullora, NSW, (www.mcwilliams.com.au).

International labelling requirements

The labels of Australian and NZ wines for international release must comply with the specific requirements of the destination. As you can imagine, such labelling can turn into a nightmare of sorts for the export manager. Here's some idea of the labelling requirements for various export markets:

✔ **France:** The label shouldn't have any mention of the additives sulphur dioxide or ascorbic acid — which goes against current Australian traditions of disclosing everything inside the bottle!

✔ **United Kingdom:** Items such as the address of the importer and the volume and alcohol content must be somewhere on the bottle. In addition, the volume and alcohol level must be in a certain sized font.

✔ **United States:** All labels must contain a government health warning, such as 'Women should not drink alcohol during pregnancy', 'People should not operate machinery or cars after drinking wine', or 'Wine may harm your health'.

You may sometimes find an over-sticker on a bottle of wine that doesn't quite match the main label. Don't worry; this information isn't an after-thought — wine companies that export their produce to other countries use this method to ensure they comply with local labelling requirements. If wine companies were to print a new label to comply with the fine print of every country, they'd be paying the label companies more than their winemakers! See the sidebar 'International labelling requirements' for more information on international labelling.

Getting into the Zone: Australia's Wine Regions

In order to give some clarity as to where all the various grapes are grown across Australia, the wine industry has developed what are called *Geographical Indications*, or *GIs*. This system divides the landmass into wine zones, regions and sub-regions.

Australia's wine zones are listed in Table 3-1. As you can see, within the zone of South West Australia (in the state of Western Australia) you have the regions of Blackwood Valley, Geographe, Great Southern and Margaret River. In order to break these regions down further to specify the winegrowers, Great Southern is divided into five sub-regions, namely Albany, Denmark, Frankland River, Mount Barker and Porongurup.

Table 3-1	Australia's Geographical Indications (GI)		
State	*Zone*	*Region*	*Sub-region*
Australian Capital Territory			
New South Wales	Big Rivers	Murray–Darling	
		Perricoota	
		Riverina	
		Swan Hill	
	Central Ranges	Cowra	
		Mudgee	
		Orange	
	Hunter Valley	Hunter	Broke Fordwich
	Northern Rivers	Hastings River	
	Northern Slopes		
	South Coast	Shoalhaven Coast	
		Southern Highlands	
	Southern New South Wales	Canberra District	
		Gundagai	
		Hilltops	
		Tumbarumba	
	Western Plains		
Northern Territory			
Queensland		Granite Belt	
		South Burnett	
South Australia	Adelaide Superzone		
	(includes Barossa, Fleurieu & Mount Lofty Ranges zones)		
	Barossa	Barossa Valley	

(continued)

Table 3-1 *(continued)*

State	Zone	Region	Sub-region
		Eden Valley	High Eden
	Far North	Southern Flinders Ranges	
	Fleurieu	Currency Creek	
		Kangaroo Island	
		Langhorne Creek	
		McLaren Vale	
		Southern Fleurieu	
	Limestone Coast	Coonawarra	
		Mount Benson	
		Padthaway	
	Lower Murray	Riverland	
	Mounty Lofty Ranges	Adelaide Hills	Lenswood
			Piccadilly Valley
		Adelaide Plains	
		Clare Valley	
	The Peninsulas		
Tasmania			
Victoria	Central Victoria	Bendigo	
		Goulburn Valley	Nagambie Lakes
		Heathcote	
		Strathbogie Ranges Upper Goulburn	
	Gippsland		
	North East Victoria	Alpine Valleys	
		Beechworth	
		Glenrowan	
		Rutherglen	
	North West Victoria	Murray–Darling	

Table 3-1 *(continued)*

State	Zone	Region	Sub-region
		Swan Hill	
	Port Phillip	Geelong	
		Macedon Ranges	
		Mornington Peninsula	
		Sunbury	
		Yarra Valley	
	Western Victoria	Grampians	
		Henty	
		Pyrenees	
Western Australia	Central Western Australia		
	Eastern Plains, Inland & North of WA		
	Greater Perth	Peel	
		Perth Hills	
		Swan District	Swan Valley
	South West Australia	Blackwood Valley	
		Geographe	
		Great Southern	Albany
			Denmark
			Frankland River
			Mount Barker
			Porongurup
		Margaret River	
	West Australian South East Coastal		

Source: Compiled from Australian Geographical Indicators, Australian Wine & Brandy Corporation (www.awbc.com.au).

Each GI is established in accordance with the definitions of zone, region and sub-region set out in the *Australian Wine and Brandy Corporation Act* and Regulation. For example, a *zone* is largely determined by a traditional name for the greater area, such as Victoria's Central Victoria zone, which reflects the common term of reference.

Included in the GI breakdown is the 'super big' zone, South Eastern Australia. You can loosely compare this super zone with those of Europe such as the vino da tavola of Italy (see *Italian Wines For Dummies* by Ed McCarthy and Mary Ewing-Mulligan, published by Wiley Publishing, Inc.) or the Vin de Table of France (see *French Wine For Dummies* by Mary Ewing-Mulligan and Ed McCarthy, published by Wiley Publishing, Inc.).

If a label states that the wine is from this zone, it means that the grapes have come from any vineyard in the state of New South Wales, Victoria or Tasmania, or parts of Queensland or South Australia — basically all the principal grape-growing regions other than those in Western Australia.

The definition of a *region* is much more specific, and may be classified as being an area between two valleys, map coordinates or roads, for example. A wine carrying a regional name must have 85 per cent of the blend of the fruit sourced from that region. So, if you discover that a label says the wine is from South Australia's Clare Valley, you can rest assured that at least 85 per cent of the grapes were grown there. And this fact is important, especially given the diversity of the winegrowing regions in Australia and New Zealand.

Don't assume that the grapes that make up your plonk are from the Barossa Valley just because that is where the winery is located. Unless the label indicates a GI of Barossa, the grapes could be from anywhere.

Further down Australia's GI index is the *sub-region*, which as you've probably guessed is a component of a region, with a more specific character. Sub-regions reflect qualities such as the differences in soil type, topography and climate within a region, and provide you with much more information than zones or regions.

Remembering that the character or quality of wine comes partly from the sub-region and also from the winemaker, you may be able to use the sub-region as a guide to source similar wines. So, if you like **Grosset Piccadilly Chardonnay**, which is from the sub-region of Piccadilly Valley in the Adelaide Hills region, hunt out other wines from that sub-region. (This wine has great longevity and a fantastic zing of acid, by the way.)

The list of regions and sub-regions in Australia seems to balloon every year, as do the discussions and even occasional court case as to who's in and who's outside the region. However, the Australian GI determination process has a successful appeal process enshrined therein to protect the fantastic reputation of some regions and the automatic credibility a new vineyard may gain just for being within a famous region. Needless to say, the regions themselves keep a very close eye on the fruit arriving on trucks to make sure that anyone making claims about producing wine from its region is really using local fruit!

For more information on GIs and current information on the GI determination process, check out the 'Wine Regions' link of the Australian Wine and Brandy Corporation Web site at www.awbc.com.au.

Breaking Up New Zealand

When people talk about New Zealand, they often refer to places as being either on the North or the South Island. Although this reference isn't considered to be an official zoning of the country's wine areas, it may act as a starting point for you to picture in your mind where a vineyard or winery is — albeit very approximately.

On a more official basis, New Zealand is broken into ten regions — six in the North Island and four in the South Island (refer to Chapter 1).

> ✔ North Island
>   • Northland
>   • Auckland
>   • Waikato/Bay of Plenty
>   • Hawke's Bay
>   • Wairarapa
>   • Gisborne
> ✔ South Island
>   • Marlborough
>   • Nelson
>   • Canterbury
>   • Otago

I do, however, foresee that these regions will be broken down into sub-regions at some point, because of the need to classify the distinct areas that exist within each region. For example, within the Otago region are Wanaka and Queenstown, which are separated by a mountain range. Consequently, the vineyards in Wanaka are a good deal cooler than those in Queenstown and they each produce quite different wines.

A quick guide to sweet serves

You may find that the amount of wine in a bottle is something you just assume. But be careful if you want to get a certain number of glasses from a bottle to serve with dessert. Some fortified wines (refer to Chapter 2) and dessert wines, such as Muscat or *botrytised* (see Chapter 8) wines, come in 300 mL or 500 mL bottles, so you need to ensure that you've got enough to go around. With dessert wines, work on the basis of a smaller serve than a table wine. I find that a standard half-bottle of 375 mL serves four to five people and a 500 mL bottle serves six to seven.

Appreciating a Good Vintage

Mistakenly, some people think that the term *vintage* means quality, and that a wine described as vintage must be good. Vintage simply refers to the year in which the grapes that make up the wine were harvested. So, if you see a label with the year 1999 marked, this means that the majority of the grapes were picked from the vine and made into wine somewhere between late January and early May in that year (depending on where in Australia or New Zealand they were grown).

In this case, as with the rules on variety and region (refer to the section earlier in this chapter 'Getting into the Zone: Australia's Wine Regions'), up to 15 per cent of the contents of the bottle can come from another year. However, if a label includes the words ' vintage wine' and shows the year of the vintage, the wine must be made solely from grapes from that particular vintage.

A wine's vintage is most often cited by wine writers talking up the greatness, or not, of a particular year. Sometimes even the PR people from the region or the winemakers themselves get in on the act. But to generalise between years doesn't always take into account how each vineyard has performed. One vineyard may have harvested their grapes a few days earlier than its nextdoor neighbour and, between one harvest and the neighbouring one, it may have rained heavily and diluted the later harvest.

Like with many things, moderation is the key to what makes a good vintage. The types of moderate weather conditions that produce a good drop include

- ✔ Some rain, but not too much.
- ✔ Sunshine, but not soaring temperatures to burn the grapes.
- ✔ Gentle breezes to allow air to flow through leaves to prevent diseases and avoid the need for chemical sprays.

With such differences in climate between each country's grape-growing regions, claiming that a great vintage was had across Australia or New Zealand in any particular year is questionable.

In 2003, for example, torrential rains in Mudgee, New South Wales, saw the grapes from established vines not only fall apart but the vines actually wash away. In the same year, down in Victoria the drought marched on, and the grape growers were crying out for a little something to wet their thirsty vine roots. The weather conditions during the year and especially just before the harvest really can make a huge difference to the wine. Consequently, not all wines from 2003 make a bad vintage and vice versa in a 'good' year.

Classifying a vintage according to the region, the individual grower and the exact time when the grapes where harvested, rather than the country of origin, is the best idea. For example, if 2000 is being claimed as being an excellent year for Pinot, ensure that it really was an excellent year in the region from where the wine comes.

For sparkling wine and fortified wines, often no vintage is claimed because the wine may be a blend of wines from across many years. In the case of Australian fortified wines such as Tokay, components that date back 50 to 80 years may be included. In fact, these blended wines are the most sought-after of all because of the complexity that comes from the older wines.

If you like a particular wine, take a note of its vintage and buy the same next time. Just be aware that shops sometimes mix vintages on the shelves when stocks of one vintage are running low and a more recent vintage is being brought in. A check on the alcohol content can also tell you whether the wines are wildly different. This check can tell you if the fruit was well ripened or not (higher alcohol equals riper fruit).

Bringing Up the Rear...Label, That Is!

Overall, as a getting-to-know-you exercise, the back label (see Figure 3-2) can give you some useful and interesting information. If you don't particularly like reds that have been matured in American oak, for example, the back label is the spot to find out whether this is the case — and save you disappointment later. Or you may be interested in the proportions of the grapes in the GSM (Grenache, Shiraz and Mourvèdre), so that next time you can look for something along the same lines — assuming you liked the wine.

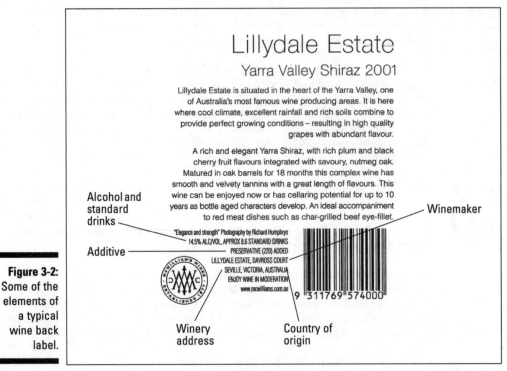

Source: Label courtesy of McWilliam's Wines, Chullora, NSW, (www.mcwilliams.com.au).

Figure 3-2:
Some of the elements of a typical wine back label.

Some labels provide you with a short story about the winemaker's dog, or the reason behind its obscure name. With some back labels I get the impression that the winemaker thinks (mistakenly, mind you) that he's a poet! The straight-laced ones tell you the wine's technical figures, such as the pH, acidity or yeast strain used to ferment the grapes. And some give you a step-by-step breakdown on how the wine is made.

More and more marketing people are writing back label blurbs rather than the winemakers themselves, so they may contain a bit of the old PR. Do your best to sift through the waffle and get to the essentials.

Scrutinising marketing propaganda

Like in any industry, a certain amount of marketing goes into selling a bottle of wine. Take, for example, one of the recent fads in Australia and New Zealand — the use of *wild yeast* for fermentation.

Wild yeast is yeast that lives in the vineyard and winery — not selective yeast that has been grown in a laboratory. Using wild yeast in wine-making has been done for centuries in Europe, and even for many years over here in the Antipodes. But with one or two successful wines being released announcing this style of fermen-tation, using the terminology is now being seen as a positive marketing tool, and every time a wine is released with 'wild yeast' written on the label, many people assume that the quality of the wine will be outstanding. Realistically, whatever the type of yeast that fermented the juice was, it comes down to the quality of the winemaking and fruit source as to whether the wine is any good. So don't be fooled by claims of wild yeast, non-filtered or whatever — the track record of the winemaker is a better tool to select your wines by.

You may find suggestions as to what types of food to serve the wine with, which can be helpful. However, I've seen labels stating 'serve with seafood, chicken or pasta' all on the same label, so be wary! Go for those that are more specific, such as 'best with garlic prawns'.

My favourite back label jottings at the moment are the ones that suggest that you share the wine with good company and with good food — a very sensible idea really!

Deciphering Bonus Stickers

More than in any other country, Australian wine producers have relied on awards to entice the consumer to buy. For some people, this stamp of approval from wine shows and competitions does help them with their purchase. Such awards are usually displayed in the form of an additional sticker of some kind. The most common sticker you may see is circular, as shown in Figure 3-2.

Type of award —
gold, silver or bronze

The show the prize
was awarded in
and class number

Lillydale Estate

Yarra Valley
750ML   Shiraz 2001

Figure 3-3:
Little gold
stickers
highlight
awards won
by the wine.

Source: Label courtesy of McWilliam's Wines, Chullora, NSW, (www.mcwilliams.com.au).

You may be under the impression that a wine bottle with a bronze sticker won third best wine in its group. Not so! As long as the wine receives a score above 15.5 points out of 20, it receives an award — sometimes along with fifteen other wines!

How the shows work

To understand where award stickers (refer to Figure 3-3) originate, you need to know about the show system. The awards are the results of a panel of trained wine judges who smell and taste the wine, and then score it according to their opinion of the wine's quality.

The awards are gold, silver or bronze. A score of between 15.5 points and 16.9 points is granted a bronze medal; between 17 points and 18.4 points, silver; and above 18.5 points, gold. Some shows also include a trophy for the wine that scored the most points in its category.

Based on the first taste, all the wines are given a score. Then the wines with scores of over 15 points are retasted for final evaluation. If the judges disagree on a score, they retaste and discuss the wine, and if they still fail to agree they call on the Chairman of Judges to adjudicate on the final score.

Any wine's score that fits into the medal parameters is awarded the appropriate medal. No pre-determined number of medals is given; if 20 wines are good enough to get a bronze medal, then 20 are awarded one. If none of the wines is good enough to deserve a gold medal, then none is awarded.

As you can imagine, this job is a very difficult and tiring one, which may sound glamorous but is, in fact, exhausting. One wine category — say the two-year-old, dry red, medium-bodied class — may constitute over 100 wines. Judges may even be left with black teeth and lips if they taste young reds all day!

Each group of wines is classified according to type, so the producer must enter the wine into the appropriate class. Consequently, a mix of varieties may be included in each class. So, you may find in the dry red full-bodied class some Shiraz, Cabernet Sauvignon and Durif, along with any other reds that are categorised as full-bodied. Likewise, in the dry white, medium-bodied class, Semillon, Pinot Gris and a lighter Chardonnay may all be bundled together. So, as you can see, judges aren't always tasting like with like.

Some of the regional shows have specific varietal classes to highlight the region's most successful wine styles. For example, the Lillydale Show, which showcases the Yarra Valley wines, has separate classes for Chardonnay, Pinot Noir and Cabernet Sauvignon — three varieties that the Yarra Valley is famous for.

What the award stickers mean

Many winemakers don't care to use award medal stickers (refer to Figure 3-3) on their bottles, and many wineries never put their wines into the show system. The reason for this is that they believe the sheer number of wines judged in one sitting is too high and, consequently, differentiating them too difficult. Judges would argue, however, that they're trained to distinguish between wines, even under these circumstances.

The wines sporting medals won in state capital city wine shows reflect well-made wines with no faults, and are a good representation of that particular wine style.

As an aid in sifting your way through the myriad bottles on sale, the little award stickers may be able to assist you in your choices. Gradually, as you become more familiar and confident in choosing wines, these stickers may become less important.

You can always plan a wine night — buy a few bottles and wrap them in foil so that you can't see — and be influenced by the labels. Then you and your friends can do the judging. You might be surprised by the results.

Lately, I've been noticing some very quirky gold stickers on some wine bottles, which look like those used to display wine awards but instead have irreverent sayings such as 'Just a damn good drop', or 'Enjoy with whoever you'd like to'. I'm not sure if these stickers are that helpful to your purchase, but they're a good example of the Aussie and Kiwi sense of humour!

Chapter 4

Bringing Home the Bounty: Modern Ways and Means

In This Chapter

▶ Shopping over the phone or over the Internet

▶ Taking advantage of wine clubs and auctions

*N*o longer is a quick trip to the local bottle shop the only way to buy wine. Sure, the specialised retail shops in Australia and New Zealand still have a good range, but with many wineries allocating a proportion of their production to the export market, some wines are becoming more difficult to find — particularly interesting ones. In this chapter, I take you through the less conventional ways and means of purchasing wine — from mail order to clubs to online auctions. So get your trolley ready!

Getting good shop service

Sadly, small local wine merchants are fading from our shopping strips, along with personal service. More and more huge chains of wine stores are taking over, which means looking a little harder, and maybe trying a few different retailers before you find one whose selections suit the type of wine that you like to drink. Let the wine assistant know a few of the wines you prefer. From this information, he or she should be able to recommend an appropriate style and price range for your taste. If you like those

recommended, go back and ask for further suggestions. This approach can help open your mind and palate.

If you live outside Oz or NZ, searching out a retailer that has a particular passion for Antipodean wines is worthwhile and shouldn't be too difficult due to the popularity of our wines. You can also contact the wineries direct to find out if they have a distributor in your country or any retail stores they sell to.

If you know the wine you're after and want to know which shops you can buy it from, check out Wine Searcher (www.wine-searcher.com). All you need to do is enter the wine and the site searches a selection of wine retailers to locate it for you.

Arranging Mail Order

Many small wineries sell their wines by mail order only, so if you find a bottle of wine you like, phone the winery.

To be placed on a winery's mailing list, just give the winery your contact details. Then, ordinarily, you're sent a newsletter along with an order form, which you can fill in and return. An added benefit to being on the mailing list is that wineries often have special open days to which only mailing list members are invited. On these days, newly released wines can be tasted and, if you're lucky, you may have a choice of aged wines that the winery has held onto in its own climatically controlled cellar.

Most wineries of this kind release their wines once a year and the amount of wine they have to sell is often limited, so don't procrastinate about your order — remember, first in, best drinking!

Bigger wineries may also have a mailing list, but you may find it easier to purchase locally if you can find the same wines at your retailer.

Don't wildly put your name on every winery's mailing list because costs are involved with this method of selling. And if you think you're unlikely to buy a winery's produce after a trial, ask to be taken off its list.

Purchasing Wine Online

Like almost everything else that is for sale these days, you can buy wine on the Internet. Most of the wine retailers in Australia and New Zealand have a Web site that you can order wine from and have it delivered to your door. And another great thing about online purchasing is that you can find wines from almost anywhere. If you're sitting in your apartment in New York or in your house in Auckland and you want an Aussie wine, you can simply log on to an Australian wine site and search one out (although the freight may be another story!).

Top online stores include

- ✔ **Cloudwine:** Offering premium and hard-to-find Australian and New Zealand wines, Cloudwine specialises in high-quality wines from small Australian wineries. The site also offers a wine search option, where you can search by winery, price range and/or specific region (www.cloudwine.com.au).

- ✔ **Kemeny's:** One of Sydney's largest retailers that is still independently owned (most of the wine stores in Australia are part of one or two large retail chains), Kemeny's has a very large selection of both commercial and small winery labels (www.kemenys.com.au).

- ✔ **Liquor King:** A site that is very easy on the eye (which has nothing to do with the Web address!) with the products well set out using clear icons. The Web site of New Zealand's largest liquor retailer, it offers a very extensive range (www.shopnaked.co.nz).

- ✔ **TLC wines:** A smaller retailer that specialises in New Zealand wines along with some mainstream Australian wines. Well worth a visit (www.tlc.com.au).

- ✔ **Vintage Cellars:** This Web site of one of the big Australian retailers has a good range of commercial wines. (www.vintagecellars.com.au).

- ✔ **Vintage Direct:** An easy-to-find-your-way-around Web site with wines grouped according to colour and price. The site also has special sections on iconic wines such as Penfold's Grange (www.nicks.com.au).

If you don't know the Web site address for a particular store, ring and ask for it. Alternatively, try entering the store's name as a Web address (for example, www.wineplus.com.au), or entering it in a search engine like Google or Yahoo.

For a more general search of what's available, enter **wine retailers** and **Australia** and/or **New Zealand** into a search engine. Then click on a match that you like and you go to a world of wine choices. (For more ins and outs of shopping online, see *Living on the Web For Dummies*, Australian Edition, by Geoff Ebbs, Wiley Publishing Australia Pty Ltd.)

After you've found a site, purchasing the wine in most cases simply involves selecting the wine and the quantity you want. You may find, as an added point of interest, that the retailer has provided a brief description of the wine and perhaps some background information about the winery itself.

Always check the currency used on the site to ensure you know how much you'll be paying. In most cases, if the site is Australian the prices will be Australian dollars, and likewise for New Zealand sites, but some sites may give prices in US dollars, so remember to check to avoid any confusion.

When shopping online, first and foremost you must make sure that you get what you order and that it will arrive in good condition. Ask the following questions to ensure the security of your order:

- ✔ **What are the delivery charges?** Usually local delivery is free, with charges imposed and increasing the further afield the wine has to travel. Delivery charges need to be taken into account so that you know the total purchase price.

- ✔ **When will the wine be delivered?** If delivery is local, how many days should it take? If ordering from overseas, will the wine be sent by airmail or by sea? Obviously, airmail is a lot faster and you can expect to see your wine sooner than by sea, but airmail is also a lot more expensive.

- ✔ **Will the wine be left on your doorstep if no-one is at home?** If so, whose responsibility is it if it goes missing? Some courier companies only leave wine if someone signs for the delivery. Other companies just leave the wine on the doorstop. Ask the vendor to specify only to leave the wine if someone is at home to sign for it.

- ✔ **Will the driver leave it out in the hot sun?** This scenario shouldn't be a problem if you specify that wine isn't to be left unless someone signs for it.

- ✔ **Who insures the wine?** As soon as you pay for the wine, you want to be sure that you're covered against any loss. Make sure insurance covers the wine while it's in transit between the winery and you. Sometimes parcels can mysteriously go missing and, if it isn't insured, you may never see your wine, or get your money back either.

- ✔ **What if some of the bottles are broken in transit?** Occasionally bottles do break, and not only do you lose those bottles but the labels on the other bottles will also be damaged. Check to see if this is covered by insurance and/or if the winery will replace any damaged bottles.

Most sites have an FAQ (frequently asked questions) section that addresses such queries. If not, contact the store.

Joining a Wine Club

Wine clubs are a great way to buy wine, particularly when you're developing your interest in wine. Purchasing wine in this way introduces you to all sorts of varieties, regions and prices. And the knowledge you gain from trying their range of wines may help you to define your likes and dislikes. For some people the club works as a simple, thought-free way of having a dozen, or more, bottles arrive on the doorstep each month. In most cases, you have to order a minimum case lot, which usually means one dozen, although some companies offer half-dozen packs.

Ordinarily, clubs offer you monthly deliveries of a mixed case of wine, but you can ask for more or less frequent deliveries. In some cases, the wines are made specifically by a well-known winery and are only available through the club.

To become a member, you may need to pay a small joining fee. The fee usually covers a monthly newsletter, any special wine dinners, tastings run by the club and the right to buy the wines through their special deals. The newsletter advises you of the mixed dozens on offer, which is a great way to choose either mixed whites, mixed reds, or more specialised grouping such as a beginner's dozen or a dozen to age (put down in your cellar).

Make sure that you read all the small print before you sign. You should be able to decline buying every month and only buy as you please. And do your own homework to ensure the prices and selections suit you.

Wine clubs I recommend include

- ✔ **Cellarbuild:** This club offers to set you up with a cellar, so you're not buying just one case — more likely six cases! Most of the wines are quite hard to get, which adds interest to the club. Contact by email info@cellarbuild.com, Web site www.cellarbuild.com, phone 61 (0)3 5931 0130 or fax 61 (0)3 5931 0131.

- ✔ **Cellarmasters:** One of the first wine clubs to offer monthly purchases, Cellarmasters deals in both big and smaller wine companies and often has wines made especially for club members. You can only contact Cellarmasters via its Web site at www.cellarmasters.com.au.

- ✔ **The Wine Society of Australia:** The Wine Society offers members a large selection of mixed prices and styles of wine, as well as wine tasting courses, social evenings, visits to wineries and a regular newsletter. Contact by email orders@winesociety.com, Web site www.winesociety.com.au, phone 1300 723 723 or fax 1300 788 988.

- ✔ **The Wine Society of New Zealand:** The Wine Society of New Zealand offers members all sorts of benefits, such as special tastings and theme dinners as well as a wine club. Its expertise is also the basis for various wine clubs that are offered by credit card companies and the like. The society has a wide selection of mainly New Zealand wines on offer. Contact by email enquiries@nz-wine-society.co.nz, Web site www.cardmember.co.nz or phone 0800 809 463.

Going, Going, Gone — Wine Auctions

The auction method of buying wine has boomed over recent times for various reasons. Firstly, some people now see wine as an investment. In Australia, even superannuation schemes are investing in parcels of certain wines. And worldwide prices for premium and cult wines have boomed. For example, when the **1998 Penfolds Grange** was released to retailers, it had a price of $450. Very few people were actually able to get any, but those who did would have been able to make a quick $100 profit if they'd sold it on within the next month or so. Sadly for wine lovers, many of the people becoming involved in this secondary market aren't even wine drinkers; they're simply around to trade in wine and make a profit.

Another reason for the boom in auctions is that an increasing number of wine drinkers want to buy aged wines. Wineries and retailers can't afford to hold wine for re-release, which makes buying aged wine straight from the source difficult. And this situation is where the auction houses step in. The great thing about the auction circuit is you can occasionally pick up, at bargain prices often, fabulous wines that have never become the darling of the investment market.

The number of bottles you can buy at an auction depends entirely on the lot up for sale — a case, one bottle, or anywhere in between. So if, for example, lot #125 is four bottles of **1996 Penfolds Grange**, you have to buy all four.

If you're keen on pursuing the auction approach to buying wine, you need to become a member of an auction house. The following is a list of auction houses that specialise only in wine — they don't deal in art or furniture or other collectibles.

- ✔ **Langtons:** www.langtons.com.au
- ✔ **Oddbins:** www.oddbins.com.au
- ✔ **Wine-xchange:** www.wine-xchange.com

As soon as you register with the auction house, you're allocated a membership number and sent out its catalogue along with a bidding sheet. You can usually make your bids either online or via fax. On the day of the auction, a cut-off time is in place, so you need to get your last best bid in before that time. Ordinarily, an estimated price is listed so that you can gauge how much you need to bid. As with most auctions, as soon as someone registers a bid, it sits as the wine's price and, if no-one else bids, the wine goes to that person. I was recently part of a online price war and was pipped at the post by $1, but I had a lot of fun watching the bids being placed by keen bidders.

If you're the successful online bidder at auction, a buyer's premium is added to the price, which is around 13 to 15 per cent. So a wine that you buy for $40, actually costs you $45 to $46 plus any delivery charges — in some cases an easy way of turning a bargain into not such a bargain. You can find the buyer's premium percentage in the auctioneer's conditions page of its catalogue.

 Make sure that you know the wine's worth before you get overexcited. The best way to do this is by checking prices after sales of the wine you want to buy. Instead of jumping in feet first as soon as you receive your membership number, have a look at the prices of recent sales of the wine you're after. Track sales over the next few auctions, if any bottles are up for sale. This approach gives you a feel for how much you should bid. And often the harder the wine is to find, the more you have to be prepared to spend.

 Buying wine without viewing it can be problematic so, if you can, go and view the wine to check the condition of the bottle. If the bottle has a bad cork, some of the wine may have leaked, making it less than desirable. If you're purchasing white wine, check the colour: the more golden in colour, the more aged it is. If the wine is relatively young, say under five years, and quite golden, stay away — it's likely to be *oxidised* (refer to Chapter 3) and over the hill.

The rise and rise of Grange

While actual prices of **Penfolds Grange** have varied on the secondary market over the years, like any form of investment, overall prices have increased. For example, in 1992, the 1971 Grange was valued at around A$130. By 1995, the average price was A$280; in 1998 around A$450; and by 2001, you would have needed to spend $520 to obtain this vintage. The main reason behind this stratospheric price rise — 300 per cent in nine years — is the increase in interest in Australian red wines, particularly Shiraz, in the overseas market. Not only do Australians want these wines but so do wealthy investors who've read glowing reviews of the wines, all of which fuels demand.

Part II

Heading to North Oz for the Wine: New South Wales and Queensland

www.moir.com.au   *Alan Moir*

In this part . . .

1n the next five chapters I explore the north of Australia's wine regions, New South Wales and Queensland. First to one of Australia's most renowned wine zones in New South Wales — the Hunter Valley — a delightful mixture of the older established family businesses, as well as the new whiz-bang tourist-focused operations.

Next, to Mudgee where the wine production is top-heavy with the reds, and the once underrated labels are making a mark for themselves at last. From there, I cover a bit of a mix of small but significant regions — such as Orange, Cowra, the cooler Hilltops and Canberra District regions. Then I take you into the vast and warm Riverina region where some of the country's most outstanding dessert wines come from.

Rounding off this part is the Queensland wine industry in the Granite Belt and South Burnett regions, which boast many varieties of grapes and interesting success stories to tell.

Chapter 5

The Hunter Valley

● ●

In This Chapter

▶ Tasting what the Hunter does best: Semillon, Chardonnay and Shiraz

▶ Enjoying the old favourites of the Lower Hunter

▶ Going for Broke and tasting some gems

▶ Meeting some of the young guns of the Upper Hunter

▶ Taking a wine holiday

● ●

*T*he Hunter Valley, about a two-hour drive north from the city of Sydney, is perhaps the best-known grapegrowing zone (refer to Chapter 3 for an explanation of the geographical zones of Australia) in New South Wales. Known simply as 'the Hunter', the zone is divided into two regions — the Upper Hunter and the Lower Hunter. The vineyards of the Upper Hunter are centred around the towns of Muswellbrook and Denman, while to the south-east, Cessnock and Branxton are the main towns of the Lower Hunter Valley.

The Hunter Valley is the oldest viticultural region in Australia. The first plantings date back to the 1820s, and Dr Henry Lindeman began planting vines in 1843. Twenty years or so later, ancestors of the Tyrrell and the Drayton families started wine businesses that still exist to this day.

The Lower Hunter is often referred to as 'the Pokolbin area', because of the large number of wineries to the north and south of the small township of Pokolbin, which lies to the west of Cessnock. The region also has its own official sub-region, Broke Fordwich, which lies north-west of Cessnock.

In the Upper Hunter, a German migrant named Carl Brecht first planted vineyards in 1864 and named them Rosemount. After the Second World War, the vineyard became neglected and the land usage reverted back to cattle farming. In 1969, the Oatley family purchased the site and re-established the vineyards, and resurrected the original name. Today, Rosemount Estate is by far the largest grapevine owner in the Upper Hunter.

In the 1960s, the Hunter struggled to remain viable as a winemaking zone. Even in the 1980s, the outlook was uncertain. Wines produced in other wine zones and regions were all the fashion and eroded the Hunter's market share. But just as the outlook began to look bleak, the 1990s saw a reversal of the Hunter's fortunes, and it continues to enjoy steady growth.

In this chapter, I introduce the wines that helped to put the Hunter on the map as a major winemaking zone and give you a taste of the grape varieties that are likely to become the stars of the future.

Defying the Odds: Climate and Location

In my opinion, you'd be mad to plant grapes in the Hunter. Now I know this sounds like a very strange remark to make, but the fact is that neither the climate nor the location of the Hunter Valley is conducive to successful grape growing — at least, not on paper.

Set between the Great Dividing Range and the Pacific Ocean, the Hunter Valley can experience extreme conditions — hail and excessive rain are just two of the elements to challenge the winemaker. Overall, the summers are hot and the winters cool. The region is also pretty dry, receiving only around 740 millimetres of rain annually.

Compared to some of Australia's other wine zones, the Hunter is largely low land. Consequently, the cooling effect that higher altitudes have on vineyards does not come into play much in the Hunter. However, in the Lower Hunter, a break in the Great Dividing Range means that some of the cooler sea breezes from the New South Wales coast flow through to the vineyards. These breezes cool the vines in the afternoon and evening, and also lower the humidity.

Battling rotten weather

Back in 1986 and 1987, I worked in the Hunter Valley during *vintage* (harvest time). The year 1986 was a dream, with beautiful weather and little rainfall. But 1987 was completely different.

Things started well, and we were picking the Semillon grapes. Then the thunder and lightening started — never have I seen such storms! Needless to say, the vineyards got drenched. When the mechanical harvesters became bogged, the vineyard managers called for 'all hands on deck';

it was essential to finish the Semillon harvest before the damp got to the bunches of grapes and rotted them. Semillon is a grape that is very susceptible to rot due to its big tight bunches and soft skins that easily split.

After a few days, fortunately, the weather improved, the vineyards dried out and we got the Semillon grapes in without losing too many to the storms.

Winning Varieties from the Hunter

The Hunter is not a great producer of grapes. The statistics say it all: The Riverina (see Chapter 7) produces about 70 per cent of the grapes grown in New South Wales, whereas the Hunter produces roughly 10 per cent. However, many of the Hunter wineries use grapes grown in other wine regions of Australia, for example, Riesling grapes from the Clare Valley and Shiraz grapes from McLaren Vale.

The Hunter Valley produces its own distinctive regional wines, and is notable for its success with white grape varieties as much as it is for its reds.

Starring white wines

Chardonnay makes up about 52 per cent of the white grapes grown in the Hunter, with Semillon at 30 per cent, Verdelho at 12 per cent — and growing — and Sauvignon Blanc making up 3 per cent.

Chardonnay

As one of the main stars of the region, a Hunter Chardonnay is a lovely and rich, nutty-flavoured wine. Murray Tyrrell introduced the Chardonnay grape to the region and today his company makes one of the best Chardonnays in Australia — Tyrrell's Vat 47. (You can find more information about Tyrrell's later in the section 'Tasting the best the wineries offer'.)

Semillon

The Hunter and the Semillon grape go together well, resulting in a wine that has evolved over the years to enjoy world acclaim. Although less Semillon is grown than Chardonnay, Semillon has made the Hunter Valley famous for its whites, and the reason stems from the inclement weather.

The Semillon grape has a thin, slippery skin, and the bunches are big with the berries packed together. These physical properties mean the grape is particularly susceptible to wet and humid weather — exactly what the Hunter Valley experiences often. (See the sidebar 'Battling rotten weather'.)

Because of the danger of them being ruined by bad weather, the Semillon grapes are picked before they're fully ripe, when the skins aren't soft and vulnerable to disease. Often the grapes get to only about 11 Baumé, which is one to two degrees lower than when the average white grape is picked (around three weeks earlier). (See the sidebar 'The sweet meaning of Baumé' for an explanation of the term, *Baumé*.)

The result is a crisp, lemony, pleasant white wine — the wine could almost be called nondescript. However, if left to age in the bottle for three, five or even up to 15 years, Semillon turns into a magnificent honeyed, soft and complex wine.

A good rule to start with is to buy more than one bottle of young wine, bearing in mind that these are often relatively inexpensive wines. Then gradually try a bottle every few years or so. I suggest you leave one for at least five years, another for eight years and then go the whole way and see how the wine is after 15 years. No magic figure exists as to how long you can age these wines for, but generally 10 to 15 years will give you an intense honeyed character. Having said that, some wines may 'live' for even longer. I've seen 30-year-old Hunter Semillons looking just fantastic — but that is more the exception than the rule.

So, did the early winemakers of this variety predict that this was how the plain young wines would transform themselves over time, or was it just serendipity? Who knows! What I do know is that a young Hunter Semillon is inexpensive and a delicious drink when aged.

Verdelho

The new kid on the block is Verdelho, originally a grape variety from Portugal. The Verdelho grape thrives in the warm weather of the Hunter and, because it can also cope with bad weather, this grape is increasingly being planted in the Hunter. Some of the best Verdelho wines come from the Broke Fordwich sub-region.

Rambunctious reds

In the Hunter, Shiraz accounts for 50 to 60 per cent of red grapes harvested. Cabernet Sauvignon is the second most planted variety with 17 per cent, Merlot follows with 12 per cent and then — strangely, given that it does best in cool climates — Pinot Noir.

The sweet meaning of Baumé

Baumé is the measurement that many wine-makers and grape growers use to gauge the ripeness of the grapes. The measurement relates to density of the juice. A higher reading in degrees Baumé means that the juice has a higher density because more dissolved sugar is found in the juice. The average Baumé that wine grapes are harvested at is somewhere between 12.5 degrees and 14 degrees Baumé. Roughly speaking, a Baumé gives a winemaker an indication of what the wine's final alcohol reading will be. So 11 degrees Baumé gives around 11.5 per cent alcohol, 13.5 degrees Baumé gives about 14 per cent alcohol, and so on.

Naming rights

If you should ever come across a Hunter Riesling bottled in the mid-80s, take a close look at the label. Many wineries labelled their Semillon 'Hunter River Riesling' even though no Riesling grapes were sighted during the winemaking process. In the 1980s, Riesling was the commonly used generic term for dry white wine, and wineries thought that consumers would be happier with this known variety rather than one that they'd never heard of.

Shiraz

Shiraz put the Hunter Valley winemaking zone on the map, particularly due to the fantastic longevity of this variety. Wine buffs still reminisce about the great years of these wines. The style is rustic with earthy-like characters and big dense flavours. In the early 1960s and 1970s, Lindemans and Rothbury Estate were particularly famous for this variety, but today you can find some of the best at Brokenwood and Tyrrells.

Merlot

Although Merlot has been planted in the Hunter over a number of years, only of late has the wine shown its suitability to the zone. A mid-season ripening variety with reasonably tough skin, Merlot can withstand rain, and the grapes can ripen into the month of March when conditions become a little drier. Merlot is being planted extensively in the Broke Fordwich area.

Cabernet Sauvignon

Cabernet Sauvignon has been part of the Hunter success story. Although the climate is a little too warm to highlight true Cabernet flavours, very fine wines are produced. Because Cabernet is a thick-skinned, late-season ripening variety like Merlot, it can withstand the sometimes difficult harvest conditions.

Sampling the Wines of the Lower Hunter

The Lower Hunter makes up the bulk of the wineries and fruit planted in the Hunter Valley, being almost double the area planted to vines compared to the Upper Hunter. Figure 5-1 (inset) shows the location of the wineries in this region.

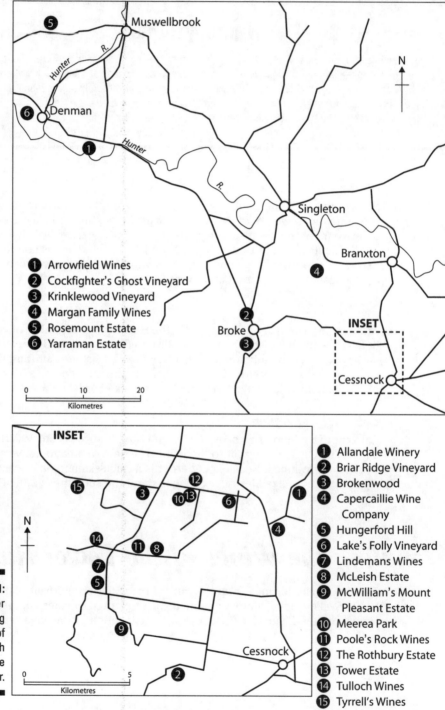

Figure 5-1:
The premier
vine-growing
region of
New South
Wales — the
Hunter.

Tasting the best the wineries offer

The wineries of the Lower Hunter vary enormously in character, ranging from small family-run businesses to vast cellar-door outlets. Many wineries have restaurants attached and a large number offer various styles of accommodation. Some of the best places to sample what the Lower Hunter has to offer include

- ✔ **Brokenwood Wines:** The key to this winery's success is its consistency. The range includes wines that are made from Hunter Valley grapes as well as wines that have been made from fruit obtained from wine regions that enjoy more consistent weather patterns during vintage, such as McLaren Vale. Brokenwood's flagship wine is the outstanding **Brokenwood Graveyard Vineyard Shiraz**, which always finds its way onto the list of the best Shiraz made in Australia.

   Also from this excellent winery come a couple of very reasonably priced wines in the **Brokenwood Cricket Pitch** range. The **Cricket Pitch White** is 60 per cent Sauvignon Blanc and 40 per cent Semillon, and has aromas of citrus and melon. The **Cricket Pitch Red** is also a blend, of which the greater part is Cabernet Sauvignon, Merlot and Shiraz.

- ✔ **Hungerford Hill:** John Parker first established The Hungerford Hill vineyards in the Hunter Valley in NSW in 1969, and the first wine release was two years later. The brand gained a good reputation for Hunter Valley Semillon and Shiraz. In 1990, the winery was acquired by Seppelts, which in turn was acquired by Southcorp. Finally, in 2002, the Kirby family acquired Hungerford Hill; a year later, they opened a stunning new winery complex in the Hunter Valley.

   Hungerford Hill offers a number of labels and a wide range of varieties. Their Cellar Door Series includes a Liqueur Muscat and a Traminer Riesling, as well as the outstanding **Hungerford Hill Hunter Valley Semillon**, a classic example of the world-famous Hunter Semillon style, made from early picked grapes and showing delicate fruit flavours.

- ✔ **Lake's Folly:** This winery was the first of the famous Hunter Valley boutique wineries, and was established in 1963 by former Sydney surgeon Max Lake. Today, the winery is under new ownership. The winery's philosophy is to keep it simple, and only two wines are made, both from fruit grown in its own vineyards. **Lake's Folly Cabernet Blend** is an excellent blend, with Cabernet Sauvignon predominating, and ages very well. **Lake's Folly Chardonnay** is excellent when young.

- ✔ **Lindemans Hunter Valley Winery:** Now owned by the giant Southcorp Wines group, this winery was originally owned by the Lindeman family. The winery was formerly known as the Ben Ean Winery — for many years, Ben Ean was also the name of its very successful wine.

Among the best to come from this winery is **Lindemans Hunter Valley Semillon**, which sets the benchmark for Semillon in the Hunter Valley. This wine is fine to drink young but is sublime after eight to ten years or longer. The other premium wine is **Lindemans Steven Vineyard Shiraz**, which comes from Lindemans Steven Vineyard at Pokolbin. This wine shows typical Hunter Valley Shiraz characters — leathery and liquorice tones and a long, dry tannin finish. This wine ages beautifully too, becoming even more savoury and textural over time.

- **McWilliam's Mount Pleasant Winery:** One of this winery's most famous range is the McWilliam's Maurice O'Shea. The wines are named after Mount Pleasant's founding winemaker. The super-premium **Mount Pleasant Maurice O'Shea Shiraz** is made solely from grapes from the ancient vines in the Old Hill Vineyard, and the **Mount Pleasant Maurice O'Shea Chardonnay** is made from the winery's best Chardonnay grapes.

The **Mount Pleasant Lovedale Semillon** and **Mount Pleasant Elizabeth Semillon** are both aged Semillons that have been in the bottle for four years before release, and so have achieved that bit of extra depth and complexity.

- **The Rothbury Estate:** Another legend of the Hunter is Len Evans who started Rothbury Estate, where some of the great Semillons were made in the 1970s. When first established in 1968, Rothbury Estate's plan was to produce a single estate Shiraz and a single estate Semillon. Now owned by Beringer Blass, Rothbury Estate produces a much wider range of varieties, although the **Rothbury Estate Shiraz** and **Rothbury Estate Brokenback Semillon** remain among its best. The Shiraz is a fruit-driven style with oak overtones, and the Semillon is intensely flavoured with distinctive fruit characters.

- **Tower Estate:** Today, Len Evans is involved in a new venture, that is the newly built and very plush Tower Estate. At this new venture the philosophy is to make premium wine using grapes from a region that is suited to that variety. So local vineyards supply the fruit for the **Tower Estate Semillon**, Adelaide Hills vineyards grow the **Tower Estate Sauvignon Blanc** fruit, a Clare Valley property is the supplier of Riesling for the **Tower Estate Riesling**, and so on.

- **Tyrrell's Wines:** Perhaps the most iconic winery in the Hunter, Tyrrell's fame is due to the late Murray Tyrrell and his pioneering vision (see the sidebar 'Profile of a local legend'). Murray's son Bruce is now in charge of the operation. While the place may seem old fashioned — parts of the winery still have dirt floors — behind the façade is a very modern winery that produces some very smart wines.

At the top of the price range are some especially good wines that are known as the Tyrrell's Vat Series, for example, **Vat 1 Hunter Semillon**, **Vat 47 Hunter Chardonnay**, **Vat 9 Shiraz** and **Vat 11 Shiraz**.

The **Rufus Stone** range was introduced as Tyrrell's production of premium red wine increased after its acquisition of new vineyards in Heathcote, Victoria (see Chapter 11), McLaren Vale in South Australia (see Chapter 16), and the Limestone Coast in South Australia (see Chapter 19). The Rufus Stone wines have been enormously successful, both within Australia and overseas.

The **Tyrrell's Rufus Stone Heathcote Shiraz** is typically peppery and spicy, while **Tyrrell's Rufus Stone McLaren Vale Shiraz** is big, bold and chocolatey — exactly the characters that you would expect in a Shiraz from this region.

Focusing on Semillon

The Hunter Valley is famous for its Semillon. Even though more Chardonnay is planted, the Hunter's Semillon is by far the better white wine.

For those who love Semillon, here's a quick rundown of Hunter Valley Semillons I've no hesitation in recommending, in addition to those noted in the previous section.

- Allandale Semillon
- Briar Ridge Early Harvest Semillon
- Briar Ridge Signature Stockhausen Semillon
- Brokenwood Semillon
- Capercaillie Hunter Valley Semillon
- Hungerford Hill Hunter Valley Semillon
- Meerea Park Semillon
- McLeish Estate Semillon
- Tulloch Semillon
- Tyrrell's Reserve Stevens Semillon

Heading for the Broke Fordwich Wines

The sub-region of Broke Fordwich is located to the north–west of the town of Broke. Having the Brokenback Range on the sub-region's western edge gives Broke Fordwich a slightly warmer aspect than the Hunter region as a whole.

Like in the Lower Hunter, most rainfall is during the growing season, which can result in problems with vine diseases. In addition, the extra fertility of the local soils, which are old volcanic soils, means that keeping excess *vigour* (growth) in the vines under control is vital, to prevent even higher disease pressures.

Choosing your style of Semillon

Don't expect your Semillon made from grapes grown in the warm Barossa Valley to age the same way as a Hunter Valley Semillon — it won't. The wines are made quite differently. Hunter Semillon is picked at what many grape growers would call 'barely ripe' status, so the resulting wines are fairly plain young wines with plenty of acid. Usually the wines have an alcohol around 11 per cent, sometimes lower.

A Barossa Valley Semillon grape is really ripe when picked, so the grape has loads of flavour and a rich fullness and texture. The alcohol is around $12\frac{1}{2}$ per cent because the grapes have more sugar in them when they're picked, and the amount of acidity is enough to balance the wine. Hunter Semillon is for ageing; Barossa Semillon is for drinking young.

So don't just grab any bottle of Semillon to stick in your cellar. Check where the grapes were grown and the percentage of alcohol. As a rough rule to follow, you can age anything under 12 per cent but over that, pull the cork!

Profile of a local legend

Murray Tyrrell was one of my favourite people in the wine industry. If you worked for him, he was simply known as 'The Boss'. (I never knew whether this was because people weren't sure whether to call him Mr Tyrrell or Murray or what.)

During vintage time, Murray would stalk through the cellars, looking for any smelly ferments or minor oversights that he could use to upbraid the winemakers. I'm sure to this day that it was just a sport for him, and that all the while he was having a chuckle at the reactions he got to his provocation. Those who called his bluff instantly became his favourites; those who didn't became Murray's targets for another day.

Murray was especially cynical about modern technology. I was once measuring the temperature of a red ferment, using a thermometer — the usual device for such a task. When he noticed, he shook his head and said: 'What's wrong with winemakers today? They all go off to university and learn too much scientific stuff. What's wrong with sticking your elbow into the grape *must* (grape juice and skins during fermentation) and using that to tell the temperature?'

Above all, Murray was one of the men who made sure the Hunter Valley was very much known around Australia as a region that makes great wine. And, he was a man who recognised what great wine was.

For the health of the plant, a vine's leaf and shoot vigour needs to be kept under control. Air circulation becomes poor with a high level of leaf density and results in a higher level of disease pressure. If air cannot freely flow through the leaf canopy, excessive humidity builds up in the centre and certain diseases happily breed away. In addition, preventative sprays seldom penetrate a dense leafy area, so leaves, shoots and grape clusters remain unprotected from potential diseases. Excessive vigour is particularly common in vines growing on soils that are too fertile. Old volcanic soils are the particular culprits here.

In spite of the problems inherent in growing vines in the sub-region, most of the main Hunter Valley wineries have vineyards in this location and rely on the area's special characteristics.

Two notable soil types are found in this area — alluvial and red basalt. The rich *alluvial* soils deposited over time by the Broke River in the valley in which Broke lies produce white wines that have a minerally and delicate style.

The *red basalt* soils over limestone in the hills have a denser structure than the alluvial soils on the flats. This basalt layer makes the soil resilient to the heavy down pours of rain so often a problem in late summer. Instead the rain runs straight off the soil and is not soaked up by the vine, which is a benefit in the late ripening period as the grape flavours don't become diluted by the uptake of this rain.

The types of soil found in the Broke Fordwich sub-region produce grapes that have great depth of flavour and colour, hence the extensive plantings of Shiraz and Merlot vines. Generally, vintage time is two weeks later here than around Pokolbin because the vines produce larger quantities of grapes and therefore it takes the vine longer to ripen this increased fruit load. Also night-time temperatures around Broke Fordwich are little lower due to a slightly higher altitude compared with Pokolbin, resulting in slowed ripening.

Overall, Broke Fordwich contributes about one quarter of the production in the Hunter Valley. The sub-region is home to many of the new and good labels. Among the wineries producing some outstanding vintages are the following:

A tough grape called Tannat

Tannat is a dark, thick-skinned, astringent, red variety of grape, which is perfect for the often inclement weather of the Hunter Valley. The tough skins can withstand heavy falls of rain without splitting. Originating in Spain, this variety is mostly grown in the southern part of France near Armagnac, and the warmth of the Hunter also suits this variety. Tannat needs considerable ageing in the barrel before bottling, typically two years. At this stage, Tannat is in the experimental phase of winemaking.

- ✔ **Glenguin Wine Company:** While not a large winery in size, the company has given itself a high profile in terms of quality. All the Hunter Valley stalwarts are represented here — Semillon, Chardonnay, Shiraz and Cabernet Sauvignon — along with the interesting addition of a little-known variety called Tannat (see the sidebar 'A tough grape called Tannat').

- ✔ Of the other wines made at this winery, **Glenguin Old Broke Chardonnay** and the **Glenguin Schoolhouse Block Shiraz** are among my favourites.

- ✔ **Hope Estate:** Hope Estate is owned and run by a former pharmacist, Michael Hope, who fled city life to pursue a life of winemaking. With a strong science background, Michael is conscious of all the important winemaking decisions needed to make full-flavoured and technically sound wines. At Hope Estate, careful consideration is taken at all times in the winemaking and grape-growing process. Best so far from this winery is the intensely flavoured and warmly textured **Hope Estate Chardonnay** as well as the **Hope Estate Shiraz** with its tones of leather and black pepper.

- ✔ **Krinklewood Vineyard:** Although a small-scale operation, the quality of the wines and the winery's growing list of wine awards is impressive. The **Krinklewood Verdelho** is very much one of the stars where the fruit salad flavours flow out of your glass. Also worth keeping an eye out for is the **Krinklewood Chardonnay** with its melon flavours and well-integrated oak.

- ✔ **Margan Family Winegrowers:** One winery that seems to be always attracting attention is Margan Family Winegrowers. Although the winery was established fairly recently, Margan makes its wines from grapes produced on 35-year-old vines. The result is wines of intensity and excellent structure, especially the reds.

  Of special note is the **Margan Verdelho**, a rich full- bodied wine; the **Margan Merlot**, which is fruit driven, full of lovely cherries and plums, and the **Margan Shiraz**, a beautifully balanced, delicious aromatic wine.

- ✔ **Poole's Rock Wines:** Poole's Rock has substantial vineyards in the Broke Fordwich sub-region, although the winery itself is situated in the Pokolbin part of the Lower Hunter.

  Poole's Rock wines are made from grapes grown entirely on the Broke Fordwich property. To date, the **Poole's Rock Hunter Valley Chardonnay** with its strong flavours of pears and nuts is outstanding. Another brand from this winery is the **Cockfighter's Ghost** range, which includes about a dozen varieties. The fruit for this label comes from the 'best from the rest', by that I mean other regions specifically selected for their fruit. For example, fruit is selected from regions that have forged a reputation for specific varieties, such as Riesling from the Clare Valley to make the excellent **Cockfighter's Clare Valley Riesling** and McLaren Vale for the Shiraz. The **Cockfighter's Ghost Chardonnay**, though, is made predominantly from grapes grown in the Broke Fordwich, and is a full of white peach characters with a hint of French oak.

Discovering the Wines of the Upper Hunter

The Upper Hunter Valley region — or Upper Hunter for short — is about 70 kilometres north-west of Cessnock. Compared to the Pokolbin area, the Upper Hunter receives over 100 millimetres less rainfall per annum, which can be a very significant factor during wet years. During the ripening season, the vineyards of the Upper Hunter are less likely to suffer from the effects of too much rain.

The Upper Hunter also has the benefit of an ever-present thin cloud cover in summer. This cover protects the grapes from the sun and avoids the risk of the grapes becoming over-ripe, which is vital to capturing flavours in the berries and resulting wines. (Over-ripe grapes lose their varietal flavour and become fairly bland tasting, resulting in nondescript tasting wines.)

The vineyards of the Upper Hunter are also 150 metres higher in altitude than those of the Lower Hunter. The constant cloud cover and the higher aspect mean that the grapes ripen a little later in the season, which allows them to build intensity of flavour. As with the Lower Hunter, you can sample excellent wines in the Upper Hunter. Refer to Figure 5-1 for the location of some of the many wineries of the Upper Hunter Valley.

Among the most successful producers in the Upper Hunter are

- **Arrowfield Wines:** One of the largest wineries in the Hunter Valley, the focus here is on Chardonnay, with Merlot and Verdelho starting to prove their value in the vineyard. The **Arrowfield Chardonnay** has rich fruit flavours with a hint of melon. Like other wineries in the Hunter Valley, Arrowfield sources a good proportion of its fruit from other New South Wales regions, notably Mudgee, Orange and Cowra.

- **Rosemount Estate:** Much of the fame of the Upper Hunter can be attributed to this winery. This large operation has built its Hunter Valley wine fame around Chardonnay and Semillon. The business also has vineyards and a winery in South Australia (which is covered in Chapter 16).

  One of Rosemount's most noted wines is the pricey **Rosemount Roxburgh Chardonnay**, which has won acclaim across the world. The grapes for this wine are harvested by hand in one of the country's oldest Chardonnay vineyards. At the more affordable end of the price spectrum is the **Premium Diamond Varietals** range, and many people see the **Rosemount Estate Chardonnay** as the quintessential commercial Australian Chardonnay. Full of tropical fruit and with melon characters, this wine is beautifully structured with a very satisfying finish.

Another Rosemount label is Show Reserve. Some consider the **Rosemount Show Reserve Chardonnay** not to be on the same level as the famous Roxburgh Chardonnay, yet for me it's the one that shows the most value for the money. While certainly not an inexpensive wine, the amount of fruit, alcohol and oak is comparatively toned down so that the wine can display a delicate, citrus Chardonnay character, along with a balanced, mid-weight texture.

✔ **Yarraman Estate:** Originally Penfolds owned the vineyard, but today Yarraman Estate owns this oldest vineyard in the Upper Hunter with vines dating back to 1958. (The original Rosemount plantings of the 1860s were neglected and it wasn't until 1969 that today's Rosemount vines were replanted.) **Yarraman Estate Black Cypress Gewürztraminer** has the intensity of flavour that can only come from grapes grown on vines over 40 years old. Like many of the other wineries of the Upper Hunter, Yarraman Estate also produces excellent Shiraz, Chardonnay and Semillon wines.

Making Wine the Focus of Your Holiday

As the Barossa is to the good citizens of the city of Adelaide, and the Yarra Valley is to those who live in Melbourne, the Hunter is very much a playground for Sydneysiders. The Hunter Valley's wineries are a real tourist magnet; people flock there to relax and enjoy good food and excellent wine.

Today, the Hunter has over 130 wineries, with around 80 located in the Lower Hunter region. The wineries range from cellar doors that are run and operated by families, to huge company complexes with sophisticated tasting and merchandising facilities.

You can eat at excellent restaurants, sample fine wine at a multitude of wineries, enjoy a wide range of recreational facilities and stay overnight in comfortable accommodation. In the summer, you can also relax while you're entertained listening to 'Jazz in the Vines' and 'Opera in the Vines'.

In addition to the wineries already mentioned in this chapter, I can't leave out the following. Not only are these wineries excellent producers of fine wines, but they also have other temptations for the visitor to the Hunter Valley.

✔ **Batchelors Terrace Vale:** This winery was one of the Hunter's first boutique wineries and is well worth the visit to sample the 100 per cent Hunter wines that, over the years, have gained more than 400 awards. Visitors are more than welcome to use the BBQ facilities here.

✔ **Bimbadgen Estate:** This winery offers fine wine, an outstanding restaurant and views to die for ('Bimbadgen' means 'lovely views').

✔ **Capercaillie Wine Company:** Capercaillie is one of the newest and smallest working wineries in Australia's oldest winegrowing region. While you sample the wines — don't miss the outstanding Semillon — you can wander about the cellar door and admire fine art, including original works by Pro Hart and Norman Lindsay.

✔ **Drayton's Family Wines:** This family-owned winery in Pokolbin has been in business for more than 150 years. Their many aged vines result in a range of premium wines. Drayton's offers accommodation and a tasting club, and has a very active events program.

✔ **Pepper Tree Wines:** Founded in 1991, this winery has been developed as one of the show places of the Hunter. The estate includes vineyards, deluxe guest house and one of the Hunter Valley's best-known restaurants. The popular cellar door annually attracts thousands of visitors who find a range of premium, super and ultra-premium varietal wines sourced from Pepper Tree's own vineyards in the Hunter, Orange, Coonawarra and Wrattonbully viticultural regions.

✔ **Petersons Wines:** A producer of some spectacular wines, this small family winery is set in beautiful surroundings. The cellar door offers a selection of quality wines, including a great Semillon.

✔ **Scarborough Wine Company:** This winery, a family-owned company, has been producing its unique style of wines since 1987, specialising in Chardonnay. The cellar door must be one of the prettiest in the Hunter; the tasting room overlooks the vineyard and gives panoramic views of the Valley.

✔ **Serenella Estate:** Formerly established in the Upper Hunter, and now re-established in the Lower Hunter by the Cecchini family, Serenella Estate wines are fresh and flavoursome. Over three generations, the Cecchini women have established a vineyard, the winery, the cellar door and a fine Italian restaurant, Arlecchino Trattoria, which gives sweeping views of the Serenella vineyard against the backdrop of the Brokenback Range.

✔ **Tamburlaine:** A small privately owned winery, Tamburlaine offers top red and white wines, as well as events such as twilight concerts and art shows.

✔ **Tempus Two Winery:** In less than ten years, Tempus Two has emerged as one of Australia's most dynamic wine brands. The wide range of wines includes classic varietals such as Barossa Valley Shiraz and Hunter Valley Semillon. The Tempus Two cellar door complex in Pokolbin includes a Japanese restaurant.

✔ **Wyndham Estate:** This winery has taken on the world with its superior winemaking and continues to impress, especially with its Chardonnays. Today, Wyndham Estate is renowned for much more than its wines: the winery has become a favourite tourist destination in the Hunter Valley, with its combination of fine food and entertainment to complement its popular wines. A major concert is held every February; you can attend 'Jazz to Shiraz' in June and 'Opera in the Vineyards' in October.

✔ **Wandin Valley Estate:** Another winery in a beautiful setting, Wandin Valley Estate has always produced premium-quality wines. In addition to the cellar door, the winery offers visitors a café, an art gallery, a swimming pool, a tennis court and a cricket ground. You can also find accommodation in self-contained Italian-style villas.

Chapter 6

The Wine Bounty of Mudgee

- -

In This Chapter

▶ Maturing Mudgee, nestling in the hills

▶ Dominating, raging reds

- -

After years of being referred to as 'Mudgee mud', grapes and wine from this emerging region are starting to turn some heads. Many people hold this region in higher regard even than New South Wales's famed Hunter Valley (refer to Chapter 5).

European migrants initially developed the wine region of Mudgee, like nearly all the grape-growing parts of Australia, as a vineyard area. Then, in time, descendants of these pioneers and other interested wine growers carried on the tradition.

During the 1970s and 1980s, the fruit from Mudgee was blended with grapes from elsewhere, and so the region was robbed of public recognition. Gradually though, the area's worth is being noted by winemakers and the drinking public. This is not surprising because some very fine wines indeed come from this beautiful part of New South Wales.

In this chapter, I introduce you to the wines of this sunny and warm region where small operators and giant wine companies alike grow the grapes.

Emerging as a Worthy Wine Region

For many years in the Australian wine world, Mudgee existed as 'the juice that arrived in a tanker during the night'. No-one proudly talked about fruit from Mudgee, because this region was considered to be an inferior place to grow grapes. However, today, wine labels proudly announce ownership of the percentage of wine in a bottle that is of Mudgee origin — such is its high reputation.

The region of Mudgee is the largest within the Central Ranges Zone. The other regions in this zone are Orange and Cowra (see Chapter 7). The main town is Mudgee with Dunedoo to the north and Kandos in the south. The name Mudgee is an Aboriginal word that means 'nest in the hills'. This meaning reflects its geographical position, surrounded by the Great Dividing Ranges and arguably one of the State's most picturesque rural areas. Every year the region shows further development and, when I was there during 2000, I was captivated by vine *rootlings* — one-year-old vines that are raised in a nursery — planted as far as I could see. Today 4,500 hectares of land are under vine, with almost 3,000 of those hectares producing fruit. (Vines take three years before really producing a crop, and more than seven years before settling down to be a reliable producer of quantity and quality grapes.)

Receiving Rain and Shine

Overall, Mudgee is a warm region, but like so many of the other inland vineyard areas, the cool nights are a big plus because the vines are allowed to really rest overnight. This rest time prolongs the ripening allowing the grape time to build up and intensify in flavours and to maintain the natural grape acidity. Ripening is fairly slow and the usual starting date for picking the fruit is early March, around four to five weeks after the Hunter Valley (refer to Chapter 5).

The vineyards of Mudgee are at a reasonably high altitude, that is, somewhere between 450 metres to 660 metres above sea level — a reason why harvest occurs in the cooler autumn time.

The Huntington Estate/ACO music festival

Music festivals at wineries is almost *de rigeur*. Huntington Estate, though, has been involved in providing music enjoyment at a sophisticated level for many years. The annual Huntington Chamber Music Festival goes over five days in early December and the town of Mudgee is totally over taken by music afficionados. The festival began quite humbly back in the early 1980s when a clarinet teacher came to try wine at the cellar door. His impression was that the barrel hall afforded the best acoustics in the world, and, from there, a small music weekend began. The arrival of Richard Tognetti in 1984 to replace a sick violinist created the internationally renowned festival as it is today. Tognetti is the Artistic Director of the Australian Chamber Orchestra and married to Susie Roberts — the daughter and winemaker of Huntington Estate, so the annual event is here to stay.

During the early weeks of vintage 2003, Mudgee experienced a once-in-a-lifetime — one would hope — occurrence. Rain fell heavily across the New South Wales vineyard areas but at Mudgee they came with such force that there were significant floods. So severe were these floods that old vines, with well-established root systems, were washed down hills. The forceful rains washed the layers of soil, along with anything that was planted in it, to the bottom of the hill. Some fortunate vineyards had harvested their fruit. In fact, the manager at the **Rosemount Mountain Blue** vineyards heeded the heavy rainfall forecast and managed to get his fruit in just as the rain began to fall, a lucky escape indeed. But that story recalls an unusual weather pattern. While rain often falls during harvest, it can more often than not act as refreshment, that is, giving the vines just a little water to help maintain the leaves as they enter the last part of their ripening. Rain doesn't have to mean disaster during vintage. If the leaves are starved of water, they start to die and the energy produced during photosynthesis of the leaves aids in the ripening of the berries.

The red wines of the region are known for their dense flavours as well as their mineral and earthy-like characters. This signature Mudgee style is attributed to the local soils.

In this region, rich, red, volcanic soils overlay quartz and gravel. Consequently, the soil is fertile so that *vigour* (the amount of leaves and shoots that the vine produces) in the vineyards needs to be well addressed to gain maximum quality. The vineyards that pay good attention to reducing shoot numbers and allowing air to circulate within the canopy, and therefore reduce disease pressure, will do well; as will the vineyards that keep crop levels at a reasonable amount. Too high a crop not only reduces the intensity of flavours in the grapes, but it also delays ripening, pushing harvest time into the late autumn when the rain can definitely impact negatively on the grapes.

The underneath soil is also important. In Mudgee this soil type is mainly quartz and gravel with a little limestone. The benefit of these soils is that they allow for good drainage before the soil profile changes into clay. The great benefit of clay is its ability to retain moisture so the older vines, whose roots have managed to reach right down into the soil, are able to sustain the vine during the dry summer time. While the talk of too much rain and then the need for the clay soil may sound a little contradictory, the need for water is more often the case. During the flowering period around November to December, vines need a source of water so that they can concentrate their efforts not just on the new leaf growth, but also on producing a good crop. Vines that are able to reach down into the soil for water will be better balanced than those that can't.

Planting the Best Grapes for the Region

Mudgee is top heavy with red wine grapes, with well over half the grapes grown being Shiraz and Cabernet Sauvignon. While Chardonnay is popular, it only ranks at about 17 per cent of the total tonnes processed.

Mudgee's claim to fame, in terms of being fashionable, is that the one time winemaker at Montrose winery, Carlo Corino, was the first to introduce the Italian red varieties to Australia. With the current boom in Sangiovese, Barbera and Nebbiolo, Mudgee can indeed boast to be a leader in the alternative red wine style stakes. While these grapes certainly don't dominate the region, they're significant within the wonderful mixture of wines available from Australia, nonetheless.

Noting stylistic reds

The best red grape varieties include

- ✔ **Shiraz:** Shiraz is the red grape leader in the area — just. In 2002, 28 per cent of Mudgee fruit was Shiraz, with Cabernet Sauvignon tallying up 27 per cent. Shiraz from Mudgee is full bodied and has a similar power of flavour as the wines from the regions such as McLaren Vale (see Chapter 16) and the Barossa (see Chapter 18) in South Australia. The flavours, while exhibiting a fruitiness, are more on the earthy side of the Shiraz style. Ordinarily, they're long livers in the bottle.

- ✔ **Cabernet Sauvignon:** Cabernet Sauvignon thrives in this region, particularly in years when the ripening is slow and the weather holds until early April, allowing full ripening of this variety to occur. The wines are generally fuller in body than those of Coonawarra (see Chapter 19) and they don't show the leafy character so often associated with this grape. You can expect a Mudgee Cabernet to be fairly full bodied with plenty of blackberry, as well as a good firm tannin structure. Like Mudgee's Shiraz, the Cab Sav ages well.

✔ **Merlot:** Merlot may not be as big player as Shiraz and Cabernet in terms of hectares grown and tonnes processed, but this variety is definitely one to watch in terms of potential. Being slightly earlier to ripen than Cabernet (by about ten days on average), Merlot offers the grape grower a chance to fully ripen and to harvest the fruit before any inclement autumn weather sets in.

Merlot has the attraction of being a fruit-driven style of wine, which is increasingly appealing to consumers. Wine-drinking statistics show that more than 85 per cent of wine gets consumed within 48 hours of being purchased from a shop. Wines in this category, such as Merlot, which can be enjoyed without needing ten years in the cellar, are becoming very much in demand.

Shining Whites

The best white grape varieties include

✔ **Chardonnay:** For white wine drinkers, Chardonnay flys the flag in Mudgee. In fact, many people attribute the boom in Chardonnay consumption to those wines originating from Mudgee in the 1970s. At that time, large tracts of land were planted to this versatile variety and the local climate suited the grape. The warmth during the day when ripening followed by cool nights allow the Chardonnay grown around Mudgee to capture intense peach and fig flavours along with a nicely balanced acidity.

✔ **Semillon:** As the lesser-planted white variety, sitting at about 9 per cent of the region's grape intake, the Semillon made in Mudgee is quite different in style to that of the Hunter Valley (refer to Chapter 5). In this region, Semillon is able to achieve a higher degree of ripeness due to the usually fine vintage conditions. So, instead of the wine being lean when young and needing time in the cellar to fill out (be a rounder, fuller tasting wine), Mudgee's Semillons are appealing for immediate drinking.

Sampling Mudgee's Top Wines

Perhaps due to the old image of playing second best to the more famous Hunter Valley (refer to Chapter 5), Mudgee wines are considered very reasonably priced. Mostly, the wines are below AUD$30, which certainly makes them value for money, especially considering the quality of some of the top red wines in the region. The highest priced wine is Rosemount's flagship Mountain Blue red and it could be argued that the price here has been determined very much as part of a marketing exercise and positioning within a select price point. See Figure 6-1 for some of Mudgee's magic wineries.

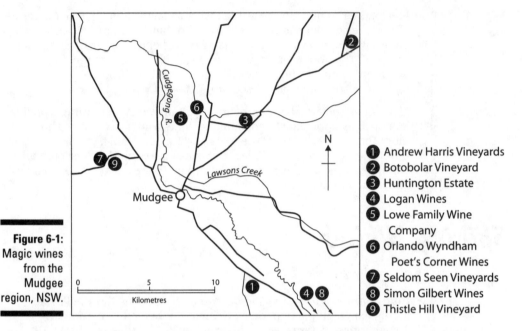

Figure 6-1:
Magic wines
from the
Mudgee
region, NSW.

① Andrew Harris Vineyards
② Botobolar Vineyard
③ Huntington Estate
④ Logan Wines
⑤ Lowe Family Wine
  Company
⑥ Orlando Wyndham
  Poet's Corner Wines
⑦ Seldom Seen Vineyards
⑧ Simon Gilbert Wines
⑨ Thistle Hill Vineyard

You can find top wines from the Mudgee wine region, which include those from

✔ **Andrew Harris Vineyards:** Large plantings by Andrew Harris Vineyards have helped put Mudgee in the spotlight. Like many of the bigger wineries in the area, the varieties that have been chosen are the ones that are well proven in the area — Chardonnay, Shiraz, Cabernet Sauvignon, Merlot and Semillon.

✔ **Botobolar Vineyard:** Botobolar was one of the first wineries and vineyards to embrace the organic style of winemaking (see the sidebar 'Controlling pesky pests without chemicals'). The best label from here is **Botobolar Shiraz**.

✔ **Huntington Estate:** One of my favourite wines comes from Huntington Estate. The wines from here have been so well made over the years, with little fanfare or promotion and low yields that keep flavours intense. The lovers of these wines are very happy to purchase their stash every year and rest them in the cellar until they slowly evolve (for at least a decade or two). The best wines are the reds, **Huntington Estate Shiraz** and **Huntington Estate Cabernet Sauvignon**, which give an honest, rustic flavour. Huntington does make a special reserve wine, which is first class but so is its standard bottling of these varieties.

These days, the founder of the vineyard, Bob Roberts, is assistant winemaker, and his daughter, Susie, takes the helm. Her style is one that continues making wines in a thoughtful yet classic method, without fiddling around using all of the latest fashions of winemaking techniques (see the sidebar 'Fashions in winemaking') and, consequently, the fruit continues to be allowed to express itself.

Logan Wines are made at the Simon Gilbert Wines winery, with a cellar door nearby. Best from Logan are the **Logan Chardonnay**, a peachy, easy-to-drink style and **Logan Sauvignon Blanc**, a tropical guava wine with good zesty acid.

✔ **Lowe Family Wine Company:** Well worth discovering are the Italian varietals of Mudgee. Wineries such as the Lowe Family Wine vineyard are favouring the new Italians with an excellent Sangiovese that has dense structure and a savoury character that is so often associated with this variety. **Tinja Sangiovese Merlot Barbera** shows sweet sour aromatics of cherry and dried herbs.

Another variety that this vineyard does well is Zinfandel, a robust red grape that is very popular in the United States. Zinfandel is a variety, though, that dislikes rain around harvest time because its reasonably thin grape skin can easily split during heavy rain — weather that can occur in Mudgee. The Lowe vineyards, however, protect a little against the effect of heavy rain as they're *dry-grown* vineyards, which means that the vine is already used to surviving without rain and can withstand, therefore, a little of natural rainfall before the grapes become saturated and split. From here comes **Tinja Zinfandel**, which shows a dusty character with a concentrated sweet fruit.

✔ **Orlando Wyndham Poet's Corner Wines:** The biggest facility in the area is the Orlando Wyndham's Poet's Corner winery. Originally known as Montrose winery, this winery has been upgraded to accommodate all

Fashions in winemaking

Like so many industries, the wine industry isn't immune to the newest and greatest way to make wine or additives to use to make wine. Some of the newer additions to winemaking are the addition of grape tannin from a packet — to increase the amount of tannin naturally found in the grapes. Another fashion is the addition of enzymes that help to extract more colour from the skins of the red grapes, so as to get deeper coloured wines. Recently the fashion in making red wines is to use a little oxygen to bubble through the wine in an attempt to gain greater colour of the final wine. And so the list goes on. Many wineries embrace these changes, sometimes only briefly before they go back to the traditional 'just let the grapes ferment without too much human intervention technique' and others swear that these new and whiz-bang methods make all the difference to the quality of their wines.

of the company's Mudgee labels — Montrose, Henry Lawson and Poet's Corner ranges. The reason for the poetry theme relates to the famous Australian poet, Henry Lawson, who grew up in the Mudgee area. The Poet's Corner range focuses on inexpensive wines that are made to be drunk young, and have good fruit-driven flavours (refer to the earlier section in this chapter, 'Planting the Best Grapes for the Region'). In the **Henry Lawson** range, Shiraz and Cabernet Sauvignon show how well they're suited to the Mudgee climate. Montrose is the premium range where the Italian varietals such as Sangiovese and Barbera shine, cementing the future of these grapes within the region.

✔ **Seldom Seen Vineyards:** A good example of Mudgee's Semillon is **Seldom Seen Semillon**, a nutty and lime wine.

✔ **Simon Gilbert Wines:** The new facility of Simon Gilbert Wines takes in fruit grown in the Mudgee region about 20 kilometres out of the centre of Mudgee. Here the area's stalwart varieties are made along with a dabbling in the Sangiovese, Barbera, Petit Verdot and Merlot (refer to Chapter 2).

✔ **Thistle Hill Vineyard:** This family vineyard, an advocate for sustainable farming, uses no insecticides, herbicides or synthetic fertilisers on its 27-acre vineyard. As a result, Thistle Hill has been classified as organic (see the sidebar 'Controlling pesky pests without chemicals ') by NASAA (National Association for Sustainable Agriculture Australia). The best from Thistle Hill is the Cabernet Sauvignon.

Controlling pesky pests without chemicals

Organic and biodynamic farming techniques have been embraced in Mudgee, notably by **Botobolar Winery**, the oldest organic vineyard in Australia, and **Thistle Hill Vineyard**. Encouraging bird and animal life, by planting trees and providing natural water areas, allows natural predators to take care of the pests without using chemicals. Alternatives to herbicide, such as mulch, are being widely adopted to help manage weeds and fungal diseases in the organic vineyard.

And biodynamically speaking, I well remember a trip here as a wine science student. For scientifically trained students, the biodynamic processes all seemed a little like witchcraft. For instance, the fertiliser was made from cow dung compost and then mixed with water. This mixing procedure had to follow a certain method with stirring one way and then the other for a certain length of time. The resulting mixture was then sprayed onto the vineyard during certain phases of the moon and/or at a particular time of the day or night.

While traditional mainstream grape growers might scoff at biodynamic and organic methods, these sustainable grape-growing practices are taking hold. While not so many vineyards go through the arduous accreditation procedure through NASAA (National Association for Sustainable Agriculture Australia Limited) — www.nasaa.com.au — to become a certified organic vineyard, the management practices of a growing number of vineyards are based on the ideal of organic practices.

Chapter 7

Rounding Out the Smaller Top Spots in New South Wales

*T*he bountiful offering of wines in this chapter feature the combined regions of New South Wales and the Canberra District (which itself is a region that takes in parts of New South Wales and Australian Capital Territory (ACT)). These wine regions cover a diversity of growing conditions, with humidity high in some areas, low in others. (Humidity depends on the flow of air through the regions, for example the higher altitude regions are able to get a good breeze throughout the vine canopy resulting in lower humidity and the coastal areas can suffer stormy conditions and higher humidity.) Mild temperatures (such as during summer when the temperatures hover around the low twenties degrees Celsius) pervade some areas and reasonably hot temperatures (above 30 degrees Celsius during summer) invade others.

A commonality of the group of wine regions is its relative youth. The frequently enjoyed migrant history, so common in Australian grape-growing regions, isn't a part of the development of these regions. Instead, Australians of Anglo-Saxon backgrounds, who have a passion for wine and see these areas as worthwhile for growing grapes, pioneered and continue to develop them.

This chapter looks at the wines that come from some of the small but interesting wine regions across alpine and river regions of New South Wales and into the ACT. The NSW regions of Orange and Cowra make up the remainder of the Central Ranges zone, (refer to Chapter 6 for wines of the Mudgee region — the largest in this zone).

I introduce wines from the Southern New South Wales zone, which takes in the higher altitude grape-growing regions of Tumbarumba, Hilltops and the Canberra District. Finally, I look at Chambourcin, a special grape variety from a winery on the coast of New South Wales, in the Hastings River region of the Northern Rivers zone.

Filling in the Central Ranges zone

The largest winegrowing region in the Central Ranges zone is Mudgee (refer to Chapter 6), but there are two distinctive regions, Orange and Cowra, based on their climate and soil types.

Discovering more than oranges in Orange

Orange falls into the Geographical Indications (GI) zone (refer to Chapter 3) of the Central Ranges. The GI, unusually, specifies a certain altitude as part of the definition for Orange. Consequently, to be accepted as part of the Orange region, vineyards must fit into the defined shire boundaries and, within these boundaries, they must be 600 metres above sea level or higher.

The Orange region is a mixed agricultural area. Beef cattle, sheep and orchards dominate the landscape. The development of vineyards is a recent trend that seems likely to continue. The first vines were planted in 1983 at Bloodwood, which, in Australian terms, is recent. Since then the region has expanded with interest from the larger wine companies, such as Rosemount Estate, investing in the area. Although many of the companies that use Orange fruit don't actually run a winery in the area, the numbers of small cellar doors (tasting facilities) are increasing. More than 30 wine businesses are run in the region but, because many of these decide to have their wine contract-made at other facilities, only a handful are local working wineries.

Chilling out in Orange

Orange is pretty mild. Snow in winter isn't uncommon and the summer temperatures aren't going to set the mercury rising too fast, with usual day temperatures often not reaching above 30 degrees Celsius. Growing grapes in Orange is cool climate viticulture. Interestingly, even though the Orange and Cowra (see the section 'Taking in Cowra' later in this chapter) regions are less than 100 kilometres apart (as the crow flies), the climatic conditions are quite different.

The mild weather in Orange is due simply to the altitude of the vineyards. As you know, the further you climb up a hill, the cooler the air temperature becomes. Orange has an average altitude of 850 metres above sea level, with many vineyards closing 1,000 metres. Few regions in Australia are this high (the Whitlands area in the Alpine Valleys region of Victoria, for example, is around 800 metres, see Chapter 12). The altitude has implications for the grape-growing season, which starts later in the year than most areas because the winter is a true winter allowing the vines to shut themselves down for the cold months. This slower start to the growing season causes the ripening of the grapes to be pushed forwards to a later date and, typically, the grapes are harvested from late March to May. The later harvest benefits the grapes with a ripening in cooler weather, which allows for the gradual build up of fruit-flavour intensity.

Rainfall is quite plentiful in the Orange region and, on average, 850 millimetres falls each year. About half of this rain falls during the growing season (September to March), and the remainder arrives in winter. The deep volcanic soils that surround the extinct volcano of Mount Canobolas mean that the soil can retain this moisture and prevent the vines from suffering water stress. The water-retentive ability of the soil allows for the vines to concentrate on the berries (rather than struggling to keep the leaves from dying off too early), resulting in good, even ripening of the grapes. (After all, the energy made by the leaves helps the plant ripen the fruit.)

Making the most of the Orange varieties

Due to slow, even ripening of grapes (refer to the previous section), the varieties that do best are those which enjoy showing their fruity flavours:

- **White grape varieties:** White grapes such as Sauvignon Blanc, Chardonnay and Riesling benefit from the mild weather (refer to the previous section), which allows the berries to build up their flavour profile and maintain it. *Sunburn* of the grapes, which volatilises the flavours from the berries, is uncommon, so expect rounded fruity whites from the Orange region.

  When the grapes become sunburnt, the soft fruit flavours of the grapes are lost to the sunshine and heat. Think of the difference between a fresh sultana eating grape and a dried sultana. The same grape variety is totally changed by the drying effect of the sunshine and the removal of the juice from the grape. The same thing can happen to wine grapes if the bunch is exposed to the sunshine, resulting in a dramatic change to the flavour of the grape, which then tastes incredibly sweet but without the usual varietal flavours that you may expect.

✔ **Red grape varieties:** Perhaps surprisingly, given the cool climate, both Shiraz and Cabernet Sauvignon can do well in the warmer years, as long as good viticultural attention is given to the vines. Usually, a region that is this cool would mean that Cabernet Sauvignon, in particular, would struggle to ripen. However, one of the strengths of the region is the long and stable weather in autumn. In most years, the weather is such that the sun continues to shine without a dramatic seasonal change that comes as autumn turns to winter and, with it, cold temperatures and rain. Instead, the grapes are able to gradually achieve all their ripeness parameters — sugar, flavour and tannin ripeness. Though, without careful site choice, which is paramount to ripening Cabernet Sauvignon, unripe flavours such as that reminiscent of green capsicum sneak into the wines making them less appealing. As Shiraz ripens a little earlier than Cabernet Sauvignon, the region is able to achieve full ripeness during the autumn period.

Pinot Noir is the other red grape variety in this region, with plantings increasing gradually. Given that this variety enjoys a cool climate, I feel that it has a bright future in the Orange region, too.

Picking from the best of the Orange bunch

A handful of wine brands and labels come out of the Orange region (see Figure 7-1).

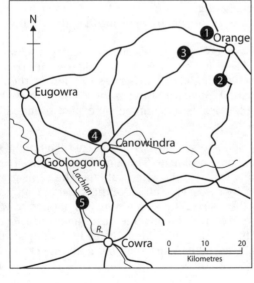

Figure 7-1: Wonderful wines from Orange and Cowra regions of NSW.

1. Bloodwood
2. Brangayne of Orange
3. Canobolas-Smith Wines
4. Hamiltons Bluff
5. Windowrie Estate

Check out the following top wines:

✔ **Rosemount Estate Orange Vineyard Merlot:** This red is one of my favourites of the Orange wines within the Rosemount Estate portfolio because of its mulberry and liquorice flavours.

The Rosemount Estate winery is increasing its plantings in the area, and continues to buy fruit from local grape growers. Rosemount Estate initially became involved through the then head of winemaking, Philip Shaw's passion for the area. His search for a new cool grapegrowing region lead him to Orange and both he and Rosemount Estate became part of the region. His own substantial vineyard was established back in 1988 covering an area totalling 50 hectares. To date he focuses on Chardonnay, Sauvignon Blanc and a trio of reds — Shiraz, Cabernet Sauvignon and Merlot. The first wines are due for release late in 2004 and will, no doubt, show the passion that has elevated Shaw to one of Australia's most internationally awarded winemakers.

An important point to remember is that many of the Rosemount Estate other labels (refer to Chapter 3 for more information about labelling requirements) — such as the **Premium Diamond Varietals** — may not actually list Orange as the region even though the grapes grown in Orange play an important part as a component of the blend in these multi-regional labels.

✔ **Bloodwood Riesling:** This particular favourite of mine shows the lovely cool-climate citrus aromas. Bloodwood was the first winery to plant in the region, in 1983. The owner, Stephen Doyle, is a real ambassador for the region, making sure that the world of wine knows about the Orange region wines and that his wines are definitely among the best.

✔ **Brangayne of Orange wines:** Wines from this local winery are highly regarded. Chardonnay and Sauvignon Blanc are planted on one vineyard — 970 metres above sea level. At a growing altitude of almost 1,000 metres, the Chardonnay fruit for the **Brangayne of Orange 'The Isolde'** shows delicate fruit flavours and a wine that ages well, too. Like so many in the region, the wine is made off site by a contract winemaker, but you can still visit a cellar door for tastings.

Home to the red grapes of Cabernet Sauvignon, Merlot, Shiraz and Pinot Noir is the company's second vineyard at a slightly lower and warmer site — 870 metres above sea level. The grapes for the Cabernet Sauvignon, known as **Brangayne of Orange 'The Tristan'**, grow here. Despite this high elevation and undoubtedly cool and late ripening season, this wine shows a great savoury character, without the green herbal flavours so often associated with cool-climate Cabernet.

✔ **Canobolas-Smith Chardonnay:** A white wine worth keeping your eye out for from another family-operated winery. This white shows the intensity of fruit it is possible to achieve when grapes are grown at an altitude of around 800 metres. Unlike many in the region, Murray Smith makes the wine on site in his small winery.

✔ **Cumulus Climbing Merlot and Cumulus Rolling Chardonnay:** The Cumulus Climbing Merlot is a terrific example of soft-fruited, berry-filled and flavourful wine, while the Cumulus Rolling Chardonnay is peach dominated with an acid lift to finish. The wines are well priced.

After a torrid past from a financial point of view, a new business (**Cumulus Wines**) has emerged from the former Reynolds Wines. This company also involves the irrepressible Philip Shaw (refer earlier).

✔ **Hungerford Hill Merlot and Shiraz:** These reds from Hungerford Hill, a winemaker that has taken quite an interest in the Orange region, producing wine from both its own vineyards and also using fruit from local growers, are worth a try. The savoury and briary Merlot is the best from here so far, with a black pepper and spice Shiraz that in warmer years shows the promise of this relatively new region.

✔ **Logan Sauvignon Blanc:** This fresh, intensely flavoured white is delightful for drinking over summer. The flavours are ripe, having lost any suggestion of those unpleasant tasting grassy or asparagus flavours often seen in under ripe Sauvignon Blanc. Instead, the wine has aromas of tropical fruits and a crisp balancing acidity. Definitely one to look out for.

Logan's is a large grape grower here. Although Logan's decided to build its winery and cellar door facilities close to Mudgee (refer to Chapter 6 for wines of the Mudgee region), the main bulk of its grape source is in the Orange region.

Taking in Cowra

Making up the trio of wine regions in the Central Ranges zone, is Cowra. (Refer to the previous section 'Discovering more than oranges in Orange', and Chapter 6, for the other two grape-growing regions of this zone.) In common with the Orange region is the fact that few actual wineries are located here. Instead, vineyards are commonly owned by out-of-town wine companies or grape growers that sell their fruit to wineries in other regions. This approach to business isn't to say that the fruit is inferior to the other regions, in fact quite the contrary. Mostly, Hunter Valley wineries (refer to Chapter 5) buy and use the fruit to make a specific single label — such as Rothbury Estate Cowra Chardonnay. The wineries also use the fruit to bolster bad years in their own region, taking advantage of the 85 per cent rule of naming where the fruit comes from (see Chapter 3 for labelling laws). Of course, spreading your grape-growing sites around different regions also helps avoid financial disaster when one region is affected by the vagaries of the weather — such as hail, excessive rain, drought and disease problems.

Cowra started its grape-growing life in 1973. These early plantings of Chardonnay showed winemakers just how good this area was for this variety and, before long, Cowra carried the title of 'Chardonnay country'; such was the degree of planting to this grape. Even today, the percentage of Chardonnay grown is 63 per cent of the white varieties and 34 per cent of total plantings. The closest rival is Shiraz, with 22 per cent of total grape plantings. In fact, such was the love affair with Chardonnay that other grape varieties have been tried only relatively recently.

The most successful grape varieties in the Cowra region are

- Chardonnay, Semillon, Verdelho in the whites.
- Cabernet Sauvignon, Merlot and Shiraz in the reds

Today, over 35 vineyard operations in the region produce around 14,000 tonnes of fruit a year. Orange (refer to the previous section) by comparison, produces around 6,000 tonnes of fruit a year.

Hotting it up in dry Cowra

In stark contrast to the winegrowing region of Orange (refer to the section 'Chilling out in Orange' earlier in this chapter), the Cowra region is considered hot and dry. Vineyards in the region need irrigation or they're not viable. As a result, the local waterways of the Lachlan River and Belubula River, as well as underground bores, are vital to the survival of vines in the region. In recent years, the *partial rootzone drying techniques* (methods used to halve the amount of water required by a vine) have been introduced to try to reduce the amount of water required for grapegrowing (see Chapter 12 for more information about partial rootzone drying). The average January day temperature in Cowra is almost 34 degrees Celsius, which is considered a hot climate. Compare this with the average Orange regional temperature of 28 degrees Celsius. Cool nights, however, temper this Cowra warmth, and allow the grapevines to rest, ensuring that the wines don't get overripe and lose their varietal characteristics (see the following section).

In Australia, viticulturists use a value of temperature to evaluate the suitability of regions for growing certain grape varieties. This measurement is known as the *mean January temperature* or the *MJT*. Don't forget Australia and New Zealand are in the Southern Hemisphere so summer time is December through to the end of February. (The Northern Hemisphere month is July for this measurement.) So the MJT is a measurement of the maximum daily temperature plus the minimum daily temperature, divided by two. Cool-climate-preferring varieties such as Pinot Noir need an MJT of less than 20 degrees Celsius, and warmer loving varieties such as Durif thrive at an MJT of 20 degrees Celsius and over. Although, the MJT is a general measurement, it does give grape growers an insight to the appropriate regions for planting certain varieties.

Making the most of the Cowra varieties

The hot and dry conditions of the Cowra region produce super fruit-flavoured grapes from the following white and red varieties:

- **Chardonnay:** Chardonnay grapes ripen during the warm late summertime months and, hence, produce Chardonnay with intense fruit flavours and high sugar levels. Consequently, the wines from the Cowra region are characteristically full-bodied Chardonnay with plenty of texture and alcohol, typically around 13.5 per cent or more.

- **Shiraz:** The second most favoured grape variety from the Cowra region is Shiraz. Unlike some regions that have a particularly distinct flavor profile for Shiraz, such as the leathery character of the Hunter Valley (refer to Chapter 5) or the black pepper tones of Heathcote in Victoria (refer to Chapter 11), Shiraz from Cowra is more mainstream. Here, the fruit flavours are berry-like with plums and blackberries dominating rather than having any peppery or earthy flavours.

Culling the best of the Cowra bunch

Top wines that come from small producers in the Cowra region (refer to Figure 7-1) include

- **Hamiltons Bluff Canowindra Grossi Unwooded Chardonnay:** This white is typical of the region, showing full flavoured white nectarine and a rounded rich palate, and is one of the best from **Hamiltons Bluff Vineyard**.

The vineyard is situated in the fertile valley of the Belubula River. Chardonnay, Cabernet Sauvignon and Shiraz are the mainstay grape varieties, with a recent inclusion of Sangiovese. Recently, the Andrews family has planted vineyards in the Orange region (refer to the section 'Discovering more than oranges in Orange' earlier in this chapter), planting Viognier and Chardonnay in an attempt to grow different, cooler styles of these varieties in comparison to those grown in the warm vineyards of Cowra.

- ✔ **Windowrie Family Reserve Chardonnay:** This white from **Windowrie** shows great freshness and liveliness of acidity with quite a dense texture. At Windowrie (one of the few working wineries in the area), the winemaker strongly believes that picking the fruit and processing it straight away (rather than delaying crushing and transporting it on a truck for contract winemaking) can make better wine.

  The Mill label is the second and lower-priced label from Windowrie. **The Mill Sangiovese** is a very good example of this savoury and earthy grape variety, perhaps heralding a future for this variety in the region.

Wines of interest from wineries that use the Cowra fruit are

- ✔ **Hungerford Hill Cowra Chardonnay:** This regionally focused Cowra label shows ripe fruit and allows the tropical notes of Chardonnay to shine through along with a full-bodied weight. The wine is quite dense and round on the palate rather than light and acidic, such as, for example, a young Riesling would be. These Cowra Chardonnays aren't wines for ageing, rather they're reasonably priced ready to drink styles.

- ✔ **Richmond Grove Cowra Vineyard Verdelho:** Orlando Wyndham's Richmond Grove label releases a special Cowra wine. This white wine is a particularly good fruity wine that should be drunk when young.

Both **Brokenwood** and **McGuigan Wines** wineries also use fruit from Cowra in their blends.

In some ways, the wines from the Cowra region are still quite unknown. Many of the big companies highly value their investment in the region, as well as the fruit that they buy from grape growers. But this involvement isn't reflected by the name 'Cowra' being listed all that frequently on the labels (refer to Chapter 3 for information about labelling). Instead, the fruit is used in that vital role of *blending*, when a bit of wine made from this sunny and ripe region can make all the difference to the final product, (see Chapter 12 for an explanation of blending). So, although Cowra isn't necessarily today's glamorous and most talked about wine region, some honest, full-flavoured sunshine-in-a-glass wines that come from here certainly speak for themselves.

Catching Up with Alpine Wines

Don't you love some of the names of the Australian towns that are almost impossible to pronounce for anyone who isn't a local. In this section, I explore the cool-climate wines from Tumbarumba, which is part of the Southern New South Wales wine zone, and wines from other main regions in this zone — Hilltops and the Canberra District.

Taking a turn around Tumbarumba

When you visit Tumbarumba as a wine tourist you may be a tad disappointed. Glitz and glamour associated with the more wine-tourist-savvy regions (such as Margaret River (see Chapter 22), Yarra Valley (see Chapter 10) or McLaren Vale (see Chapter 16)) aren't really on the Tumbarumba menu. Most of the fruit produced in the region is sold pre-harvest and shipped out and made mainly at the Charles Sturt Winery in Wagga Wagga or to Hungerford Hill in the Hunter Valley. Regardless, Tumbarumba surely is one of the most beautiful small winegrowing parts of Australia.

Cooling down in Tumbarumba

The Tumbarumba wine region is situated at the foothills of the Australian Alps, not that far from the majestic Mount Kosciuszko (Australia's highest mountain). Not surprisingly, this winegrowing region is a cool-climate one, sitting at about 680 metres above sea level. But the region isn't vines, vines and more vines, as far as you can see. Instead, because the entire region isn't suited to vines, pockets of vineyards tumble around here and there. Growing grapes here means that careful site selection is important to ensure that the vines are able to maximise sunshine. As a result, you find vines on the undulating hills, mostly facing north or east to expose the vines to the sun's rays.

Knowing the best of the Tumbarumba varieties

Over 70 per cent of the grapes growing in the Tumbarumba region are used for sparkling base wines (see the sidebar 'Giving a base wine its sparkle'). The reason for success of these varieties is the coolness of the region. These cool conditions enable the grapes to ripen so that the fruit flavours develop intensity at lower sugar ripeness while, at the same time, allowing the grapes to maintain their acidity.

TECHNICAL STUFF

Giving a base wine its sparkle

As grapes ripen, the sugar level increases, as does the amount of flavour in the berries. At the same time, the acid level decreases. Grapes are picked when the winemaker feels that the right balance between these three components is met. For sparkling base wines, less sugar is required; flavours need to be ripe but not too fruity, and acidity levels must still be quite high.

In the right cool climate these components can come together at the same time. In a warmer climate, while the grape grower is waiting for full flavour development, the sugar levels rise too quickly and the acid drops away too fast. So a cool climate, such as is found in the Tumbarumba winegrowing region, is vital for making top quality sparkling base wine.

The grape varieties that like it cool are

- ✔ **Chardonnay:** Typical Chardonnay is delicate in flavour and weight. Fruits are in the citrus and melon spectrum with some nutty influences from the slow grape ripening.

- ✔ **Pinot Noir:** Table wine and Tumbarumba get along well, too. The cool climate allows the Pinot Noir fruit to mature without the occasional super hot day that so often plagues grape growers in other Pinot Noir regions such as the Yarra Valley (see Chapter 10) and Mornington Peninsula (see Chapter 13) in Victoria.

  Pinot Noir is sought after from Tumbarumba for sparkling wine, too, because of its delicate flavours and good acid.

- ✔ **Sauvignon Blanc:** The signature flavour that these grape growers get for their Sauvignon Blanc is gooseberry along with a good zesty acidity.

Taking to Tumbarumba's top pickings

Tumbarumba wines aren't made in the Tumbarumba region. The fruit produced in this winegrowing region is shipped to wineries outside the region. The lack of wineries means that very few wines actually acknowledge the region on the label. Partly, too, this lack of acknowledgement is due to the grapes being used to make sparkling wines, which are usually a blend of wines across many regions.

Wines to check out that acknowledge the Tumbarumba region on the label are

- ✔ **Chalkers Crossing Tumbarumba Pinot Noir:** This red is a wine that I like, especially as it is an inexpensive Pinot Noir, a rare thing indeed in Australia. Although situated in the Hilltops region (see the next section), this winery uses grapes that have been grown in the Tumbarumba region, which the winemakers believe is more suited to producing cool-climate specialists such as Pinot Noir and Chardonnay.

- ✔ **Hungerford Hill Tumbarumba series:** This series includes a Chardonnay, Sauvignon Blanc and Pinot Noir. The Pinot Noir shows a degree of fruitiness along with some good tannin structure.

Sparkling wines that incorporate the fruit from Tumbarumba for you to try are

- ✔ **Charles Sturt Chardonnay Sparkling** wine.
- ✔ **Seppelt Salinger Sparkling** wine.

Heading into the Hilltops

An emerging wine region in the Southern New South Wales zone is Hilltops. Centred around the town of Young, the Hilltops region is about 400 kilometres west from Sydney. In terms of size, the region is small with only five wineries in the area. The biggest landowner is McWilliam's with its Barwang property. The fruit, other than what goes to McWilliam's, is mostly sold on to the larger winemaking companies such as Southcorp Wines and the Hardy Wine Company. At present, 400 hectares are under vine.

The Hilltops winegrowing region is considered to be a cool to mild area. (During the ripening season, the daily temperatures never get much higher than the high twenties Celsius.) Rainfall in this region is uniform during the growing season. Situated at around 440 to 600 metres above sea level, this altitude gives the region a touch of coolness that tempers the warm summer days, allowing gradual ripening of the grapes.

The best grape varieties from the Hilltops region where the red soils tend to give these grapes depth of flavour and a strong berry aroma are

- ✔ Cabernet Sauvignon.
- ✔ Shiraz.

Wines to note in the region are

- ✓ **McWilliam's Barwang Merlot:** This red shows fantastic depth of flavour with real blackberry tones and fine tannins and its success proves that this variety may soon be more extensively planted.

- ✓ **Chalkers Crossing Hilltops Cabernet Sauvignon:** Shows a ripe cherry and blackberry aroma with hints of peppermint and soft tannins.

- ✓ **Chalkers Crossing Hilltops Shiraz:** Shows liquorice, spicy and peppery flavours. Planted as recently as 1997, these two wines are the best from the Chalkers Crossing winery, which has made a strong reputation for itself already. (Refer to the previous section for Chalkers Crossing wines that use grapes from the Tumbarumba region.)

Uncorking in Canberra

This is the third of the four winegrowing regions in the Southern New South Wales zone (refer to 'Taking a turn around Tumbarumba' and 'Heading into the Hilltops' for two other regions that I cover within this zone). The Canberra District doesn't just comprise vineyards in the ACT. As a region it also provides wines from some of the countryside of New South Wales, around the towns of Yass and Murrumbateman. So although the entire ACT is in the Canberra District region, the region itself isn't exclusively Canberran. In fact, most of the wineries (see Figure 7-2) are on the north and north east of the state and territory border and are, therefore, geographically in New South Wales.

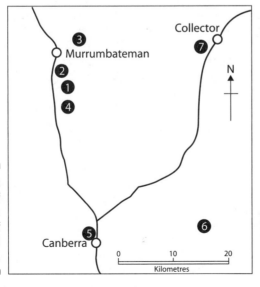

Figure 7-2:
Wineries of the Canberra District of ACT and NSW.

1 Clonkilla Winery
2 Doonkuna Estate
3 Helm's Wines
4 Jeir Creek Wines
5 Kamberra
6 Lark Hill Winery
7 Madew Wines

The passion of the sipping scientists

One of the unusual snippets of interest about the Canberra District region is the make-up of the winemakers. Nearly all are doctors, either retired or hoping to retire soon. But they're doctors of science and hold PhD degrees in scientific research. The reason for this phenomenon is related to the nation's capital, Canberra, being the home to the Commonwealth Scientific and Industrial Research Organisation, known as the CSIRO. So the passion for wine and winemaking is backed up by some seriously clever scientific minds.

Cold times in Canberra, or not?

Although winters in the Canberra District are bitterly cold, with minus 5 degrees Celsius a common breakfast temperature, the weather warms up come summer time. During spring, many of the vineyard sites are prone to frost and the newer planting sites were made to take this need for springtime sun into account. As soon as the cold winter is finished, the rainfall totals begin to diminish, and the vines can't survive the region's hot dry summers without supplementary irrigation coming either from surface dams or bore water.

The tempering of these warm days comes from the use of higher altitude plantings that allow the vines some respite from the warm days and give that all-important night-time cooling. On average the vineyards are sited across altitudes ranging from 500 metres to 800 metres above sea level. So, instead of the grapes ripening too fast, they slow after the sun goes down and maintain their fruit flavours. The other reason for the need of a bit of altitude is the risk of spring frosts. Being a little elevated means that the potentially damaging cold air drains down to the valleys and away from the vineyards.

Catching up with the best of the Canberra District varieties

Out of the over 200 hectares planted to grapevines, the dominant varieties across the Canberra District that make up around 50 per cent of the annual crush are

- Cabernet Sauvignon
- Chardonnay
- Shiraz

Other significant plantings are

- Merlot
- Riesling

Uncorking Canberra's cork forests

On the edge of the city of Canberra is the Glenloch Cork Oak plantation. Originally, it was planted in 1917 under the direction of American architect and town planner Walter Burley Griffin as a way of making Canberra commercially self-sufficient. The plan for the harvest of these trees wasn't wine-related though. Instead, the cork was used as part of a rifle assembly.

Wine corks, on the other hand, are produced using the bark of a cork oak tree — *Quercus suber.*

In Spain and Portugal, where the majority of cork oaks grow, the bark is carefully stripped from the tree every nine years and used to produce wine corks.

All five of these varieties I consider to be 'mid-climate' varieties, which means they're suited to a climate somewhere between cool and warm. All these varieties need a certain amount of summer into autumn warmth and stability (in terms of low rainfall) in the ripening months. The Canberra District region offers these conditions and so, not surprisingly, these grapes do well.

A few outsider varieties that do well in these climatic conditions, and that make wine lovers take note as a result, include

- ✔ **Pinot Noir:** Probably, this region is, in general terms, too warm for top Pinot Noir, but Lark Hill Pinot Noir is a consistently top quality, fruity yet savoury Pinot Noir.

- ✔ **Riesling:** Another point of difference is the Brindabella Hills Riesling which shows great zesty lemony fresh character.

- ✔ **Viognier:** In the early days, Clonakilla Shiraz Viognier was considered quite an unusual blend. Today, many Shiraz makers are adding a touch — somewhere between 5 per cent and 10 per cent — of Viognier to give the mid-palate some sweetness of fruit. This wine is truly one of the pioneers of this blend and has set the standards high for winemakers also endeavouring to make this style of wine.

Casting for Canberra District's pick of the bunch

One of the most recent, and without doubt the largest, winegrowing venture in the region is that by the **Hardy Wine Company** — formerly BRL Hardy, before the merger with the US-based Constellation Brands. The company's vineyard development includes plantings of 20 hectares of vines and establishing a large winery. So far, the outstanding wines from this venture are

- ✔ **Kamberra Chardonnay:** A soft peachy and nutty wine that you're best to drink young — within two or three years of production.

- ✔ **Kamberra Meeting Place Pinot Noir/Chardonnay Sparkling Wine:** A yeasty, biscuity and lemon tangy wine with a lovely long flavour.

Until the Hardy Wine Company's own vines are producing significant crops, local fruit from other Southern New South Wales Zone vineyards, Tumbarumba (refer to 'Taking a turn around Tumbarumba' earlier in this chapter) and Hilltops (refer to 'Heading into the Hilltops' earlier in this chapter), go into making these wines.

The main group of wineries of the Canberra District region are in the Murrumbateman area. Notable producers are

- ✓ **Clonakilla Winery:** This winery's excellent offerings include

  - A blend of Shiraz and Viognier that has the typical pepperiness and spice of a Shiraz but with the added pear-like mid-palate flavour that comes from the 6 per cent Viognier that has been blended with the Shiraz.

  - An excellent spicy and savoury straight Shiraz.

  - A Riesling that shows how the cool nights are able to maintain the natural acidity in the fruit to produce a zesty and vibrant drop.

- ✓ **Doonkuna Estate Shiraz:** A savoury style Shiraz that is a specialty from **Doonkuna Estate.**

- ✓ **Helm's Wines:** The region's most renowned winery, in terms of the profile and character of the owner — Ken Helm. Enjoy the atmosphere being bailed up to hear information-packed lectures on the latest analysis of the government's changes to the wine taxation system, or the history of the area and Helm's ancestors.

  The best from here is **Helm's Riesling** that shows great lime tones and bright acidity.

- ✓ **Jeir Creek Wines:** Shiraz is again the wine to try from here with the **Jeir Creek Shiraz** showing that the region is making good spicy earthy and liquorice style Shiraz.

The key to cool-climate style of wines from Bungendore and Lake George areas is that the grapes ripen late into autumn — some years as late as June. Fruit flavours are delicate and the acid maintains a long finish of flavour. You can find top wines from these areas from

- ✓ **Lark Hill Winery:** The high altitude of this winery at Bungendore — 860 metres — means that this vineyard has the ability to make fine Pinot Noir and a very refined Chardonnay.

- ✓ **Madew Wines:** The best varieties, so far, from this winery at Lake George, are both the Chardonnay and the newly released Pinot Gris, a variety that loves the coolness of this site.

Meandering to the Northern Rivers — Hastings Out on Its Own

The sub-tropical climate (ample rain and high humidity) of the Northern New South Wales wine zone seems an unlikely place to find vineyards. However, you can find table wines from small wineries dotted along the coastal region of New South Wales, a pleasant diversion from the beautiful white beaches.

The climate in this winegrowing region is sub tropical with temperatures moderated by influences from the afternoon sea breezes. Largely, though, the vineyards of the region experience high humidity, and rainfall during the growing season, which reduces the need for irrigation. The concern for winegrowers is that these conditions pave the way for disease and a prevalence of natural pests (see the sidebar 'Chambourcin — a modern-day French Résistance').

Grape varieties harvested at Hastings River include Chardonnay, Semillon, Sauvignon Blanc, Verdelho, Cabernet Sauvignon, Cabernet Franc, Merlot, Pinot Noir and Chambourcin.

Chambourcin — a modern-day French Résistance

High humidity and rainfall provide perfect conditions for pesky pests to thrive in vineyards. Wanting to beat natural pests and diseases, a French hybrid grape variety, Chambourcin, was bred to withstand powdery mildew, a disease that is prevalent in the Hastings River region. The Chambourcin grapes are dark red and thick skinned, which means they can withstand relatively high amounts of rainfall.

One standout vineyard in the Hastings River region, with a national reputation, is **Cassegrain Wines**. This vineyard (near the town of Port Macquarie) pioneered the variety of Chambourcin in Australia. Also, Cassegrain follows biodynamic principles (see Chapter 6), and uses non-chemical strategies such as its choice of vine varieties, and pruning methods to facilitate airflow and the sun's penetration.

This **Cassegrain Chambourcin** red wine is medium-bodied in weight with dominant fruity aromas and soft tannin.

Chapter 8

The Bouquet of the River Region

● ●

In This Chapter

▶ Bearing fruit from Italian heritage

▶ Growing great volume reduces cost to you

▶ Sampling the 'sticky' best

● ●

*T*he most renowned wines from the Big Rivers zone are from the Riverina region. (This winegrowing zone also includes the Murray-Darling and Swan Hill regions — a part of Victoria, which I cover in Chapter 12.)

The Riverina produces the lion's share (more than two-thirds) of the state's wines and, being larger than all of the other states' wine regions put together, its sheer geographical size takes your breath away. Out on the hot plains, around the town of Griffith (the regional capital of the Riverina), is an amazing array of huge winery facilities producing large volumes of technically good wines, including the well known Botrytis Semillon dessert wines. Here, even rain falls on fertile soil and warm temperatures prevail throughout the ripening season. These conditions support eight of the biggest wineries — three of which are still owned by the families that established them. These family-owned vineyards, such as De Bortoli Wines and Casella Wines, which were started by seriously hard-working Italian migrant winemakers, are all into their second or third generation winemakers. All have worked to transform the small operations into some of the largest makers and exporters of Australian wine.

Griffith is the centre of the expansion and, today, the wonderful feeling of the early migrants still exists with plenty of ancestors bearing the names of the old home country of Italy. The winemaking has been passed down over generations, and checking out the wines from this region is especially rewarding because the hospitality is flavoured with Italian-inspired restaurants and architecture dotting the countryside.

In this chapter, using some of the big wines, I show the expansive size of the Riverina region and blow the myth that says big has to be bad.

Warming Up and Staying Hot

The town of Griffith is the 'capital' of the Riverina wine region. Griffith isn't close to any other main cities, with Sydney around 650 kilometres away to the east and Melbourne 400 kilometres to the south. The Riverina region is an inland region, whose existence is due to the irrigation system known as the Murrumbidgee Irrigation Area (MIA). The MIA was established in 1912, and uses water from the mighty Murrumbidgee River, allowing the transformation of the semi-arid region into fertile land.

Around Griffith, the climate is pretty hot and stable. The official term for the climate of the area is *Mediterranean,* which is typically a long warm-to-hot summer with plenty of sunshine. Griffith and the surrounding winegrowing areas fit well into this description of a Mediterranean climate with the summery days being hot and dry. And the summer days *are* hot. For example, the main indicator for heat during the growing and ripening season is a measurement of the mean January temperature. For the Griffith area, the mean temperature is 23.8 degrees Celsius, and for Tasmania (see Chapter 15) the mean January temperature is 18.8 degrees Celsius. When compared using this method, the difference between these two areas doesn't seem huge, but in viticultural terms, each one degree of difference has quite an impact on the styles of wines that are grown and the varieties that are successful. Griffith, along with the Swan Valley in Western Australia (see Chapter 21), is the hottest grape-growing area in Australia.

The rain falls mostly in the winter, although the annual rainfall totals are considered to be relatively low. The annual rainfall is only 400 millimetres compared to a wetter climate such as that of the Yarra Valley (see Chapter 10), which receives 900 millimetres.

The great thing about being hot, as well as having a good supply of water, is that lots of grapes can be grown on each acre. This means that ample sunshine is available to ripen the grapes and, along with regular water from the MIA, the vines are able to cope with large crops. This dry climate has the added benefit of creating a low disease risk. As a result, little intervention is needed to protect the vines from fungal diseases meaning that few chemicals are required. Removing the need to have someone operating the sprayer on a regular basis also reduces labour costs. These conditions mean that the cost of growing grapes in this climate is reduced, which means lower priced wine for you and me.

Not surprisingly, some of Australia's largest wine companies are established in the Riverina region because these large wineries make the bulk of wine to meet a price in the market place. So, the region is home to eight of Australia's top twenty biggest wine processing facilities. In order of size, they are Buronga Hill Winery, Buronga (McGuigan Simeon Wines); Stanley Wine Company, Buronga (Hardy Wine Company); De Bortoli Winery, Bilbul (De Bortoli); Casella Wines, Yenda; Riverina Estate, Griffith (Riverina Estate); Wickham Hill Winery, Griffith (Orlando Wyndham); Miranda Family Winemakers; and Hanwood Estate (McWilliam's Wines).

Surviving the Heat with Grapes That Grow the Distance

A warm climate means that many tonnes of fruit can be grown on each acre of dirt, and some varieties do particularly well. Being able to make a good wine over varying ripeness and flavour profiles is the criterion for surviving in the heat. For example, Riverina Chardonnay can be made in a ripe style, with the honeyed and peachy tones evident. Compare this Chardonnay to one grown in the cool parts of the state, such as the Orange region (refer to Chapter 7), where you see quite a good acidity, and more flinty and minerally types of flavours. These two wines represent different styles of Chardonnay, but both secure a place in the market.

Most of the wines from the higher cropped vines of the warm Riverina wine region though, it is fair to say, are less intense in flavour than areas that have a milder climate and have less grapes per vine. The higher cropped vines have more fruit to deliver flavour to. In comparison, in the cool areas (for alpine wines, refer to Chapter 7), the longer growing season allows the vines a longer period of time to put maximum amount of effort into producing depth of flavour. So the higher intensity of flavours is with these lower cropped vines.

To a degree, this region represents winemaking to a price, and the wines from regions like the Riverina make up the bulk of the wines consumed by the Australian wine scene.

Wines from the Riverina region come from the following major grape varieties:

- ✔ **Semillon — the dry and the 'sticky' ones:** Semillon is second only to Shiraz as the most grown grape variety in the Riverina region. The dry climate suits the characteristic big bunches of the Semillon (in wet climates, Semillon can be attacked by fungus and the resulting mould that quickly spreads through the big bunches damages the thin skins). The great Semillon that comes from this area is the botrytised *sticky* Semillon. The term *sticky* is an Australian colloquial word, which refers to wines that are made using grapes that have been affected by *Botrytis cinerea* — see the sidebar 'What rot — the good, the bad and the sticky'. The dry climate during ripening works perfectly to make this type of wine, and many wineries in the region have a good deal of success with it. Often the wines are labelled with a reference to 'golden', such as the **Golden Mist** by Westend Estate and **Golden Botrytis** by Miranda Wines.

  Semillon is also a variety that can make a reasonably flavoured wine, even at high crop levels. Semillon also works well as a variety to blend with others. For example, you often see Semillon and Chardonnay blends, or winemakers use Semillon in a generic blend of white varieties. That is, no specific grape variety is claimed on the label, which simply refers to the wine as *dry white wine,* or a name such as Barramundi with no varieties mentioned on the label. These sorts of generic wines are at the bottom end of the price point. Their success relies on someone *realising* that the wine is white, simply by seeing the colour through the glass. The fact that the consumer is happy to simply have a glass of white wine, without thinking too much about what grapes went into making it, supports the wines' success, too.

- ✔ **Chardonnay:** Close on the heels of the popularity of Semillon is Chardonnay. The Chardonnay grapes grown around the Riverina region seem to be at the centre of the Australian wines' world reputation as being 'sunshine in a glass'. The Chardonnay grapes have no difficulty ripening in the region's sunshine. And irrigation from the Murrumbidgee River guarantees that the vines flourish while supporting quite heavy crop loads.

- ✔ **Colombard, Traminer and Muscat Gordo Blanco (*white blenders*):** Out of the 101,000 tonnes of white grapes grown in the Riverina, the third, fourth and fifth most planted collectively make up 21,500 tonnes of fruit (which also represents 11 per cent of the total red and white grapes grown). Yet, you hardly ever see the varieties written on the label. They are, in order of importance, Colombard, Traminer and Muscat Gordo Blanco. Most of these wines find their way into the famous '2 to 4 litres cask wine' or 'bag in a box' wine (in the United States these wines are referred to as 'jug wines'). The wines are a classic example of grapes grown and wines made to a cost.

- **Shiraz:** Making up over 51 per cent of the red grapes grown and 25 per cent of all the grapes grown, the work-horse of the Riverina region plantings is Shiraz. Shiraz, like Chardonnay and Semillon, is a versatile grape, working well in this hot climate under the high production regime.

- **Cabernet Sauvignon:** In this Mediterranean-like warm climate, true Cabernet flavour can get a little lost in the heat. That isn't to say that the Cabernets made in the Riverina aren't good red wines, they are. But because of the heat and the higher cropping levels, they tend to lose their identity as being true Cabernet Sauvignon. The best producers are keeping the crops a little lower and are trying to get a little more Cabernet into the glass. As the region's second most planted red variety, you also find good inexpensive blends of Cabernet and Shiraz, and Ruby Cabernet.

Ruby Cabernet variety is a cross between Cabernet Sauvignon and Carignan. Carignan was selected for this cross breeding because of its heat tolerance and high yielding ability. The result is that Ruby Cabernet grows well in the Riverina and is part of many red wine blends. You hardly ever see the name Ruby Cabernet on a label because this variety is much more useful as a component of a blend, rather than a wine by itself.

- **Merlot:** Merlot is the most recent to make an impact on the varieties planted in the region. Like Cabernet Sauvignon, Merlot does lose some of its typical mulberries and plum-like fruit in the hot climate but, again, it plays a part in making flavourful red wines at a price.

- **Durif:** Durif is one of the varietals (along with Shiraz) most suited to the region. As a variety that is from the southern parts of France, and hence quite a warm district, Durif thrives in the heat of the Riverina. The wines are for lovers of the big and gutsy styles of red wine. Consumer demand helps to keep the number of hectares planted relatively low (producing about one-eighth as many grapes as Shiraz produces). But as more Durif is made, and the wine drinker begins to become aware of this style of wine, demand is increasing. In fact, in the 2003 vintage, the demand for Durif was higher than the amount that could be supplied.

TECHNICAL STUFF

What rot — the good, the bad and the sticky

Botrytis cinerea (usually shortened to simply *botrytis*) is a bunch fungus commonly found to attack berries. Botrytis comes in two forms. The first, unwelcome form is when the fungus develops during a wet spell at ripening of the grapes. The fungus causes the berries to go mouldy, brown/grey and mushy, giving the subsequent juice a nasty mouldy flavour. In this form botrytis is known as *grey rot*, and definitely isn't a welcome part of the vineyard. Grey rot is quite a problem for the grape grower and then the winemaker because removing the mouldy flavours from the wine is difficult.

The second, good form of botrytis occurs in dry conditions. In this form, the fungus has the name of *noble rot*, which may sound rather like a contradiction of terms. The ideal climate occurs when the autumn weather gives misty mornings and the afternoons remain warm. The humidity during the early part of the day encourages the growth of the botrytis, and the afternoon warmth prevents the mould from going soggy and turning to grey rot. If the noble rot botrytis infection increases, the berries shrivel and the intensity of their flavour, and their sugar levels, skyrocket. You hear these wines being referred to as *honeyed, orange marmalade* and *apricot-like*. The final wine still has quite a level of sweetness left in it, somewhere around 150 grams per litre of sugar in Australian styles (a dry wine has less than 2 grams of sugar). The wines are stunning for their intense fruit flavours, their rich viscosity and texture. The 'sticky' term relates to this dominance of sweetness and thick texture of the wine. Botrytised wines can be made from any white variety — the classic variety is Semillon but increasingly other varieties are used.

Enjoying Some Impressive Drops

The Riverina region producers 60 per cent of the state's grape crop, and 15 per cent of Australia's total tonnes. But producing more grapes doesn't necessarily mean that the wine quality suffers. Despite being the biggest producer of grapes in New South Wales, some pretty good wines come from the area, proving that the right skills, technology and fruit combine for impressive drops.

The history of this wine region shows an ever increasing pursuit of quality. Although the first winemakers in the region were largely self-taught Italian migrants, future generations have gradually become scientifically trained. Today, all the winemakers in the region have degrees in wine science, and the technology they're using to improve the way they make wine is ever increasing. Large investments of money are made into the winery facilities. Simple developments such as having big enough refrigeration plants that adequately cool the juice during fermentation have led to huge improvements in the quality of the finished wines. The wines are able to maintain their fruit flavours (for a fresher wine) when fermentation is properly controlled.

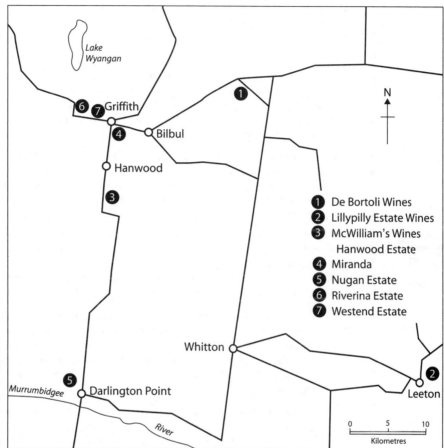

Figure 8-1:
Big is
beautiful in
the Riverina
region, NSW.

Map labels: Lake Wyangan, Griffith, Bilbul, Hanwood, Whitton, Murrumbidgee, Darlington Point, Leeton, River, N

1 De Bortoli Wines
2 Lillypilly Estate Wines
3 McWilliam's Wines
   Hanwood Estate
4 Miranda
5 Nugan Estate
6 Riverina Estate
7 Westend Estate

0   5   10
Kilometres

Nearly all of the wineries in the Riverina region (see Figure 8-1) are on the big side of the big scale. *Tank farms* (groups of enormous stainless steel tanks) loom up out of the flat horizon and, at night during harvest, the lights and action coming from the wineries give a real sense of excitement.

You can find quality wines from the following wine makers:

✔ **Barramundi Wines:** Formerly Cranswick Estate Premium Wines, **Barramundi** is part of the publicly listed Evans & Tate company which also owns the Milburn Park Winery in Victoria (see Chapter 12). Barramundi doesn't have a history steeped in tradition or generations of winemakers that are so often a part of the Riverina region. Originally, the winery was set up by Cinzano as a vermouth-producing facility but, as the market for vermouth faded, the demand for wine increased. In stark contrast to many of the other wineries in the region, Barramundi was built with technology and modern equipment right from the start. So, the facility doesn't have that added-on look that is so apparent with fast expansion.

In the vineyards, an emphasis on low input of sprays and human intervention is possible because of the hot dry climate. Like the majority of producers in the region, a whole range of standard varieties are grown. Mostly, their wine is destined for export under labels such as Barramundi and Image. At the time of writing, the wines haven't been released, but I expect them to be fruit-filled, easy-quaffing wines.

✔ **Casella Wines:** Before Casella's success with Yellow Tail wines (see the sidebar 'Hopping to the USA'), few Australians had heard of Casella wines. But the fruity and easy-to-like **Yellow Tail Chardonnay** quickly became one of Australia's biggest selling wines on the export market, making Casella the fifth biggest exporter by volume of wine.

✔ **De Bortoli Wines:** De Bortoli's is often credited for making some of the best examples of the inexpensive wines made from white blenders (refer earlier, in the section 'Surviving the Heat with Grapes That Grow the Distance'). The outstanding wines, however, from this Riverina winery, are those to do with botrytis and Semillon.

- **De Bortoli Noble One** continues to be a leader in its field in Australia with a reputation for making a truly intense wine. The flavours of marmalade and lime tang flow along with the luscious and decadent texture. This wine has been at the pinnacle of dessert-style wine from the first time it was made, more than 20 years ago.

- **Rare Dry Botrytis Semillon** has an extra richness and texture compared to many other Semillons even though the fruit hasn't been allowed the same amount of noble rot development as for the Noble One. Not easy to find but worth looking for.

✔ **Lillypilly Estate Wines:** This not-so-big winery is situated at Leeton, south-east of the town of Griffith. Top wines from here are

- **Lillypilly Estate Tramillon**, made from Traminer and Semillon. This medium-dry white with a pale yellow colour is floral and spicy with a lively finish.

- **Lillypilly Estate Noble Muscat of Alexandria**, made from the grape Muscat of Alexandria (a grape variety that is also known as *Muscat Gordo Blanco*). This sweet white with a golden colour carries a flavour of dried fruits and a refreshing tingle to finish.

✔ **McWilliam's Wines Hanwood Estate:** Although wines from here boast no claim to Italian ancestry, McWilliam's is Australia's second biggest family-run winery, after De Bortoli Wines. Back in 1913, John James McWilliam, one of the founders of the McWilliam's wines, was so impressed by the Riverina region's ability to grow plants that he's quoted as saying: 'Plant a six-inch nail in the soil, water it and in a year you will have a crowbar.' I doubt any of today's grape growers would disagree. McWilliam's produces wines from wineries dotted across Australia — one in the Hunter valley (refer to Chapter 5), another in the Yarra Valley (see Chapter 10), one in Coonawarra (see Chapter 19), another in the Hilltops region (see Chapter 7) and, here, at the Hanwood Estate.

At Hanwood, McWilliam's has developed quite a following for its inexpensive yet always well made **Hanwood** range of wines that includes Cabernet Sauvignon, Chardonnay, Merlot, Sauvignon Blanc, Shiraz, Semillon, Verdelho and a few blends of these. Of the Hanwood range, I suggest the Chardonnay and the Merlot as good easy quaffing wines. Also fabulous from the McWilliam's stable is the **McWilliam's Limited Release Riverina Botrytis Semillon**, which oozes fresh ripe fruits with a balance of sweetness and acid tang to finish.

✔ **Miranda:** Before the sale to McGuigan Simeon Wines in 2003, the third generation of yet another Italian family ran this winery.

The bulk of Miranda's production comes from the Griffith area where a couple of refreshing and affordable styles of wine, quite forgotten in the rush for sophisticated varietal wines, are

- **Somerton** brand wines, known as 'sunshine in a bottle', which includes Lambrusco (a sweet, semi-carbonated red wine).

- **Miranda Raisined Muscat** (also a bit fizzy and sweet), which is made from partially dried Muscat grapes.

- **Miranda Mirrool Creek Reserve Durif**, an inexpensive red.

Although these wines aren't considered spectacular by serious wine tasters, they're nevertheless well made and fit a niche in the market that enjoys a lower-alcohol, slightly sweet, full-ripe wine style with zesty fruit flavours.

Other well-made wines from Miranda, for a price, are

- **Miranda Varietals** label.

- **Firefly** label.

Miranda wines, although based in Griffith, continues to see the benefit of purchasing and growing fruit in other regions and its **King Valley** label has always been seen as a well-priced wine (see Chapter 12).

✔ **Nugan Estate:** A relative newcomer to the region, the Nugan family began in this area in 1940 growing fruit and vegetables. In 1993 they planted vines and, more recently, started making wine, too. Situated at Darlington Point, just south of Griffith, **Nugan Estate** is right on the banks of the Murrumbidgee River, so the temperatures are a little lower than the regional mean (refer to the section 'Warming Up and Staying Hot' earlier in this chapter), being moderated by the water.

A couple of standout wines from Nugan Estate are

- Cookoothama — the main label in the Nugan Estate range. A sticky (refer to the section 'Surviving the Heat with Grapes That Grow the Distance', earlier in this chapter) from this label that stands out is the **Cookoothama Botrytis Semillon**, a lush and fruity wine that has enough acid to balance the sweetness. Also worth finding is the **Cookoothama Chardonnay**, a not over-oaked fruity Chardonnay. A flavourful red at a price is the **Cookoothama Pigeage Merlot**

- **Nugan Estate Manuka Grove Durif** — a powerful wine with sturdy tannins.

✔ **Riverina Estate:** This huge facility boasts a storage capacity of 30 million litres — tiny in comparison to the largest in Australia at Berri Estates in South Australia (see Chapter 20), which has 120 million, but enormous when compared with the average small winery's 20,000 litres. Yet, despite its size, the top grapes for this winery are still largely hand-picked and the winery controls most of the vineyards from where they source their fruit.

The best from this winery are

1164 Family Reserve range, especially the Shiraz and Cabernet Sauvignon.

Warburn Show Reserve Merlot, Durif and Semillon.

The Wagga Wagga institution

Here in Australia, we're pretty good at finding unusual place names. Of course, mostly you find that the names relate back to Aboriginal sources. The city of Wagga Wagga (translation: the place of many crows) is no exception. Just outside Wagga (as it's more commonly known), is the Charles Sturt University. This university is one institution that teaches the wine science degree. Part of the experience here includes a working winery (**CSU Winery** — check out the Web site at www.csu.edu.au/winery), so it's a relief to know that the wines (table wines, fortified and sparkling) coming from this commercial — as well as teaching — winery, are worth trying, for example, the impressive **Charles Sturt Orange Chardonnay**.

- **Westend Estate:** As a second-generation winemaker, Bill Calabria still makes wine in a traditional manner. His red grapes are fermented in open fermenters, which means quite a lot of manual labour. But the results are in the glass because his reds are some of the best in the region. Unlike most of the other producers, the Westend wines are only made from grapes grown in the Riverina so they're true examples of what the region can do.

The best drops from Westend Estate are

Reds under the label of **3 Bridges** — the Durif, Cabernet Sauvignon and Shiraz.

Golden Mist Botrytis Semillon (refer earlier to the sidebar 'What rot — the good, the bad and the sticky' for information on the botrytis process), possesses a soft lemon/lime nose with honeyed character — a good choice to finish any meal.

Selecting a dish for your botrytised sticky

In Australia and New Zealand, we often think of serving a sweet wine with dessert. But in France, which is home to the famous Sauternes wines, and the inspiration for these Griffith stickies, a glass of Sauternes is just as likely to be served as an aperitif because logic says that sweet is gentle on an empty stomach. The French particularly like to pair it with rich pâté de foie gras and, I must say, that combination certainly is rather a delicious experience. In Australia, to my mind, we too often serve our sweet wines with overly sweet foods, so that all you're left with is a big mouthful of sugary thickness. More recently, though, matches such as botrytised wine with creamy blue cheese are becoming popular. And for me, you can't go past a simple poached fruit, such as pear with a sprinkle of roasted almonds and a glass of one of these luscious flavoured and textured sticky wines.

Hopping to the USA

Casella Wines built its international market share using its Yellow Tail range, which was named after the Yellow-Footed Rock-Wallaby and also known as Yellow Tail. The winery has shown huge growth and has taken the United States export market by storm, and all of this in a few short years. As recently as 2000, Casella wasn't even in the top twenty Australian wine companies, yet by 2002 they were ranked as the ninth biggest in terms of tonnes of grapes crushed. This ranking is a considerable effort when you consider that the wineries that export more than Casella do so with a huge combined portfolio of wines. For example, Southcorp Wines is the largest exporter of wine, but it achieves this status by combining all their portfolio such as Penfolds, Lindemans, Wynns, Rosemount Estate, Seaview and Seppelt together. Not a bad achievement at all for a family-run winery.

Chapter 9

Travelling North to Sunshine and Wine in Queensland

In This Chapter

▶ Discovering Granite Belt greats

▶ Taking to the best from South Burnett

*W*ithout a doubt, Queensland's fame centres around the image of sun, surf and bikinis. But, inland from the coast, two other sun worshippers are contributing to this state's rich history — the emerging wine regions of the Queensland wine zone delivering a variety of wines from varying climes. In the southwestern hinterland of Queensland's capital, Brisbane, and close to the Queensland and New South Wales state border, is the older and more prominent of the two regions — the Granite Belt wine region. And further north, about two hours drive inland from the beautiful Sunshine Coast, is the newer wine region known as South Burnett.

Although these two regions built their businesses on the flow-on from the large tourist market that wends through the state each year, the quality of wines from here contribute to a healthy texture for the wine industry at large. In this chapter, I give you a run-down on some of the quality wines from this northern zone.

Unveiling Climatic Variety in Queensland

Don't be surprised when you hear the Granite Belt winemakers telling you that snow isn't uncommon in the winter months. Even though Queensland carries the labelling of the Sunshine State, the cool, high-altitude region around Stanthorpe gets mighty cold indeed. This altitude allows the vines to really shut down for the season and have a proper winter, one you'd commonly see in the southern states. The other main region of Queensland, the South Burnett, while not as cold, does have its share of below 5 degrees Celsius nights and early mornings across winter. The low temperatures are a shock when you visit in August from cold Victoria, as I did, with little thought of packing anything warm. For us southern-state dwellers, we just always think that Queensland represents sun, sun and more sun.

Cool clime and later harvest in the Granite Belt

The Granite Belt boasts 37 wineries with almost as many cellar-door operations (refer to Chapter 2 for information about visiting a cellar door), associated cafés and restaurants. The region is the largest of the Queensland winegrowing areas, with 700 out of the total of 1380 hectares in 2003. As an agricultural region, the Granite Belt has a deserved history as a provider of beautifully ripe stone fruits and apples — an image that's hard to imagine given that I'm talking about Queensland, the state known for its heat and blazing sunshine.

The fruit *is* very good and the grapes maintain their fruitiness because of the cool location of the region. The Granite Belt wine region and its main town of Stanthorpe are part of the western fringe of the Great Dividing Range and sit around 750 metres above sea level. Contrary to what most people may think, the Granite Belt is considered a mild, even cool climate (with temperatures 5 degrees Celsius to 10 degrees Celsius below coastal districts), depending on the individual vineyard site. Grapes are picked later, from early March to mid-April, on the Granite Belt.

A distinguishing characteristic for the region is soil type. Up on the Granite Belt the soil is, not surprisingly, granite-based with huge outcrops haphazardly but scenically plonked by nature across the landscape. Indeed, I imagine the task of ramming in the trellis posts around the vineyards is still a feat in itself given the rocky structure of the soil. The locals claim that this soil gives their fruit a more minerally tone, a secondary flavour to simple fruitiness. This rocky soil also means that the spring-time rains can drain away quickly from the vines' roots, preventing the waterlogging around the root base, something that vines hate.

Warmth and high humidity in South Burnett

Northwest of Brisbane is the South Burnett region. This wine region is still really in its infancy (begun in the mid-1990s) and one that has largely been based around the tourist trade. To date the region has 11 wineries, with a few established in no-man's-land just outside the declared South Burnett Geographical Indication (GI) boundaries. (Refer to Chapter 3 for an explanation of the GI indicator.) The region is the second biggest player in the vineyard area with 400 hectares planted to date. The climate is warm and sub-tropical, leading to high humidity during the growing season. In comparison with the Granite Belt (refer to the previous section), harvest time for these wine growers is from late January to early March.

In the South Burnett region, the soils are rich and often red, which indicates very fertile soil. This can pose a problem if the vines aren't trellised and managed well, as the vine *vigour* can be extreme. In a region with high spring rainfall and high humidity, this excessive leaf and shoot growth can spell disaster, causing devastating crop loss to the vine fungal diseases of powdery mildew and *Botrytis cinerea* (refer to Chapter 7).

Planting Grapes for an Unusual Wine Region

One thing that both of these regions have in common is the variety of wines they make. For example, at **Ballandean Estate Winery** in the Granite Belt, the range of wine styles at any one time is around 18, and at **Crane Winery** in the South Burnett the number of grape varieties some years is even greater. Largely, this varietal choice is driven by the tourist market, with the popular sweet whites and reds featuring heavily on some cellar door wine selection lists.

Growing grapes on the Granite Belt

The Granite Belt winegrowing region was started by that familiar story of Italian migrants who came to Australia and saw the chance to make a bit of their own wine — just like in their homeland. Back in 1920s, grapes were planted for eating but also for making wine. The market wasn't for the local Anglo-Saxon population, rather for the large Italian community that had arrived in Australia and had found work in the Queensland sugar cane fields. But, in this region, wine really wasn't thought of as a serious commercial venture until the late 1960s.

Ripening reds

The main red varieties grown in the Granite Belt are Shiraz and Cabernet Sauvignon. Merlot is having some success, as is the new darling of the nation — Sangiovese. Ironically, only some of the Italian varieties, such as Sangiovese, are being planted, after the mostly Italian grape growers planted Shiraz 30 years ago.

The reason these mid-climate varieties, Merlot and Sangiovese, do well is that they're not ripening during the warm weather. In comparison, an early-ripening variety, such as Pinot Noir, would have berries that are becoming physiologically ripe in January and the warm climate would destroy the grapes' subtle flavour — so vital in making top quality Pinot Noir. So, Shiraz does well, showing some good ripe, yet not too ripe, jammy flavour. Cabernet Sauvignon is a late-ripening variety and the Granite Belt is able to make some well-ripened versions of this grape. In fact, on the higher-altitude vineyards, the climate is so cool that in some years the Cabernet Sauvignon grapes fail to fully ripen.

Welcoming whites

The best of the white varieties from the Granite Belt region so far are Verdelho and the ubiquitous Chardonnay. The Verdelho grape enjoys the warmth available to the area, giving those delicious ripe tropical flavours. I anticipate other mild-climate-loving varietals such as the French Rhône whites of Roussanne, Marsanne and Viognier showing a bit of a presence in this region's vineyards in the future.

More than peanuts in South Burnett

South Burnett enjoys fame as both the peanut growing capital of Australia and the home of one of Queensland's most controversial politicians, Sir Joh Bjelke Peterson. The main town of Kingaroy is full of things bearing his name such as references to the man, street signs and a local swimming pool. The famous peanut vendor is also there working from a caravan selling to the passing trade on the side of the road. In some ways, these slightly dubious claims to fame have helped establish the vineyards in the area. The tourist trade has always been pretty steady, so the idea of cellar doors and something other than peanuts holds appeal.

You can find a fruit salad list of the varieties grown in the South Burnett region, no doubt due to the desire to please everyone on the tourist bus. The best red variety is Shiraz, and Chardonnay and Verdelho are the most successful whites.

Finding Wines Worth the Search

Most Australians, outside of Queensland's wine drinkers, are pretty unaware of the wines coming out of Queensland's wine regions. The interest in the Queensland zone is lead mostly by the wines from the Granite Belt region (see Figure 9-1), which is centred around the town of Stanthorpe on the New South Wales Queensland border.

Clearing of the scrubby woodland and granite boulders that characterise the region began in the 1800s — for table grapes and orchards, rather than wine. The pioneering of the wine industry goes to Italians and their descendants, beginning around the 1920s. Producing wine for their own enjoyment was just the beginning, from which modern-day winegrowing began with plantings of Shiraz in the 1960s.

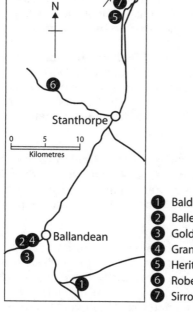

Figure 9-1: Wines to discover from the Granite Belt wine region, Queensland.

1. Bald Mountain Vineyard
2. Ballendean Estate Wines
3. Golden Grove Estate
4. Granite Ridge Wines
5. Heritage Wines of Stanthorpe
6. Robert Channon Wines
7. Sirromet

Sunshine in a glass — the wines of Stanthorpe

To date, the highest profile wines from the Granite Belt and its main town of Stanthorpe are from **Robert Channon Wines**. Planted in 1998, wines from this young grower and winemaker are becoming known to people all over Australia, chiefly because of a legal battle between the French Champagne company, Moët & Chandon, and the then-named Channon Wines. The dispute centred around the name on the label, Channon. For the French company, the Australian winery's name was far too similar to its own label and, so, off to court both parties went. The situation was resolved by the owner of Channon wines changing its label to his full name, thus Robert Channon Wines.

Despite this leap to notoriety by other means, the wines from the winery, too, are very good. The entire vineyard, which makes up around 8 hectares, is under a permanent net. The thinking behind this approach is that hail in the area isn't infrequent. Also, at the high altitude, of around 950 metres above sea level, strong winds, which damage the soft shoots on the vines, are common. Finally, the unwelcome visits from hungry birds are a nuisance. So, to avoid all of these damaging influences and to enable the fruit time on the vine until it is absolutely ripe, rather than being forced to pick the grapes just because the birds are getting too hard to control, permanent netting is installed. Although the vineyard is planted to Chardonnay, Merlot, Cabernet Sauvignon and Verdelho, it is the **Robert Channon Verdelho** that is making the winery famous all over again. Just as Queensland is known as the Sunshine State, this wine personifies sunshine in a glass, with loads of tropical fruit flavours and enough acidity to refresh the palate.

The oldest plantings in the region are at **Ballandean Estate Wines**, having been established as a table grape vineyard in the 1920s. These days, only wine grapes are grown, and 18 styles of wines are made including sparkling wine, dry white, sweet wine, reds and even a fortified Muscat. One of the best for its freshness and zing of acidity is the **Ballandean Estate Semillon Sauvignon Blanc**.

The Shiraz from **Bald Mountain Vineyards** and **Golden Grove Estate Shiraz** are showing the sceptics that this fine red variety can be grown in places other than South Australia (see Chapters 16 to 19 for wines from this zone). **Granite Ridge Wines** and **Heritage Wines of Stanthorpe** are producing good varietal Cabernet Sauvignon.

The biggest and most ambitious winegrowing venture to date is that of **Sirromet Wines.** With a vineyard of over 140 hectares, these plantings are easily the largest in the region. Like other winegrowers in the area, a bit of a fruit salad of varieties is planted in the vineyards. From the selection, the whites that is beginning to show some strength in quality are Verdelho and Viognier. These two *Vs* have a strong future as important wine varieties in the region.

Looking bright in South Burnett

To date, the wines from this young region are a little uninspiring. However, the region (see Figure 9-2) is full of enthusiastic people and, as the winemaking attracts qualified winemakers, the quality of the wine and the vineyard management are likely to improve. The climate is a tough one for vines (refer to 'Warmth and high humidity in South Burnett' earlier in this chapter), being humid and susceptible to rain during the ripening months. If the grapes are affected by wet weather and, hence, mildew and bunch rot, then these growing conditions are going to benefit from experienced winemakers.

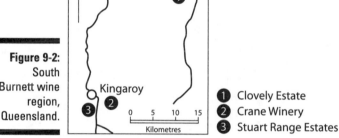

Figure 9-2:
South
Burnett wine
region,
Queensland.

One of the best wines from the region is the **Clovely Estate** Chardonnay from a large newly established winery. This winery is a very ambitious venture, having established over 170 hectares of vines in the region, with over 40 per cent of those hectares bearing another favourite, Shiraz. Certainly, the wines from here are worth watching for as the vineyards gain some age and, hence, produce full flavoured fruit.

Like Clovely Estate, **Stuart Range Estates** was established by a large group of investors. An experienced winemaker is in charge and this experience is showing through in the wines as the knowledge of what tricks to use in the less-than-perfect weather years are applied to making the wine. Verdelho is showing as its best variety to date.

Part III
Victoria and Tasmania: Something Devilish about Those Wines

www.moir.com.au   Alan Moir

In this part . . .

Victoria is home to quite a diverse group of wine regions. In this part, I take you to wine regions located around the state's capital city of Melbourne and to other of the state's regions further afield.

First and nearest the capital is the cool Yarra Valley. Then I take you to the heart of the state, the warmer regions such as Nagambie and Heathcote, where the vineyards are still quite small and the winemakers are making themselves known for their Shiraz wines. A little further north are the luscious wines of Rutherglen and the diversity of the King and Alpine Valleys, where the wines are deliciously overwhelming. On then, as far north-west as you can, to the state border, where you find vines and more vines around Mildura — a region where wines are made for a price.

Then I take you to the surf coast with the top wines of the Bellarine Peninsula. And, finally, to the cool Mornington Peninsula, the warmer Sunbury and cool Macedon regions.

Don't skip the last chapter in this part because it's there I cover the most beautiful island in the world — well, in my opinion anyway — Tasmania. Stunning sights and beautiful Pinot Noir. Not to be missed.

Chapter 10

The Wines of the Yarra Valley

The Yarra Valley lays claim to being Victoria's first grape-growing region. The men behind these vineyards were migrants from Switzerland, one of whom was Guillaume de Pury, whose family still operates and makes wine at the original Yeringberg property (albeit with modern-day improvements!). In 1838, the Ryrie brothers planted vines at Yering Station (this vineyard has since been re-established and you can visit it today in its modern state), and by 1863 a total of 430 acres of vines covered the region.

By 1921, the 1,000 acres or so that had been planted across the valley were reverted to pasture land for cattle, as the global economy went into decline and wine wasn't so sought after. Then, in the early 1960s, vines began to reappear in the Yarra's landscape, with the majority of plantings undertaken by wine enthusiasts from the city looking for a new challenge. And as their winemaking success grew, so did the Yarra's reputation.

Today, with significant investment from both Australian and international companies, the Yarra is no longer made up of the odd small, owner-operated winery. Rather, the region is a significant player in both the quantity and quality of the Australian wine scene. The Yarra undoubtedly makes some of the best cool-climate wines in Australia.

Cool-Climate Produce

The Yarra Valley prides itself on having a cool climate because this allows a certain style of wine to be produced. With a cool climate, the region's seasons change gradually. Ordinarily, the winters (June to August) are wet, which has little effect on the grapevines, as they lie dormant during this season. Instead, the winter and spring rains saturate the soils, preparing the ground for the forthcoming dry summer as well as filling up the dams in preparation for the possible irrigation demands of the season.

Along with the arrival of spring (September to November) comes the endless discussion of the type of season the vineyards may have. Spring is the most vigorous growing season and the weather conditions during this time are critical. Though the mornings stay cold, the days gradually warm over the spring months and the buds on the vines start to burst.

As the new vine shoots lengthen and the vines go into flower, grape growers hope for fine weather with only moderate winds. Too much wind or rain can mean that flowering is poor, leading to reduced numbers of berries formed. By the end of November and into December, the bunches are pretty well formed, albeit still just tiny clusters. Over the next few months, the grapes swell and ripen, and during this period a cool climate is important.

The flavours of the grape varieties planted in the Yarra are considered mostly at the delicate or elegant end of the spectrum. Consequently, from February through to the end of April, the weather needs to be sunny and warm during the day and cool at night, with the odd spell of mild weather. These conditions provide for a ripening that is stretched out over many weeks, allowing the flavours in the grapes to gradually build up, giving them some intensity.

Early-ripening grape varieties such as Pinot Noir and Chardonnay are picked around mid-March, as is Sauvignon Blanc. Cabernet Sauvignon and Petit Verdot are late-ripening varieties so are the last to be picked — often not until late April on many sites around the valley. Sometime in between the Merlot, Cabernet Franc, Pinot Gris, Riesling, Marsanne and Shiraz grapes ripen.

The timing of the ripening depends on the vineyard site, and the Yarra Valley is quite a diverse area. Properties on the Yarra floor are typically warmer than those perched atop of the valley's hills, which means they can ripen their fruit fully in nearly every season. The higher altitude vineyards are naturally cooler so their fruit ripens later in the season. For this reason, grape growers in the hills don't plant Cabernet Sauvignon, which is a late ripener, because the grapes would struggle in eight out of ten years to really ripen fully.

The rough rule is that for each 100 metres above sea level, the temperature drops by one degree Celsius. Vineyards in the Yarra vary from 50 metres to 400 metres above sea level. So, for a vineyard such as St Huberts, which is on the valley floor at 55 metres above sea level, the Pinot Noir ripens around the last week in March. At the other end of the altitude spectrum is the winery Gembrook Hills, which is 190 metres above sea level. The Pinot Noir at this winery, on average, isn't ready for picking until around the second week of April, about two weeks later than St Huberts.

This comparison is a little simplistic as all vineyards are tended in different ways, but it gives a good general idea of how altitude affects grape ripening. And with over 90 wineries in the region, each located on a slightly different site and having slightly different growing conditions, these facts add interest to all the wines made in the district.

What the Yarra Does Well

The most popular varieties planted in the Yarra are Pinot Noir, Chardonnay, Cabernet Sauvignon, Sauvignon Blanc and increasingly Shiraz. Alongside these mainstays you also find varieties such as the little-known Roussanne and Marsanne.

Some producers are concentrating on making a true Bordeaux blend, which means that their Cabernet Sauvignon will also contain Petit Verdot, Cabernet Franc, Merlot and maybe Malbec, varieties you find planted in smallish quantities. The attractive and fruity white variety Gewürztraminer is also sprinkled across the valley, as is the newly fashionable Pinot Gris. All in all, the Yarra is becoming quite a diverse valley.

Here's some more information on the more popular varieties in the region:

- ✔ **Consistent Chardonnay:** You may find, as I have, that drinking Chardonnay is unfashionable. Quite frankly, though, Chardonnay from cool-climate regions is a seriously good drink, and certainly one of the Yarra's most delicious wines. (See also the section on wines from the Adelaide Hills in Chapter 17 and those from the Margaret River in Chapter 22.)

    Unlike many Australian Chardonnays, those from the Yarra typically age very well. As a young wine they may appear a little subdued but, with a little time — say three to six years — they turn into complex yet softly sophisticated wines.

- ✔ **Stylish Sauvignon Blanc:** An increasingly popular choice both with the public and among growers, the Yarra's Sauvignon Blanc is better made today than it was when introduced to the area 10 to 15 years ago. Back then it was quite herbaceous, reminiscent of crushed leaves and green grass, whereas today the leafy tag is gone and the variety is much more fruit flavoured, with tropical fruits in particular more apparent on your tastebuds. This shift in style has mostly been due to the increase in knowledge of how to grow the grape properly.

    The cooler parts of the Yarra Valley are especially good for growing this variety, as the crisp and very fruity characters are caught before the grapes ripen too far and lose these distinctive characters. So look for Sauvignon Blanc from the higher areas of the Yarra, such as up around Hoddles Creek.

✔ **Pleasurable Pinot Noir:** If any winegrowing region is to be acknowledged for the appearance of Pinot Noir on our tables, the Yarra is that region. The pioneers of the Yarra were all lovers of Burgundian wines, and having been seduced by these Pinot Noirs they set out to create a bit of this magic in the Yarra. So, armed with land and vine cuttings, they began the challenge of making elegant and complex Pinot Noirs. While it is fair to say that the early makings weren't a patch on the wines made today, they proved that the Yarra had the climate to make great Pinot Noir.

Move forward 20 years or so from those early plantings and the Yarra's Pinot Noir has a definite personality of its own — and interestingly, many of those early producers are still making some of the best today. None of the wines is a blockbuster in terms of tannin and big fruit but they show that gorgeous and, can I say it, feminine character that, like the fairer sex, is always intriguing. (After all, I am a female winemaker of Pinot Noir!)

The most noticeable thing about growing Pinot in the Yarra Valley over the past few years (since around 1997) has been the seeming change in the weather. A string of summers (excluding 2000) have been much warmer than usual. Out of all the varieties, Pinot proves to be the biggest test for grape growers. Since Pinot needs the cool weather to allow its flavours to evolve slowly, grape growers have had to ensure that adequate water is available to the vine so as not to allow the vine to stress, thereby causing the fruit to take on an almost cooked flavour.

✔ **Classy Cabernet:** The Yarra's Cabernets have always been regarded as some of Australia's finest. Given the flavours and tannins that build up from the long ripening facilitated by the cool climate, you can expect the Cabernets to be of subtle blackberry and cigar box character. The tannin is apparent but not so gritty that your mouth feels that it has been attacked with sandpaper. The Cabernet is delicious whether a few years old or stored in your cellar for eight to ten years. (Although, they're wines that test your self-discipline if you attempt the latter!)

✔ **Sassy sparkling:** A relatively new venture in the Yarra is the production of sublime sparkling wines. After the injection of big dollars (millions of them) by Moët & Chandon back in 1986, the Yarra stamped its claim on these wines. The tradition caught on and several years later another Champagne company, Devaux, invested plenty more French francs. The Yarra had already proven itself in terms of the required grape varieties, namely Pinot Noir and Chardonnay. Some Pinot Meunier was also planted in 1986 and a little bit of France was established in Victoria. Today, the Yarra's sparkling wines are rated among some of the best made in the world, as well as being admired by the French (albeit a quiet admiration!).

Revealing a Cabernet's true colours

The use of the term *Cabernet* is fairly broad ranging these days. Strictly speaking, Cabernet refers to wine produced from the Cabernet Sauvignon grape. However, the term is also used for a Cabernet Merlot wine (which is a blend of the Cabernet Sauvignon and Merlot grapes). In addition, to make things more confusing, only 85 per cent of the grape varieties used have to be listed on the label. (Refer to Chapter 3 for information on the ins and outs of labelling.) So you may find that a wine called 'Cabernet' contains not only Cabernet Sauvignon grapes but also other red grapes. The most common addition is Merlot but Cabernet Franc, Malbec and/or Petit Verdot are also used.

Diving into the Yarra Valley

Every time I drive along the main highways of the Yarra the number of new plantings amazes me. Vines seem to sprout from paddocks that were once home to sleepy sheep and cattle. And when I venture down any of the little side roads, which are often very lumpy and dusty dirt roads, vines are evident as far as the eye can see.

Melburnians are lucky enough to be able to take the Yarra for granted — being less than an hour's drive from the centre of Melbourne, a day trip is just too easy. Figure 10-1 shows the Yarra's location in the state of Victoria.

The Yarra Valley has a few pockets of wineries. Closest to Melbourne are the Diamond Valley wineries, then, around the increasingly suburban Coldstream, is a group of both new and older wineries. The towns of Healesville and Yarra Glen are probably considered the central part of the Yarra Valley, and the Seville and Hoddles Creek areas are the outposts. Each area has quite distinct characteristics and, increasingly, the bigger wineries take fruit from across many of the districts to add complexity to the grapes they grow on their own home plots.

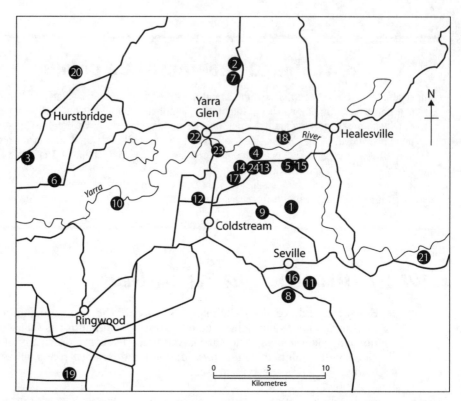

Figure 10-1:
The Yarra
Valley region
in Victoria.

1 Coldstream Hills
2 De Bortoli Winery
3 Diamond Valley Vineyards
4 Domaine Chandon
5 Dominique Portet
6 Evelyn County Estate
7 Fergusson Winery
8 Five Oaks Vineyard
9 Giant Steps

10 Kellybrook Winery
11 McWilliam's Lillydale
    Vineyards
12 Mount Mary
13 Oakridge Estate
14 The Yarra Hill
    (Punt Road Wines; Sticks)
15 Rochford
16 Seville Estate

17 St Huberts Vineyard
18 TarraWarra Estate
19 Wantirna Estate
20 Wedgetail Estate
21 Yarra Burn Winery
22 Yarra Ridge
23 Yering Station
24 Yeringberg

Venturing along the main trail

The Yarra Valley region (refer to Figure 10-1) is in the Port Phillip Zone.
The region borders on the towns of Emerald and Cockatoo to the south,
the Plenty River marks the western boundary, and the Yarra River, which
begins in the region's east, flows through its centre on the way to Melbourne.

Most producers are located around the towns of Coldstream, Healesville and Yarra Glen, and the historic Lilydale. The valley is surrounded by the Great Dividing Range to the east, the Plenty Ranges to the west and the Dandenongs to the south, and the altitude range is from 50 to 400 metres.

Wines of Coldstream

Names of towns are funny things. Without much thought about the name, I referred to the town of Coldstream for many years. However, when I started to work there I began to realise that the name held true meaning. At about the same time, the Australian Bureau of Meteorology set up a weather station in Coldstream and started including it in the forecast region. As I rose from my warm bed, I began to realise how apt the name was: Coldstream would frequently be the coldest place in the Melbourne forecast region — and usually by several degrees. Some mornings would be minus 4 degrees Celsius! As a result, the wineries around this town often experience very cold night-time conditions.

Here's a list of the top wines from wineries in the Coldstream region:

- **Coldstream Hills:** I feel that this winery's best wines are from the reserve rather than the standard range. Look for the **Coldstream Hills Reserve Pinot Noir**, an intensely textured dark cherry flavoured wine, the nutty complex and citrus **Coldstream Hills Reserve Chardonnay** and the briary and tobacco leaf-like **Coldstream Hills Reserve Cabernet**. Wine writer James Halliday and his wife Suzanne initially owned the vineyard but Southcorp, Australia's largest wine company, now owns it. These days, the original vineyards are supplemented by plantings in other parts of the valley.

- **Domaine Chandon:** I have to declare a bias: I was once a winemaker with this winery. Chandon not only has a stunning visitors' centre (see Chapter 28 for information about the best cellar doors) but also a range of seriously good sparkling wines:

   - **Chandon Blanc de Blancs** (my favourite), which means white of whites, is made only from Chardonnay grapes and shows complex flavours of stone fruits and nuts.

   - If you like your wine a little sweet, the unique **Chandon Cuvée Riche** is making headlines as a lovely luscious aperitif or to have with dessert.

   - The excellent **Chandon Vintage Brut** follows the classic blend of Champagne, that is, a blend of Pinot Noir, Pinot Meunier (both red grape varieties) and Chardonnay.

   - The romantic **Chandon Vintage Brut Rosé** shows red berry fruit flavours.

- **Chandon Z*D Vintage Blanc de Blancs**, a recent release — the name referring to the wine having zero *dosage* (sugar syrup) added during the final winemaking process so the wine is bone dry and a stunning aperitif. The wine also comes with a *crown seal stopper*, like the seal you see on beer bottles, as an alternative to the often-problematic (for thirsty picnickers who forget to pack the corkscrew) cork stoppers.

✔ **Dominique Portet:** This winery, which is named after its owner, is one of the newcomers to the area. For many years this Frenchman was at the helm of Taltarni (see Chapter 10), before setting up his own business in the Yarra. The wines to note are

- **Dominique Portet Yarra Valley Cabernet Sauvignon** has a long mouthful of flavour with intense cassis and plummy flavours.

- **Dominique Portet Sauvignon Blanc** is made in a French style where, instead of fermenting in stainless steel to capture the fruity aromas as is done in most Australian wineries, the grapes are treated more like a Chardonnay with the juice transferred into oak barrels for fermentation — with an eye on giving the wine a denser texture and less dominant fruitiness.

✔ **Giant Steps:** Nearby to Coldstream Hills is the Giant Steps winery. The owner Phil Sexton's background is one of beer brewing and he started one of Australia's most successful small breweries — Redback. But beer was replaced by his and his wife's love of vines and wine, from which Giant Steps evolved. The wines are better and better each year with the cherry and blood plum-like **Giant Steps Pinot Noir** being a highlight along with the high quality, citrus and oak dominated **Giant Steps Chardonnay**.

✔ **Yeringberg:** I suggest that you get on this winery's mailing list and try the medium-bodied blackberry and cigarbox-reminiscent **Yeringberg Cabernet Merlot** and the slightly different spicy, pear and quite full-bodied **Yeringberg Rousanne/Marsanne** blend. Guill and Catherine de Pury own the winery. Guill is the grandson of Guillaume de Pury who planted grapes at the same site back in 1862. Today the vineyard is partly managed by Guill and Catherine's children. In the early days, the wines were top class, and they still are today. If you're ever lucky enough to visit this winery, grab the opportunity. The original buildings are still standing, along with ingenious grape transport systems.

✔ **Mount Mary:** Regarded by many as one of Australia's premium wineries, Mount Mary makes beautiful wines with the utmost care and thoughtfulness, such as:

- The not-so-well-known **Mount Mary Triolet** — a blend made from Sauvignon Blanc, Semillon and Muscadelle — produced in the tradition of the white wines of Bordeaux, France.

- **Mount Mary Quintet**, a beautiful wine with elegance and well worth cellaring for five to eight years

- **Mount Mary Chardonnay**, a zesty and balanced barrel-aged wine.

- **Mount Mary Pinot Noir**, which tends to be a lighter more fragrant style of Pinot Noir

✔ **Oakridge Estate:** Yet another winery that has had a reincarnation. This time the headquarters were originally what is now the Five Oaks Winery in Seville (see 'Exploring in yonder hills'). The move to the Yarra floor has meant more exposure to the passing tourist trade, as well as having a vineyard in the warmer part of the Yarra Valley. Today the wines that are the pick of the crop include

- **Oakridge Yarra Valley Cabernet Sauvignon**, an easy-to-drink wine reminiscent of cassis, and with a touch of mintiness, finishing with soft tannins.

- **Oakridge Yarra Valley Chardonnay**, a zesty citrus-like wine — both refreshing and satisfying at the same time.

- **Oakridge Yarra Valley Shiraz**, a medium bodied blackberry and all spice fragrant wine.

✔ **Rochford:** Rochford was established in the Macedon Ranges. In 2001, Rochford purchased the winery formerly known as Eyton to make its headquarters. The winery has two labels: the Rochford E label wines are made predominately from grapes from the Yarra Valley, and the less expensive Rochford V label wines are made from grapes grown across Victoria. The best wines so far are the black cherry and truffles **Rochford E Pinot Noir** and the pear and jasmine blossom **Rochford Arneis**.

✔ **St Huberts Vineyard:** St Huberts is on the site of some of the earliest vineyards planted in the Yarra. For a wine that is a change from the more usual varieties, look for the densely textured and honeyed **St Huberts Roussanne**.

✔ **The Yarra Hill:** Two well-made labels currently come from this patch: Punt Road and Sticks. The Sticks label shows fantastic value for money, especially the fruity **Sticks Pinot Noir**. The Punt Road wines are a step above the Sticks, being aged a little longer in oak and bottle before they're released for sale. Particularly good are the richly textured **Punt Road Pinot Gris** and the blackberry and briary **Punt Road Cabernet Sauvignon**. Although this winery is relatively new, the fruit being used is largely from mature vineyards belonging to old-time grape growers, and its reputation is getting bigger by the moment.

Wines from Yarra Glen

Many of the vineyards around Yarra Glen sit pretty low on the Yarra Valley floor, so if anyone is going to be frosted or flooded, they're the most likely candidates. However, this location also makes these some of the warmer sites, so you can expect riper, richer-flavoured wines than those in the hills.

Top wines from this area come from

- **De Bortoli Wines:** The biggest Yarra Valley producer and one that has endless energy to keep on planting more and more vines. The wines, though, don't suffer in quality despite the large winery. A few labels come from here:

  - The De Bortoli Yarra Valley range. Here you find a rich, savoury and earthy **De Bortoli Yarra Valley Pinot Noir**, a creamy and soft **De Bortoli Yarra Valley Chardonnay** and, in the warmer years, a leafy and tannin rich **De Bortoli Yarra Valley Cabernet Sauvignon**.

  - The second tier of wines is the De Bortoli Gulf Station. The fruit is still from the Yarra Valley, but the wines are more aimed at drinking earlier than the Yarra Valley range (these can be aged for around five years). The **De Bortoli Gulf Station Pinot Noir** is released earlier than the De Bortoli Yarra Valley Pinot Noir and the result is a more fruit-filled wine showing raspberries and cherries. New from the stable is the **De Bortoli Gulf Station Sangiovese**, which is a spicy and fruit dominated wine.

  - The third-tier label from this winery is the De Bortoli Windy Peak range, a range of wines that have some Yarra Valley fruit supplemented by fruit from other regions. The wines are not expensive at all with the **De Bortoli Windy Peak Chardonnay** being hard to beat in quality and drinkability.

The Italian dynasty — the De Bortoli family

In 1927, Vittorio De Bortoli started what would today be one of Australia's most successful wine companies, **De Bortoli Wines**. Although you could find a couple of wineries in the region then, mostly the area was growing fruit and vegetables. A surplus of grapes in 1928 lead Vittorio to make some of his own wine, for himself and the whole Italian community that came south from the Queensland sugar cane fields in the off season to find work as fruit pickers. Many of these workers purchased wine from Vittorio and, by 1936, he was able to make his first big crush of fifteen tonnes of Black Shiraz fruit. Using the land that he bought in 1927 and gradually added to, Vittorio and later his son Deen just kept on growing the business. Today, the company runs a wine producing facility and vineyards in Victoria in the Yarra Valley as well as having vineyards in the King Valley, and in Griffith, New South Wales (refer to Chapter 8). The tradition continues today with all of Deen and Emery's children working in the business.

✔ **Fergusson:** The winery has set itself up as one of the main tourist destinations within the Yarra Valley, offering lunches and functions to the passing tourist buses. The wines are well made and the best is the **Fergusson Benjamyn Cabernet Sauvignon**, a briary and soft-tannined wine.

✔ **TarraWarra Estate:** Specialising in Chardonnay and Pinot Noir, this winery has grown in size and stature over the years. Both varieties are made in a weighty, intense style with the intention that they should rest in the cellar for a few years before being opened. Look out for the well-priced second label known as Tin Cows, especially the **Tin Cows Shiraz**.

✔ **Yarra Ridge:** Owned — along with the nearby St Huberts — by another significant player in the Australian wine scene, Beringer Blass (which, incidentally, Foster's Brewing Company owns), this winery has had a period of mediocre performance, as is often the case after a corporate changeover. But after much shuffling and hard work, the wines produced are now back to form. Yarra Ridge's wines are doubtlessly, and unashamedly, of a commercial style with loads of fruit flavours and immediate appeal.

The best from Yarra Ridge over the years are the Chardonnay and Sauvignon Blanc, with Merlot also making a play of late. On occasion, the standard Pinot Noir can also be a good buy.

✔ **Yering Station:** Like many wineries, Yering Station cellar door offers wines not sold elsewhere (see Chapter 28 for the top ten cellar doors). Look out for

- **Yering Station Pinot Noir Rosé:** The winery is a strong supporter of rosé and this wine is a light and fruity example of rosé made from Pinot Noir. Perfect in the summertime.

- **Yering Station Reserve Pinot Noir:** An opulent, dark plums and truffle like wine with slightly obvious oak.

- **Yering Station Shiraz Viognier:** Like many other producers of Shiraz, Yering Station blends a bit of Viognier with the Shiraz. The result is a full-bodied wine showing some pear from the Viognier along with black plums and berries from the Shiraz.

- **Yering Station Viognier:** A really fruity and rose-petal-like wine.

Yering Station is also the Australian home of the excellent Devaux Champagne house and its **Yarra Bank Sparkling** wine.

Exploring in yonder hills

What is most noticeable in and around Seville and the Diamond Valley (south of Hurstbridge) (refer to Figure 10-1) is that the countryside isn't wall-to-wall vines as it is in other areas in the Yarra. Rather the opposite: You're hard-pressed to spot a vine! Instead, this area abounds in fruit orchards and berry farms, and the roads are dotted with roadside vendors and signposts inviting you to pick your own produce.

Wines grown around Seville

Top wines from Seville include those from

- **Five Oaks:** Look out for **Five Oaks Riesling** and **Five Oaks Chardonnay**. This vineyard site can sometimes be a little too cool for Cabernet, making the wines taste a little herbaceous — that is, quite herbal-like without the berry fruit flavours you'd expect.

- **Gembrook Hills:** Without doubt one of the coldest vineyards in the Yarra. When the valley floor hits 30 degrees Celsius, you can be sure the temperature here barely gets past 20 degrees Celsius. The wines are terrific — herbal and citrus **Gembrook Hills Sauvignon Blanc** is one of the best around. Also, look out for the truffley and raspberry leaf-like **Gembrook Hills Pinot Noir**, which seems to get better each year.

- **McWilliam's Lillydale:** Owned by the McWilliam's family company, the fifth largest wine company in Australia, this winery produces good quality, non-complicated wines. And it hasn't been lost among the big McWilliam's wine portfolio, as this winery makes the company proud to be part of the Yarra. One of my favourite wines from the range is the spicy, floral **Lillydale Estate Gewürztraminer**, a terrific change from the more common white wine varietals. Back in the 1980s this grape was an unusual choice to plant; however, it proves to be a good one, giving the winery a stamp of individuality.

- **Seville Estate:** One of the cooler vineyards in the valley, in terms of climate, is Seville Estate, which is situated up in the hills among the cherry and stone fruit trees. As a result, varieties such as Cabernet Sauvignon struggle to ripen. The **Seville Estate Shiraz**, however, with its cool climate spiciness is very good, and the **Seville Estate Chardonnay** is one to stash in the cellar for five years.

- **Yarra Burn Winery:** Purchased by The Hardy Company, Yarra Burn continues to flourish. Today, the winery has access to fruit from the high-altitude Hoddles Creek Vineyards, which means that the wines have an increased delicacy and interest. Some of the wines are still made at the winery, but one of the best — particularly commercially — is the **Yarra Burn Pinot Noir Chardonnay** sparkling wine. Of note, also, is the Yarra **Burn Bastard Hill Chardonnay** (named after a vineyard high in the hills that pushes the vineyard manager to the limit of his patience because of the marginal climate).

Wines from the Diamond Valley

Top wines from the Diamond Valley include those from

- ✔ **Diamond Valley Vineyards:** Diamond Valley made its name as a top-class Pinot Noir producer. These days it makes a standard version of the wine from fruit sourced all over the region, but better still is its **Diamond Valley Estate Pinot Noir** made from fruit off the Diamond Valley property. Typically, this wine is medium-bodied as well as having some raspberry and toasty oak flavours.

  For the top drop, try the **Diamond Valley Close-Planted Pinot Noir**, which is produced from grapes grown in the style of the vineyards in France. This method involves planting the vines closer together so that the vines produce less fruit per vine but theoretically more intense flavours. At Diamond Valley this is definitely the case, with the wines showing plenty of dense fruit flavours.

- ✔ **Evelyn County Estate:** As you veer around a bend in the road towards this winery, the first thing you notice is a stunning building looming out of the landscape. Inside this architect-designed building (which is built with materials and colours sympathetic to the landscape) is a restaurant where you can enjoy lunch daily as well as breakfast on the weekend. As well as the restaurant, you can taste the wines. Make sure you include the following from the Black Paddock range:

  - **Evelyn County Estate Black Paddock Pinot Noir**, intensely flavoured with plums, truffles and a long finish.

  - **Evelyn County Estate Black Paddock Cabernet Sauvignon**, some briary and blackcurrant flavours with a soft tannin finish.

- ✔ **Wedgetail Estate:** Wedgetail Estate is a small producer tucked away in the hills making good, reasonably priced wines. Both the **Wedgetail Estate Pinot Noir** (showing plums, cherries and a touch of mint) and **Wedgetail Estate Chardonnay** (with a complex mix of nuts, peaches and a touch of oak) are all too easy to drink. The casual, simple lunches are well worth the detour.

Out all alone

What would a good winegrowing region be without a couple of isolated outposts? The following vineyards are quite removed from the rest of the valley (refer to Figure 10-1). Both areas were planted early in the Yarra's history and now have suburbia creeping ever so slowly towards them. Additionally, both can now lay claim to second-generation status.

- ✔ **Kellybrook Winery:** Initially this winery made its fame as a cider and apple brandy maker — a spirit based on the calvados digestifs of France — which makes sense since the Kelly family set up its vineyard among apple orchards and were self-confessed Francophiles. Now second-generation winemaker Phil Kelly has revitalised many of the apple trees to continue the tradition as well as tending the vines. Still very much a family-run concern, Kellybrook produces some good honest wines, particularly blackberried and savoury **Kellybrook Shiraz** and the peachy and melon **Kellybrook Chardonnay**.

- ✔ **Wantirna Estate:** I'm letting you know this information up front: My family owns this small winery and I make the wines with my pioneering father. Now, because I'm way too shy and retiring to comment on my own wines, here's what Jeremy Olivier has to say in his book *OnWine Australian Wine Annual 2002*: 'There's a distinctive winemaking stylist's footprint in the fineness, tightness and elegance of their wines, which are some of the most intensely flavoured and complex in Australia.'

  Our history is such that our Cabernet Merlot blend is often the one people know. But with more than just a touch of passion for the wines of Burgundy in France, we also make both Pinot Noir and Chardonnay.

The fun of the grape-grazing festival

The Yarra's grape-grazing festival is an annual tradition. Held in either February or March (for details, check the tourism Web site www.yarravalleytourism.asn), the idea is to graze your way around the valley during grape-picking season. Each of the wineries teams up with a restaurant — often some of Melbourne's best — and you're able to choose a glass of wine with a suitably matched, entrée-sized plate of food. Then, all you need to do is sit under a tree and enjoy. A pretty divine way to spend a Sunday. For more information, check out www.grapegrazing.com.au/map.html.

Chapter 11

Victoria's Wine-Diverse Heartland

*T*he wines of the western and central parts of the state of Victoria in Australia are as diverse and stunning as the region itself. From Heathcote's seriously good Shiraz and Australia's best Gewürztraminer in the Central Highlands, to the Rhône Valley influenced red and white varieties of the Goulburn Valley, you're sure to find a wine to please.

Varieties That Prosper

Australia's Central Victorian wine zone includes the regions of Goulburn Valley (and its sub-region Nagambie Lakes), Bendigo, Heathcote, and Strathbogie Ranges (which includes the Central Victorian mountain country). Across to the west of the state is the Western Victoria zone, which includes the regions of the Pyrenees, the Grampians, Ballarat and a tiny area on the south-western coast of Victoria known as Henty. (For more information on Australia's geographical wine zones, refer to Chapter 3.)

Although each Central Victorian region has a unique climate, overall the regions are quite dry, receiving rainfall primarily during winter (June to August) and spring (September to November). As a result excessive leaf growth isn't a problem, and the risk of disease is lower than in areas receiving high rainfall and/or where there is too much foliage and air can't easily circulate. All the regions have well-structured soils, that is, soils that allow free drainage of water down into a clay base, which allows it to be stored for the roots to access in the dry summer months.

Temperature-wise, at the coolest end of the spectrum are the wineries in the Strathbogie Ranges, the Pyrenees and the Grampians, with the warmer ones located in Heathcote and the Goulburn Valley. One commonality is that the warm days are followed by cool nights, which allows the all-important slow ripening of the berries for a gradual build-up in intensity of fruit flavours.

Reds rule

Red wine is the star performer in Central Victoria, given the mild to warm temperatures. Consequently, Shiraz is a strong performer, as is Cabernet Sauvignon. In the cooler Strathbogie and Ballarat vineyards, Pinot Noir does well and produces many a fine base for sparkling wines. The reds of the area have the following characteristics:

✔ **Shiraz:** Arguably some of Victoria's best Shiraz is grown in these parts. The regions that do Shiraz with style include

- **Goulburn Valley:** Long-living Shiraz is grown around here. The fruit is full of rich-ripe plum flavours and is often blended with the sweet Grenache or the savoury Mourvèdre grapes. The **Mitchelton Crescent** blend is definitely one to look for.

- **Bendigo:** You're not going to be disappointed by the amount of flavour that you get per sip from the Bendigo reds, such as the **Sutton Grange** wines. Typically spicy with a savoury background that keeps the fruitiness of the wines in check.

- **Heathcote:** If you're after a blockbuster Shiraz, the Heathcote reds might suit. Full of flavour with a backbone of tannin, they often have a high alcohol content. The **Jasper Hill** Shiraz for example has more than 15 per cent — now that is ripe fruit!

- **Pyrenees:** The reds from this region are always lovely and ripe, with flavours that move from rich plum and ripe blackberries to spicy and black-pepper tones with a fair whack of tannin. Particularly good are those from **Dalwhinnie**. What I enjoy most from the Pyrenees Shiraz is the ability of the winemakers (or maybe the clever grapes themselves) to show a degree of sophistication so that the second glass is as interesting as the first. Many of these wineries also add charm to their wines by blending a touch of Mourvèdre or Viognier with the Shiraz. (See the sidebar 'The Rhône Rangers come to Victoria' for more information on this technique.)

✔ **Cabernet Sauvignon:** Often unfairly forgotten in all the fame of the district's Shiraz wines, the local Cabernet Sauvignons are full-bodied and ripe, showing blackberry and cedar flavours, occasionally with a touch of mint. While they don't have the reputation of South Australia's Coonawarra Cabernets (see Chapter 19), the richness is something that many welcome. A few of the best come from the wineries **Taltarni**, **Red Edge** and **Dalwhinnie**.

Arousing, aromatic whites

The aromatic varieties such as Sauvignon Blanc, Riesling and Gewürztraminer all show their strengths in the cooler regions of these areas, and the results are some very stylish wines. By comparison, Chardonnay produced in the area is a little ho hum, except when the grapes are used for sparkling wine. The white wine highlights to look out for include those from

✔ **Strathbogie Ranges:** The cool, almost cold nights make this area perfect for capturing and maintaining a fruity, acid, zingy Riesling. The **Alexander Park** wines, in particular, show these traits.

✔ **Central Victorian Mountain Country:** My prize for the most delicious Gewürztraminers in the district goes to those from **Delatite Winery**. This wine has a charming, lychee-like fruit and a soft textured palate.

✔ **The Pyrenees:** The climate of this region suits the fruity style of Sauvignon Blanc, making wines without the passionfruit, herbaceous tones that you see in so many examples of this variety. Both **Mount Avoca** and **Taltarni** do this variety well.

A newcomer with potential is Pinot Gris — a very versatile grape in regions such as the Grampians and the Pyrenees. Wineries that are doing well with this variety include **Redbank** and **Mount Langi Ghiran**.

The wonderful white varieties from Southern France — Marsanne, Roussanne and Viognier — have moved beyond being fashionably new and are now acclaimed as serious wines. They're particularly at home planted in the warm Goulburn Valley and Heathcote regions.

✔ **Goulburn Valley:** These varieties really have stamped a name for themselves in this region, and **Mitchelton** has been at the forefront, blending the varieties to make the Airstrip blend. Also look out for the age-worthy Marsanne that **Tahbilk** has been making for years — inexpensive and has fantastic cellaring potential.

✔ **Heathcote:** The Viognier in this region has seen itself as that added extra. Added to Shiraz at a proportion of something less than 10 per cent, Viognier gives the Shiraz a certain fullness and subtlety through the mid-palate. **Heathcote Winery** was one of the pioneers of this style in Australia.

Central Victoria Up Close

The Central Victoria zone is located roughly to the north-north-east of the city of Melbourne. The main towns include Bendigo, Heathcote and Goulburn Valley, and the cooler Strathbogie and Central Victorian Highlands (see Figure 11-1).

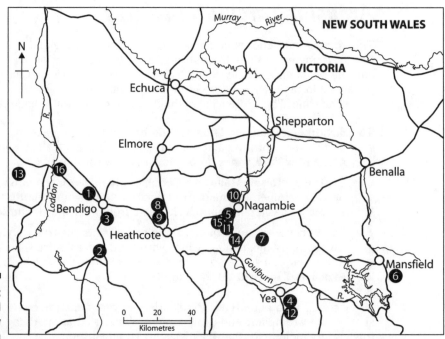

Figure 11-1: Delightful diversity from Goulburn Valley, Bendigo, Heathcote and Strathbogie Ranges wine regions of Victoria.

① Balgownie Estate
② Blackjack Vineyards
③ Chateau Leamon
④ Cheviot Bridge Wine Company
⑤ David Traeger Wines
⑥ Delatite Vineyard
⑦ Dominion
⑧ Heathcote Winery
⑨ Jasper Hill Vineyard
⑩ Kirwan's Bridge
⑪ Mitchelton Wines
⑫ Murrundindi Vineyard
⑬ Passing Clouds
⑭ Plunkett Wines
⑮ Tahbilk Winery
⑯ Water Wheel Vineyards

Goulburn Valley produce

The Goulburn Valley region is located in the middle of Victoria, pretty well due north of Melbourne and runs from the town of Seymour — about 120 kilometres from Melbourne — up to the Victoria–New South Wales border town of Echuca on the Murray River, another 150 kilometres or so north.

The main focus for quality wine in this region is around the sub-region known as Nagambie Lakes, just north of Seymour and 150 kilometres north of Melbourne. The wines of this region are known for their rich and intense weight and fruit flavours.

When I think of the Nagambie region, I think of warm, dry summers and autumns. Summer day temperatures average in the high 20 degrees Celsius to low 30 degrees Celsius, and during this season the vines are exposed to an average of nine hours of sunshine a day.

The vineyards around the Goulburn River actually have their climate tempered by being close to two waterways — the Goulburn River and the Nagambie Lakes. Both waterways act to take the edge off the hot summer days, allowing the grapes to ripen just a little more slowly, thereby ensuring that a concentration of fruit flavour is reached before harvest.

Tahbilk Winery planted the first vines in this region way back in 1860, although most of the planting has been done over the past 30 years. Today, the region has 19 wineries, contributing to a vineyard area of 700 hectares, but these statistics are growing every year.

Though the oldest winery in the area, Tahbilk hasn't stayed still. The winemaking is up to date, and both the **Tahbilk Marsanne** and **Tahbilk Shiraz** are worth buying. I suggest you buy a few — some for the cellar and a couple to drink now because the Marsanne changes from being lemon and grapefruit dominant when young into a richly textured honey and toasty wine with five plus years in the bottle.

While the **Mitchelton** winery has always had a high reputation for its Shiraz and Blackwood Park Riesling, the so-called new varieties hailing from the Rhône Valley in France have done much for this winery's success. The Airstrip white (consisting of Marsanne, Roussanne and Viognier) and Crescent red (Shiraz, Mourvèdre and Grenache) really back up the locals' conviction on the suitability of these varieties to this warm, dry climate.

Within the quite large portfolio of wines made at Mitchelton is the **Preece** range, which is always a reliable choice in a less expensive restaurant or cafe, or to take to a party when you want good inexpensive wine.

The lousy problem

Central Victoria is an active *Phylloxera* region — its vines and soil contain a vine louse that is partial to eating vine roots and, over time, kills the vine. Most of Australia's other grape-growing areas are free of this louse, except Geelong (which had it in the 1800s but is thought to be free of the pesky problem now), King Valley Rutherglen, and Strathbogie.

Unfortunately, no spray or cure exists to eradicate this pest. As a result, affected regions have road signs telling visitors not to take vine material (cuttings, grapes, leaves) out of the area. By trying to contain *Phylloxera* to currently affected areas, the Department of Agriculture hopes to

keep the louse isolated. Unfortunately, it can hitchhike undetected, catching a ride on the soles of shoes or the tyres of cars. So if you visit this region, change your shoes when you leave and before you go walking in the vineyards of *Phylloxera*-free areas.

Interestingly, this pest doesn't kill the vines immediately. Some vines at Mitchelton have had evidence of *Phylloxera* on their roots for years, but still produce fruit every year, albeit with much reduced yields. The one available cure is that of planting the vines on resistant rootstock, so vineyards that have the problem will gradually replant using this rootstock.

In keeping with a good work ethic, Tahbilk chief executive Alister Purbrick has his own smaller winery, **Dalfarras**. The Tahbilk value-for-money theme continues with the spicy and cinnamon like **Dalfarras Shiraz** and a wine that is reminiscent of lemon zest and fresh herbs — **Dalfarras Sauvignon Blanc;** both particularly good.

Although now part of the Dromana Estate consortium, **David Traeger Wines** is still run as a small affair. My first introduction to its wines came via the Verdelho, at the time a little-known variety in Australia. Since then, this label has paved the way for this variety, every year making a wine that seems to burst with sunshine. The **David Traeger Shiraz** is very good, too, showing the region's famous pepper and spice.

For the local heroes of Viognier, Roussanne and Marsanne in the whites and Shiraz, Grenache and Mourvèdre in the reds, search out those from the smaller identity in the region, **Kirwan's Bridge Wines.**

The best of Bendigo

Bendigo (refer to Figure 11-1) has four major wine centres: south-east around Harcourt, further north around Bendigo, north-west around Bridgewater, Inglewood and Kingower, and to the south-west around Maryborough. Most affairs in the area are small, and nearly all are family owned and run.

Bendigo's climate is warm, almost hot, in the summer time. The vineyards situated on low-lying country make the most of the heat for ripening their grapes, while those located on the hills utilise the altitude to develop their style. In addition, the granitic soil of the region is tough and not very fertile, so grape yields are low per vine and fruit intensity is high.

Perfumed Shiraz and well-structured Cabernet Sauvignon are just two of the highlights of this region. Look out for those from

- ✔ **Balgownie Estate:** Expect well-made, concentrated wines, with the Shiraz and Cabernet Sauvignon being of particular note.
- ✔ **Blackjack Vineyards:** Another winery that offers value. The wines are powerfully flavoured, showing what a warmer-than-average vineyard site can do in this region.
- ✔ **Chateau Leamon:** True to regional style, the Cabernet Sauvignon shows blackberry and violets while the Shiraz is spicy with a touch of mint.
- ✔ **Passing Clouds:** One of the northernmost vineyards in the Bendigo region. Owner Graeme Leith is something of a local personality with his unique way of doing things. But his way works, as his reds show strong regional character and depth of flavour, along with a touch of mintiness.
- ✔ **Sutton Grange:** Given this vineyard's location in the foothills of the Mount Alexander range, the climate isn't so different to the warmer parts of the Macedon Ranges (see Chapter 14). So, instead of the big weighted wines more common to the Bendigo region, this winery offers a more restrained, savoury style of wine.
- ✔ **Water Wheel Vineyards:** Well worth the modest price, the Cabernet Sauvignon has rich, ripe, blackberry flavours, while the Shiraz is concentrated and aniseed-like.

The Rhône Rangers come to Victoria

I remember in my early wine-drinking days the pleasure of buying French Rhône Valley wines for an absolute bargain price. Apart from France, no other country, including Australia, seemed to have discovered these delicious spicy wines at that time. Alas, a good review here and there saw prices of these French wines skyrocket.

Thankfully, some of Australia's top winemakers shared in my passion and, today, in the warmer climes of Victoria, the gorgeous red grape varieties of Grenache and Mourvèdre (also known in Australia as Maltaro) are blended with Shiraz to make a densely flavoured yet spicy and balanced red wine. And in the whites the mix of Viognier, Roussanne and Marsanne makes for some full-bodied, textural whites.

Hunting down Heathcote

The Heathcote region's (refer to Figure 11-1) boundary (after much dispute and discussion) runs between the Bendigo and Goulburn Valley region on the northern side of the Great Dividing Range. This situation means that rainfall is low, although what does fall is usually evenly spread across the seasons. Luckily for the local grape growers, the region's red soil retains water, so during dry spells the vines' roots can still find water down deep in the soil.

The top local producers don't opt for irrigation, instead preferring their vines to produce less fruit, smaller berries and, hence, more concentrated wines. Consequently, many of the wines from this area aren't cheap.

Perhaps the most famous, particularly internationally, are the wines from **Wild Duck Creek**. This quiet grape grower hit the news with a wine called **Wild Duck Creek Duck Muck**, which reached huge price heights after rave reviews from American critics. (The owner David Anderson still seems a little bemused by the whole thing, and quietly continues to make his wine in his humble surrounds.) The wine isn't for lovers of the elegant styles of wines; instead, it is incredibly intensely flavoured and dense in texture with a huge mouthful of blackberrry, chocolate and liquorice.

One of the top Shiraz from this area comes from **Jasper Hill Vineyard**, which has slowly but very surely being building its reputation. Despite being almost wiped out by a fierce bushfire in the early establishment days, these winemakers weren't to be put off and they continue to build their following by the day. These days the vineyard is run with an emphasis on biodynamic viticulture practices. (Refer to Chapter 6 for more information about this type of grape growing.)

Jasper Hill Shiraz gets a decent dose of oak during its winemaking procedure and this flavour is a little obvious when the wine is young. But, with four or more years in bottle, the wine tends to marry all the components together to give a rich flavour of chocolate, savoury meats and a spicy finish.

For a straight and very richly textured Viognier, look out for that from **Heathcote Winery**, one of the earliest producers in the region. Also of note is the **Heathcote Curagee Shiraz**, a Shiraz with a touch of Viognier added that fills out the peppery Shiraz with a pear-like rounded middle palate.

A small producer that is making intensely structured and well-priced Shiraz and Cabernet Sauvignon is **Red Edge.**

The Central Victorian Mountain District

The Central Victorian Mountain District is quite diverse, spreading east from Seymour across to Mansfield. Around the towns of Seymour and Yea, the temperatures are warm, but to the east the temperature cools down around the town of Mansfield at the foothills of the Great Dividing Range and the ski resort Mount Buller. In these areas, the winters deliver frosts and the occasional snowfall, and in spring the growing season is slow to get going because the days are still cold. Consequently, ripening occurs much later in autumn, so the grape growers can take advantage of the cold nights.

Yay! We're in Yea

I don't know a single child that has gone through this town without saying, 'Yay, we're in Yea!' (The next town is called Yarck, so it follows with 'Yuck, we're in Yarck!') Anecdotes aside, Yea is an interesting area with wines that are something to watch out for. Most of the vineyard activity occurs in the rolling hills off the Melba Highway, and the area with its cool nights in summer and autumn, along with plenty of daytime sunshine, is very suitable to viticulture.

The **Cheviot Bridge Wine Company** is a commercial-sized operation in the Yea Valley that has been unashamedly set up to make and sell wine at a price and profit. Three tiers of wine are on offer: the **Cheviot Bridge Yea Valley** range, which is the most expensive; the medium-prized **CB** range; and the inexpensive **Kissing Bridge** range. For my money, the CB range offers the best value for quality wines, particularly its Shiraz.

As a test of the potential of this area, **Murrundindi Vineyard** was planted back in 1984. To date, the citrus and melon **Murrundindi Chardonnay** proves to be its best wine.

Strolling through Strathbogie

Most people first became aware of the Strathbogie Ranges in the late 1970s when the Tisdall wine company planted its Mount Helen vineyard. Many grape growers thought it was ludicrous to plant in such a cool spot but, as is so often the case, those critics were proved wrong.

Although plantings are still small and the wines from the area are hardly threatening dominance of wine store shelves, the region is nevertheless making itself known as an area where fine cool-climate (if you've lived there you'd say freezing!) wines are being made.

In the mid-1990s, when I was making wine at Domaine Chandon in the Yarra Valley (refer to Chapter 10), we planted vineyards in Strathbogie, and today that fruit is a very significant quality addition to the blend of Chandon sparkling wines.

For wines that show loads of full, ripe, fruity flavours, my picks are the Merlot and Shiraz from **Plunkett Wines**, a winery slowly establishing itself as a significant winemaker in the Strathbogie Ranges. Also, look out for **Alexander Park Riesling**, a fruity bombshell from **Dominion Wines**.

Up in the Victorian High Country

In the foreground of the imposing stature of Mount Buller is **Delatite Vineyard**. The cold winter and early spring weather deliver the bulk of the rain to this area, and as the summer days draw near rain becomes a distant memory. Summer days are quite hot with low humidity, yet the nights are cool thereby letting the vines slow down the ripening process overnight. By autumn the days are getting shorter and the nights cooler, allowing varieties such as Gewürztraminer to maintain their powerful flavours.

A favourite of mine is **Delatite**, located a few kilometres from the town of Mansfield. Ever since planting in 1968, the wines produced here have been first class. The aromatic whites, especially the lychee and jasmine floral aroma **Dead Man's Hill Gewürztraminer** and the lime and lemon **VS Riesling** are without doubt among Australia's finest. The reds show good cool-climate flavours with that regional touch of mintiness.

Out in the Wild, Wild West

The western part of Victoria makes up quite a large parcel of land (see Figure 11-2). The towns that feature in this area are Bendigo, Ararat, Stawell, Ballarat and, in the south-west, Portland. See Figure 11-2. Other than in the Henty region, no sea is in sight, so the climate is *temperate*, that is, mild to warm. The region's topography, however, is quite varied. Some vineyards are located on the warm, flat plains, while others have opted for higher elevations with their cooler microclimates.

Pyrenees

Although this wine region doesn't really resemble the French Pyrenees region (some of the earlier settlers thought it did, hence the name, but in fact the French Pyrenees are much higher and more rugged), plenty of Gallic involvement has occurred in these wineries over the years. **Taltarni Vineyard** had Frenchman Dominque Portet at the helm for many years and, until recently, the Remy Cointreau Group owned **Blue Pyrenees Estate**, formally known as Château Remy.

The region is about 175 kilometres from Melbourne, and the area's 16 wineries surround the small townships of Avoca and Moonambel. Most of the vineyards are on flat land at the foot of the Pyrenees Ranges, and experience cool nights that slow down the ripening after the day's warmth. The soil is gravelly with some clay underneath, which allows rain to drain freely to the clay where the moisture can be retained for use in dry months.

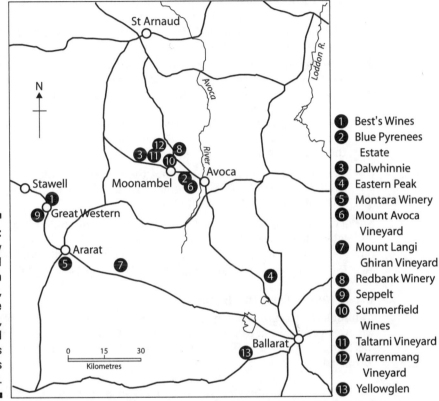

Figure 11-2: Highly regarded wines from the Ballarat, the Grampians, Henty and Pyrenees wine regions of Victoria.

Some of the best Shiraz in Australia comes from around this region, with **Dalwhinnie** and **Warrenmang Vineyard** leading the charge. Both wineries produce excellent 'standard' release Shiraz, but really outstanding are their special-release wines such as the **Dalwhinnie Eagle Shiraz** and the **Warrenmang Black Puma Shiraz**. Both wines have a full fruit style but with a backbone of restraint that keeps your interest in the Shiraz for more than one glass.

Dalwhinnie also makes a fine Chardonnay and, over at Warrenmang, I'm quite taken with its inexpensive Vinello — a blend of the Italian varieties of Sangiovese, Barbera, Nebbiolo and Dolcetto — which is a great food wine.

Other top drops of the region include the following:

- **Redbank Winery's Sally's Paddock** is an original Australian wine blend of Cabernet Sauvignon, Shiraz and Malbec. This drop has become quite an institution among wine lovers over the years. In addition, one of its most commercially successful labels has been the **Long Paddock** range of whites and reds, along with the ever-reliable, inexpensive lemon and toast-like **Emily's Sparkling Wine**.

- The aromatic variety of Sauvignon Blanc and the Shiraz from **Mount Avoca Vineyard** and **Blue Pyrenees Estate**. Located just west of the small town of Avoca, both vineyards are planted at the foothills of some very beautiful mountains. The Blue Pyrenees vineyard is the coolest in the region, situated at an altitude of around 400 metres above sea level. Being surrounded by a mountain range protects the vines from some of the hot summer winds and also creates coolness at night.

- The spicy and peppery Shiraz and the long-living Cabernet Sauvignon from **Summerfield Wines**, a winery which has been making a name for itself over the past 20 years or so.

- The sparkling wines from **Blue Pyrenees Estate** and **Taltarni,** both of which make first-class, finely textured wines. At Taltarni you also find robust reds along with its inexpensive second label, **Fiddleback**, which is top value-for-money, easy-drinking white and red wines.

Great things from the Grampians

Although the Grampians may not be the largest region in terms of number of wineries (it has 16 in total), it can lay claim to some of Victoria's finest, including **Best's Wines**, **Seppelt Great Western** and **Mount Langi Ghiran Vineyard**.

Those grapes that ripen a little later in the season, such as Shiraz and Cabernet Sauvignon, really benefit from the tempering of the weather with the change of seasons in this region.

As mid-March approaches, the days become shorter, and a few degrees cooler, with maximum temperatures in the mid- to high-20 degrees Celsius. In addition, the night-time temperature regularly drops well below 10 degrees Celsius. The grapes respond beautifully to these temperatures, soaking up the sunshine during the day and completely ceasing any ripening at night, thus prolonging the harvest date and building their flavour intensity. Despite limited natural water sources, water is no problem given the Grampians' reclaimed water system. Treated town wastewater simply ends up on the vineyards as summer irrigation.

Then and now

The Grampians area has some serious history in vineyards. Take Best's Wines vineyard, now into its fifth generation of Thomson family grape growers — not a long time compared to European standards but in this young country quite a feat. And miners who had come to the area in search of gold dug the underground cellars at Seppelt Great Western. Instead of goldmining, they found employment building the underground cellars, which were to be used as they are in Champagne, that is, for ageing sparkling wine. Today these cellars are very much in use and are well worth a look if you visit the area. Being part of the huge Southcorp company, the Seppelt cellar door offers a huge array of wines to taste. I suggest you focus on the wines of the region, such as the famous **Seppelt Show Reserve Sparkling Shiraz**, and the **St Peter's Shiraz**.

For some fine Pinot Noir and Shiraz that carry the regional touch of eucalyptus mintiness, try those from **Montara**. Located 350 metres above sea level on the slopes of Mount Chalambar, the vineyard is cool enough to make these varieties successfully.

To date, the **Mount Langi Ghiran** vineyard's densely flavoured peppery Shiraz and cassis Cabernet Sauvignon have stood out, but recently its pear, spice and appley Pinot Gris has also begun to impress.

Bubbly Ballarat

Ballarat is tiny in terms of its number of wineries, having nine at last count, with only a couple reaching any quantity. The climate isn't dissimilar to the Grampians region, where the autumn nights are cold, prolonging ripening and allowing an intense build-up of fruit.

Ballarat is most famous for **Yellowglen** and its sparkling wines, so both Pinot Noir and Chardonnay feature as important grape varieties. While the grapes aren't processed into wine in the area any more (these days all the grapes for Yellowglen go to one of the many Beringer Blass wineries that the brand produces), Ballarat is the heart and soul of the second part of the sparkling wine production process.

The finished base wines are transported back to the Yellowglen winery for blending, bottling and ageing on *yeast lees* (the dead yeast cells from the yeast that carried out the bottle fermentation. By leaving the wine on these lees over time, the wine develops terrific *mouthfeel*, a soft bubble and some toasty flavours, all great attributes to making top sparkling wine).

Compared to Yellowglen, **Eastern Peake** is a tiny part of the local wine scene. Nevertheless, this winery has made a bit of a name for itself over the years, particularly for **Eastern Peake Pinot Noir Rosé**. Often rosé made from Pinot Noir is just a simple Pinot Noir, not really a rosé style nor a Pinot Noir, just an average wine. But the Eastern Peake wine is a light and perfumed Pinot Noir, worthy of a slight chill before serving.

All alone in Henty

Henty is one of Victoria's most isolated vineyard areas. Located in the southwestern corner of Victoria, it is approximately 330 kilometres from Melbourne and just 100 kilometres east of the South Australian border. The nearest towns are Portland, on the coast, and Hamilton, inland.

Only six wineries exist in the Henty region, although it does have a few vineyards planted by companies whose wineries are based in other regions (such as the Seppelt vineyards at Drumborg). The reason for this is probably the unpredictable weather — the area often experiences either drought conditions or heavy rains that tend to floods, making the viability of the region a little dubious.

Despite the isolation and conditions, the Crawford River Riesling from the Henty region is one of the most highly regarded and renowned wines of this variety in Australia. The Crawford River Riesling has the floral side of Riesling, with jasmine flower, and orange blossom aromas and palate flavours. The acid is quite high but softens beautifully with time.

Chapter 12

Heading North to Northern Victoria

. . . .

In This Chapter

▶ Finding out what the northern regions do best

▶ Entering bushranger territory in north-east Victoria

▶ Viewing the vastness of the Murray-Darling basin

▶ Indulging in treacly Tokay

▶ Sampling wines that thrive in the heat

. . . .

*T*wo distinctly different winemaking regions are found in the northern part of Victoria: The region in the north-east that is centred around the town of Rutherglen, just south of the New South Wales border, and the region in the north-west of the state that has the town of Mildura as its centre. The north-west is bordered by New South Wales to the north and South Australia to the west, and Mildura sits almost on the New South Wales border.

The north-east is steeped in a proud viticultural history. Many of the wineries date from the 1850s and generations of winemakers have passed through their gates. Much of the winemaking knowledge has been handed down from father to son (and to the occasional daughter). The region has varied topography and enjoys a range of climates.

In the north-west, vast tracts of flat land are planted to vines that rely for their survival on water from the nearby Murray River. It is a dry, almost arid part of the country. Yet, back in the 1880s, Californian irrigation engineers realised the potential of the region for growing crops — as long as water was around. European immigrants began to grow grapes, loving the effect of the intense heat on their table grapes. Although subsequent generations have opted to change the plantings to wine grape varieties, you can still see the occasional high-trellised vineyard producing grapes for the table grape and dried fruit business.

In this chapter, I introduce you to the wonderful grape varieties produced in these two regions — such as the fortified wines of Rutherglen, the Italian-flavoured wines of King Valley, the fruity Muscats, and rich Shiraz, the most-grown red from around Mildura, in the Murray-Darling basin.

Celebrating North-East Specialties

The grape-growing region of north-east Victoria is made up of five official wine regions, namely the Alpine Valley, Beechworth, Glenrowan, King Valley and Rutherglen. The area around Rutherglen enjoys a warm climate for growing grapes, whereas further to the south-east towards Beechworth and along the Alpine Valley towards Mt Buffalo the climate is much cooler.

In this section, I describe some of the best-known and most popular wines varieties from this diverse region.

Fortifyingly fabulous: Tokay and Muscat

The famous fortified wines known as Tokay and Muscat are made only in Australia. (Refer to Chapter 2 for the full story of Australia's fortified wines.) The varieties needed to make these wines are Muscadelle for Tokay, and Muscat Blanc à Petit Grains (also known in Australia as Brown Muscat) for Muscat.

The grapes that result in these fortified wines need warmth to bring them to the full ripeness they require, and the warm climate around Rutherglen produces them very successfully. For these types of wines, the grapes need to be super ripe, and that means staying on the vine a lot longer than usual. The weather conditions for the last stage in ripening is vital — little or no rain and lots of warmth.

Migrating to well-known Italians

The King Valley was originally an area of tobacco plantations established by the predominantly Italian migrant population. Over time, however, the tobacco plantings made way for vineyards and the tobacco-drying sheds have been transformed into wineries.

TIP

Managing your Port intake

The two main types of Port are Vintage and Tawny. Tawny Port is aged in a similar way to Tokay, so that you can open and drink it over time. Vintage Port, however, is aged in a similar way to red wine so, as soon as you open the bottle, the wine gradually oxidises — consequently, you really should drink Vintage Port within a day or so of opening.

Now I know that recommending you demolish a bottle of Vintage Port in a couple of days is a big ask, given its sweetness — not to mention its high alcohol content (around 18 to 20 per cent). So, if, like me, you rather like the odd glass of Vintage Port, I recommend that you invest in some small screw-top mixer bottles. These bottles hold around 375 millilitres, which is half a standard wine bottle. After you open your Port, fill one of these bottles and seal it. Because very little oxygen can get into the bottle, your Port is protected from oxidation and remains fresh until the next time you feel like having a glass.

Many second- and third-generation Italian migrants established wineries in the King Valley region, in such towns as Whitfield and Cheshunt. Most of today's winemakers started off as grape growers though, planting their vineyards and selling their fruit to wine producers. Now, by producing their own wines, they keep a winemaking focus on the region.

Interestingly, by planting the varieties so well known by their ancestors, the winemakers have carved out quite a niche for themselves. The Italian red grapes of Sangiovese, Barbera and Nebbiolo, and the white grapes of Arneis and Pinot Grigio are putting the King Valley on the winemaking map. And, in true Australian style, where diversity is celebrated, the King Valley also produces some fine Chardonnay, Merlot and Shiraz.

Basking in some sunny reds

The north-east produces excellent full-bodied reds, primarily because of the climate. During the ripening season, temperatures get quite high and the air is usually dry. The grapes can ripen with high levels of sugar that, in turn, produce high levels of alcohol in the finished wine.

REMEMBER

During fermentation, yeast uses the sugar in the grapes to produce alcohol, which means the greater the amount of sugar, the higher the level of alcohol.

The sunny disposition of the north-east produces the following red grape varieties:

- **Durif:** The region's most famous red wine variety, this little-known French grape is incredibly dense in flavour. However, the tannins are aggressive and quite unpleasant if not well handled during winemaking. Such is the denseness of this wine that whenever I do a Durif tasting I end up with temporarily black stained teeth!

- **Shiraz:** Rutherglen Shiraz is quite different in style to that of, say, the cooler Victorian vineyards around the Yarra Valley (refer to Chapter 10) and the sweet-fruited Shiraz of South Australia (see Part IV). Rutherglen Shiraz is earthier in character, displaying the variety's savoury style.

- **Cabernet Sauvignon:** These reds seem to lose their typical Cabernet flavours in this warm climate, resulting in an excellent wine that is more like a dry red wine than a typical Cabernet Sauvignon.

Sampling the Best from the North-West

The north-west grapegrowing region divides into two regions. The Murray-Darling region is so called because the Darling River meets and flows into the Murray River north-west of Mildura. Vineyards here and in the Swan Hill region cover land in both New South Wales and Victoria.

Mildura and Swan Hill are in the hottest part of Victoria. As summer heats up, days where the temperature doesn't drop below 40 degrees Celsius are common. Being so far inland — approximately 500 kilometres from the south coast of Victoria — the climate is considered *continental*. Swan Hill is somewhat south of Mildura, so temperatures are marginally less.

Most of this region experiences large variations between day and night temperatures — a 40-degree day will cool to 20–25 degrees at night (which is still pretty hot). The weather is also dry, especially during the growing season, which means that humidity and, consequently, the risk of fungal disease is low. And while the roots of the vines are getting water through irrigation, the foliage remains dry, thus reducing the need for fungicide sprays — another benefit.

In this section, I describe some of the good quality, popular grape varieties produced in the dry, flat region of north-west Victoria.

Making much of Chardonnay

The most favoured grape variety in north-west Victoria is Chardonnay, a versatile grape that can be grown quite cheaply and the wine made cost-efficiently on a large scale.

As a variety, a Chardonnay vine can happily produce a lot of bunches of grapes and still maintain good fruit flavours. Although the grapes may not end up making the world's most complex wine, the end product is good-quality wine — the stand-out example is the ever-popular Lindemans Bin 65.

Blending the white varieties

The north-west region is also well known for its multipurpose grapes such as Sultana, Colombard and Muscat Gordo Blanco. These varieties are rarely used to make wines on their own; they're used more commonly to bulk up the very commercial labels that are sold at rock-bottom prices.

TECHNICAL STUFF

Blending basics

If a wine is blended, more than one grape variety has been used to make the final wine. Often the various grape varieties are declared on the label. For example, you may see 'Semillon/Sauvignon Blanc' listed. Winemakers are happy to declare the origins of these classic varieties as both have well-established followings as distinctly flavoured white wines.

However, in other cases, the actual varieties may be less clear because of an Australian law that states that only 85 per cent of the contents need be listed. So, what you think may be a bottle of Chardonnay may actually contain 15 per cent of another grape variety.

The workhorse varieties such as Colombard and Sultana are often used as 'fillers' (on their own they produce very non-descript white wines). By adding a percentage of these varieties to a more tasty wine like Chardonnay, winemakers can stretch the whites a little further. Besides, calling a wine 'Chardonnay/Sultana' just doesn't have much consumer appeal!

Don't be put off by blended wines, which are often inexpensive because this technique keeps costs down. In fact, blending is one of the oldest winemaking tools around. The great wines of Bordeaux are a mixture of Cabernet Sauvignon, Cabernet Franc, Merlot, Petit Verdot and Malbec. Champagne is a blended wine, too. In fact, the Champenois will tell you that blending — often from several hundred different wines — is what makes Champagne magic. In addition, fortified wines have a little bit of intensely flavoured wine from aged barrels added.

Only 85 per cent of the contents of a bottle of wine has to be from the variety claimed on the label; the other 15 per cent can be any variety. (Refer to Chapter 3 for lots of interesting information about wine labels.)

The wine made from Colombard and Sultana grapes is pretty bland, allowing it to blend in without altering the flavours too much. Muscat Gordo Blanco is very fruity, so it can boost the flavours in a wine that might be lacking.

Painting the region red

Like Chardonnay, Shiraz is a very significant grape variety in the north-west and can also make pretty decent wine even when lots of grapes are grown per vine. Shiraz grapes love the sunshine, which allows them to ripen into the resulting rich, full-flavoured wine.

The other varieties that thrive up here are Cabernet Sauvignon and, increasingly, Merlot, Grenache and Tarrango. Rising crop levels start to affect the true varietal flavour of Cabernet and Merlot, yet they're both still able to make a quality red wine.

Growing the perfect grape

Like any plant, a vine must have water to keep healthy. In arid areas that are not irrigated or are only lightly irrigated, vines are naturally limited in their growth and in the number of grapes they can produce by the amount of water they have access to.

However, in the north-west of Victoria, access to water hasn't, in the past, been an issue. (I say 'in the past' because, as water becomes a more and more precious resource in Australia, increasing pressure to reduce water consumption is being brought to bear on those agricultural pursuits with high water usage.)

Because of the ready availability of water, the grape-growing region of north-west Victoria (along with the Riverina region of New South Wales that I discuss in Chapter 8 and the Riverland in South Australia, see Chapter 20) can grow large quantities of grapes on relatively few vines — and the sun guarantees ripeness.

The result is that the fruit is less intense in flavour because the vine has to divide its energy to provide flavour among many more bunches. Consequently, the grapes are sold by the grape growers at a reduced price compared to grapes from other regions, and the resulting wines are less expensive. That's not to say that the wines aren't good — they're some of the best quality, reasonably priced wines available.

Grenache doesn't seem to mind how hot it gets — the fruit just gets riper and riper and the flavours build into an incredible sweetness that, if not harvested in time, acquires a raspberry jam character. Tarrango is the relative newcomer to the region — and indeed to Australian vineyards in general. At last count, Brown Brothers, the main producer of this variety, just couldn't get enough Tarrango grapes to meet demand.

Exploring the Wineries of the North-East

Like many wine regions across Australia, the number of hectares of vines planted in the north-east seems to explode each year. An exciting aspect to this growth is the movement away from the obvious grape choices. Instead of just planting more of the varieties that the rest of Australia grows, winemakers explore the Italian varieties, increase their experimentation with the Spanish Tempranillo grape on warmer sites, and lean towards such lesser-known French varieties as Gamay on the cooler sites.

Today the five winemaking zones of north-east Victoria — the Alpine Valley, Beechworth, Glenrowan, King Valley and Rutherglen — boast over 60 wineries, ranging from tiny family affairs to some of the huge wine companies. Figure 12-1 shows many of the wineries from these wine regions.

South of the border

Just below the New South Wales border are the regions of Rutherglen and Beechworth, with Glenrowan south of Wangaratta.

In total, this area has 37 wineries. Many more vineyards than that, though, are owned by grape growers who have decided to grow the grapes and sell them, leaving the winemaking side to others.

In this corner of Victoria, the weather from late spring onwards is generally fine and stable. The biggest risk in the flat valley areas is spring frost, which, on the occasions it has occurred, has frozen the young shoots, resulting in low crops.

Rutherglen, land of full-bodied reds

The Rutherglen region is in an area of land known as the golden triangle — Rutherglen forms one point of the triangle, with Yarrawonga in the west and Wangaratta in the south forming the other points.

The region boasts 19 wineries and is the warmest part of the north-east region. Not surprisingly, some pretty powerful reds as well as the famous fortified wines come from this part. For many years this region was popular with young males whose idea of a red wine was a high-octane, full-bodied red — think of the biggest-bodied, most tannic red you've ever tasted and then double it! Fair to say that this was the style of wine that was once made . . . thankfully, times have changed.

Even though the wines that are being produced these days are more refined and more sophisticated, they can never be accused of being shy and are still a memorable wine experience.

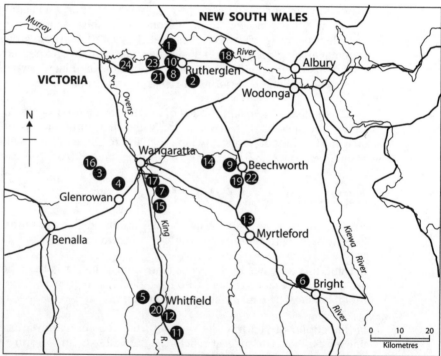

Figure 12-1: Popular wines from the Alpine Valley, Beechworth, Glenrowan, King Valley and Rutherglen grape-growing regions of north-east Victoria.

1. All Saints Estate
2. Anderson Winery
3. Auldstone Cellars
4. Baileys of Glenrowan
5. Boggy Creek Vineyards
6. Boynton's Winery
7. Brown Brothers
8. Campbells Wines
9. Castagna Vineyard
10. Chambers Rosewood Vineyards
11. Chrismont Wines
12. Dal Zotto Estate Wines
13. Gapsted Wines
14. Giaconda Vineyard
15. John Gehrig Wines
16. Judds Warby Range Estate
17. Miranda King Valley Winery
18. Morris Wines
19. Pennyweight Winery
20. Pizzini Wines
21. R. L. Buller & Son
22. Sorrenberg Vineyard
23. Stanton & Killeen Wines
24. Warrabilla Wines

The outstanding wines of the Rutherglen region can be found at the following wineries:

- ✔ **Campbells Wines:** Of late, a fantastic surprise has been the refined — if I can use that term for this variety — Durif coming from Campbells Wines. Not only does Campbells make a straight Durif that must be cellared for at least ten years, but it also offers a blended wine of Shiraz, 'Campbells SDC' Durif and Cabernet. Campbells also makes some of the best fortified wines of the region with stocks of old Tokays and Muscat for use during blending. These include **Campbells Merchant Prince, Campbells Merchant Prince Rare Rutherglen Muscat NV** and **Campbells Isabella Rare Rutherglen Tokay NV.**

- ✔ **Morris Wines:** Another winery that can't be forgotten is Morris Wines (see the sidebar, 'Legend profile: The Morris family' in this chapter). My most vivid memory of visiting this winery was the 100-year-old Tokay that Mick Morris gave my university group to try. The wine was like treacle it was so viscous. Needless to say, only a drop was needed to appreciate what this incredibly complex wine offers. These old stocks of Tokay and Muscat are vital in the making of the wines of today, as just a tiny bit of these in a blend — less than one-half of a per cent — can boost the whole wine remarkably.

- ✔ **Stanton & Killeen Wines:** If you're looking for another Durif, then visit Stanton & Killeen Wines. The **Stanton & Killeen Durif** has everything — big, full-flavoured and with plenty of tannin. Allow this one to develop in your cellar.

Legend profile: The Morris Family

The Morris family entered the wine business in Rutherglen in the 1880s, planting vines in the same vineyards that are in use today. The current living legend of the family is Mick Morris, although his son, David, heads up the wine-making these days. The historic winery is famous for its Tokay and Muscat.

Mick Morris remembers the days before mechanisation. In order to carry out vineyard work in those days, a horse had to be bridled up and the plough attached — rather more work than is needed today, when you simply fire up a tractor.

The pace of life is still relatively slow around here, which is all well and good. The magic touch at this winery is to age the wine by simply leaving it alone. Given that they've been aged and cared for over many years, many of the older wines are quite expensive. But don't let this stop you from trying this uniquely Australian product.

- ✔ **All Saints Estate:** Like many of its neighbours, the winery at All Saints was established back in the 1860s. The style in which the winery is built, resembling a castle, looks somewhat odd, sitting as it does in the middle of rural Australia! However, full marks for originality. The wines are very well made, especially the Durif. Don't forget to try the white wines, such as the peach and melon mid-weighted **All Saints Chardonnay** that becomes honeyed with age, as well as the apple and toasty **All Saints Marsanne**.

- ✔ **Anderson Winery:** The specialty here is Anderson Methode Champenoise Shiraz: Using the densely flavoured local Shiraz grapes, the wine is firmly structured with good balancing sweetness.

- ✔ **Chambers Rosewood Vineyards:** Perhaps the biggest character of the region is Bill Chambers at Chambers Rosewood winery. Well, it's barely a winery in the sense of today's high-tech winemaking facilities. Here the wine is literally made in a tin shed, in big old barrels that slowly age the world famous and simply stunning fortified wines. In fact so good are the wines that the famed American wine critic, Robert Parker, has given Chambers' fortified wines the perfect score of 100, something rarely achieved by any wine in the world.

- ✔ **R. L. Buller & Son:** One of the best all-round places to find well-priced red wines is the winery of R. L. Buller & Son. Many of the reds are a blend of one or more varieties. A couple of the best are the Shiraz/ Grenache/ Mourvèdre and the Shiraz/Cabernet. The fortified wines, too, are very good and relatively inexpensive.

- ✔ **Warrabilla Wines:** For seriously robust wines, try those from Warrabilla Wines. The wines at this winery are made the old-fashioned way with the relatively modern introduction of new oak maturation.

Beechworth, rolling country and special wine

Beechworth is one of the smaller winemaking regions of Victoria, having only eight wineries in mid-2003. The landscape is all rolling hills and valleys. During the ripening season, the winemakers rely on the cool nights to temper the warm days.

The topography around Beechworth also encourages breezes to flow through the valleys, and these breezes help to control vineyard diseases. As summer turns into autumn, the weather is often quite dry and the vines rely on the soil in which they grow, which is partially clay, to give up some of the rainfall that has been retained from the spring rains.

Four excellent wineries in the Beechworth region are

- ✔ **Castagna Vineyard:** Like a growing number of vineyards across the world, Castagna Vineyard operates under a biodynamic regime. (Refer to Chapter 6 for explanation of organic and biodynamic regimes.) The line-up is small, offering a Syrah, Sangiovese and a rosé.

  The Syrah (or Shiraz) is made in a style that is a little different to the blockbuster wines so common in the warmer regions of Australia: The winemaker uses new oak only as a background effect with the result that the wine tastes savoury rather than bursting with very ripe fruit.

- ✔ **Giaconda Vineyard:** The most famous vineyard in the area is the Giaconda Vineyard. On this relatively small vineyard, attention to detail is paramount, and this is demonstrated from the siting of the vineyard through to the winery. Currently, the best wines you can find at Giaconda are the incredibly intense nutty, peachy and quite oak dominant **Giaconda Chardonnay** and savoury, truffley, yet still fruity, **Giaconda Pinot Noir**.

- ✔ **Pennyweight Winery:** Although Beechworth may have only a handful of wineries, each one does something a little different from the others. The owner of the Pennyweight Winery is a descendant of the famed Morris family of Rutherglen (see the preceding section), so expect to see some excellent fortified wines. Of note, here, is the range of Sherries as well as a full-bodied Cabernet Sauvignon and Shiraz — another throwback to the Rutherglen origins.

- ✔ **Sorrenberg Vineyard:** This winery was established in 1986, just after Giaconda. The **Sorrenberg Chardonnay** from this vineyard is always full flavoured and also possesses a lovely nutty character. In addition to the wines usually produced in this region, Sorrenberg makes a Gamay that has the appeal of a soft red wine.

Fending off fungus

Fungal disease such as the two mildews of *downy* and *powdery mildew* and the mould *Botrytis cinerea* are the main diseases that plague Australian vineyards. Preventative sprays are available as well as ones that control the disease once it appears.

The best method of disease control, however, is prevention. Allowing air to circulate freely through the vine canopy is one of the best ways in which to lessen the risk of fungal disease.

Glenrowan, from bushrangers to brews

Probably more famous for Ned Kelly and the bushrangers of the 1800s, the town of Glenrowan is on the Hume Highway, south-west of the town of Wangaratta (refer to Figure 12-1). Glenrowan, like Beechworth, is one of the smaller winemaking areas of Victoria. In mid-2003, this area had only four wineries. The following are highly recommended:

✔ **Auldstone Cellars:** Worth a visit is Auldstone Cellars, which makes a sparkling Shiraz as well as a deeply concentrated Cabernet Sauvignon and Shiraz.

✔ **Baileys of Glenrowan:** Baileys vineyard has the reputation for making some of the best Muscat in Australia — **Baileys Founders Series Muscat** — super intense in texture, and with flavours of coffee and dried muscatel grapes. In addition, you can find an excellent **Baileys 1904 Block Shiraz** made from vines planted back in 1904. Nowadays, these old vines only produce a few bunches on a vine, but these few bunches produce a wine that is super-concentrated in flavour. The result is a Shiraz that is intensely flavoured, big in body and worth cellaring.

✔ **Judds Warby Range Estate:** This winery flys the Durif flag, making a dense wine with loads of flavour and tannin.

The valleys to the mountains

South-east of Wangaratta and in the direction of the high country going towards Mount Buffalo, are two valleys that take advantage of varying topography to produce a range of excellent varieties of wine: King Valley and Alpine Valley.

King Valley, from the plains to the hills

The King Valley can be split into two different areas — the flat valley floor around Milawa, a small town south-east of Wangaratta, and the Whitlands area around the tiny town of Whitfield, on the King River south of Wangaratta.

After you read this section, you may well understand why the King Valley is one of my favourite areas. In terms of beauty, this area is breathtaking — and the wines are pretty good, too! However, the region is also significant for its focus on the varieties that flourish, and for taking a gamble by doing something different.

In most areas of Australia, new grape growers planted varieties that were in high demand and hence commanded high prices per tonne of fruit. The best example is Chardonnay — no matter where the land was located Chardonnay was planted. Inevitably, by the mid-1990s, Chardonnay production exceeded demand, at which time everyone promptly stopped planting it. Needless to say, by the early 2000s, there was a shortage of premium Chardonnay . . .

Although the King Valley growers weren't immune to this rush to cash in on the popular grapes, they had the foresight and courage to plant varieties that were not only unfashionable but were actually almost unknown to not only most wine drinkers but also to most winemakers. The varieties planted in King Valley include the Italian Sangiovese, Barbera, Arneis, Verduzzo and Nebbiolo. Today these varieties are in vogue and gaining more followers by the day.

The floor of the King Valley, at around 140 metres above sea level, enjoys warm days and cool nights. The area has a reputation for being a reliable grape-growing area in terms of climate — rain is not usually a problem during the ripening months and sunshine is abundant. The land here is flat, which allows large acreage of vines to be planted, thus keeping costs down.

The great thing about the King Valley is that the surrounding hills allow for a varying climate that gives each vineyard its own personality. For example, some pockets are warmer than others as they're protected from the Alpine winds. Other vineyards flourish in the Alpine breezes as they help keep the incidence of disease down by allowing air to circulate through the vine leaf canopy.

The Whitlands vineyards are much cooler, being situated above the snow line at 800 metres above sea level. Fittingly, the pioneers in the Whitlands area were also Milawa's pioneers — the Brown family, or the winery known as Brown Brothers. Brown Brothers planted the Whitlands vineyards in 1982, using it as a trial initially to see just how well some varieties did in the cooler climate.

And they certainly did well and continue to do well — the grapes make the most of the sunshine enjoyed in the region and the evening coolness experienced at this altitude slows down the ripening process. Ripening slowly means that all the grape flavours are captured, a particularly important factor in aromatic grape varieties such as Gewürztraminer, Riesling, and the softer reds such as Pinot Noir.

The Whitlands vineyards produce grapes for the sparkling base wines — Pinot Noir, Pinot Meunier and Chardonnay, and Riesling, Pinot Gris and Merlot. The success that Brown Brothers has had with these vineyards has encouraged others to plant on the higher slopes, and you find many a well-priced wine coming from this area that offers real value for your money.

Among the stand-out wineries in the King Valley (refer to Figure 12-1) are the following:

- **Boggy Creek Vineyards:** Situated at an altitude of 350 metres above sea level, Boggy Creek Vineyards has for years been supplying grapes to sparkling winemakers such as Domaine Chandon. The higher altitude ensures that the grapes build up plenty of flavour before the sugar levels get too high, which is perfect for sparkling wine.

  More recently, the owners have been making wine under the Boggy Creek label. The best wines so far have been the savoury **Boggy Creek Pinot Gris** and the fruit-driven **Boggy Creek Sauvignon Blanc**.

- **Brown Brothers:** In terms of sheer size, length of experience in the region and experience with experimental grapegrowing, Brown Brothers leads. Now into its fourth generation of winemakers, Brown Brothers is a winery that is not happy to rest on past achievements. The winery offers an impressive range of wines, with upwards of 45 wines in its portfolio. Some of the unusual wines are for sale only at the cellar door (see Chapter 28), until the winemakers and marketing department can assess the promise of the grapes. A few you might come across are Cienna, Ruby Cabernet and Tempranillo.

  As part of its commitment to experimental winemaking, the huge winery at Brown Brothers now has what is called the 'kindergarten winery'. Here small tanks are used for making small batches of wine from new varieties that the vineyard has planted, or for trialling different winemaking techniques. The amusing thing about this kindy winery is its huge size when compared to the size of many family wineries.

  The wines from Brown Brothers are always good and of a consistent quality. The best from the King Valley vineyards are the Pinot Noir/ Chardonnay Sparkling wine and the Riesling. From the Milawa vineyards, where the climate is comparatively warmer, Shiraz, Grenache and Cabernet Sauvignon do well.

  At the Mystic Park vineyards of Brown Brothers (further north near Swan Hill and described in the section 'Crossing state lines: The Swan Hill wineries'), the warmth produces the grapes for the unique sweet Orange Muscat and Flora, and for the Tarrango, a light summery red wine that is exceptionally popular in the export market.

- **Chrismont Wines:** A little further up the Valley past Cheshunt is a branch of the Pizzini family that owns Chrismont Wines. Not surprisingly, the flagship wines, **La Zona** wines, represent all things Italian. This range includes the berry-filled Barbera, a delicate Pinot Grigio and a savoury Marzemino (Marzemino is an Italian red variety that has traditionally only been grown in northern Italy).

✔ **Dal Zotto Estate Wines:** More Italian winemakers, who make a range of Italian varietals. The stand-outs are the very good nutty **Dal Zotto Chardonnay** and the **Dal Zotto Merlot** that shows full-of-fruit characteristics.

✔ **John Gehrig Wines:** In line with the trend in King Valley, things are done differently here, too. The influence, however, isn't Italian and instead the winery has developed a following for its 100 per cent varietal wines of Petit Verdot, Gamay and Pinot Meunier — varieties that are more often found in a blend of wine varieties rather than alone.

✔ **Miranda King Valley Winery:** Just to prove my earlier point about good wine for a price, Miranda King Valley Winery is worth mentioning. Here you find well-made, straightforward wines, the best being the Chardonnay and the Merlot.

✔ **Pizzini Wines:** Further up the King Valley at Whitfield is Pizzini Wines, which is where the Pizzini family initially grew grapes for sale to other wineries, like many of the region's other winemakers. While these sales are still part of their income today, so is winemaking. Particularly good red wines are the savoury **Pizzini Sangiovese** and rose petal-like **Pizzini Nebbiolo**; in white wine, you can't go past the honeyed and floral **Pizzini Arneis** and the richly flavoured **Pizzini Verduzzo**.

To successfully make sparkling wine, grapes that have low sugar content are required to produce sparkling base wines that are lower in alcohol. But these base wines still need to have plenty of flavour, which is possible to achieve when grapes are grown at this altitude. Check out *Wine For Dummies, 3rd Edition,* by Ed McCarthy and Mary Ewing-Mulligan (published by Wiley Publishing, Inc.) for an explanation of the sparkling wine process.

Alpine Valley, going up and cooling down

In this section, I show you some cool-country wines. The principal towns along the Alpine Valley are Myrtleford and Bright, south-east of Wangaratta. The Ovens River flows through both towns, while the Kiewa River flows to the north. The smaller Buckland and Buffalo Rivers also water the region.

Grapes crossing state borders

Vineyards from the King Valley and Alpine Valley regions of north-east Victoria are often mentioned on the back labels on bottles of wine made by producers whose winery is based elsewhere. For example, the **Tyrrell's Lost Block Cabernet Sauvignon** is made from fruit sourced in the region. As Tyrrell's has no winery established in the region, a contract facility processes the grapes into juice or wine and then transports it to Tyrrell's Hunter Valley premises in New South Wales. The production of the wine then takes place in the Hunter Valley.

Like the Whitlands in the King Valley, the higher altitude (most vineyards are at least 250 metres above sea level) means that the region is distinctly cool. The cold winds that blow straight off the Victorian snowfields also influence the low temperatures. Consequently, the ripening of the grapes is slow, which allows them to mature gradually and concentrates the fruity flavours. Generally the ripening months from late March to May are fairly dry, which means disease at this time isn't a problem.

The most planted varieties are Merlot, Cabernet Sauvignon and Chardonnay, along with increasing amounts of Pinot Noir. As of mid-2003, eight wineries had been established in the region.

Two of the most impressive wineries (refer to Figure 12-1) in the Alpine Valley region are

- **Boynton's Winery:** At the southern end of the Alpine Valley near Bright is Boynton's. While not the first winery in the region, Boynton's was the first to bring the area to the notice of the wine-drinking public. The vineyard is perched on the side of a hill with the vines receiving good morning sunshine. While Boynton's produces a number of wines, the stand-out so far is mulberry and olive-like **Boynton's Merlot**. In the right year, when the grapes are able to fully mature, Boynton's produce an excellent blend of Cabernet, Merlot and Petit Verdot.

- **Gapsted Wines:** By far the largest producer in the region is Gapsted Wines. Established only in 1997 and so a fairly new winery, Gapsted has already established itself as a good producer. The success of this winery is partly due to a good understanding of the local area as well as the realisation that to make good wine in this region, certain 'normal' viticultural practices need to be modified.

  At the Gapsted vineyards, the vines have been trellised to allow the early morning rays of the sun to penetrate the vine canopy and so reach the grapes, and to also shade the grapes from the stronger, harsh afternoon rays. Many of the Gapsted wines are made from a blend of wines from its King and Alpine Valley vineyards, using the attributes of each area to boost wine quality and diversity. So far the best from this very promising vineyard are the soft and medium-bodied **Gapsted Shiraz**, honey and pear-like **Gapsted Pinot Grigio** and crisp and herbal **Gapsted Sauvignon Blanc**.

Heating Up: The North-West Region

Without the irrigation system established in the Murray-Darling basin (that is, the system that pumps water from the Murray River and the Darling River) the north-west wine region wouldn't exist. The region is regarded as arid and, other than seasonal crops such as wheat, nothing could flourish.

The number of wineries in the region may not be large, but the wineries that exist are large — really huge, in fact. If the Lindemans Karadoc Winery was the first winery you saw, any illusions you had that winemaking and grapegrowing are romantic activities carried out by happy peasants who regularly prance around on grapes at wine festivals would be shattered.

The Lindemans Karadoc complex is reminiscent of an oil refinery. The sheer size of the tanks is mind-boggling, and the factory (as many people call it) is so vast that you practically need a compass and map to find your way around. However, the loss of romance is compensated for by the fact that here wine is made very cost effectively and is the type of wine that is most commonly consumed by the wine-drinking public.

The north-west region is flat, between 50 and 85 metres above sea level, and uniformly low, so no breezes flow from higher ground. However, the flat terrain means that the rows of vines can march on forever, allowing the vineyards to be principally managed by machinery. Mechanical pruners, mechanical grape harvesters and mechanical canopy trimmers are seen far more often than a real, live vineyard worker. Input costs can be low and, as a consequence, wine costs are kept down.

Today, more than 21,500 hectares are planted to wine grapes in the Murray-Darling region. If you compare this with the almost 6,500 hectares of the high-profile Barossa Valley (Chapter 18), you get the enormous size of this region in perspective. See Figure 12-2.

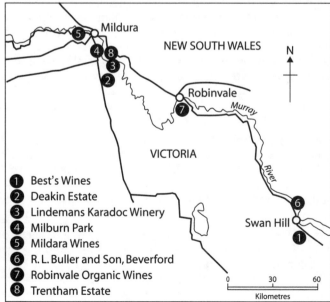

Figure 12-2:
Popular wines from the Murray-Darling and Swan Hill grape-growing regions of north-west Victoria.

1 Best's Wines
2 Deakin Estate
3 Lindemans Karadoc Winery
4 Milburn Park
5 Mildara Wines
6 R. L. Buller and Son, Beverford
7 Robinvale Organic Wines
8 Trentham Estate

A landscape of vines: The Murray-Darling region

The landscape of the Murray-Darling region is filled with hectare after hectare of vines, stretching away as far as the eye can see. Visitors are often struck by the odd appearance of the vines. Being mechanically managed, the vines look a little unloved compared with those that are tended by hand. With pruning all done by machine, the winter wood tends to get bunched together and the vine looks a little mangled. In the growing season, the vines sprawl everywhere, shading some fruit yet exposing other bunches to the full assault of the hot sun.

The wineries of the Murray-Darling have adjusted their techniques and vine management to cope with local conditions. Some of the wineries that are doing this very successfully are the following:

- **Deakin Estate:** The company that owns Deakin Estate has Katnook Estate in Coonawarra (see Chapter 9) as its flagship winery so, not surprisingly it knows how to make good wine. The standard wine from Deakin is very good, particularly the melon and peachy **Deakin Estate Chardonnay**. The top tier of wines, **Deakin Select**, is reasonably priced and offers wines with more depth of flavour — these wines are made from vines that have been deliberately cropped at lower levels to achieve the extra depth of flavour. (Less fruit per vine gives more intensity of flavour.)

- **Lindemans Karadoc Winery:** What an enormous place this winery is — one of the largest, most modern winemaking facility in the country. Yet size doesn't detract from the quality of the wines produced here, and you can find some pretty palatable ones, including the hugely successful **Lindemans Bin 65**. An all round quality wine that greets you with good peach and melon aromas and flavours — as you would expect from a Chardonnay. Amazing value for money. The other Bin range wines are also made here, as are many of the cheaper Southcorp products (Lindemans is part of Southcorp Limited).

- **Milburn Park:** Although the name of this winery has changed recently (formerly it was known as Alambie Wines), the name Milburn Park is building quite a reputation. The quality is consistent across the various labels — the top labels are Milburn Park and then Salisbury — with the Chardonnay and Shiraz being the leaders. Milburn Park is part of the large Evans & Tate Company.

- **Mildara Wines:** For a good quality Chardonnay, at a keen price, try **Mildara Chardonnay**. Like the other big players in the region, Mildara makes considerable amounts of wine at this facility, and one vineyard in particular produces around 4,000 tonnes each year — something like 20,000 litres of wine. Rather a lot really.

- **Robinvale Organic Wines:** If you're interested in organic and biodynamic wines, then Robinvale Organic Wines may be of interest.

- **Trentham Estate:** Trentham Estate is considered part of the Mildura winemaking district even though you find it situated across the Victorian border in New South Wales. One of the smaller vineyards in the region, Trentham Estate makes not only the stalwarts Chardonnay and Shiraz, but also varieties such as Nebbiolo, Noble Taminga and Petit Verdot. The **Trentham Estate Noble Taminga** is made as a dessert-style wine, so is fruit driven with an edge of sweetness.

Noble Taminga is a man-made variety being a cross between Traminer, Riesling and Farana (a Spanish variety). This wine was developed through work done at the Commonwealth Scientific and Industrial Research Organisation (CSIRO).

- **Zilzie Wines:** One of the labels to emerge over recent years, Zilzie Wines was originally a grape grower selling its fruit to others. This winery has now placed itself on the map in terms of wine quality and is certainly producing quality Shiraz that shows plenty of typical Shiraz flavours — plums, spice and black cherry — a top wine from the region under the **Zilzie Show Reserve** label. The **Buloke Reserve** range (named after a conservation park within the estate set up to protect the endangered Buloke tree) includes good Merlot and Sangiovese varietal wines.

Doing a bit for the environment

Those who use the waters of the Murray–Darling basin to irrigate crops attract a certain amount of bad press. Not just grape growers — the growers of crops such as cotton and rice also come under fire. The point of contention is the amount of water used to irrigate an area that is basically arid.

Being well aware of these problems, the Department of Primary Industries has done much research and has found a way to more than halve the water required by a grapevine.

The method is known as *partial rootzone drying*. By applying water to only half of the vine's roots,

the vine is tricked into thinking that it's under water stress, and responds by shutting down its rate of internal water loss. The vine does this by closing the pores on the surface of its leaves that lose water into the atmosphere. This internal control also turns off the vine's own leaf production — fewer leaves means less water lost.

As a result of this, not only is water saved but the concentration of flavour in the grapes and their colour has been found to be better — so potentially the wine is better. Consequently, the vines are using less water in these areas of high water dependence while producing better fruit. A clever bit of science.

Crossing state lines: The Swan Hill wineries

The Swan Hill winemaking region (refer to Figure 12-2) is tiny in comparison to its northern neighbour. Vineyards cover around 500 hectares, which is incidentally about the same as the plantings in Tasmania (Chapter 15). Much of the grape supply comes from contracted grape growers who sell to the big wineries. In mid-2003, the region boasted six wineries, though a core group of three businesses makes most of the wine.

Like the Murray–Darling region, vineyards of the Swan Hill winemaking region extend across the Victorian–New South Wales border. The similarities don't end there — Swan Hill experiences hot weather too, albeit a tiny bit less so than further north in Mildura. Humidity is low and irrigation, of course, is vital.

Like their neighbours to the north, the winemakers of Swan Hill adapt their processes to the climate. Some of the most successful wineries are the following:

- ✔ **Best's Wines, Lake Boga:** Interestingly, the best producers in Swan Hill are those who have vineyards elsewhere. Best's Wines St Andrews vineyard (see the section on the Grampians in Chapter 11) was the first to be planted in the Swan Hill region. The wines in the Best's portfolio that claim they come from the state of Victoria are from this region, at least in part. Like the southern arm of the business, **Best's Shiraz** is a terrific berry-filled wine, and the tropical fruited **Best's Chenin Blanc** is also excellent.

- ✔ **Brown Brothers, Mystic Park:** As discussed earlier in the King Valley section, this vineyard is where the really fruity grapes are grown for some of Brown Brothers biggest sellers — the Orange Flora and Muscat and the Tarrango. Other grapes that come from this vineyard for the Victorian blend of wines include Cabernet Sauvignon and Grenache.

- ✔ **R. L. Buller and Son, Beverford:** Another winery with two locations (see the preceding section, 'Rutherglen, land of full-bodied reds'), this winery produces wines that are really good value and easy to drink. Make a point of looking for the Cabernet Sauvignon and the Shiraz.

Counting white grapes by the tonne

The white grape variety with the largest number of tonnes processed in Australia in 2003 was Chardonnay with 235,921 tonnes (or 17.3 per cent of the total amount of grapes grown in 2003, followed by Semillon at 5.5 per cent. Colombard was next with 4.1 per cent, then Muscat Gordo Blanco with 3.3 per cent. Sultana was in fifth position with 2.4 per cent of white grapes. These figures may surprise those who think only of the premium side of the Australian wine scene.

Making wine with chips and planks

So that a good wine may be made inexpensively but still undergo a satisfactory maturation process prior to bottling, winemakers have come up with a clever solution. The result is that many inexpensive wines rarely see the inside of a real barrel. Instead, they're matured with what the Australian wine industry refers to as *oak chips* or *planks*. And the wine styles that have this treatment are the cheaper versions of the wooded varieties — reds, except rosé, and wooded whites such as Chardonnay.

Instead of ageing the wine in oak barrels, which are relatively small vessels that are both costly to buy and, due to high labour costs, costly to maintain, the oak is cut into small pieces, known as oak chips. The chips are then put into what look like giant tea bags made of hessian and placed in the wine, which is stored in large stainless steel tanks, and left to soak.

Stainless steel tanks are relatively inexpensive; they come in a range of sizes and don't need replacing every few years, as would be the case with oak barrels. And oak chips are also inexpensive — an important consideration when making wine for a price.

Planks are used to achieve a similar effect. Instead of little oak chips, long planks of oak are submerged in the tank of wine. The amount used is determined by the winemaker after considering the oak impact he or she wants in the final wine. While this is undoubtedly ingenious, this process may miss the mark. Although the wines treated to an oak bath are getting better all the time, to my mind, they often taste a little raw.

Chapter 13

Down by the Sea: The Peninsulas and Gippsland

In this Chapter

▶ Understanding the effects of maritime climate on grapes and wines

▶ Finding some of the seaside's best-kept secrets

*W*ithout a doubt, vineyards situated near the sea are pretty special. The views from the vines out across the water, the blustery winds that somehow make you feel part of the weather and the diversity of the coastal landscape all contribute to the feeling that you are somewhere unique.

The grapevines of coastal areas produce very distinct wines. The Mornington Peninsula is a cool region and the choice of the vineyard site is paramount to producing top-quality wines. Over on the Bellarine Peninsula, the weather is much milder and drier, allowing for a bit more freedom in the choice of site. The smallest region of this trio, in terms of hectares under vine, is Gippsland, whose climate, not infrequently, goes from drought to floods.

In this chapter, I highlight the reasons why these three regions in Australia's state of Victoria produce such great wines, and provide you with some tips as to the best wines and wineries.

Seaside, Surf and Serious Wine

The Mornington and the Bellarine Peninsulas both fit into the Port Phillip wine zone (along with the Yarra Valley, Sunbury and the Macedon Ranges, which are discussed in Chapters 10 and 14, respectively). Mornington is part of the Mornington Peninsula region and the Bellarine Peninsula is part of the Geelong region. Gippsland, despite its small size, is its own wine zone. (Refer to Chapter 3 for more information about Australia's geographical wine zones and regions.)

All of these areas were better known for their beaches and weekenders, until a booming interest in wine saw many professionals from the capital city of Melbourne become weekend vignerons. Some retired from the daily suit and tie to become full-time vineyard workers. Those with romantic ideals of a vineyard life largely bought and then sold their vineyards, realising that the work required took much more than a weekend pottering among the vines. Today, the weekend vignerons in all three regions have largely been replaced by some very serious business ventures.

Grappling with the geography

Gippsland and the Mornington and Bellarine Peninsulas are located about one hour's drive from the city of Melbourne — all in different directions. The Mornington Peninsula sits to the south-south-east of Melbourne, the Bellarine Peninsula to the south-west, and Gippsland spreads itself out to the east. Port Phillip Bay, Bass Strait and Western Port Bay surround the region, which is a 100 per cent *maritime,* or mild, climate. (See the sidebar 'Making for mild, in the maritime' for more on this type of climate.)

TECHNICAL STUFF

Making for mild, in the maritime

Gippsland and the Mornington and Bellarine Peninsulas are located by the sea. As such, they're all classed as having a *maritime* climate. Generally this phrase means that the temperatures are mild, and that the difference between the daytime and night-time temperatures is less than it is in inland areas, because the nearby sea and sea breezes buffer the land from the extremes that you may get inland. So, instead of high temperatures of, say, 35 degrees Celsius on summer days, followed by quite cool nights of 12 degrees Celsius, the days and nights down by the sea don't quite reach the same extreme temperatures. The days are more like 30 to 32 degrees Celsius, and the nights remain warmer, somewhere around 20 degrees Celsius.

This climate of milder weather means that grapes ripen more gradually, thereby allowing the fruit flavour to develop intensity. It also means that harvest time is later in the season — more towards the middle of autumn.

The downside of this climate is that if an early break in the weather occurs as the seasons begin to change from autumn to winter, the grapes may not reach maximum ripeness and the late ripening varieties just won't come through. On top of this, excessive rainfall can ruin crops.

Being seaside also means dealing with wind — and strong wind, at that. Young shoots that develop on the vine in spring, which is the windiest part of the year, can easily be ripped straight off the vine. Wind also affects the number of bunches of grapes formed: the stronger the winds during October to November, the fewer the berries. On a positive note, these natural climatic circumstances keep crop levels down, allowing the vine to concentrate its ripening efforts on fewer berries and thus giving the grapes intense flavours. So, these sometimes-difficult grape-growing circumstances may actually be one of the reasons why these areas produce such excellent wines.

The Mornington Peninsula seems to expand its vineyards at a stratospheric rate in comparison to those on the Bellarine Peninsula and Gippsland. The Bellarine Peninsula has been expanding gradually, with most of the growth being done as large single vineyards as opposed to many new small land holdings. Many of the vineyards are simply being planted to sell the grapes rather than to make the grapes into their own wine label. Over on the Mornington Peninsula, the opposite seems to be happening, where small wineries are developed often with a tasting room and a restaurant as well. Gippsland is very much the sleepiest among the trio, with only tiny expansions each year.

Sea-swept varieties that work

Like the other cool climates in Australia, such as the Yarra Valley (refer to Chapter 10) and around Adelaide in South Australia (see Chapter 17), the very fact that the weather may be cool during the ripening season limits the grapes that do well. So if the winemaker is going to have any chance of producing a really good wine, the grape grower must choose early ripening varieties.

Climate also magnifies just how well varieties that like it cool, such as Chardonnay and the Pinot family of Noir, Gris and Meunier, can grow.

Climatic differences also showcase how the same variety can excel in quite different situations, as is evident with Shiraz. In a cool climate, Shiraz shows its refined side. Grow it in a warmer climate, such as McLaren Vale (see Chapter 16), and you'll struggle to find a wine that is bolder.

Complex Chardonnay

While the Peninsulas and Gippsland are quite different in many ways, I believe a streak is common through all their wines — that being flavour without obvious fruitiness. So instead of finding a Chardonnay that oozes fruit salad, you're more likely to find one that is somewhat nutty or biscuity.

- ✔ **Mornington Peninsula:** As a region, these Chardonnays often have oatmeal characters and may need to be left to age for two or so years to develop their potential.

- ✔ **Bellarine Peninsula:** Over here, be tempted to drink their Chardonnay straight away or age it for a number of years to see a wonderful complex flint-like nose and generous texture develop.

- ✔ **Gippsland:** Chardonnay from Gippsland, such as that from the Narkoojee vineyard, is often quite full and luscious, tending towards some sweetness of fruit, depending on the season the grapes were harvested.

Pretty in Pink Pinot

Many regard the Pinot Noir grown around these areas as some of Australia's finest.

- **Mornington Peninsula:** You can find a mixture of the pretty Pinot style, such as those made by **Tuck's Ridge**, where the wines are full of strawberry and raspberry-like fruit. Other Pinots, such as the **Stonier** range, are spicy and beetroot in flavour with more tannin backbone.

- **Bellarine Peninsula:** The wines produced at **Bannockburn** have firm structure and must be aged for at least four years.

- **Gippsland:** Also of merit are the few small winemakers of Gippsland, particularly Phillip Jones of **Bass Phillip** who has a reputation for making a very distinct, meaty style of Pinot Noir.

Gorgeous in Grey Pinot

The Mornington Peninsula is Australia's centre for Pinot Gris, though a little is grown in Tasmania, too (see Chapter 15 for more information). Of those made in this area, **T'Gallant** on the Mornington Peninsula is both the pioneer and the leader of this variety in Australia.

If you want to be sure about the style you're getting, I suggest checking the alcohol content. The closer it is to 12 per cent, the more likely the wine will be light and delicate. Up around 14 per cent and the wine will be much more like lychees and honey.

Determining the shades of Pinot

Some terms just don't translate well — take Grey Pinot for instance. I prefer to call it by the French name, Pinot Gris, or the Italian name, Pinot Grigio, depending on the style of wine.

Every time I mention any of these Pinots, someone always asks me what the difference is between them. The simple answer is that they're the same grape variety, and you can take your pick whether you call it Pinot Gris or Pinot Grigio. The variety can go by either name and what you choose to call it really depends on whether you swing to the French or the Italian way of thinking.

The French style, Pinot Gris, is a rich and ripe style of Pinot, principally made in Alsace. In Italy they produce Pinot Grigio, which is a more delicate wine picked early before the honey-like tones develop, and is likely to be quite low in alcohol — about 12 per cent.

But you can't necessarily use the names as a guide here for Australian Pinots. I've seen Australian wines called Pinot Grigio that have 14 per cent alcohol and resemble the Pinots of France much more than those of Italy.

Shiraz and all that spice

Many a dedicated Shiraz drinker would scoff at the idea of Shiraz grown on the Mornington Peninsula, on the basis that the region is too cool to produce *real* Australian Shiraz. And that is true, mostly. However, a couple of wineries are making a decent Shiraz, one being **Paringa Estate** at Red Hill on the Mornington Peninsula. The style from the cooler climes is more elegant and often quite European in character, with some peppery/cherry-like tones.

Cross Port Phillip Bay to the Bellarine Peninsula and the Shiraz is much more reliable. Wineries such as **Scotchman's Hill** are making Shiraz that is a little bigger in flavour with some earthy, spicy and plum-like tones, more akin to France's Rhône Valley Shiraz than Australia's South Australian regions (see Part IV).

Sensational new arrivals

As is happening all over the two countries, interest is growing in some of the 'new' grape varieties. One variety that's making a name for itself, particularly in the Geelong region, is Viognier (vee-OH-nyay). So far Viognier has been made as a white wine, but increasingly this white grape variety is being used as a boost to Shiraz wines, with up to 10 per cent blended into the wines. Some of the best white wine Viognier of the region is being made under the Bannockburn by Farr label.

Although not actually grown on the Mornington Peninsula, the 'i' range of Italian grape varieties is developing a big reputation for itself. This range includes the varieties Sangiovese, Barbera, Nebbiolo and Arneis. The grapes are grown in the warmer King Valley (refer to Chapter 12), but their winemaking home is the Dromana Estate winery on the Mornington Peninsula.

Mornington Peninsula

The Mornington Peninsula is a tract of land that flows south from the city of Melbourne and is shaped a bit like a boot, like Italy. Surrounded by Port Phillip Bay, Bass Strait and Western Port Bay, the region's climate is 100 per cent maritime. Starting just past the urban sprawl of the city of Melbourne in a suburb called Mount Eliza, the Mornington area continues southwards to include the areas known as Dromana, Main Ridge, Red Hill South, Merricks and Moorooduc.

Site selection on the Mornington Peninsula has been particularly important for the vignerons. Around Red Hill, some of the soil is the very fertile, red volcanic type, which makes grapevines prosper far too much. Too much vigour in the vines means excessive foliage, which in turn leads to potential disease issues, shading of the fruit and uneven ripening.

As a result, vineyards in this area need to ensure that they address any potential risks. For example, during winter the vines should be pruned to a certain number of buds only, somewhere between 25 and 30 buds per vine. As each bud yields one shoot, this is the first method of controlling excess vigour and hence foliage. Then, as a follow-up during spring and early summer, shoot and leaf thinning may be adopted, again to remove some of the foliage. These vineyard practices mean that both wind and sunshine can flow through the leaf canopy, dramatically decreasing disease issues and allowing uniform ripening in the fruit zone. Added to these mechanical adjustments is the need for a vigilant preventative spray program. By using preventative sprays, potential disease problems can be avoided.

Although the Mornington Peninsula is not Mount Everest, it does have some vineyards on higher altitudes, especially around Red Hill. This environment makes for lower temperatures, which means slower ripening of the grapes. For this reason, the aspects of the vineyards in this area face north in order to get plenty of northern sun. (In the Southern Hemisphere, the sun moves from east to west, via the north.) If the vineyard faced south, you'd have no hope of getting fully ripened grapes.

Other areas of the Mornington are lower lying, such as Dromana and parts of Moorooduc. Here the temperatures are warmer and so the grapes ripen earlier.

Mornington has earned its reputation as a top wine region based largely on Chardonnay and Pinot Noir wines, which I believe will always be the case. Some movement into other varieties, however, has occurred, namely the white wines of Pinot Gris and Viognier and, on the warmer sites, Shiraz.

A no-grow red area

Without doubt, a few grape growers can make a decent Cabernet Sauvignon on the Mornington Peninsula. Many grape growers give the variety a go but most have to graft it onto one of the darlings of the Peninsula — Pinot Noir, Chardonnay or Pinot Gris. Even over on the Bellarine Peninsula, where it's a tad warmer, the Cabernet that survives more often than not tastes a little weedy and like green grass.

Cabernet Sauvignon ripens late in the growing season. Often before the grapes have ripened, the wintry touch to autumn has begun and the vines just don't want to put any more effort into fully developing their flavours. Instead, herbaceous and green blackcurrant flavours prevail with astringent tannins.

Having said all that, those few determined producers who are still pursuing the elusive great Cabernet do have some success. Largely, they're from the warm low-lying area around Dromana and they crop the vines very low. Whatever energy the vine can muster can then be put into ripening less fruit, sooner, while the sun is still warm. For grapes to get the same ripe flavours at higher crop levels, the vine has to work harder as more fruit exist to ripen. This simply means that the harvest date is pushed out towards the coolness of late autumn and the grapes may never reach the same ripe taste. A few reliable labels are Turramurra Estate, Willow Creek Vineyard and Dromana Estate.

Moving around Mornington

Once better known for its beaches, the Mornington Peninsula today has 51 cellar doors (refer to Chapter for some information about visiting a cellar door) and over 175 vineyards of varying sizes. Some are very small concerns that grow grapes either to sell or to be made into wines under contract at a nearby larger vineyard.

Tourism is very much part of the whole Mornington Peninsula wine scene, and many wineries have developed their business to include anything from a café to a small restaurant. So I recommend you take your appetite with you if you get a chance to visit. Figure 13-1 shows the location of the area's major wineries.

Down in Dromana

The Dromana area is one of the warmest on the Peninsula. Vineyards established in this area are on flat ground, pretty much at sea level. The vines also face the warmer Port Phillip Bay, so the weather is milder. As a result, the grapes ripen earlier than those in vineyards on other parts of the Peninsula.

One of my absolute favourite wineries in this area is **Turramurra Estate**, owned and run by David and Paula Leslie. David's other life was as a pathologist so not surprisingly the scientific aspects of his winemaking are spot on, while still allowing the wines have plenty of individual character.

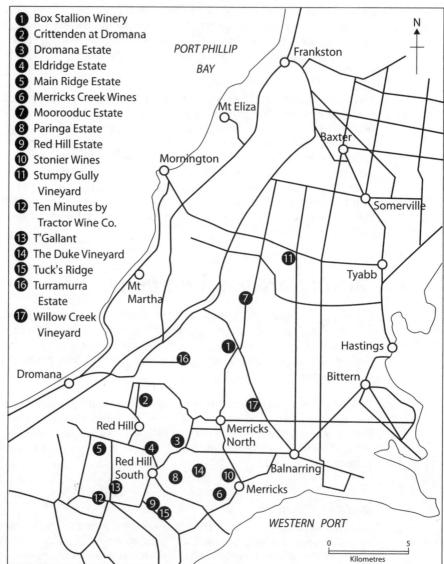

1. Box Stallion Winery
2. Crittenden at Dromana
3. Dromana Estate
4. Eldridge Estate
5. Main Ridge Estate
6. Merricks Creek Wines
7. Moorooduc Estate
8. Paringa Estate
9. Red Hill Estate
10. Stonier Wines
11. Stumpy Gully Vineyard
12. Ten Minutes by Tractor Wine Co.
13. T'Gallant
14. The Duke Vineyard
15. Tuck's Ridge
16. Turramurra Estate
17. Willow Creek Vineyard

Figure 13-1:
Major wineries of the Mornington Peninsula, Victoria.

The **Turramurra Pinot Noir**, with a balanced amount of fruit, tannin and firm structure, shows the warmth possible from this site. A great surprise is the **Turramurra Cabernet Sauvignon**, which in most years achieves ripeness due to this vineyard's warmer aspect and the attention to detail in the vineyard intended to optimise all the warmth available to ripen this variety.

For Viognier, try **Elgee Park**, renowned for being Australia's earliest producer of the variety and today still making one of the best around. Planted in the early 1970s, this vineyard kicked off viticulture on the Mornington Peninsula.

Although established in 1982, many years after Elgee Park, **Dromana Estate** was one of the first wineries to really make everyone take notice of the Peninsula wines. Planted by experienced horticulturist Garry Crittenden, Dromana Estate has made top-quality wines from the very early days. Recently, the winery was sold to become part of a larger consortium, but the winemaking is still in the family, with Garry acting as a consultant to his son, Rollo Crittenden. Check out the smart Pinot Noir and Chardonnay in Dromana's Reserve and normal ranges. In early 2004, Garry released a label of his own, again. Not happy to simply retire and enjoy the Peninsula, Garry has a new venture called **Crittenden at Dromana.** Using the fruit from his original plantings of 20 years ago, he is making high quality, reasonably priced Chardonnay and Pinot Noir.

The Garry Crittenden 'i' range, which is the Italian varietal range, is made from grapes principally grown in the King Valley (refer to Chapter 12) in the north of Victoria. The range includes reds made from Nebbiolo, Barbara, Sangiovese and Dolcetto, with one white from the little-known Arneis grape.

Up on Main Ridge

The Main Ridge area stretches between Arthur's Seat and Red Hill. The area is quite high, with some of the coolest vineyard sites on the Peninsula, but is also quite beautiful and serene. In among the vines, you find strawberry farms and cherry orchards, all offering their wares direct to the public — you can even pick your own fruit at some orchards.

Main Ridge is considered to be the Mornington Peninsula's first commercial winery. Established back in 1975 by then-engineer Nat White, it now focuses on making Pinot Noir and Chardonnay. Although still very small, the wines have carved out a niche for themselves in the wine lovers' world. Lately, Nat has relied more heavily on letting the vineyard express itself through the fruit, which he then allows to ferment on wild or indigenous yeast. (Refer to Chapter 3 for more about this method of fermentation.)

The winemaking duo Kathleen Quealy and Kevin McCarthy were seen as quite renegade when they set up shop in this area in the late 1980s. One of their first releases under the label **T'Gallant** was an unwooded Chardonnay. At the time, they couldn't afford the high price of new French oak and saw an opening in a market that was bursting with over-oaked Chardonnay. Full of initiative, they then developed the first of the successful Pinot Gris wines, especially from this area, over the following years. In early 2003, the multi-national Beringer Blass purchased T'Gallant, but all reports are that the Quealy/McCartney team is to stay on. While far from conventional, all the wines are well made, with my particular favourites being the T'Gallant **Imogen Pinot Gris,** a richly flavoured wine of honey and minerals and **T'Gallant Tribute Pinot Gris** which is a wine with a lychees, herbs and a good acid to finish.

Try the top Pinot Noir from **Eldridge Estate** and **Ten Minutes by Tractor**. The latter label is a strange name indeed; however, as with most wine labels, a reason exists behind it. The story goes that three neighbouring vineyards pool equipment, and the time taken to drive the shared tractor from one vineyard to another is never more than 10 minutes. All three vineyards — the Judd, McCutcheon and Wallis families — grow Chardonnay and Pinot Noir. However, the Judds also grow Sauvignon Blanc and the Wallis family some Pinot Gris. Some of the wines released are a blend from all these vineyards, and the best parcels are kept as designated vineyard releases.

Centring around Red Hill South and Merricks

As you meander across the Mornington Peninsula and through Red Hill, you come out at the other side of the ridge that separates the Port Phillip Bay facing vineyards from the Western Port Bay-facing vineyards. The roads are named after the beach they lead to, such as Point Leo Road, and Shoreham Road.

The vineyards sitting at the top of the ridge, namely **Paringa Estate** and **Red Hill Estate**, are cooler than those on the flat land, such as **Stonier Wines**.

The **Stonier Chardonnay** shows typical Peninsula nutty and oatmeal characters that have plenty of flavour but with a good backbone of cool climate acidity. The Stonier winery is now owned by the Lion Nathan Group, which also owns Mitchelton in the Goulburn Valley (Chapter 11) and Petaluma in the Adelaide Hills (Chapter 17).

For some intensely flavoured wines, especially the Pinot Noir, try those from **Merricks Estate** and **Tuck's Ridge**. **Merricks Shiraz** is surprisingly good, full of spices and blackberry, given the cool climate. The vineyards face Western Port Bay, which in some years can mean that the wild spring winds reduce the flowers and hence the bunches to perishingly low numbers. But the conditions can have a good result, when they allow low crops to maximise everything the vine has to give to the fruit.

Also from the Tuck's Ridge portfolio is a range of cheaper wines under the label of **Callanan's Road**. While the wines lack huge amounts of complexity, they're terrific value at under $20.

A newcomer to the region is **Scorpo Vineyard**. So far, the wines here are promising and, like other vineyards in the area, doing well with Shiraz, having planted it on the warmest part of the property. The **Scorpo Chardonnay** is typical of the region, being rich and nutty.

Embracing the Italian is **Box Stallion Winery**. Among the winery's white wines is the spicy, full-bodied **Box Stallion Arneis** and the lightly fizzy number, **Box Stallion Moscato**. Low in alcohol with less than six per cent, Moscato makes a fabulous wine to have with a summer lunch.

The **Paringa Estate** wines are very fine indeed, with the more expensive ones being from Estate-grown fruit and a regional range showcasing fruit from vineyards across the region. The winery's **Paringa Estate Pinot Noir** is ripe and raspberry-like with a generous and soft texture — a black pepper dominant Rhône-like Shiraz that has covered itself in wine awards over the years.

Meandering around Moorooduc

Along with the Dromana vineyards, those around Moorooduc are among the warmest. The area has mainly duplex or sandy clay soils, which means that they retain water poorly and the amount of vigour is much reduced. The combination of warmer climate and poorer soils gives this area the benefit of ripening earlier than Main Ridge and Red Hill. Typically, the red wines are more powerful in flavour as well as higher in tannin.

Moorooduc Estate offers great value Chardonnay and Pinot Noir. The label is called **Devil Bend Estate** and the grapes are sourced from all over the region. The wines have good, pure fruit flavours that will surpass many more expensive competitors.

The owner of the Moorooduc Estate, Richard McIntyre, is something of an institution on the Mornington Peninsula. Not only was he one of the first people to set up a winery and vineyards, he has also either consulted to or made wine for many of the local wineries. Recently, Richard and his wife Jill have expanded their winery to include a rammed-earth building housing Jill's restaurant and accommodation with views over the vineyards.

By Mornington Peninsula standards, **Kooyong** is a big vineyard. It also has a large, modern winery with all the latest winery technology. At present the 93-hectare property has one-third planted to grapes and, as in so much of the area, the focus is on Pinot Noir and Chardonnay. Typical of the area, the vineyard is on poor soils that are relatively dry, but as the vineyard is situated on the flat, winds from neither bay cause much of a problem. So far, it has been the **Kooyong Pinot Noir** that has shown how good an area this is. The extra warmth of the vineyard's location aids in making a full flavoured, silky textured wine reminiscent of black cherries and dark plums.

For Pinot Noir with strong structure and plenty of tannin, and a generous Pinot Gris, try **Yabby Lake**. Like Kooyong, this vineyard has taken advantage of the warmer site, which while still maritime, doesn't get blasted by cold winds straight off Western Port Bay. The man behind this venture is

---

A winter wine weekend

The Queen's birthday weekend (celebrated in Australia on the second Monday in June of each year) is set aside by Mornington Peninsula's winegrowers as their time to showcase the best they have to offer — and what a great way to spend a holiday weekend! A number of vine-yards are open to the public, and the local tastings are a fabulous way to acquaint yourself with the diversity of the region. Most wineries hold a special event, along with music, or participate in a theme lunch. In 2003 it was 'Pinot Noir and Pies' — and sophisticated pies, I might add!

Australian-born New Zealand resident, winemaker Larry McKenna. (See Chapter 23.) In early 2004, Todd Dexter, (formerly making Stonier Wines' top quality wines) came to Yabby Lake as winemaker. I'm expecting some pretty outstanding wines to come from the team from here.

Reasonably big, in Mornington Peninsula terms, is **Willow Creek Vineyard** with over nine hectares of Chardonnay, Pinot Noir and Cabernet Sauvignon. The top label is the **Tulum** range which comes from vineyards on a warm protected site. Both the **Willow Creek Tulum Chardonnay** and **Willow Creek Tulum Pinot Noir** are intensely flavoured with good acidity.

At **Stumpy Gully Vineyard** the best wines are the pear and mineral **Stumpy Gully Pinot Gris** and the **Stumpy Gully Chardonnay,** which is best when young because the melon flavours and soft acidity are in good balance. At 25 hectares, the family-run winery has dabbled in many a variety — Cabernet Sauvignon, Merlot, Sangiovese, Pinot Noir, Shiraz, Sauvignon Blanc, Chardonnay, Pinot Grigio, Riesling and Marsanne.

Bellarine Peninsula

The main focus of the Bellarine Peninsula is the town of Geelong, which is located on the western side of Port Phillip Bay. At the bay's widest part, it separates Bellarine from the Mornington Peninsula by 75 kilometres, but this distance is a great deal less as the bay comes around and the Peninsulas almost join at the head of the Port Phillip Bay. Bass Strait, the water tract that sits between mainland Australia and the island of Tasmania, also has quite a climatic influence on the area.

Method behind more than one label

Offering many different wines from one winery isn't the domain of the big wineries alone. Some of the small producers also have a choice of labels. For example, Moorooduc Estate has three tiers of labels. The top, at least in terms of cost, is **The Moorooduc**. The fruit for this wine comes only from a specific vineyard site, one that the winemaker has identified as being his best plot of land. The second label is **Moorooduc Estate**, and the fruit comes from the vineyards owned by the winemaker. The third, and least expensive, is the **Devil Bend Creek** range, the fruit of which is sourced from all over the Mornington Peninsula. These different tiers of wines are all made with the same amount of care and expertise as the top-priced wines, while still retaining the individual stamp of a smaller producer. The wines offer great value for money and are a way of buying from top small producers without having to pay a premium price. Keep your eyes open for these differently priced wines.

The Mornington and Bellarine climates are quite different. For example, Bellarine receives only 550 millimetres of rain each year, compared to 850 millimetres on the Mornington. And, as the majority of this rain falls in winter, the growing season on the Bellarine Peninsula is dry and a little warmer than the Mornington. For this reason, the area is able to grow later ripening varieties such as Shiraz and Cabernet Sauvignon with more success, as these varieties have a chance to ripen before autumn turns to winter.

The Geelong area isn't very well known for its wineries, and its reputation has been based largely on individual wineries rather than the region as a whole. Bannockburn, Scotchman's Hill and Pettavel come immediately to mind and all produce quality wines. But don't overlook the produce of other Geelong wineries, which comprise the 300-plus hectares planted to vines in the area. See Figure 13-2 for their location.

Stranded, all alone, is **Shadowfax Wines**, which isn't strictly part of the Geelong region but is part of the greater zone known as Port Phillip. I mention it here simply because the Geelong region is really its closest neighbour. Although the winery itself is very modern, Shadowfax Wines is part of Werribee Park, one of Victoria's historical mansions, which has magnificent grounds. So a visit not only guarantees some great wines but also a touch of Victoria's history.

A small vineyard has been established at Shadowfax but the wines are mostly produced from fruit brought in from McLaren Vale, the Yarra Valley and Geelong. Look out for medium- to full-bodied savoury **Shadowfax Pinot Noir** and the elegant **Shadowfax Shiraz**.

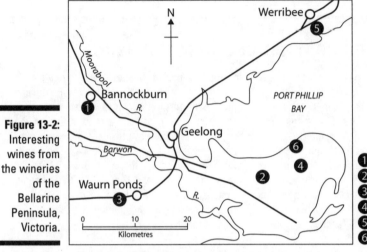

Figure 13-2: Interesting wines from the wineries of the Bellarine Peninsula, Victoria.

1 Bannockburn Vineyards
2 Leura Park Estate
3 Pettavel Winery
4 Scotchman's Hill
5 Shadowfax Wines
6 Spray Farm

Around Bannockburn

The fame of the Bannockburn winery makes it pretty difficult to separate the township from the winery. Suffice to say that the town itself isn't much more than a pub and a shop. The reputation of the Bannockburn wines, however, has touched most parts of the wine-drinking world.

Gary Farr is the face behind **Bannockburn Vineyards**, having been the winemaker for longer than he probably cares to remember. The grapes sourced for these wines are grown only on the Bannockburn vineyards. The **Bannockburn Pinot Noir** is a complex wine of savoury mushrooms, dark plums and balanced tannin while the **Bannockburn Chardonnay** is rich in flavour but with enough acidity to keep this richness in balance. Both are very special wines and the winemaking of each has been influenced by Farr's many working trips to Burgundy.

The top of the range is the expensive **Bannockburn Pinot Noir,** known as **Serré**, which means *tight* in French. This wine takes its name from a small vineyard that has been developed very much in the style of those of Burgundy. The vines are planted close together to allow them to naturally control each other's *vigour* (vine growth), and are tended only by hand. The resulting wine is intense and full flavoured.

Other varieties produced at Bannockburn are Shiraz, Cabernet Sauvignon and Sauvignon Blanc, which, apart from the Shiraz, play very much second fiddle to Farr's love of the Burgundy varieties. You can find the Bannockburn wines in top wine stores and on restaurant wine lists.

So as not to be considered lazy, Gary Farr also decided to establish his own label — **Bannockburn by Farr** — from vineyards that he himself owns. (The Hooper family largely owns Bannockburn vineyards.) And so the pleasure of Farr's passion for all things Burgundian continues with some lovely Pinot Noir and Chardonnay wines. Added to these is **Bannockburn by Farr Viognier**, a lesser known white with some terrific pear flavours along with a warm, generous texture.

Waurn Ponds

The Waurn Ponds area is about 15 kilometres south-west of Geelong, and sits the same distance inland from the southerly coastal town of Torquay. This close proximity to the water, namely Corio Bay at Geelong and Bass Strait at Torquay, play a big influence on grapegrowing in this area. The maritime climate allows the vines to develop a little more slowly, giving the grapes time to build up their fruit flavours. The area still has only a handful of vineyards, but this is gradually changing as more people see the promise of the area.

For full-flavoured wines, try those from **Pettavel Winery**. Many of the grapes supplying this winery come from established vines, which produce better structured fruit than grapes harvested from young vines. The owner, Mike Fitzpatrick, was also involved in grapegrowing for many years before building his own winery.

For an excellent Pinor Noir, try one of Australia's earliest advocates of the grape — **Prince Albert**. This tiny specialist producer has gradually evolved in this style of wine, as those around it have introduced new winemaking methods, and produces a lighter style of wine that has lovely Pinot Noir perfume and delicacy.

Phylloxera's role in Geelong's downfall

The Geelong region established itself as a wine-growing region way back in the 1840s. Like the Yarra Valley, Swiss immigrants chose the area as suitable for growing grapes. By 1869, 400 hectares were planted to vine. Unfortunately, the area's demise came by way of a pest called *Phylloxera*, a creature world renowned for enjoying a feast on the vine roots, which gradually kills the plant. The vines of the region were replanted in the 1960s, this time on a vine rootstock resistant to *Phylloxera*, but haven't yet regained the 400-hectare coverage they once reached.

Drysdale Way

The vineyards around Drysdale are located towards the tip of the Bellarine Peninsula but still close enough to Bass Strait to be affected by the strength and coldness of the winds from the water. Many are right on the coast, which makes for some pretty spectacular vistas, and the best known is **Scotchman's Hill**.

Established by the Brown family in 1982, Scotchmans Hill really put this area on the map. Today Robin Brockett, viticulturist-cum-winemaker, runs what has developed into quite a sizeable business. Of the 300 hectares planted to grapes in the Geelong region, more than 40 per cent are turned into wine made at this vineyard. The vineyards have been carefully and thoughtfully established, with a good deal of emphasis on the planting of trees to form windbreaks. While the winery makes some Shiraz and Sauvignon Blanc, it's most famous for the grapes of Burgundy — Pinot Noir and Chardonnay.

The cheaper range from Scotchman's Hill is called **Swan Bay**. If you're looking for something a little less expensive, Swan Bay is worth trying because it's still the product of an experienced winemaker.

For the area's top drops, try the **Leura Park** wines, which are made under contract by De Bortoli's Steve Webber — an assurance of quality. The **Leura Park Chardonnay** is toasty and citrus-like, while the **Leura Park Pinot Noir** shows truffles along with some dark cherry flavours.

Gippsland

Simply no comparison exists as to the number of vineyards and hectares under vine on the Mornington Peninsula and the Gippsland area. But while Gippsland is the smallest of these three in terms of number of vines planted, the actual landmass of the area is very large. However, only 250 tonnes or so of grapes were processed in 2003, which is as much as many single wineries on the Peninsulas would crush.

As yet, no specific regions have been declared for the Gippsland wine zone, which covers an area from the New South Wales–Victoria border, inland to the Great Dividing Range and along the coast to Wonthaggi. (For more information on Australia's wine zones and regions, refer to Chapter 3.)

Long known for its cattle grazing, dairy products and rainforests, Gippsland's lush grassy paddocks are unlikely to be overrun by vineyards. Although no agricultural area likes to have extremes in rainfall, vines are particularly sensitive.

Of all the soil conditions that can be endured by grapes, wet feet is the hardest. Consequently, local grape growers are very game fellows and, well aware of this drawback, have made site selection paramount.

The vineyards established in Gippsland are mainly pretty small affairs, usually of less than 8 hectares. This is principally because of the variable weather: Gippsland is always either in drought or under flood! Overall, the weather is pretty cool and windy, especially when the wind comes up from the chilly Bass Strait. Consequently, varieties such as the cool climate specialists, Pinot Noir and Chardonnay, do best.

The three areas of Gippsland — South, West and East — have slightly different climates, with East Gippsland being quite dry in comparison to the other two.

Most of the wineries in Gippsland are situated around the towns of Bairnsdale, Leongatha and Warragul, with the odd renegade isolated winery on the outskirts. See Figure 13-3.

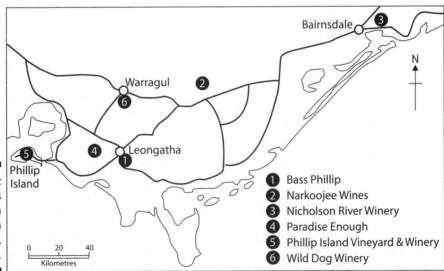

Figure 13-3: Top wines from wineries in Gippsland, Victoria.

1. Bass Phillip
2. Narkoojee Wines
3. Nicholson River Winery
4. Paradise Enough
5. Phillip Island Vineyard & Winery
6. Wild Dog Winery

Stunning South Gippsland

The area of South Gippsland centres around Leongatha and Foster. The weather is *maritime* (see the sidebar 'Making for mild, in the maritime' for more on this type of climate), and is close to the windiest part of Victoria. As a former rainforest, not surprisingly, the area is wet, especially in winter.

The wines from **Bass Phillip** are probably the most discussed wine in Victoria — people either love them or have some reservations. The vineyard outside Leongatha was originally planted to Cabernet Sauvignon and Merlot, due to founder Phillip Jones's passion for the wines of Bordeaux. He quickly realised that the marginal climate would rarely ripen these late maturing varieties and within six years had transformed his vineyard into 90 per cent Pinot Noir, with the remaining 10 per cent Chardonnay.

The wines from **Paradise Enough** are undoubtably some of the region's best. The **Paradise Enough Chardonnay** shows a lovely mineral tone, the **Paradise Enough Pinot Noir** has some game-like flavours and the sparkling **Paradise Enough Pinot Noir/Chardonnay** is delicate and refined. Added to that, the wines are extremely good value.

Discovering East Gippsland

This area's close proximity to the Great Dividing Range means that, contrary to the rest of Gippsland, East Gippsland gets low rainfall. The rain clouds basically empty themselves onto the hills before arriving in the area! When it does rain, it usually happens in one event, and locals pray that enough falls to fill the dams.

A couple of tiny vineyards exist in the area, but only **Nicholson River Winery** is making any decent quantities of wine. The Nicholson River wines are rich, textural wines, especially the Chardonnay and Semillon. You may have to search a bit to find them, but you can always call in to the winery and pick some up for yourself.

The secret of Nicholson River

I met the owner of Nicholson River, Ken Eckersley, in 1986. The venue was the National Wine Show. Standing among all the highly trained winemakers who were mainly representatives from the big technically correct wine companies, Ken was expounding what were then some pretty outlandish winemaking views, such as barrel fermenting white wines, a popular technique nowadays but not so well known at the time. Above all else, Ken aims to make wines with an individual stamp to them — for him, simply making wine by recipe misses the point.

Netting West Gippsland

The area around Warragul is where the bulk of the Gippsland wineries exist. The rainfall is high and the soils are red, which makes a pretty interesting challenge for grape growers. These conditions give rise to a high amount of vine foliage growth and, hence, the possibility of poor fruit production and ripening, so vineyard attention is paramount.

A relatively new vineyard to the area, **Narkoojee Wines** make a full-flavoured Chardonnay with a dense texture and a soft finish — reflective of the style of this area. For a spicy and full-flavoured Shiraz, try the **Wild Dog Shiraz**, the product of a small, family-run vineyard and winery where everyone is hands-on — from the vineyard to the winemaking and the service at the cellar door.

In addition, the **Phillip Island Vineyard & Winery** has a range of well-made wines including Pinot Noir, Sauvignon Blanc and Chardonnay. (Interestingly, this vineyard is completely covered in permanent netting, which is one way of protecting vine shoots and grapes that are welcome fodder for the voracious appetite of local wildlife and affected by strong resident winds.)

Chapter 14

Sunbury and Macedon Ranges

In This Chapter

▶ Introducing Australia's top Shiraz
▶ Wallowing in sparkling wine

*A*lthough close to each other and to the city of Melbourne in terms of distance, the wine regions of Sunbury and the Macedon Ranges are very different. Sunbury is on the warm, dry plains around 40 kilometres north-west of Melbourne and the Macedon Ranges vineyards are a further 40 kilometres down the highway.

The Macedon Ranges vineyards are situated at an average altitude of around 500 metres above sea level. Consequently, this region is one of the last areas in Australia to harvest their grapes each year. I can remember a year in which Macedon had snow on the ground in early May — before they had finished picking the grapes! Now that's cold!

Not surprisingly, the styles of wines made in the two districts are very different. Sunbury is famous for its Shiraz, while Macedon makes renowned sparkling wines from Pinot Noir and Chardonnay. In this chapter, I provide some insight to the secrets of these wonderful regions.

Sunbury: Little Known but Lovely

These days, Sunbury is practically a part of the urban sprawl from the city of Melbourne in Victoria. The region isn't new to grapevines — even in the 1800s, vines were very much part of the landscape.

In 1863, state politician James Goodall Francis established Goona Warra vineyard. Knowing that vines enjoyed sunshine, he planted on the terraced land around today's Goona Warra site, as well as constructing a beautiful large bluestone winery. In keeping with the theme, just across the road at Craiglee, another politician, James Johnston, established 16 acres of vines along with his own bluestone winery. Thankfully, both historical buildings still exist and are put to use by their current owners.

As with so many of the Victorian wineries, the economic depression of the 1920s, along with a change of taste from table wines to the fortified wines of Rutherglen (which I discuss in Chapter 11), saw the Sunbury vineyards go to ruin, and soon sheep replaced the vines.

Grapevines stayed away from Sunbury until the late 1970s, when Pat Carmody re-established Craiglee in 1976 and then the Banniers re-established Goona Warra in 1983. (See the sidebar 'Craiglee winery design' for more about these wineries.)

Today, the Sunbury *viticultural* area — the area of land planted to grapevines — is small, with only a few family-run affairs. Most of the vineyards are on flat ground on *alluvial* river soils, which are free draining, allowing water to drain away from the vines' roots in wet winters but requiring irrigation in hot, dry weather.

The region's weather is classed as *Mediterranean,* which means that the winters are cool and the summer days are long and hot. Rainfall is limited in the growing season, with little rain during the ripening period, around February. That means that the varieties selected must be resilient to dry spells, and the grapes' flavour must be able to stand up to the heat without a loss in intensity. So, not surprisingly, the sun-loving Shiraz grape, in particular, does well.

Chief grape varieties of the Sunbury region

Without doubt, the Sunbury area is most famed for its Shiraz grapes, which are full of flavour with a streak of elegance. One of the strongest and most common descriptors that people use to describe a Sunbury Shiraz is that it's 'peppery'. By 'peppery', they sometimes mean like white pepper and at other times just a lovely reminiscence of freshly cracked black pepper.

Cabernet Sauvignon and Merlot grapes also do well in Sunbury, with Wildwood one of the best producers. And a few wineries with higher altitudes and hence a cooler climate grow Pinot Noir successfully — most notably Wildwood and Ray-Monde.

Star performers in Sunbury

The Sunbury region has a rich history and, surprisingly few wineries are established around the area today. See Figure 14-1 for where the main wineries are in the region. Perhaps, fearing the sprawl of Melbourne's size forced grape growers to other regions, I'm not sure. But size doesn't matter in this case, especially given that one of Australia's finest Shiraz wines — namely that of Craiglee — comes from the area.

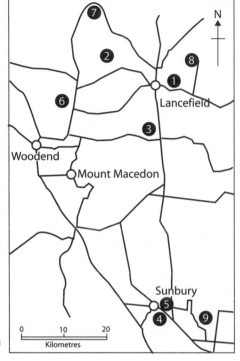

Figure 14-1: Variety from the wineries of the Sunbury and Macedon Ranges, Victoria.

1 Cleveland Winery
2 Cobaw Ridge Winery
3 Cope-Williams Winery
4 Craiglee Vineyard
5 Goona Warra Vineyard
6 Hanging Rock Winery
7 Knight Granite Hills Wines
8 Portree Vineyard
9 Wildwood Vineyards

Make it a wine weekend at the Sunbury Wine Festival

Held on the weekend of the last Sunday in August, the Sunbury Region Festival is a low key yet very interesting wine weekend. The Friday night is reserved for special dinners where old mansions are transformed to host guests in a wine and food evening. The Saturday features a centralised tasting where all the local wineries, from small in size to tiny, get together to showcase their wines. On the Sunday, a few of the wineries are open to the public for light lunches, music and, yes, more wine. The Sunbury festival may not be in the blockbuster style of those in other regions but it more than makes up for that with personalised attention.

Typical warm climate Sunbury wines include the following:

- **Craiglee Shiraz,** the winery's top wine, always finding a place among selections of Australia's finest Shiraz. The wine is elegant, ripe without being overly so and has a trademark black pepper spiciness.
- **Goona Warra's** sparkling Cabernet Franc is first class, showing rounded wine of blackberry, blueberry and cloves.

Typical cooler climate Sunbury wines include the following:

- **Wildwood Pinot Noir** is generous in palate with savoury and dark berry flavours.
- **Wildwood Chardonnay** has a nutty aroma with a soft and generous texture.

  Located just beyond Melbourne, the **Wildwood Vineyard** has an altitude of 130 metres above sea level, which means that the vineyard is high enough to benefit from the cool breezes that blow in from Port Phillip Bay. This elevation provides the vineyard with a mild to even cool climate, allowing it to make a pretty decent Pinot Noir and Chardonnay.

- **Ray-Monde Pinot Noir** grows only with this variety and does a good job of making a truffles and savoury Pinot Noir, balanced by a good dose of black cherries.

  The Ray-Monde vineyard is at a higher altitude than most others — 350 metres above sea level. This higher position means that the grapes experience a cooler climate, which makes producing very good Pinot Noir possible, albeit in a bigger, richer style than from true cool climates.

Craiglee winery design

The original Craiglee winery was constructed on the side of a hill, and used gravity to turn the grapes into wine. First, the fruit arrived by horse and cart at the top entrance to the winery. The grapes were then tipped into a crusher and fermented on the level below. After pressing the skins from the finished wines, the wine was gravity-fed down to the bottom level where the barrel storage was located. All in all, the building design facilitated a very simple as well as a gentle way of handling the grapes. An added benefit of the building was the insulation. Not only were the bluestone bricks thick, but the soil surrounding them also ensured that the natural coolness of the winery could be maintained. Today, owner Pat Carmody is unable to use this building as his winery due to the need for modern-day equipment, but the building still stands. If you get the chance, take a look.

Macedon: Bubbling Up to Meet You

The Macedon Ranges wine region is quite a contrast to Sunbury. Situated just under one hour's drive from Melbourne, the area has an elevation at between 120 metres and 620 metres above sea level. Consequently, the region is specified as a *cool climate,* and you know you're alive when you visit on a winter's morning!

The region branches off to the east and west from the Calder Highway and takes in towns such as Kyneton to the north, Lancefield to the east, Gisborne to the south and Daylesford to the west. At last count, 21 wineries are situated in Macedon. All are planted on unique plots of land with varying soil types and altitudes, so each winery makes quite individual and different wines to those of its closest neighbours. Refer to Figure 14-1 for where the main wineries are in the region.

The Macedon Ranges are most well known for their sparkling wines. The local association has agreed to give the sparkling wines of this region the regional *appellation* of 'Macedon', as a way to showcase the region. By doing this they have also identified their sparkling wine as a distinctive product from a specific winegrowing region — just like the Champagne makers of the Champagne region did all those years ago.

Vineyards and varieties

Most of the vineyards in the Macedon Ranges (refer to Figure 14-1) are situated at somewhere between 300 to 620 metres above sea level, which means that their climate is cool bordering on cold so only certain grape varieties can be grown with success.

The area is becoming famous for its sparkling wines, which are made from the classic champagne grapes of Pinot Noir and Chardonnay. Both varieties of grapes are cool-climate specialists. Not only do these grapes work well when they're used for sparkling wines, but they also make some pretty good table wines. Vineyards such as **Bindi** in the Gisborne area are testament to this.

Along with Chardonnay and Pinot Noir, you can also find some Sauvignon Blancs that are made in the intense fruit-flavoured style that finish with a zing of acidity. **Hanging Rock 'Jim Jim' Sauvignon Blanc** is a fantastic example with a tropical, herbal and acid style.

A little further afield is a patch of the Macedon Ranges that's a little warmer. Kyneton (although still cool to my mind) is able to produce some very good Shiraz, especially those coming from **Knight Granite Hills Wines**. Although still at a high elevation, this vineyard makes use of being on the other, warmer side of the mountain range, and has planted its vineyards to face north to optimise the warmth of the sun.

Being on the cool side of grapegrowing, all the vineyards in the Macedon Ranges region must ensure that their viticulture is absolutely spot-on. By that I mean the vineyard manager needs to be able to utilise every bit of sun that shines on the vines during the ripening season. Certain viticultural practices are used, such as removal of leaves from around the clusters as the grapes ripen. This process allows the sun to filter through onto the fruit and allow the grapes' flavours to fully mature. Vineyards that pay this extra attention to detail are without a doubt making the best wines in the region.

Pioneering the history of Kyneton

As you drive through the country to Kyneton, you see many an old hay store and barn, falling down but oozing with charm and providing a reminder of the farmers who established the area. The region has a mixture of climates with cold winters, hot summers and long, hot autumns. As such, the area is slow to get into the growing season compared to other Victorian regions. Consequently, the grapes are not too advanced during the heat of summer, and the real ripening comes during the gentle temperatures of autumn when days are warm but nights are cold — perfect ripening weather. Like the other parts of the Macedon Ranges, the Kyneton area is one of the last on mainland Australia to harvest their fruit.

While **Knight Granite Hills Wines** make a few different varieties, the Knight family is best known for its Shiraz and Riesling. The long ripening period shows through with both wines, which show such strong intensity and full ripeness, yet aren't overblown in texture, and which both maintain good fine structure. Llew Knight took over the day-to-day running of this vineyard from his father, Gordon, who established the vineyard in 1970. The vineyard was planted at an elevation of 550 metres above sea level, and at the time of planting was the highest vineyard in Australia.

Discovering hidden treasures of Gisborne

The vineyards of Gisborne sit on top of the ranges surrounding Melbourne and look back over the city. All are very small affairs, making wine from their own plots of land, and making it well. The last time I visited the area was one early June, and as I walked through the vineyards, the cold of the earth seeped through the soles of my boots — and I might add that there were no holes in my boots! Come summer the weather warms, but like some of the other vineyard sites chosen around the area, the higher altitude means that the vines still benefit from cold nights.

The **Bindi Pinot Noir** (from **Bindi Wine Growers**) shows great length of flavour with extremely good backbone. Search out a bottle and you'll be well rewarded — I promise! The Bindi vineyard sits at 520 metres above sea level, so the climate is cool, and they grow only Chardonnay and Pinot Noir. Harvest occurs well into the autumn month of April, which is considered late in Australian terms.

Not far from the Bindi vineyard is the very similar **Mount Gisborne**, which also only grows Chardonnay and Pinot Noir. The cold nights experienced here mean that ripening is delayed until the autumn weather arrives. So, instead of the fruit being almost ripe during the hot months when delicate flavours get burnt out of the grapes, the real flavour-ripening phase is pushed into the cooler autumn days, making the wines truly reflective of the variety. Both wines are made by consultant Stuart Anderson, a pioneer of winemaking in Victoria, having set up his own (since sold) winery called Balgownie back in 1969.

Hanging Rock events

Every February, thousands upon thousands of Melburnians flock to the famous Hanging Rock for the annual Harvest Picnic. A concept developed over ten years ago, small providores, farmers of all sorts and wineries display their wares. The idea is to take along an empty picnic basket, wander the stalls, selecting a bit of this and a bit of that before finding that perfect spot for the picnic rug. Spread out the goodies and sample the best of the new gastronomical treats being developed around country Victoria.

Twice a year, on New Year's Day and Australia Day (26 January), the picturesque Hanging Rock country racecourse is open for business. Away from the hype and fashion of Flemington Racecourse's famous Melbourne Cup, this country race meeting is truly an Australian tradition. Picnics, children, and the odd small bet set amongst a bush setting make for a fantastic day. Of course, if you go, make time to visit the odd local winery beforehand!

Lazy days around Lancefield

The Lancefield area takes in the small towns of Lancefield to Hanging Rock and Romsey. Without doubt this area is the coolest part of the Macedon Ranges, with vineyards existing as high as 630 metres above sea level. Cold is the only description for some of their weather. I remember waiting to receive fruit from the Hanging Rock vineyard during one vintage in the 1990s. Picking had been delayed due to an unseasonal burst of cold weather that bought snow to the vineyards in May. Now that is cool-climate viticulture! While that sort of cold blast isn't an annual occurrence, the types of grapes planted around this region are very much those which benefit from this type of climate.

For a pretty decent sparkling wine, try one of those from the **Cope-Williams Winery** or the **Hanging Rock Winery** (refer to Figure 14-1). The latter are made in an unashamedly French style by owner John Ellis, who lets the wine age in barrels for many a year before its second fermentation in the bottle. The result is a wine nothing like the usual fruity Australian bubbly. Instead, it has a dominance of nuttiness and aged wine character, somewhat similar, dare I say, to the Bollinger wines of Champagne. Along with sparkling wines, the Hanging Rock Winery is known for its 'Jim Jim' Sauvignon Blanc and Shiraz.

Another good sparkling wine comes from the **Cleveland Winery,** most notably its **Cleveland 'Macedon'** sparkling wine. Also worth trying is the range of table wines, including Pinot Noir, Chardonnay and more recently Pinot Gris. Like the Hanging Rock Winery, Cleveland also sources Shiraz fruit from the Heathcote region to make a full-bodied, spicy red.

Portree Vineyard has a **Macedon Blanc de Blanc** sparkling wine worth trying. One of my favourites from this small vineyard is its **Portree Damask Rosé**. Made from Pinot Noir, the wine is purposefully light in body yet plenty of flavour — definitely a summer treat to search out.

Tucked away among a natural forest is **Cobaw Ridge Winery**, a vineyard oasis with plantings of Shiraz, Viognier and Chardonnay. Added to these is a little-known Italian variety called Lagrein, hailing from the north-east region of Trentino-Alto Adige (see *Italian Wine for Dummies*, by Mary Ewing-Mulligan and Ed McCarthy, John Wiley & Sons Inc.). The Lagrein grapes typically produce sturdy, savoury wines with a good backbone of tannin, for example, the **Cobaw Ridge Lagrein**, which is well worth trying (as is visiting the small cellar door).

Chapter 15

Tasmania:
Wines of a Cool Climate

● ●

In This Chapter

▶ Discovering delicacy of flavour that cool climates bring

▶ Toasting top Pinot Noir and Chardonnay

▶ Tassie's finest from the north, east and south

● ●

*T*he vine plantings in Tasmania are very small affairs, some as small as one hectare, and many of the winemakers are amateurs dabbling in the wine game. But some of Australia's finest wines are made in Tassie, a fact not overlooked by the big mainland companies that are gradually investing in the island and fuelling the rise in prominence of its wines.

Being isolated from the mainland and having a relatively small population has enabled Tasmania to maintain its pristine environment — the rivers remain largely unpolluted and the air is clean. And this purity comes through in the state's produce. In the past decade, Tasmania's wine industry has come of age and its wines are now more than ready to take on the best of the mainland.

The Purity of Tasmania

Located south of eastern mainland Australia, Tasmania comprises one official wine zone. This Geographical Indication means that no specified regions break up the island. (Refer to Chapter 3 for more information on this classification system.)

Tasmania, however, can roughly be divided — unofficially — into three wine regions:

- The north coast, including the Tamar Valley of Launceston and the Pipers River area to the north-east of Launceston.
- The east coast, stretching from north-east of Hobart north up to Bicheno.
- The Hobart region, which includes the Coal River Valley, the Derwent Valley and the Huon Valley.

Broadly speaking, most of Tassie specialises in Pinot Noir and Chardonnay wines. However, the aromatic whites, such as Riesling, Gewürztraminer and Pinot Gris, do very well in the Tamar Valley.

Contributing less than 0.5 per cent of Australia's total grape crush, Tasmania has less than 1,000 hectares planted to vines, as compared with Australia's largest farmer, South Australia, which has around 67,000. With over 75 wineries and 156 vineyards, 70 per cent of Tasmania's vineyards are smaller than five hectares. Increasingly, bigger vineyards are being planted and today notable wine companies such as Yalumba, the Hardy Wine Company, Taltarni and Domaine Chandon rely on fruit grown in Tasmania.

Contract winemakers make much of the wine from Tasmania, which means the vineyard owner hands over the grapes to a contract winemaking facility to produce wine according to the grower's specifications.

Prime Climatic Conditions

The climate across Tasmania is best described as *temperate,* which means that the highest daily temperature is rarely above 20 degrees Celsius. In addition, the difference between day and night temperatures is minimal. Such a climate means little shift in temperatures during the growing and ripening season, and few extremes from day to day.

Broadly speaking, the northern part of the island is warmer than the southern. Being so far south of the equator, autumn in Tasmania consists of long days of sunshine. This allows grapevines to soak up the soft sunshine while ripening gradually. A dry autumn in Tasmania, which is likely in at least three out of five years, is heaven for the grape growers as the fruit can just hang on the vine, developing just a touch each day. Harvest takes place in early April to late May.

Site selection for vineyards in Tasmania is critical to the quality of the final wines produced. The most successful are those on a slope, which allows for good cold-air drainage into a valley below and eliminates the risk of frost.

Spring frosts burn and kill new shoots, while autumn frosts damage grapes on the vine by breaking down the skin — the most important part of the grape for wine flavour.

Protecting vines from wind is important, particularly when new shoots are growing in spring and when the vines are flowering, a process that determines the amount of berries per bunch. Strong winds can easily break off new shoots, and the loss of one shoot is equivalent to the loss of two potential bunches. (As a rule, most shoots will have two bunches on them. Pinot Noir is known occasionally to form three.)

Many vineyard sites in Tasmania have gravelly or rocky soils that provide good drainage. In addition, the rocks absorb the sun's rays and radiate it back onto the vines as a secondary source for ripening. Given that Tasmania's annual rainfall (the average being 600 millimetres) is much lower than in many parts of mainland Australia, many vineyards need to irrigate during the ripening period.

Toasting Tassie's Top Grapes

Those grape varieties that ripen in the early to mid-season, such as Chardonnay and the red Pinot Noir, produce the best wines in Tasmania because its cool days allow the fruit to ripen steadily. Rarely do late-in-the-season grapes such as Cabernet Sauvignon and Merlot, however, produce truly ripe wines in this region.

The best varieties include

- **Pinot Gris:** With similar climatic conditions to the two places that forged this variety's reputation — Alsace in France and Fruili in Italy — Pinot Gris is Tassie's star. The long, sunshine-filled autumn days produce a style full of nutty flavours and a soft and generous texture.

- **Gewürztraminer:** More than any other variety, the flavour of the Gewürztraminer grape is revealed in the final wine, albeit with the rounded texture that alcohol gives.

- **Riesling:** As with others from a cool climate, Tassie's Rieslings are citrusy, full of fresh lemon and lime with a good backbone of acidity.

- **Chardonnay:** Although climatically a very versatile grape, some of the best are grown on cool sites, as the grapes are able to develop more subtlety of character. Needless to say, Tasmania meets this criterion, and produces some delicious and long-living Chardonnays. With 35 per cent of the island planted with Chardonnay, it is a very significant variety.

✔ **Sparkling wine:** Sparkling wine and Tasmania go hand in hand, with the climate allowing the fruit to develop loads of flavours at low sugar levels. Consequently, Tassie's sparkling wines have a denseness of flavour and lovely full texture that sits alongside the bubbles. The early days of the excellent **Jansz** label was under the guidance of the famous Champagne company of Louis Roederer, and these wines established Tasmania's ability to produce fine sparkling wines.

✔ **Pinot Noir:** Tasmania is increasingly gaining a reputation for its Pinot Noir — still the only viable red variety on the island. One hundred different brands are made in Tasmania, and 36 per cent of the island's total plantings are of Pinot Noir, with a high percentage made into table wines and sparkling wines.

Research shows that the enzymes responsible for flavour and pigments in grape skin switch off when temperatures go above 22 degrees Celsius — a process that accounts for the often very deep colour of Tasmania's Pinot Noirs.

The Wonderful Wines on Offer

The areas under vine across Tasmania vary considerably due to differing climatic conditions. In the north around the Tamar River, the wind is quite ferocious on some vineyard sites and crop levels are therefore kept quite low. Consequently, production is small but the wines are usually full of flavour, especially the sparkling wines.

The mildest weather is found along the east coast. The coast tempers the weather and fewer fluctuations in temperature occur. The weather is also reasonably predictable — well, as predictable as any weather can be — so vintage to vintage variation is less pronounced. So, when you buy wine from top Tasmanian producers, such as Freycinet (see the section 'East coast charmers', later in this chapter), the year-to-year variation in quality is much less than it is in a vineyard where each season varies dramatically.

Around Hobart the weather is quite mild, with sunny yet cool autumn days. In summer, temperatures may creep up into the high twenties degrees Celsius, but this isn't when the main ripening occurs. The ripening occurs in the cooler autumn days, which prevents the fruity flavours from being *volatilised* out of the grape — burnt away. Instead, ripening occurs slowly, and you're likely to find delicate varieties such as Riesling and Gewürztraminer intensely flavoured.

North coast novelties

Tassie's north coast wine region is centred around the city of Launceston, which is located on the Tamar River. North-west of the city is the Tamar Valley and to the north-east is Pipers River. The largest wine area in Tasmania in terms of hectares planted and tonnes produced, the north coast's vineyards made up 72 per cent of the total in Tasmania in 2002, with 68 per cent being greater than ten hectares in size. Figure 15-1 shows the locations of the region's wineries.

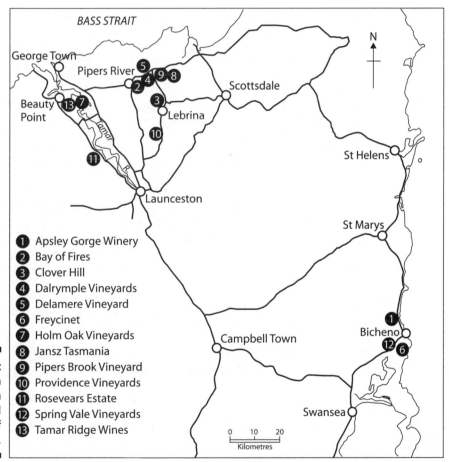

1. Apsley Gorge Winery
2. Bay of Fires
3. Clover Hill
4. Dalrymple Vineyards
5. Delamere Vineyard
6. Freycinet
7. Holm Oak Vineyards
8. Jansz Tasmania
9. Pipers Brook Vineyard
10. Providence Vineyards
11. Rosevears Estate
12. Spring Vale Vineyards
13. Tamar Ridge Wines

Figure 15-1: Wineries on the north coast and east coast of Tasmania.

Located over on the Pipers River side of the Tamar Valley is one of the biggest players in the area, **Pipers Brook Vineyard**. This company owns vineyards in both the Tamar Valley and the cooler Pipers River region. The winery is particularly famous for aromatic whites such as Riesling and Gewürztraminer. The **Pipers Brook Chardonnay** is very good, although it needs a few years of cellaring to allow the crisp acidity to meld into place. Also of note from this vineyard are the Pinot Noir and Pinot Gris wines.

The second label from Pipers Brook Vineyard is the **Ninth Island** range. None of the varieties offered under this label have ever disappointed me — this top winery offers fantastic value. Look out for the two Pinots, Noir and Grigio.

Next door to Pipers Brook is the home of **Jansz Tasmania** wines, which is owned by the Yalumba wine group from South Australia (see Chapter 18). Jansz produces only sparkling wines, with both the non-vintage and vintage continuing to impress with their quality of fruit and lovely soft bead.

Still in the Pipers River region is another top sparkling winery, **Clover Hill**, owned by the mainland wine company, Pyrenees-based Taltarni. This property is one of the most beautiful in Australia, and I was lucky the day I visited — the usual high-speed winds were non-existent! Clover Hill sparkling wines are made well and have a great creamy texture and flavour. Also good is **Lalla Gully Chardonnay,** rich in nutty and honey flavours with a good dose of balancing acid.

And the last big, wine company-owned property in Tasmania is the **Bay of Fires,** owned by the Hardy Wine Company. This site is the main source of fruit for its excellent sparkling wine, Arras, as well as for a good range of well-made, full-flavour wines. Search out the Riesling and, in the cheaper **Tigress** range, the Pinot Noir.

Other small wineries on the eastern side of the Tamar Valley making particularly good Chardonnay and Pinot Noir are **Dalrymple Vineyards**, **Providence Vineyards** and **Delamere Vineyards**.

Over on the western side of the Tamar River, and mostly a little further south than the vineyards of the Pipers River region, are the **Tamar Ridge Wines**.

With around 65 hectares of vines, **Tamar Ridge** is by far the biggest vineyard planting in West Tamar. Although established relatively recently (1994), the wines have well and truly developed a name for themselves. Yet again, the strength of Pinot Noir leads the pack in quality at this winery, with the Pinot Gris and Chardonnay being the best of the Tamar Ridge whites. Prices are reasonable, too.

While Tamar Ridge is established a little distance from the river, **Holm Oak Vineyards** is close to the banks of the river. The winery is named after the amazing large old oak trees that protect the vines from the sometimes wild winds in this region. Like its neighbours, Holm Oak specialises in Pinot Noir.

Further south towards the city of Launceston is **Rosevears Estate**. With over 22 hectares of vines (the vast majority of Tasmania's vineyards are less than four hectares), this reasonably sized Tasmanian business produces top Chardonnay, Pinot Gris and Gewürztraminer, with the old favourite Pinot Noir also showing some fine quality.

East coast charmers

The area that follows the coast road from Hobart in the south-east to St Helens on the east coast is loosely considered the east coast wine region, and is without doubt among the most beautiful and relatively untouched parts of the world (refer to Figure 15-1).

Top-class wines from this region include those from:

- **Apsley Gorge Winery:** Pinot Noir and Chardonnay are the only two varieties produced. If you ever visit, you might find that freshly caught crayfish and oysters are also on offer. The owner was an abalone fisherman in his previous life so seafood plays a big part at this winery.

- **Freycinet Vineyards:** Located 20 kilometres inland from the coast, the maritime influence prevents the vineyard from experiencing large climatic fluctuations. Yet despite this close proximity to the coastline, the actual property is nestled away, and is protected from the usual windy wildness of the coast. The red wines are very deep in colour given the extended cool ripening season, which allows the grapes to ripen slowly and the pigments in the skin to intensify.

  The **Freycinet Pinot Noir** is full of fruit flavour yet with enough tannin to ensure that it will age well for ten or so years — without a doubt this is one of my personal favourites. In keeping with the wine styles of Burgundy, the Freycinet Chardonnay is also lovely and will age well.

- **Spring Vale Vineyards:** Like Freycinet, this vineyard has been at the forefront of putting Tasmanian wines, particularly Pinot Noir, on the minds of wine lovers across mainland Australia.

Hobart's finest

In the south of Tasmania (which incidentally is the second most southerly grape-growing district in the world, the Otago region in New Zealand being the most southerly; see Chapter 25), the long autumn allows intensely flavoured and well structured wines to be produced (see Figure 15-2). The Coal River Valley wineries are grouped together to the north-east of Hobart, around the town of Richmond. This winery area is the second biggest in Tasmania after the Tamar–Pipers River region.

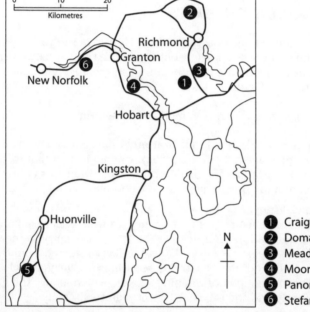

Figure 15-2: Wineries of southern Tasmania.

1 Craigow Wines
2 Domain A
3 Meadowbank Estate
4 Moorilla Estate
5 Panorama
6 Stefano Lubiana Wines

Top producers in the south include

- **Craigow Wines:** Still a relatively new label, this winery is making an excellent full-flavoured Pinot Noir and a spicy and lychee Gewürztraminer.

- **Domaine A:** A winery with one of the biggest reputations in Tasmania, it shot to attention a number of years ago with its Cabernet Sauvignon–Merlot blend, an unlikely wine at such limits of viticulture. Such late-ripening varieties are a challenge to Tasmanian winemakers, and only in certain years can the Cabernet Sauvignon ripen past the stage of herbaceous green flavours.

At Domaine A, a second tier of label is known as **Stoney Vineyard** (the first is Domaine A). The name comes from the physical appearance of the vineyards: the soil is literally covered with stones to help ripening by absorbing the warmth of the sun and re-radiating it back to the grapes. **Stoney Vineyard Sauvignon Blanc** shows how well this aromatic variety can do in cool climates allowing the herbal flavours to come through with a kick of acid to finish, as does the **Domaine A Pinot Noir**, which is a well-ripened, dark cherry reminiscent wine.

✔ **Meadowbank Estate:** The **Meadowbank Riesling** is quite European in style, with citrus-like fruit as well as a good zing of acidity.

✔ **Wellington Wines:** The energetic Andrew Hood produces myriad wines for others under the company name **Hood Wines**. But he does find time to produce a few for himself under this label, the most famous of which is the dessert-style Iced Riesling, made in the style of the icewine (see the sidebar 'Icewines of the north and south').

Two of Tasmania's best-recognised wineries are in the Derwent Valley. The one closest to Hobart is **Moorilla Estate**, whose vineyard and winery overlook the Derwent River. As well as the grapes grown on this site, Moorilla Estate also owns the St Mathias vineyard in the northern Tamar Valley region. Moorilla Estate was one of the earliest wineries to be established in Tasmania and remains one with a big reputation, pioneering Gewürztraminer in Tasmania. I love the musk and spice of the **Moorilla Estate Gewürztraminer** and the lime-dominant **Moorilla Estate Riesling**, while the **Moorilla Estate Pinot Noir Reserve**, which is only made in years of exceptional fruit, is well worth trying for its full ripe flavours of plum and trufffles.

The other strong-on-quality winery is **Stefano Lubiana Wines**, particularly for its Pinot Noir, Chardonnay, Riesling and Pinot Gris. The site of the vineyard is a big factor in the quality of its produce: the vines are planted on a gentle slope that allows for sun exposure, and the Derwent River acts to keeps the summers cooler and the winters warmer.

You find the location of a group of wineries that make up the Huon Valley wine region south of Hobart. The temperatures here get very cold and, in some years, even the stalwart early-ripening varieties struggle. Consequently, vineyard choice is paramount, with the must-have criteria being a sloping piece of land that receives maximum sunshine and shelter from coastal winds, and soils that can absorb and re-radiate warmth.

TECHNICAL STUFF

Icewines of the north and south

Originating in Germany in 1794, icewine is the result of pressing grapes that have been left on the vine to freeze in winter. The freezing of the grape intensifies its sugar and flavour, and leaving the ice crystals in the wine press further enhances this intensity. Today, Germany, Austria and, increasingly, Canada lead the market in this type of wine.

Down in Tasmania, however, another winemaker is attempting his own style of icewine. Given that the weather doesn't allow freezing to occur, Andrew Hood freezes his grapes in a cool store after harvest. The result is Iced Riesling, a sweet, dessert-style wine bursting with an array of tropical fruit and citrus lift. Look out for this one under Andrew's **Wellington** label.

Formally a microbiologist and lecturer in wine science, Andrew established his own winery in 1994. As a contract winemaker, he consults with the grape grower and aims to produce exactly the style of wine they're after. Wines that have his mark include **Tinderbox**, **Elsewhere**, **Meadowbank** and **No Regrets**.

The key grape varieties in the south are Pinot Noir, Chardonnay, Gewürztraminer, Riesling and Sauvignon Blanc. Table wines and sparkling wines are the predominant styles.

All the wineries in this region are small affairs, with the largest being **Elsewhere Vineyard** with 13 hectares. The name came about because the owners felt that the weather report often forecast that it would be fine and sunny 'elsewhere'. The best of the Elsewhere range is the Pinot Noir, as it is at **Panorama Vineyard**. Noted other wineries in this region that produce tiny amounts are **Tinderbox**, **Two Bud Spur** and **No Regrets**.

Part IV
The Wine Regions of South Australia and Western Australia

www.moir.com.au

Alan Moir

In this part . . .

The immense wine zones of South Australia and Western Australia are as diverse as several small countries.

I take you first to South Australia's larger-than-life grape-growing region of McLaren Vale, where the reds rejoice. Then, to other large and small plantings of Fleurieu, and a dip into the Mount Lofty Ranges. I visit the popular wines of the Barossa Valley with two other less famous wine-producing valleys, Clare and Eden Valley, to reveal the regal Rieslings. Next, to the Limestone Coast where Cabernet's top in Coonawarra country and Chardonnays shout in Padthaway. New plantings from seaside Mount Benson are for followers of Sauvignon Blanc and Shiraz. Riverland is vast, beautiful and a haven for both Chardonnay and Semillon to thrive in its Continental climate.

Over in Western Australia, I take you to Greater Perth where lower volume and high quality Chenin Blanc, Verdelho and Shiraz all make the grade. Then to coastal regions where Margaret River flaunts her stylish wines, and the Great Southern area quietly gains some recognition for itself, too. A fruit salad of wine, food and scenery delights all wine lovers.

Chapter 16

Meandering through McLaren Vale

· ·

In This Chapter

▶ Finding value and choice where beauty abounds

▶ Thriving reds, with colour and flavour, to put away

▶ Whispering whites for early consumption

· ·

*W*ith more than 66,000 hectares of vineyards in South Australia —
the largest grapegrowing state in the country — the McLaren Vale
region, which is part of the Fleurieu wine zone (see Chapter 17 for other wine
regions in this zone, such as Kangaroo Island and Langhorne Creek), manages
third place in the ranking of size. With nearly 6,500 hectares under vine,
I call this region large, especially when making a comparison with the total
plantings across Tasmania (refer to Chapter 15), which are yet to reach
1,000 hectares.

Less than an hour south from the state's capital, the scenic wonder of the
plantings of McLaren Vale provides one of Adelaide's favourite weekend
visiting spots with some readily accessible fabulous ocean views. Nearly all
the wineries have a cellar door (for tastings and purchases), many with some
sort of café or restaurant attached. Although the region does have some
presence by the big wine companies — such as the Hardy Wine Company
(Hardys) and Rosemount Estate — the majority of the winemakers are small
to medium in size.

In this chapter, I take you through the McLaren Vale region and introduce
you to a few lesser known labels as well as the area's famous rich and full-
bodied reds.

Where the city meets the Vale

Poor old McLaren Vale seems to be consumed by the city sprawl. The last time I visited the region, I was shocked by the residential living that had been constructed, right next to wineries and vineyards. Although quite a green land gap was still apparent between the suburbs of Adelaide and the beginning of what is only a smallish town of McLaren Vale, the town seemed to be surrounded by new housing. But don't be put off — at this stage, the buildings are centralised around the town. Drive on for five minutes and the landscape again becomes vine laden, and the obvious local pursuit is grape growing and winemaking.

Looking for Suburban Sanctuary in McLaren Vale

McLaren Vale is a wealth of geographical diversity (rivers, ocean proximity, hills) as well as technological variety. You find winemakers in this region using traditional methods alongside those using the most modern facilities. Since 1838, when the first plantings were made in this region, the wine region's proximity to Adelaide meant the sprawling residential development from the city (see the sidebar 'Where the city meets the Vale') towards the tiny township of McLaren Vale was inevitable. The Tintara Cellars, which was started by Thomas Hardy in 1876, and is now part of Hardys, offers a stunning step back in time. The bluestone buildings ooze history and, for those lucky enough to get a peep, the inside cellars are built from huge chunks of wood, and the underground cellar boasts all sorts of rare wines dating back to early in the twentieth century.

Relying on Warm and Sunny Weather

McLaren Vale is only about 12 kilometres from the sea and this close proximity helps to moderate the quite warm climate. McLaren Vale is regarded as having a Mediterranean climate, with summer daytime temperatures regularly in the mid-30 degrees Celsius. These warm conditions provide a reliable climate for growing vines. And, for the technically weather-minded, little *diurnal temperature fluctuation* occurs. In other words, the daytime and night-time temperatures don't show a large difference. The tempering of this heat comes in the afternoon by the sea breeze that blows in from the nearby Gulf St Vincent.

A *Mediterranean* climate indicates a warm and dry summer with cool, wet winters. McLaren Vale fits the bill here, too, with only about 180 millimetres of the annual 650 millimetres of rain falling in the crucial October to April growing season. So the spring into summer and early autumn weather is typically dry and warm, leading to the need for irrigation on most properties. Those vineyards that don't irrigate tend to have old vines where the vines' roots have searched deep into the ground over the years, looking for water. The yield per vine is tiny, but what berries the vines produce have incredible concentration of flavour and colour.

By not irrigating in a low rainfall region, the vine can *stress*. The vine shows this stress by being less vigorous in the amount of leaves that are produced; by producing less bunches and by producing smaller grapes. Smaller grapes mean a high skin to grape pulp ratio. And, as the flavour and the colour for the resultant wine comes from the skin, the greater amount of skins in the fermenter means a higher amount of colour and flavour extraction. The final wines are typically deep dark red, bordering on black in colour and have unbelievable flavour. Naturally stressing, the grower must carefully monitor the vine to avoid all the leaves falling off too early and making conditions difficult for the grapes to ripen.

The soils across the region vary from sandy and extremely free draining to red soils and clays. The sandy soils are another reason for the need to irrigate as the rainfall disappears very quickly through the soil. None of the soils is excessively rich in nutrients, which means *high vigour* (strong vine and leaf growth) isn't usually a problem. Dense leaf canopies are less common in McLaren Vale than they are in more lush regions. The combination of the low humidity that the region experiences and the sea breezes mean that air flows well through the leaf canopy and outbreaks of leaf mildews and grape moulds are rare.

The Bushing Festival

The Bushing Festival, held in October each year in McLaren Vale, is one of the Fleurieu region's wine celebrations. The festival started as a throwback to the medieval times when tavern owners hung ivy outside the tavern to welcome the new wine and *mead* (a low-alcohol mixture of fermented honey and other ingredients). In McLaren Vale they use the local olive branches instead. The festival coincides with the local wine show, where the region's wines are showcased. After the results of the wine show are finalised, a bushing king or queen is selected. During the celebration, the old monarch is de-robed while the newly-anointed monarch is crowned — an event that takes on all sorts of hilarity, as I'm sure you can imagine.

Top olive oil, too

In the past, the McLaren Vale winegrowing region was covered in almond trees. Although evidence of this early choice of crop still exists today across the region, the favoured non-vine crop is now olives. Not surprisingly, in the warm climate, olives are thriving. The partnership between wine and food is strong, too, with those who enjoy making and growing wine, nearly always interested in everything to do with the table. So olive groves dot the horizon and a few of the wineries show a hand at making olive oils. Notably, the two most involved are also the two most influenced by Italian wines and wine-making, **Coriole Vineyards** and **Primo Estate**. So if it isn't enough to have a lesson on wine when you visit, you can now learn about the growing, tasting, blending and intricate ways to fashion top quality olive oils.

Growing a Mighty Mix of Great Grapes

Varying conditions for growing grapes, from soil to climate to exposure, due to slope aspect or influence from nearby sea breezes, means nearly all red and white grape varietals have a chance to flourish in the McLaren Vale.

Rewarding reds

Red varieties that thrive in the McLaren Vale wine region include

- ✔ **Shiraz:** This red is without doubt the king of McLaren Vale, making up 60 per cent of the red grapes crushed and 45 per cent of all grapes grown in the region. The warmth of the climate allows for the build up of fully ripe, rich and intense flavoured berries. Tannin development isn't restricted either so the wines that result are big and bold, filled with sweet fruit and plenty of texture. Mostly, the wines have been made utilising American oak barrels for the oak ageing. Typically these barrels impart an aromatic flavour, often referred to as coconut-like. The style of much of the McLaren Vale Shiraz is of super ripe wines. The criticism of this style of wine is that it can be jam-like with fruity sweetness (see the sidebar 'One for all and two for some').

- ✔ **Cabernet Sauvignon:** This popular grape is the second most grown red variety in McLaren Vale. These wines are a long way from the Cabernet Sauvignon of Coonawarra — South Australia's renowned Cabernet centre (see Chapter 19). The typical leafy and fine-grained tannins are gone, instead Cabernet from McLaren Vale is velvety, blackberry and mulberry-like and has soft tannin. The wines are an expression of soft fruit and a ripe mid-palate.

✔ **Grenache:** This red grape variety is made in a similar vein to the McLaren Vale Shiraz. Big and fruity. Grenache, intrinsically, has very sweet-flavoured fruit with a touch of spicy clove and nutmeg. You find some of the Grenache wines are so ripe that they border on being Port-like in character. Certainly the odd Grenache has alcohol levels around 16 per cent by volume. In comparison to Shiraz, which deepens in colour as it becomes riper, Grenache doesn't. The variety is actually quite a pale red grape and winemakers have to work the skins hard during fermentation to try to extract as much colour as possible. You also find that winemakers use Grenache in blends with grapes such as Shiraz and Mourvèdre.

✔ **Sangiovese, Petit Verdot, Merlot, Tempranillo, Cabernet Franc:** These grape varieties are just some of the 'other reds' that are slowly infiltrating the red vines plantings across the McLaren Vale region. All have great potential to thrive, especially those that love the warmth, like Italy's Sangiovese.

Whetting whites

White varieties that thrive in the McLaren Vale wine region include

✔ **Chardonnay:** This white variety is pretty lonely in McLaren Vale. Chardonnay is the second most planted grape, taking 16 per cent of the total, and the grape variety works well in the region. As an early ripening variety, winegrowers achieve rich fruitiness in the wines with ease. Typically the wines are soft, low acid wines ready for early consumption.

✔ **Semillon, Verdelho, Viognier, Marsanne and Roussanne:** These white varieties are all planted, to some degree, in the region. Although Semillon is the other white of choice for the local grape growers (making up 16 per cent of white grapes; 3 per cent of all grapes), white grapes make up only 20 per cent of the total. Some white varieties are grown principally to make a crisp, dry white to sell at cellar door. Increasingly, though, the Rhône Valley varieties of Roussanne, Marsanne and Viognier, are likely to be embraced by the locals, given the region's suitably warm climate as well as the broadening of Australian wine-drinkers' palates.

One for all and two for some

Red wines aged in oak have been made to be dry red wines — that is, without grape sugars in the wine due to all the sugar being converted to alcohol during fermentation. The apparent sweetness comes from the ultra-ripe fruit flavour rather than actual sugar. Also, alcohol gives your mouth a sensation of sweetness and these wines are generally high in alcohol.

For me, this style of wine can be a little tiring. The first glass is impressive in its full-throttle style, but a second glass can border on too much. Depends on your taste, though.

Enjoying the Local Lovelies

McLaren Vale is a terrific mixture of wines. You can find both the icon wines that demand big prices and some bottle bargains from many wineries (see Figure 16-1). Somewhere in the middle is the still well-priced-for-the-quality wine. The region itself is quite beautiful and when you take the chance to visit, you discover almond trees, olive groves, quaint cellar doors in bush settings and some great restaurants. And, not to mention the beach, just down the road.

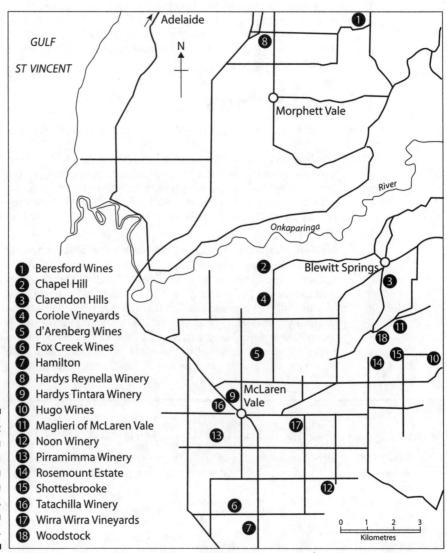

Figure 16-1: Wines from majestic McLaren Vale wineries, South Australia.

1. Beresford Wines
2. Chapel Hill
3. Clarendon Hills
4. Coriole Vineyards
5. d'Arenberg Wines
6. Fox Creek Wines
7. Hamilton
8. Hardys Reynella Winery
9. Hardys Tintara Winery
10. Hugo Wines
11. Maglieri of McLaren Vale
12. Noon Winery
13. Pirramimma Winery
14. Rosemount Estate
15. Shottesbrooke
16. Tatachilla Winery
17. Wirra Wirra Vineyards
18. Woodstock

Catchy Coriole wines

One of my favourite places is **Coriole Vineyards**. Apart from the cellar door (see Chapter 28 in which I talk about ten of the top cellar doors), the wines are consistently very good. From the top of the range come

- ✔ **Coriole Mary Kathleen Cabernet Sauvignon Merlot:** A fragrant wine with berry and chocolate flavours. Good to cellar for five to seven years and decant as an older wine.

- ✔ **Coriole Lloyd Reserve Shiraz:** A wine with a touch of refinement on the usual style of Shiraz, showing a good concentration of ripe berry fruit and sweet spices with firm tannins and a lingering finish. You can look forward to the flavours improving even further after cellaring for the next ten to twelve years.

The standard bottling wines of choice for value are

- ✔ **Coriole Shiraz:** A good-value choice, and not too ripe and plummy.

- ✔ **Coriole Redstone (a blend of Shiraz and Cabernet Sauvignon):** An even lower price than Coriole Shiraz, yet still maintains an excellent quality, plenty of fruit definition and a good soft texture.

The reasonably new **Coriole Sangiovese** and **Coriole Nebbiolo** wines fly the flag for the Italian varieties here. Their savoury characters, rather than big fruity ones, show why these varieties are such food-friendly wines

Prima Primo vino

A winery based in the McLaren Vale, but with most of its vineyards in the Adelaide Plains (in the Mount Lofty Zone, see Chapter 17) is **Primo Estate,** a winery with that touch of the different. Owner Joe Grilli, whose ancestry roots are in Italy, makes all his wines with a touch of class, toning down some of the region's typically super-ripe flavours by monitoring the grapes' ripeness. Grilli also owns vines in the cooler region of the nearby Adelaide Hills. Bravely he makes Colombard — a white grape that doesn't excite many other winemakers, due to its lack of obvious fruit flavours. But Grilli makes this grape variety shine.

Success comes as a first-class drop from Primo Estate winery when you can find

- **Primo Estate La Biondina Colombard:** An example of Colombard that shows that white wines don't always have to burst with fruitiness to be good. This wine is minerally complex and a terrific food wine that doesn't dominate your dinner.
- **Primo Estate Joseph Moda Amarone Cabernet Sauvignon:** A red wine made by harvesting the grapes and then partly drying the fruit on racks, before fermenting the grapes. The result is a savoury wine with long living potential.

Delightfully idiosyncratic d'Arenberg

Enjoying the wines from the McLaren Vale means a meander to the slightly unusual side of the region — to **d'Arenberg Wines.** Nowhere in Australia can you find such an array of wines with such individual names. Wines like **The Lucky Lizard Chardonnay**, **The Footbolt Old Vine Shiraz**, **The Laughing Magpie Shiraz–Viognier** and so the 'story behind a name' list goes on. But the winery is focused on the quality of the wine as well as delighting its wine followers with creative names.

Highlights from the range of well-named, good-tasting wines include

- **d'Arenberg The Olive Grove Chardonnay:** A best from the McLaren Vale comes this rich and rounded Chardonnay, typical of the warm climate of the region. The wine has loads of texture along with a great nutty finish.
- **d'Arenberg The Custodian Grenache:** A quintessential McLaren Vale Grenache — juicy, spicy, and very ripe and bold.
- **d'Arenberg The Dead Arm Shiraz:** The winery's flagship wine. The name 'Dead Arm' refers to a disease that some old vines can get whereby the *cordons* (branches of the vines) slowly die. The disease is called *Eutypa lata.* When vines have this disease, they produce less fruit than a healthy vine would and, in doing so, the resultant fruit is incredibly intense in texture and flavour. Being big and ripe, and super concentrated, this wine isn't for the faint-hearted.

Good value red and white drinking wines from d'Arenberg that are worth tracking down are

- d'Arenberg The Stump Jump Riesling/Sauvignon Blanc/Marsanne.
- d'Arenberg The Stump Jump Grenache/Shiraz.

d'Arenberg The Stump Jump Riesling/Sauvignon Blanc/Marsanne and d'Arenberg The Stump Jump Grenache/Shiraz are both rich and fruity wines with the red having soft tannins. They're made to be drunk on purchase, instead of cellaring for your child's wedding five years in the future. Also, the Rhône varieties can't be missed — look for **d'Arenberg Hermit Crab Marsanne Viognier** and **d'Arenberg Money Spider Roussanne**.

A touch of town types

Right in the middle of the township of McLaren Vale is **Tatachilla Winery**. The wines made here are for the lovers of seriously big and soft wines. Generously proportioned wines that are quintessential McLaren Vale are

- ✔ **Tatachilla Foundation Shiraz.**
- ✔ **Tatachilla McLaren Vale Cabernet Sauvignon.**
- ✔ **Tatachilla Keystone Grenache/Shiraz.**

Nearby is another town-based winery, although like Tatachilla the fruit comes from all over the region and beyond. The **Hardys Tintara Winery** is one of the oldest buildings still standing in McLaren Vale being built from sturdy bluestone. Look for

- ✔ **Tintara Reserve Grenache:** A juicy, ripe, berry-filled wine.
- ✔ **Tintara Reserve Shiraz:** A wine with intense structure, showing both plenty of tannin and loads of sweet, ripe fruit to fill out the palate. Certainly one to stash in the cellar for ten years.

At the gateway to McLaren Vale, if you're travelling from Adelaide, is Hardys other winery — **Hardys Reynella**. The vast range of Hardys sparkling wines come from this winery, albeit from grapes that have been grown all over the country. For example, the fruit for the premium ranges of Arras and Sir James comes predominantly from the Victorian Hoddles Creek vineyards in the Yarra Valley (refer to Chapter 10) and Tasmania (refer to Chapter 15 for Tassie treats). The multi-regional labels made at this facility are

- ✔ Hardys Eileen Hardy Shiraz.
- ✔ Hardys Eileen Chardonnay.

Hardys Eileen Hardy Shiraz and **Hardys Eileen Chardonnay** both have iconic status among wine drinkers who love the big and rich side of Australian wines. The wines are made in the fruit-dominant, ripe style with a good lashing of new oak. Some may find this oak dominance a bit too much, but if aged for five to ten years, the wines seem to fit the oak better.

Well-priced lively locals

Fox Creek Wines makes a range of well-priced, local wines, with Shiraz being the stand-out, so far. As part of the range, is a vibrant **Fox Creek Verdelho** and, as an every day drink, is the **Fox Creek Shadow's Run Shiraz/Cabernet**, named after the favoured dog that lives on the property.

Also producing Verdelho is **Chapel Hill** winery. Chapel Hill was one of the first wineries to produce a Verdelho and, because many people discovered the variety through this winery, Chapel Hill continues to have a good following. Sitting up on the hill, overlooking McLaren Vale, Chapel Hill is a modern winery that makes honest wines year after year, albeit at times quite heavily oaked.

At Chapel Hill, new oak barrels are used in both red and some white winemaking. The usual percentage winemakers use is somewhere between one-third to one-half of all the barrels used each year. For example, if a winery makes 15 barrels of Chardonnay or Shiraz, five to seven barrels would be made using new oak. Some wineries, of course, opt to use more or fewer than this, depending on the style of wine it prefers to make. The influence on a wine's taste and smell from the new barrels shouldn't be too obvious. Sure, a touch of toastiness, char or a mocha-like smell enhances the wine but, when you sniff the glass and all you smell is freshly cut oak, well, you know the winemaker has gone too far. The trick is to balance the amount of oak in the wine; after all, wine is made from grapes not trees. Try the **Chapel Hill Unwooded Chardonnay**, a fresh and white peach wine with medium body — another best from the region — and the **Chapel Hill Verdelho,** an apple and mixed tropical fruits wine.

On the flats of the Vale, is the ever-present, ever-high quality **Wirra Wirra Vineyards**. I'd be amazed if any regular drinker of Australian wine hasn't tried the wine that made Wirra Wirra famous, that is, **Wirra Wirra Church Block** red, a quintessential Australian red blend of Cabernet Sauvignon, Shiraz and Merlot. Always top quality and at a reasonable price.

If you love ripe and soft reds, find yourself a bottle of **Wirra Wirra RSW Shiraz**. The **Wirra Wirra Chardonnay** is quite a full-bodied wine with toasted nut flavours.

Shiraz to stash from Clarendon

Clarendon Hills is a winery whose Shiraz needs to be hidden away in your cellar and left there for a future celebration. The wines aren't cheap, and their popularity in the United States, due to very favourable wine reviews, means they're harder to find in Australia.

The **Clarendon Piggott Range Syrah** is the wine that some people yearn to have, given the reputation it now has for itself. The wine is immense in structure with enough tannin and fruit intensity to keep it living for another 15 to 20 years, at least. However, this wine's expensive.

Other small-quantity, high-quality wine producers

Rounding off the small quality producers are the following:

- **Beresford Wines** is among the new cellar door outlets to pop up in McLaren. Currently, the company sources fruit from McLaren Vale and other regions such as the Clare Valley (Chapter 18), but in the future it expects to have a premium level of label that is solely McLaren Vale fruit. Look for the **Beresford McLaren Vale Shiraz**, a big ripe wine with stacks of chocolate and black berries, and soft tannins.

- **Hamilton** wines are showing great promise of late since the arrival of its new winemaker. The wines have been taken up to the next level of quality with generous, rich-fruited reds, such as the **Hamilton Centurion Shiraz, Hamilton Lot 148 Merlot** and, among the whites, is the minerally and lime-like **Hamilton Slate Quarry Riesling**.

- Long-time McLaren Vale grape grower, David Paxton, who knows how to grow great grapes, owns **Paxton Vineyards**. The family owns and runs vineyards across the country and sells the grapes to wineries. Their biggest venture is the McLaren Vale vineyards. (To diverge a little, to promote the quality of the Shiraz grape from this vineyard, Paxton makes a wine made under contract — **Paxton McLaren Vale Shiraz** — a wine with plenty of instant appeal with fruit, soft tannins and a round texture.)

- **Hugo Wines** makes ripe wines that use a good dose of oak, but without overdoing it. The **Hugo Cabernet Sauvignon** is worth finding.

- **Mitolo** specialises in making very individual wines with extremely intense flavours. Whilst the wines might be made from well ripened grapes, they don't slip into the 'overripe-and-jammy-and-all-too-much-of-everything' bag. Instead, these wines manage some refinement. Look for the **Mitolo GAM McLaren Vale Shiraz**, **Mitolo Savitar McLaren Vale Shiraz** and the **Mitolo Serpico McLaren Vale Cabernet Sauvignon**.

- **Mr Riggs** is the new venture of the former long-time **Wirra Wirra** winemaker, Ben Riggs. Along with various consultancy jobs, he makes the **Mr Riggs Shiraz**, a quintessentially McLaren Vale red showing ripe berries, chocolate nuances and just a very appealing 'I'll have another glass, please' sort of wine.

- **Noon Winery** is the home of some blockbuster reds, with ripeness that at times hits the 17 per cent alcohol mark (most reds are between 13 to 14 per cent alcohol). The wines are concentrated in fruit power, tannin and are almost sweet, given the high alcohol (see the sidebar, 'One for all and two for some'), such as **Noon Eclipse Grenache Shiraz** — as soon as you taste them, you never forget them.

- **Pirramimma Winery** is known for its 100 per cent Petit Verdot — the first Australian winery to make this variety by itself. Ordinarily, Petit Verdot finds itself as a small part of a Cabernet Sauvignon blend, rather than a stand-alone wine. But grown in the warmth of McLaren Vale, this winery makes a rich yet sophisticated medium-bodied **Pirramimma Estate Petit Verdot**.

- **Shottesbrooke** consistently makes good wine year after year. The outstanding drop from here is the **Shottesbrooke Eliza Shiraz**, which offers berry and spice and a good backbone of soft tannin.

- **Woodstock** on the flat, hot part of the region makes juicy, rounded **Woodstock Grenache**.

Joy-filled giants

At the larger end of the winery size spectrum are

- **Maglieri Wines:** Owned by giant wine company Beringer Blass, this winery reliably makes **Maglieri Semillon**, **Maglieri Shiraz**, **Maglieri Chardonnay** and **Maglieri Cabernet Sauvignon** each year. The wines are definite crowd pleasers with full fruity flavours and a judicious use of oak.

- **Rosemount Estate:** McLaren Vale is the home to its prestigious Balmoral Syrah, a wine that is oak-dominated when young but which, after five years or more, begins to balance the fruit and the oak weight for a generously flavoured wine. The other good product from this winery is the **Rosemount Estate GSM** — Grenache, Shiraz and Mourvèdre.

Chapter 17

Ambling around Adelaide

. . . .

In This Chapter

▶ Blending and making wines in Langhorne Creek

▶ Discovering Shiraz and Cabernet on Kangaroo Island

▶ Finding variety in Adelaide's bounty

. . . .

Most people who know about South Australian wines recognise the names McLaren Vale (refer to Chapter 16) and Barossa Valley (see Chapter 18). Fewer people, though, have heard of the interesting group of winegrowing regions I outline in this chapter. Here, I complete the regions of the South Australian Fleurieu wine zone — Langhorne Creek (with its fruit-driven reds), Kangaroo Island, and touch on Currency Creek. I also take you to the Mount Lofty Ranges zone's region of the Adelaide Hills, where the elegance of the cool-climate mix of reds and whites stars. (You can find information about wines from Clare Valley in Chapter 18, the other regions in this zone.)

The wines you can expect from Langhorne Creek are typical of the wine that Australia has built its reputation on — fruit-driven wines that are soft in tannin, which allows the wines to be consumed at a young age. Shiraz, Cabernet Sauvignon and Merlot stand out in this region dominated by red grapes. The Adelaide Hills has built its fame on elegant, cool-climate wines and offers a mix of whites and reds, where the stars are Sauvignon Blanc, Chardonnay in the whites and Pinot Noir in the reds.

I also introduce you to some wines from a few wineries that are established right in the centre of the capital itself. In time, lovers of Australian wine are going to be just as familiar with the quality drops from these lesser-known regions.

Appreciating Adelaide's Delightful Surrounds

Langhorne Creek, 70 kilometres southeast of Adelaide, and Kangaroo Island, a small island to the south of Adelaide, are two of the winegrowing regions of the Fleurieu zone, and the Adelaide Hills — literally in the hills, which are in the Mount Lofty Ranges zone — are just behind the South Australian capital.

To put the regions into perspective, in terms of their largesse within South Australia, here is an idea of their current sizes and production capabilities:

- **Langhorne Creek:** The region ranks fourth in the state, with more than 5,500 hectares of vines. As recently as 1990, just 450 hectares were planted. Industry advice indicates that this figure is still growing rapidly and the region is placed to soon overtake McLaren Vale (refer to Chapter 16) as the third largest South Australian region.

  For years the region has been a large grape-growing area, but not many of the Australian wine-drinking public would recognise the name. The reason is because, until recently, nearly all the grapes grown in the region were sold to other companies, wineries that made wine out of the Langhorne Creek region and who used the valuable, flavourful grapes to blend with others. Although over 70 per cent of the grapes grown in the region are still sold on, more of the locals are keeping some grapes for themselves, and making and marketing Langhorne Creek wine.

- **Kangaroo Island:** This region is tiny and is likely to stay that way given the isle has limited available land.

  Kangaroo Island is the domain of tiny vineyards run as a passion of the owner rather than as a full-scale business proposition.

- **Adelaide Hills:** The region ranks seventh with 5 per cent of the state's planting, or around 3,500 hectares. Growth in this area is likely to slowly increase but, due to the very hilly nature of the region, only a finite number of sites are suitable for growing grapes.

  The Adelaide Hills is made up of small to medium wineries that have carved out a market for themselves by delivering consistently high quality wine, albeit at reasonably expensive prices.

Varying the Climate

By definition, Kangaroo Island is influenced by a maritime climate. Langhorne Creek is across the mainland and close to Lake Alexandrina (an almost enclosed bay on the South Australian coastline), which means this region is also strongly influenced by its maritime location.

Up in the Adelaide Hills, things are really cool; in fact some pockets are marginal in their ability to consistently fully ripen some varieties. What the three climates do have in common is that they're all cool. The coolness in the maritime climates, however, comes from the sea breezes, and in the hills, the coolness is due to the altitude.

Appreciating cooling maritime climes

If it weren't for the closeness of the Southern Ocean, Langhorne Creek would be a warm vineyard region. Certainly, the days are warm, but you need to don a thick jumper for a night-time stroll. The sea breezes are cool, beginning during the mid-afternoon. Also, Lake Alexandrina is a large body of water, and its sheer mass keeps the surrounding area a few degrees cooler than countryside further inland. The climate is a bit like McLaren Vale's (refer to Chapter 16) warmth tempered by sea breezes, except much cooler at night. The reds from here are particularly good because the mild temperature suits Merlot and Cabernet Sauvignon — two varieties that, while they grow well in warm areas, can show their true varietal colours in cool climates. Shiraz, from warm climates such as McLaren Vale (Chapter 16), Barossa (Chapter 18) and Heathcote (Chapter 11) is big and bold and delicious. But in slightly cooler conditions Shiraz can also thrive, showing plenty of fruit flavour but without the big bodied texture and alcohol hit that the warm areas give.

The water connection in Langhorne Creek is particularly interesting. The vineyards are largely established on floodplains, made because of the diversion of the Bremer River. Each winter, the floodgates of the Bremer River are opened and the winter rainfall from the Mount Lofty Ranges pours through. At **Lake Breeze Wines**, for example, they allow the water to sit and soak for a day or two before releasing it to the next vineyard plot. This super saturation gives the vines a thorough watering and allows them to survive throughout the dry summer months.

Another wine region within Fleurieu's zone is Currency Creek. The climate in Currency Creek is also maritime because the region is right on the coast of South Australia, and climatically very similar to Langhorne Creek. So far, only three wineries exist but, with the large tracts of flat land available, Currency Creek may become a more prominent player in the future.

Across the waterway is Kangaroo Island. Only certain parts of the island are available for grapegrowing, partly because of the National Parks that occupy much of the island and also due to the fierce wind that buffets the ocean side of the island, making native grasses the only viable vegetation. Grape growing that does exist on Kangaroo Island has to contend with wet and cold winters and wind, which are quite fierce. The main vineyard area is on the northeast coast of the island and the island is a little protected here by the Australian mainland. (Refer to Chapter 13 for an explanation on how wind affects the vineyard.)

Understanding the hilltop altitude attitude

Like some of the other winegrowing regions across Australia, the grape growers choose the Adelaide Hills ('the Hills' as it is often shortened to) because of the coolness. Here is a region that, unlike its relative neighbours, such as the Barossa Valley (Chapter 18) and McLaren Vale (Chapter 16), can excel in the cool climate varieties such as Pinot Noir, Chardonnay and Sauvignon Blanc. The later ripening variety of Cabernet Sauvignon tends to struggle in the Hills, except on very specifically selected sites.

The main criterion for coolness comes from the region's altitude, which varies from 350 to 700 metres above sea level, depending on site selection. Another moderating factor to the climate is the breeze from Gulf St Vincent — the same breeze that cools the adjacent McLaren Vale region.

Most of the wineries claim simply the Adelaide Hills as their region. A few have opted to identify with one of the two sub-regions within the Hills — Lenswood and Piccadilly Valley. Generally speaking, Lenswood is a little warmer than Piccadilly Valley with steep slopes and an altitude of between 400 to 560 metres above sea level. Piccadilly Valley's landform is more undulating and the altitude ranges from 400 to 710 metres above sea level. Therefore, on the whole, Piccadilly Valley is cooler than Lenswood, and wetter, too. In fact, the Piccadilly Valley is the coolest sub-region in South Australia.

Harvesting Great Grapes

Cool climates, whether from maritime or altitude influences, allow wine producers to grow a variety of grapes successfully. The varieties that have a reputation in these wine regions are

- **Pinot Noir:** The king of the Adelaide Hills, in reputation and being the most planted red grape. The variety loves the cool climate, slowly ripening and developing all the nuances that Pinot Noir must develop to succeed as a wine. The subtle flavour and structure of Pinot Noir can't be found in a warm climate as the grape simply ripens too quickly and the core of great Pinot Noir is volatilised out of the grape by the heat of the sunshine. So the coolness of the Hills is perfect for making fragrant, feminine styles of Pinot Noir.

- **Chardonnay:** The principal white grape of both the Adelaide Hills and Langhorne Creek. In Langhorne Creek, despite its dominance of the white grapes of the region, Chardonnay only accounts for 8 per cent of total plantings; it's almost impossible to find a Langhorne Creek Chardonnay. Most of the crop is used in multi-regional blends. Conversely, the Adelaide Hills does Chardonnay very well, and you can find many top local wines to choose from.

  The key to Chardonnay in the Hills is similar to that of Pinot Noir — cool ripening weather to retain the delicacy of the grape flavours and to maintain the acidity. Chardonnay from the Adelaide Hills is typically fine and elegant in style and can age well.

- **Sparkling:** The other reason for growing Pinot Noir in the region is for sparkling *base wine* (see the sidebar 'Bottling bubbles for a sparkling surprise'). The coolness of the region means that the Pinot Noir grapes retain their acidity and don't become too full of flavour in the mid-ripening phase (which is important for sparkling base (refer to Chapter 7)). For the same reasons, Chardonnay is grown for sparkling base wines, because the coolness of the Adelaide Hills means that the grapes' natural acidity is retained, an attribute for this style of wine.

- **Sauvignon Blanc:** From the Adelaide Hills, and often toted as being Australia's best. The variety loves the coolness of the days, since these temperatures allow the vines to keep all the fresh fruity grape flavours and the acidity. The Adelaide Hills region isn't one that creates high vigour vines so the crop per vine is usually quite low. This low vigour, along with the coolness, acts to give the variety a definition of gooseberry and passionfruit that isn't overly herbaceous.

- **Cabernet Sauvignon:** A red with a niche for itself in Langhorne Creek, making up 44 per cent of red plantings and 39 per cent of plantings of all grapes in the region. For years, the local grape growers have known of this region's ability to grow great red grapes. Time passed before the locals set up wineries and now actually make the wines themselves. Although the region is cool, it can ripen Cabernet Sauvignon comfortably each year. Cabernet Sauvignon from the region is typically red berry dominant with a touch of mint creeping in, in the cooler years. Tannins are usually dusty and fine textured.

Over on Kangaroo Island Cabernet Sauvignon is the main grape. Here the climate is a little fierce, which aids in keeping the vines' vigour down and keeps the crop levels low. With still little wine coming off the island, the quality is hard to judge, but the recent Cabernets (see the section 'Hopping over to Kangaroo Island', later in the chapter) are promising.

In the Hills, Cabernet is a site-by-site proposition. Mostly, the region is too cool for this late ripening variety with a year every so often cooling down early in autumn and not allowing the grapes to fully ripen. The warmer sites are vital and those on the eastern slopes near the town of Mount Barker are promising.

✔ **Shiraz:** Makes up 37 per cent of the red plantings in Langhorne Creek (second to Cabernet Sauvignon) and 32 per cent of all grapes in Langhorne Creek. Again the story is the same for Shiraz as for Cabernet — nearly all the Shiraz grown in Langhorne Creek is sold to other companies and is blended. Out of those wines made locally, many of them are blended, too, but with locally grown Cabernet Sauvignon, making that quintessential Australian red blend of soft fruit flavours with a touch of mint. From a straight Shiraz you should expect plenty of ripe fruit flavours, some chocolate, earthiness and spiciness.

✔ **Merlot:** The third grape of choice in Langhorne Creek. Ripening a little before Cabernet, Merlot is able to show its full mulberry-like qualities and its soft tannin. Mostly, this variety is made as part of a blend where it does its job of filling out the middle palate of Cabernet, admirably. I imagine that, as the region develops, the winemaking side of grapegrowing is going to reveal some 100 per cent Merlots from this region.

Bottling bubbles for a sparkling surprise

A base wine is the beginning of a sparkling wine — red or white. The base wine for a sparkling red wine, for example, is made just the same as a red wine would normally be:

✔ The grapes are crushed, fermented on skins and probably aged in oak, resulting in still wine.

✔ The still wine goes through a traditional process to turn it into one with bubbles by inoc-ulating it with yeast (that is, a yeast culture goes in), adding sugar and bottling the wine.

As with all fermentation, the yeast converts the sugar to alcohol and carbon dioxide is produced. But, because this process takes place in a sealed bottle, the carbon dioxide can't just disperse into the air. Instead, the carbon dioxide dissolves into the wine and, hey presto, the base wine becomes deliciously bubbly.

Discovering Praiseworthy Local Wines

Langhorne Creek ranks as the fourth biggest vineyard region in terms of hectares under vine. Kangaroo Island has only one working winery. And by far the largest region, in terms of number of wineries, is the Adelaide Hills.

Linking up in Langhorne Creek

Langhorne Creek wine region has only eight wineries, and a further nine labels are made off site (see Figure 17-1). Leading the pack in terms of age, being the second oldest family-owned vineyard in Australia, is **Bleasdale Vineyards.** Goodies from here are

- ✔ **Mulberry Tree Cabernet Sauvignon:** My favourite from the Bleasdale range is this aptly named red. Although the name comes from the elderly mulberry tree on the property, the wine has fantastic mulberry and ripe berry flavours with a soft tannin finish. None of its wines is overpriced either.

- ✔ **Bleasdale Generations Shiraz:** The most expensive from here, and inexpensive considering the price of many Australian reds, which shows the regions classic ripe, soft fruity character along with an earthy tone.

- ✔ **Bleasdale Malbec:** You don't often find this red variety being made all alone. This wine shows a terrific fruit making and is a wine that's all too easy to drink.

Figure 17-1:
Wineries in
Langhorne
Creek.

Lake Breeze Wines is another winery that sells the majority of its fruit and has of late made its own label, too. Like its neighbours, the wines are all fruit and soft texture. The **Lake Breeze Bernoota Shiraz Cabernet Sauvignon** is all of those things and, like nearly all Langhorne Creek wines, this red is inexpensive.

Now in its fifth generation of farmers and grape growers is the Adams family vineyard of Metala fame. This family isn't the winemaker responsible for making the original Metala wines (a brand now owned by the Beringer Blass company and which typifies the classic Australian red of easy drinking — fruit-filled and a short-term ageing wine). The fruit for the Metala wines, though, has always come from this vineyard and for decades wine lovers have been enjoying the wine, probably never considering the region in which the grapes were grown. Today, the grapes are still sold to Beringer Blass to make the wine, but the Adams family has expanded its product. Since 1998, the family has used its vineyards, some as old as 115 years, to make its own wine. In doing so, the family business, along with others, is raising the profile of Langhorne Creek. The vineyard's new wine label is **Brothers in Arms** and has definitely made a big entrance onto the wine scene. The **Brothers in Arms Shiraz**, from the original Metala block, has definite fruit flavours but is underwritten by a savoury and earthy character that gives it a step above many simpler wines.

The winemaker at Brothers in Arms has his own little vineyard, too. David Freschi has had considerable international winemaking experience and makes the **Casa Freschi** wines. These wines are worth looking for, although hard to find:

- ✔ **Casa Freschi La Signora:** An interesting blend of Cabernet Sauvignon, Shiraz with a touch of Nebbiolo and Malbec. The result is a wine demonstrating more the European savoury perfumed style of wine, rather than the blockbuster fruit bomb typical of many South Australian wines.

- ✔ **Casa Freschi Profondo:** Top of the line and an expensive red made only when the fruit is top-notch quality. The blend is mostly Shiraz with some Cabernet Sauvignon, and is full of ripe fruit and a long liquorice backbone.

Established in 1988 is the relative newcomer to the region, **Bremerton Wines**. Like its neighbours the focus is on the red wines, with the particularly successful being

✔ **Bremerton Old Adam Shiraz:** Strikingly packaged, this wine is the label's flagship wine — generous in texture but without an over-ripeness that can lead to jamminess.

✔ **Bremerton Verdelho:** A good find is this tropical fruity and acid fresh wine.

✔ **Bremerton Tamblyn:** A ready drinking and fruit-packed wine that is a blend of Cabernet/Shiraz/Malbec and Merlot.

One of the pioneers of the organic grapegrowing practice in Australia is David Bruer who, in his former life, was head of the Oenology Department at the Roseworthy College in Adelaide. So his grapegrowing and winemaking theory should be good! The highlight of the **Temple Bruer** label is the **Temple Bruer Cabernet Sauvignon/Petit Verdot** blend.

A newcomer to the region is **Step Road Winery.** Among the reds made here is the **Step Road Sangiovese**, a medium-bodied wine with sour cherries and savoury tones.

Hopping over to Kangaroo Island

Over on Kangaroo Island, **Dudley Partners** is the only working winery. The eight remaining wine labels send their grapes to the mainland to be made under contract at another winery. A tiny industry was born where the only winery started life in a shearing shed. At **Dudley Partners Kangaroo Island** winery, a group of local sheep farmers and farm brokers came together to diversify their land holdings. The result is a small winery, now in more appropriate surroundings and with consultancy advice from the mainland. Some better-than-average Shiraz and Cabernet Sauvignon come from here.

Not far away is the **Cape d'Estaing** vineyard whose wines are exported to Europe and the United States and, although rarely seen in Australia, finding a recent Cabernet from this label is rewarding.

Probably the best, so far, is **Kangaroo Island Trading Company Special Reserve Cabernet Merlot**, being made and owned by the Adelaide Hills winery **Chain of Ponds Wines**.

Getting some altitude in the Adelaide Hills

Recently, the number of wineries in the Adelaide Hills region totalled just fewer than 50 (see Figure 17-2). One of the highest profile wineries in the Adelaide Hills is **Petaluma Wines** (in the Piccadilly Valley sub-region).

Petaluma Wines was started by a well-known identity in the Australian wine industry, Brian Croser. Today, the winery is owned by the brewing company Lion Nathan. Nothing seems to have changed, though, in the quality of winemaking and the style of the Petaluma wines.

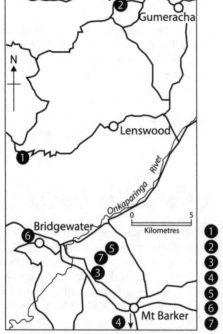

Figure 17-2: Wineries in the Adelaide Hills.

① Ashton Hills
② Chain of Ponds Wines
③ Hillstowe Wines
④ Longview Wines
⑤ Nepenthe Vineyards
⑥ Petaluma Wines
⑦ Shaw and Smith Winery

The fruit for the wines doesn't all come from the Adelaide Hills:

- **Croser Sparkling** wine is the top of the range, and uses fruit from Adelaide Hills in origin.

- **Petaluma Coonawarra** is a Cabernet blend, which, as the name says, is grown at the company's Coonawarra vineyards.

- **Petaluma Hanlin Hill Riesling** is one of Australia's best, and the fruit comes from the famed Clare Valley.

- **Petaluma Piccadilly Valley Chardonnay** is locally grown and shows the tight citrus flavours of the Hills with some stone fruit.

The second label from Petaluma is **Bridgewater Mill.** The wines come from grapes grown across many regions, and are always clean, well-made wines. Particularly popular is the **Bridgewater Mill Three Districts Sauvignon Blanc.**

Nepenthe Vineyards has made a bit of a stir since arriving on the wine scene. The winery sits atop a beautiful hilly range just outside the town of Hahndorf.

Wines to look for from Nepenthe are

- **Nepenthe Vineyards Sauvignon Blanc**, a consistently high quality with a zesty acidity, and gooseberry fruit flavours.
- **Nepenthe Vineyards Pinot Noir**, a savoury and brooding fruit driven red.
- **Nepenthe Vineyards Tempranillo**, one that adds a twist to its range as a fruity and spicy wine with touches of earthiness.
- **Nepenthe Vineyards Lenswood Zinfandel**, sweet fruited, with plenty of the variety's trademark alcohol weight — usually around 16.5 per cent alcohol.

A small producer in the area is **Ashton Hills Vineyard**. The best from here are

- **Ashton Hills Pinot Noir**, a fragrant style of Pinot Noir, typically with hints of cherries and truffles.
- **Ashton Hills Riesling**, a white from the cool Adelaide Hills that has the lime and lemon zesty acidity.
- **Ashton Hills Salmon Brut**, a deliciously strawberry and soft, sparkling wine.

Next door to Nepenthe is the new, state of the art, **Shaw and Smith Winery** (see Chapter 28 where I talk about the ten top cellar doors). The cousins Martin Shaw, an experienced winemaker in Australia and one of the original 'flying winemakers' ('see the sidebar Flying Aussie/Kiwi winemakers'), and, Michael Hill Smith (part of the Yalumba family) set up the winery. So, neither is shy to the winemaking game.

Renowned wines from here are

- **Shaw and Smith Sauvignon Blanc**, showing the crispness of fruit and acidity typical of cool grown Adelaide Hills grapes.
- **Shaw and Smith M3 Vineyard Chardonnay**, a consistently high quality with delicate fruit, barrel toastiness and an ability to age for more than five years.

Near the town of Lenswood is **Geoff Weaver** wines. The cool climate at the altitude of around 500 metres means that the Sauvignon Blanc is bursting gooseberry fruits and an acid zing. The **Geoff Weaver Chardonnay** has a reputation for being long-living.

Knappstein Lenswood Vineyards is another winery that reinforces the fact that the Adelaide Hills does Sauvignon Blanc very well. Also excellent is the savoury, soft tannined **Knappstein Lenswood Vineyards Pinot Noir**.

Tim Knappstein is the winemaker and owner of Knappstein Lenswood Vineyards winery. His first winery was called Knappstein Wines, which he sold to the Petaluma group. Knappstein Wines continues to trade under this name and is located in the Clare Valley (see Chapter 18). A little less confusing, now.

Chain of Ponds Wines rose from nowhere to establish itself as a reliable winemaking company. Some of the best in the range are the easy, early drinking wines:

- **Chain of Ponds Novello Rosso**, a rosé blend of Sangiovese and Grenache.
- **Chain of Ponds Novello Nero**, a fruit bomb wine made from Barbera, Grenache and Sangiovese.

Longview Vineyard, although a new addition to the Adelaide Hills region, is also a fine winery. Currently, the wines are made under contract at a few local and McLaren Vale wineries. Look for these colourfully named wines:

- **Longiew Black Crow Nebbiolo**, with a spicy and cinnamon nose that opens up to plenty of cherries and long-living tannins.
- **Longview Devil's Elbow Cabernet Sauvignon,** with plenty of oak to show when young, and which integrates well after two or more years in bottle.
- **Longview Whippet Sauvignon Blanc**, with plenty of tropical fruits as well as balancing of herbal flavours and a fresh acidity.

The giant brewing company Lion Nathan, which incidentally also owns Petaluma, Stoniers and Mitchelton wine companies, owns **Hillstowe Wines**. The quality across the portfolio hasn't suffered since the 'big took over the small', either. A few wines to search out are:

- **Hillstowe Udy's Mill Pinot Noir**, a medium weighted Pinot with a quite savoury and dark plum nature.
- **Hillstowe The Scrub Block Lenswood Pinot Gris**, a citrus and honey flavoured wine with good acid balance.

Flying Aussie/Kiwi winemakers

A phenomenon that arose in the mid-1980s was the concept of a 'flying winemaker'. Australian and New Zealand winemakers have always travelled to Europe during the Northern Hemisphere's vintage to see how things are done over there. Originally, this visit meant just a wander through the district with perhaps an opportunity to work a week in a French winery. Gradually, though, this journey became almost *de rigeur* for young graduates from the winemaking degrees.

Australian and New Zealand winemakers are less busy in their own wineries during the August–September months, perfect to venture to Europe to broaden their horizons. Added to this benefit, is the reputation of the winemakers from the Antipodes to work hard and long hours, and to keep the wineries spotlessly clean, a basic winemaking tool that was sometimes overlooked

in many European wineries. The added benefit to the overseas employers is that these young winemakers are all highly qualified, having gone through a four-year science-based tertiary degree.

The initial destinations for these flying winemakers was Southern France and Italy but the idea soon spread to lesser-known wine countries such as Hungary and Moldova. Before long, agencies were set up to recruit winemakers to work for the whole vintage, sometimes with absolutely no knowledge of the language. Indeed, many new graduates spend the first years of their qualified winemaker's life travelling between vintages, starting the year in the warm regions of Australia before moving south to the cool regions, then a brief holiday before arriving in Europe in their autumn.

Making and growing — or not

As a twist to the usual winegrower–winemaker routine, Adelaide has a few wine labels that either don't own any vineyards or don't own a winery, or both. Some winery addresses are a central Adelaide location where, other than one operator, no wineries actually exist. A few scenarios explain this phenomenon:

- **Lengs and Cooter:** The owners of this label undertake another slant on the method. They're happy to make the wine, they just purchase the fruit from various regions — Riesling from Watervale in the Clare Valley, Pinot Noir from Adelaide Hills and so on.

- **Peter Rumball Wines:** This winery is situated right in the middle of the city of Adelaide. Rumball's specialty is sparkling red. His hands-on involvement begins about mid-way through the winemaking. Firstly, he buys the fruit from the grape growers, then he has the base wine made at a regional winery. Rumball then takes over to create the second fermentation in the bottle, ageing the wine on the lees and the final disgorging. The wines are a fantastic example of this quirky Australian wine, where full-bodied Shiraz wine is made into a rich, soft and luscious sparkling wine.

✔ **Will Taylor Wines:** The owner of the label owns neither vineyards nor a winery, nor is he a winemaker — Taylor's a city lawyer who specialises in wine law. Instead, he recognises the top grapegrowing regions for specific varieties and buys grapes from trusted vineyards. He then takes his fruit to a well-admired local winemaker who does the winemaking for him. As a result, Taylor has the **Will Taylor Riesling**, made from Clare Valley fruit by Knappstein winemaker, Andrew Hardy. Over in Victoria, Martin Williams makes the **Will Taylor Pinot Noir** from Yarra Valley and Geelong fruit. All are top-flight wines.

Chapter 18

A Tale of Three Valleys: Barossa, Eden and Clare

*H*ere is a story about three valleys which are quite close in terms of distance but which are all very different from each other — the Barossa, Eden and Clare Valleys. The Barossa Valley and Eden Valley regions are part of the Barossa zone, and the Clare Valley is part of the Mount Lofty Ranges zone. (For more information on the classification of Australia's geographical wine zones, refer to Chapter 3.)

The Barossa Valley is probably the best-known winegrowing region in South Australia — it certainly is the most visited region.

The Eden Valley lies to the south-east of the Barossa Valley. Actually, Eden Valley is the name of the central town and it's far from being a valley — the boundaries of the region are in the Barossa Range at an altitude of 400 metres above sea level! Two sub-regions lie within the Eden Valley — High Eden and Springton.

The Clare Valley is located a little to the north of the Barossa Valley. At the time of writing, five sub-regions are under consideration to be so designated (see the section 'Classy Clare Valley', later in this chapter).

In this chapter, I take you on a tour through these famous South Australian wine regions, introducing you to some of the well-known and not-so-well-known Australian wineries — the common denominator is that they're all producers of good wine! For some reason, people drop the word 'Valley' when they talk about the Barossa and Clare Valleys, but Eden Valley always gets its full title. This chapter, then, is all about the Barossa, the Clare and Eden Valley.

Big, Bold and Brassy: The Barossa Valley

Like so many of the Australian and New Zealand wine regions, the Barossa was pioneered by immigrants, many of them from Germany and Silesia (now called Poland). Johann Gramp planted his first vines at Jacob's Creek in 1847; little did he know that these early plantings would be the start of what is today one of the world's biggest-selling red wines (**Orlando Jacob's Creek**).

Many settlers from England were also involved in the early days of the Barossa. The English brewer Samuel Smith planted a vineyard and called it **Yalumba**; this winery is today still owned by the Hill Smith family.

The centre of the Barossa is the town of Nuriootpa. Don't worry about trying to pronounce it — the locals simply call it Nuri. Other townships of note are Tanunda and Rowland Flat.

Finding the climate hot and dry

The Barossa is definitely a hot and dry climate. Annual rainfall is moderate, with most rain falling during the winter months. Summer heat leads to considerable loss of water due to evaporation, so any rainfall the Barossa gets during the growing season is gratefully received. Most of the vineyards are located across the broad flat land that is the Barossa Valley floor. Other vineyards are located in the surrounding low hills at altitudes of up to 350 metres above sea level, which makes them a little cooler.

The generally applied rule is that for every 100 metres above sea level that you travel, you drop about one degree Celsius in temperature.

The warm-to-hot weather — summer daytime temperatures of 25 to 35 degrees Celsius are normal — lasts into autumn and the harvest time. For this reason, mechanical harvesters do much of the grape picking in the cool of the night. Harvesting at night means the grapes are processed before they get too warm and the juice begins to oxidise; this is particularly important for white grapes, which are more susceptible to *oxidation* than are red grapes (see the sidebar 'Oxidation explained').

Some of the older vineyards are unable to be machine harvested due to the style of trellising used and vineyard management systems. The fruit from these vineyards is harvested at first light so that the fruit is brought to the winery while it's still cool from the night before.

TECHNICAL STUFF

Oxidation explained

Oxidation of the juice occurs as soon as the skin of a grape is split. The nature of machine harvesting is that, depending on how efficiently the machine operates, a certain proportion of the grapes are damaged and split, allowing their juice to run.

This juice is then susceptible to oxidation, which occurs at a faster rate at higher temperatures. Oxidation of the juice means that some of the fruit flavours are lost to the air; the browning of the aromatic acids in the skin also leads to some bitterness in the resulting wine.

Showing off with some top drops

The fertile valleys and gently rolling landscape of the Barossa produce a wide diversity in its wine. The region is renowned for its reds, but it produces some mean whites, too. In this section, I describe some of the varieties produced by the wineries of the Barossa.

Cabernet Sauvignon

In some ways, Cabernet Sauvignon plays second fiddle to Shiraz in notoriety as well in the amount of fruit devoted to its making. However, Cab Sav makes up 14 per cent of the grape intake from the Barossa vineyards, and over 20 per cent of all the red varieties grown.

In a warm climate, Cabernet Sauvignon can tend to loose its classic trademark elegance. The fruit flavours are certainly ripe so you won't taste any herbaceous tones in Barossa Cabernet. Instead, you get quite a high-alcohol wine, blackberries and some dry, dusty tannins. (*Dry tannins* are those that feel as if they're drying up the saliva in your mouth.) Much of the Cabernet fruit goes into making blends of wines; it's most often blended with Shiraz. For those who love the pure expression of Cabernet Sauvignon, the Barossa may not be you, but if you like it big, ripe and full flavoured, look for Elderton Wines and Peter Lehmann Wines.

Grenache

I've always had a bit of a soft spot for Grenache, and its unashamedly fruity, perfumed and spicy style. Some of the oldest Grenache vines in Australia are in the Barossa, because Grenache has always been part of the Barossa story. Today, Grenache ranks as the third most-grown red grape, and much of it makes its way into a blend.

For some reason, Grenache spent many years unloved and unrecognised, being used merely as one of the grapes in a blend. Few winemakers bothered to name it on their labels. However, fashions change and wine lovers have recognised this rather appealing grape variety for what it is. The rise in profile of France's Rhône Valley wines, of which Grenache often plays a significant part, has certainly helped its profile here.

Yalumba is one of the wineries that makes a straight Grenache. Charles Melton Wines and Turkey Flat Vineyards both produce a rosé-style Grenache, while Charles Melton makes a blend of Grenache, Shiraz and Mourvèdre.

Semillon

Semillon thrives in the heat of the Barossa — in fact, the climate of the Barossa could ripen any grape variety, such is its warmth! A Barossa Semillon is quite a different wine from those famous Hunter Valley Semillons (refer to Chapter 5). The grapes are fully ripe and the resulting wines are full-bodied and ready to drink. The climate is also dry which means there is less of a threat of the fungal disease *Botrytis cinerea* (refer to Chapter 8 for more information about this fungus), which often afflicts Semillon in regions that get high rainfall.

Semillon is prone to the *Botrytis cinerea* fungus, due to its large berries that are packed tightly within the bunch. In a wet climate, if one berry splits and subsequently mould develops, all the berries in the bunch develop mould or rot. The infection then spreads to adjacent bunches, and so on. In the Barossa, rain at vintage isn't common, so Semillon can stay on the vine without much risk of fungal disease, and so the fruit can ripen fully.

Some of the best Barossa Semillon comes from the wineries of Peter Lehmann and St Hallett.

Shiraz

Shiraz is the 'monarch' of the Barossa, making up 40 per cent of all grapes planted. The warmth of the region, the lack of rain and the low cropping levels all conspire to making the intensely structured wines.

A low-cropped vine would produce less than 2 tonnes to the acre (grape growers most often talk about metric tonnes to the imperial acre). To describe this output in metric measurements, as young viticultural graduates do, this is about 5 tonnes per hectare.

The Barossa crop levels are low due to a shortage of useable irrigation water to supplement the low seasonal rainfall. However, the best grapes in the Barossa are grown without much extra water, which allows the grapes to concentrate in intensity.

Barossa Shiraz usually has a fairly high alcohol content, at 14 per cent or more. The flavours tend to be a mixture of savoury, spice and liquorice. Often the choice of oak for maturation is American oak, so expect some of the sweet coconut flavours that are typical with this style of oak. Barossa Shiraz can easily be drunk young and also ages well in the medium to long term.

Among the best producers of Shiraz are Torbreck, St Hallett, Peter Lehmann and Hewitson, and Penfolds range of Bin wines.

Touring some well-known wineries

The Barossa is full of history — even some of its ancient vines have interesting stories to tell. In addition to some very interesting old buildings that have fascinating historical connections going back to the 1800s, you're also surrounded by some very interesting wineries producing some very fascinating vintages (see Figure 18-1).

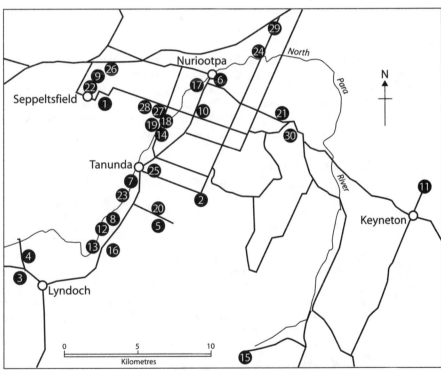

Figure 18-1: Fascinating vintages from wineries of the Barossa Valley and its lofty neighbour, Eden Valley, South Australia.

❶ Barossa Valley Estates	⓫ Henschke Wines	㉑ Saltram
❷ Bethany Wines	⓬ Jacob's Creek	㉒ Seppeltsfield Winery
❸ Burge Family Winemakers	⓭ Jenke Vineyards	㉓ St Hallett
❹ Charles Cimicky wines	⓮ Langmeil Winery	㉔ The Willows Vineyard
❺ Charles Melton Wines	⓯ Mountadam	㉕ Turkey Flat Vineyard
❻ Elderton Wines	⓰ Orlando-Wyndham	㉖ Two Hands Wines
❼ Glaetzer Wines	⓱ Penfolds Wines	㉗ Veritas Winery
❽ Grant Burge Wines	⓲ Peter Lehmann	㉘ Whistler Wines
❾ Greenock Creek Cellars	⓳ Richmond Grove	㉙ Wolf Blass
❿ Hamilton's Ewell Vineyards	⓴ Rockford Wines	㉚ Yalumba Wine Company

Charles Melton Wines

One of the top wineries in the Barossa must be **Charles Melton Wines.** Everything about this winery smacks of a passion for winemaking. Like so many of the Barossa wines, the wines here are made from both winery-owned vineyards and contract growers. And without a doubt, this is one vineyard that regards its grape suppliers highly, as year after year the wines are top class.

Favourites of mine include the **Charles Melton Nine Popes**, which is a blend of Grenache, Shiraz and Mourvèdre. This wine has a great spiciness, good tannin backbone and lovely rich fruits. Also the **Charles Melton Rose of Virginia**, a rosé made from Grenache grapes that are fruity without being lolly-like and sweet. The **Charles Melton Shiraz** definitely has its origins in the Barossa but is balanced in weight without too much oak influence.

Elderton Wines

Another quintessential Barossa winery that makes wines that are unashamedly big in alcohol, oak use and fruitiness, Elderton has as its flagship wines the **Elderton Command Shiraz** and the **Elderton Ashmead Cabernet Sauvignon**. The Command Shiraz is massive in its weight and has loads of new oak flavours, while the Cabernet, made from ripe fruit, is in more of a blockbuster style than varietal. Both wines need time in the bottle.

Leo Buring Wines

Leo Buring has long been a name synonymous with extremely high-quality Riesling. Leo Buring's long-time winemaker, John Vickery, built up this reputation and the current winemakers have kept the quality high (these days, John is semi-retired and consulting to Richmond Grove).

The top of the range is the **Leo Buring Leonay Riesling**, a wine that ages incredibly well and develops with bottle age from a wine that is lemon-dominated wine to one with soft mouthfeel and toasty flavours. Also worth looking for is the citrus and floral **Leo Buring Eden Valley Riesling** and the herbal and musk-like **Leo Buring Clare Valley Riesling** (incidentally, both wines also age very well).

Orlando-Wyndham

This large Australian wine company, which also owns Richmond Grove (see later), has its headquarters in the Barossa. Part of this winery's portfolio is the world-famous **Orlando Jacob's Creek,** which (as the marketing people aren't backward in telling you) is poured into a million wine glasses across the world every day. So, clearly, this is a wine that appeals!

The Jacob's Creek label that initially attracted all the attention was the **Jacob's Creek Shiraz/Cabernet** blend. Over the years, while this blend still leads the pack, the entire range has gained worldwide success. A number of varietals have been developed under the brand name, including **Jacob's Creek Riesling**, **Jacob's Creek Semillon Sauvignon Blanc** and **Jacob's Creek Chardonnay**, all well made and good value.

No-one at the winery expects you to sit and pontificate on the aromas, hue or flavour profile of the wines; the Jacob's Creek range is made directly for the value-for-money section of the market, and has to this day never missed a beat when judged by this criterion.

Buoyed by the success of the 'standard' Jacob's Creek, a **Reserve** label has been added. And, yes, for value — albeit at a higher price — wines bearing the Reserve label are a good drop. Look for the **Jacob's Creek Reserve Cabernet Sauvignon**.

Another well-priced range (around $14 per bottle at the time of writing) from this wine company is the **Orlando Gramp's** line of wines. The **Gramp's Barossa Grenache** is typical of this variety in this region, with simply loads of cherries, raspberries and a soft tannin finish. If you're looking for a mid-priced sparking wine, the **Orlando Trilogy Brut Non Vintage** isn't expensive (approximately $13) and has biscuity flavours with a fresh citrus finish.

One of the top wines from this company is the **Orlando St Helga Eden Valley Riesling**. Year after year, this Riesling is a zingy and citrus wine that shows great potential for ageing.

Penfolds Wines

The headquarters of this large Australian wine company is on the main street that goes through Nuriootpa. The owners of Penfolds are Southcorp Wines, and its Barossa facility is indeed mammoth.

A huge range of labels come under the Penfolds banner, from the lower range but good-quality Penfolds Koonunga Hill Shiraz Cabernet to the famous Penfolds Grange. Much of the Penfolds range is made from a blend of grapes grown in many regions; blending is very much part of the Penfolds winemaking culture. Some of the company's best wines are

- ✔ **Penfolds Yattarna Chardonnay:** This wine was dubbed the 'white Grange' by many, such was the hype that surrounded its 1995 release in 1998. The first few releases of this wine were quite dense in flavour, lacking the right balance of acid and subtlety and they aged quite quickly. However, by 1998, the wine had become more restrained in flavours when young, showing hints of citrus, peaches and new oak, and developing over time into a soft textured wine reminiscent of toast and honey.

✔ **Penfolds Grange:** How can Penfolds' wines be discussed without a mention of what has become one of Australia's best-known wines? To this day, Grange is still the most sought-after wine on the wine-auction circuit. Buyers are desperate to get a bottle of each vintage so they can have the whole collection.

Penfolds Grange was made as an experimental batch in 1951, and the first commercial release was from the 1952 vintage that was released a few years later. Today, it still holds iconic status. Each new release is eagerly awaited, despite the price tag (often over AUD$400 per bottle).

The Grange is a blend of Shiraz and, depending on the year, some Cabernet Sauvignon. No one wine region can claim to be the sole producer of grapes for Grange, though it's fair to say that grapes from the Barossa Valley are almost always a part of the blend. The wine is robust when young, showing loads of blackberry and new wood. Over time, these flavours evolve into nutty, meaty, liquorice flavours.

✔ **Penfolds St Henri Shiraz:** Considered 'poor-man's Grange', this wine retails for around AUD$60 a bottle. I must say that I often think of this wine as more satisfying than Grange — perhaps it just seems to deliver a lot for the price. Expect a blackberry and spicy aroma with a generous and soft mouthfeel of liquorice and dry tannins. The wine also ages well for at least 15 years.

✔ **Penfolds Bin 407 Cabernet Sauvignon:** A wine that has had quite a loyal league of followers over the years, because many people look to Penfolds for their Cabernet Sauvignon. The Bin 407 is fruit dominant with blackberry and violet aromas, along with a blackcurrant-flavoured palate. You can drink it young or age it in your cellar for 10–15 years.

✔ **Penfolds Koonunga Hill Shiraz Cabernet:** Always terrific value at less than $15, Koonunga Hill is an easy, everyday drinking wine. The wine is fruity and has soft tannins to balance.

Peter Lehmann Wines

One of the best-known characters and long-time ambassador for the region is Peter Lehmann. His winery offers a vast array of wine types, all made to a high quality, from the zesty and citrusy **Peter Lehmann Semillon** to the richly weighted **Peter Lehmann Chardonnay**.

The **Peter Lehmann Cabernet Sauvignon**, **Peter Lehmann Merlot** and **Peter Lehmann GSM (**a spicy and raspberry-like blend of Grenache, Shiraz and Mourvèdre) are all top notch and well priced. The flagship **Peter Lehmann Stonewell Shiraz** shows the Barossa at its best, with lashings of blackberries and spice, and an undercurrent of oak.

Richmond Grove

This winery comes under the Orlando-Wyndham banner. The **Richmond Grove Barossa Shiraz** is true to the Barossa style — big and juicy fruited, though these days this Shiraz is less oak dominated.

The jewel in Richmond Grove's crown is the **Richmond Grove Watervale Riesling**, a refined wine that captures the delicacy of Riesling and lives on in the bottle for years. (Watervale is in the Clare Valley, described later in this chapter.)

Rockford Wines

One of the region's most renowned wines is made at Rockford, the **Rockford Basket Press Shiraz**. While the wine is definitely full in body, it isn't a big fruit bomb of a wine; instead the wine is savoury and earthy. The name refers to the old style of grape presses that were used before the advent of today's pneumatic bag presses. Rockford Wines still uses the basket press for this wine, believing that this method gets the best results.

St Hallett

One label that can always be relied on for value and reliability is St Hallett. For a long time, St Hallett has honed its winemaking skills on its flagship wine, **St Hallett Old Block Shiraz**. As is the case across the Barossa, the vines are up to 100 years old and are cropped at low levels to make the fruit flavours very intense.

The **St Hallett Faith Shiraz** is a blend of fruit from both the Barossa and Eden Valleys, the Eden Valley fruit making the wine a little more restrained in weight and power than the Old Block Shiraz. In terms of white wines from the Barossa, **St Hallett's Blackwell Semillon** is one of the leaders. Unlike many Semillons that are made in a fruit-driven style, this wine has been barrel fermented and aged on lees giving it more of the nutty tones.

St Hallett's lower priced everyday drinking wines are the **St Hallett's Gamekeeper's Reserve**, a red blend of a Grenache, Mourvèdre, Shiraz and Touriga, and the **St Hallett's Poacher's Blend** made from Chenin Blanc, Semillon and Sauvignon Blanc. Both are well-made, fruit-filled wines that are well worth trying.

Saltram Wines

Owned by the Beringer Blass Wine Estates, this winery is making a vast array of wines across all price points.

The **Saltram No. 1 Shiraz**, their current flagship wine, is the quintessential 'fruit bomb' Barossa Shiraz, layered with loads of American oak and, at the time of writing, costs about AUD$65. Saltram has plans to release a higher-priced wine as its flagship in the future.

The **Pepperjack** label is one of the Saltram range of wines. All are fruit-filled and soft in tannin wines that are ready to drink when you buy them. Look for the **Pepperjack Shiraz** and **Pepperjack Cabernet Sauvignon**.

Seppeltsfield Winery

About 2 kilometres of date palms line the road to the historic Seppeltsfield winery, where the buildings have all been faithfully restored. Along the way, you see a majestic building that turns out to be the mausoleum of the Seppelt family.

Seppeltsfield is well known for its range of fortified wines. Although Sherry isn't a particularly fashionable style of wine these days, the **Seppelt Show Amontillado Sherry DP116** is absolutely one of the best. The Sherry is luscious, nutty and very well priced for the high quality. (*Note:* The 'DP116' is simply a winery bin number that has carried through to the naming of the wine.)

Also made by Seppelt is the famous 100-year-old **Para Liqueur Port**, which is the highest-quality batch of Port that continues the style of the line established. The oak barrel is larger than the average wine barrel, being 480 litres rather than the usual 225 litres. The twist here is that the wine isn't released for 100 years, so the current release is the 1904 vintage.

Not surprisingly, this century-old Port comes with a price tag attached; the 1904 vintage is selling for just over $1,000. If you're lucky enough to be able to try it, you find a thick and dense texture, almost treacly, while the palate is jam-packed with chocolate, rich fruit cake and toffee. Worthy of a once-in-a-lifetime experience if you can find a bottle — and some friends to share it (cost and all) with.

A less expensive yet still delicious Port is **Seppelt Show Tawny Port DP90,** which offers the flavours of dried fruits and roasted nuts and which has a luscious but not dense texture. (The 'DP90' indicates the winery bin number.)

Turkey Flat Vineyards

Along with the Charles Melton Rose of Virginia rosé (refer earlier) is the other famous Barossa rosé, the **Turkey Flat Rosé** from Turkey Flat Vineyards. Fruity and with a touch of sweetness, this rosé is a perfect wine for the Australian climate.

Also in the Turkey Flat range is the **Turkey Flat Semillon/Marsanne**, a rich and peachy white wine that is excellent value.

Fair play and pay in the vineyards

The relationship between the grape grower and winemaker is very important. In the days when supplies of grapes were plentiful, it wasn't unknown for winemakers to drop the grower who had supplied them with grapes in the past in favour of some other grower who promised to give them a better deal.

At that time, of course, the winemaker saved some money. However, times change and as the saying goes, 'what goes around, comes around'. With the boom in wine exports, grapes came to be in short supply. Now it was the grape growers who held the upper hand. Not unexpectedly, the grape growers were less inclined to do any favours for winemakers who had cast them aside in the past.

On the other hand, winemakers who had remained loyal to their grape growers and had supported them, even when they could probably get grapes cheaper elsewhere, reaped the rewards of their loyalty.

A good working relationship, where both parties strive to produce and use the best possible grapes, benefits everyone, especially the wine lover, for this harmonious state of affairs can only mean consistently good wine.

Wolf Blass Wines

Headquartered in the Barossa and owned by the Beringer Blass Wine Estates, Wolf Blass Wines makes a huge number of quality wines across several price ranges, from the low-priced **Wolf Blass Yellow Label Riesling** (a fruity, ready-to-drink summery wine) to the very expensive **Wolf Blass Black Label Cabernet Sauvignon Shiraz** (a Cab Sav dominant wine, aged in the bottle for four years before sale) and the **Wolf Blass Platinum Label Adelaide Hills Shiraz** (an ultra-premium and ultra-expensive — AUD$175 — Shiraz with an ultra-ripe and full style).

In the medium price range is the **Wolf Blass Grey Label Cabernet Sauvignon,** which has a blackberry and minty character and is made essentially from Langhorne Creek grapes (refer to Chapter 17). The house style of Wolf Blass is a wine that is big in fruit and flavour intensity.

Yalumba Winery

Despite being Australia's twelfth-biggest wine company, the Yalumba Wine Company is still family owned, being run by Robert Hill Smith, one of the descendants of the original owner, Samuel Smith.

Yalumba's headquarters are a little off the beaten track, through the town of Angaston. The company has a range of brands: From the **Oxford Landing** range and **Y** series at the lower end of the price scale, through to regional

Yalumba Barossa and **Yalumba Eden Valley** labels, and then individual flagship wines such as **Heggies, Pewsey Vale** and the **Octavius Barossa Shiraz**.

One wine that Yalumba has always made with great skill is Riesling. Two that are top quality are the individual vineyard selection **Pewsey Vale Eden Valley Riesling**, a Riesling with lemon and lime flavours made from grapes grown in the Pewsey Vale vineyard, and the **Heggies Eden Valley Riesling**, also a wine with lime-dominant flavours and long palate intensity. Both wines show great potential to age well.

Yalumba's skill with making white wine and its passion for the white grape Viognier have combined to make the glorious **Yalumba Eden Valley Viognier** and **Yalumba The Virgilius Viognier**. Both these wines are luscious in weight and packed with apricots, lychees and spice flavours.

Added to Yalumba's portfolio is the **Yalumba D Sparkling Wine** which, along with the recently acquired Jansz label, is made from fruit largely grown in the cool climates of Tasmania and Victoria. Both are finely beaded, delicately flavoured wines of high quality.

In the regional range, Yalumba has some noteworthy Barossa reds. The company was one of the first to release a wine that was 100 per cent Grenache, before the grape had gained its now-fashionable status. The **Yalumba Barossa Bush Vine Grenache** is full of ripe Barossa fruit that at times borders on jammy. This full type of wine has a strong following, especially among those who believe that if big is good, bigger is better.

Going off the beaten track and finding gold

Although the Barossa may be full of old vines and links to third-, fourth- and fifth-generation winemaking families, the region is also attracting many newcomers seeking lifestyle changes.

Great wine with unforgettable names

Particularly notable are **Torbreck** and **Two Hands Wines**, both of which are fond of giving the wines unusual names. As well as being good with names, both wineries make expensive, full-bodied blockbuster Shiraz. Most of the labels are made from Shiraz from different individual vineyards and at varying price levels. If you're after big-flavoured, high-alcohol, juicy-fruited and tannin-full wines, then the Shiraz from these two wineries is for you.

The Torbreck range includes wines with names such as

- ✔ **Torbreck Runrig:** The flagship wine from Torbreck Vintners, this wine is made principally made from Shiraz, with just a 3 per cent addition of Viognier to give even more fruit flavours on the palate. The texture is rounded and the flavours bold. Cellar this one for 10 years or more.

- ✔ **Torbreck 'The Juveniles':** No oak has been used to make this blend of Grenache, Shiraz and Mataro (also known as Mourvèdre). The wine is very fruity and spicy and ready to drink when young.

- ✔ **Torbreck Woodcutters Red:** The least expensive wine within the Torbreck range, this wine of 100 per cent Shiraz is easy to drink young, showing plenty of ripened blackberries and well-integrated soft tannin.

Two Hands produces wines with names that are quite different, also, such as

- ✔ **Two Hands 'Bad Impersonator' Single Vineyard Barossa Valley Shiraz:** Made from Barossa Valley fruit, this red is one of those big and powerful wines that are synonymous with much of the Barossa Valley — lush black berries, liquorice and earthiness sum up this wine

- ✔ **Two Hands 'The Bull and The Bear' Barossa Valley Shiraz Cabernet:** This blend of Shiraz and Cabernet Sauvignon allows the wine to be a little more refined than the other 100 per cent Shiraz wines made at this winery. The more elegant Cabernet Sauvignon tones down the overtly fruity Shiraz. This is a medium-bodied wine with aromas of cinnamon and herbs.

The Quiet Achievers

Throughout the Barossa Valley, you come across smaller wineries, often family owned, that are making exceptional wines, not only super Shiraz. The wineries listed here are some of those in the Barossa that are quietly going about making top wines.

- ✔ Barossa Valley Estates
- ✔ Bethany Wines
- ✔ Burge Family Winemakers
- ✔ Charles Cimicky Wines
- ✔ Glaezter Wines
- ✔ Grant Burge Wines
- ✔ Greenock Creek Cellars
- ✔ Hamilton's Ewell Vineyards
- ✔ Jenke Vineyards

✓ Langmeil Winery

✓ The Willows Vineyard

✓ Veritas Winery

✓ Whistler Wines

Small, Subdued and Sassy Eden Valley

The Eden Valley is tiny in comparison with its lower-altitude neighbour of the Barossa, and not only in area. In 2003, the total amount of grapes crushed in the Eden Valley was almost 9,500 tonnes, whereas in the Barossa, the amount was close to 50,000 tonnes. However, size doesn't necessarily matter and a number of very high-profile wineries have chosen to make the Eden Valley their home. In addition, many of the wine companies based in the Barossa source fruit from the Eden Valley (see the section 'Big, Bold and Brassy: The Barossa Valley').

For a while, the local grape growers considered calling the Eden Valley region the Barossa Ranges, as this more accurately describes the location of the region. But since the success of early Leo Buring Rieslings, which were made from fruit grown in vineyards adjacent to the town of Eden Valley, the name became associated with a place that produced high-quality wines, so the name stuck.

Cooling off in the Eden Valley

The Eden Valley is situated to the east of the Barossa Valley and its eastern boundary is 400 metres above sea level in the Barossa Ranges; the highest point in the region is around 600 metres above sea level. The altitude naturally means temperatures are a good deal lower than those on the floor of the Barossa floor, and rainfall is higher, as the rain clouds drop their rain at the higher altitude. In an average year, the winter rainfall is about 520 millimetres, with another 180 millimetres falling in the growing season of October to March.

The soils of the Eden Valley region are, for the main part, rocky and free draining, therefore vines established in the region have their vigour, or the amount of leaf growth they produce, naturally controlled. In a region with such high rainfall, extremely fertile soils would be a problem for the winemaker — the combination of rain and fertile soils leads to excessive vigour. The infertile soils therefore naturally manipulate the crop levels, reducing the amount of fruit the vines can grow and allowing the fruit that does form to be intense and concentrated in flavour.

Doing what the region does best

If the Barossa is defined by Shiraz, then the Eden Valley is just as strongly identified by its talent for Riesling. Shiraz, however, isn't overlooked.

Riesling

Riesling is the star of the white varieties from the Eden Valley. The cool weather allows for the citrus flavours and the zingy, fresh acid to be captured and retained in the grapes as they ripen. You can expect tight and citrus-dominated Rieslings, but with great potential to age. In the past, Riesling was often considered to be the poor cousin of Chardonnay. However, the Eden Valley has certainly turned that view on its head and Eden Valley Riesling is highly sought after.

Riesling is the most-grown grape in the Eden Valley, making up well over half of the total white grapes planted. The best Eden Valley Rieslings are from Pewsey Vale and Orlando St Hilary, as well as the blend known as *Mesh*. (See the sidebar 'Messing around for Mesh'.)

Chardonnay

The other white grape that enjoys the cooler climate of the Eden Valley is Chardonnay. The lower temperatures mean that the grapes ripen slowly and retain their natural acidity. In comparison to harvest time in the Barossa, harvest time for Chardonnay grapes is at least two weeks' later, which allows the grapes to ripen in the cooler days. An outstanding Chardonnay producer is Mountadam Vineyards.

Shiraz

Of the red grapes, Shiraz is the most planted in the Eden Valley. Most of the Eden Valley Shiraz is used as part of a blend with Barossa Shiraz. The Eden Valley fruit takes on a more spicy and peppery flavour and is more medium weight compared to the full-bodied Barossa Valley Shiraz. When the two regions are blended together, the result is a toning-down of the overt fruitiness and ripeness of the Barossa fruit.

Pinot Gris

Pinot Gris from the cool Eden Valley is able to produce a soft and elegant wine. The cool climate allows the grapes to maintain their acidity so you won't find an Eden Valley Pinot Gris that is dense in weight. The wine is quite refined, allowing the more minerally flavours to come through rather than loads of pineapple and honey, flavours which are more common in the warmer climates.

Merlot

Merlot from the Eden Valley makes wine with savoury and quite herbal flavours. The cool climate prevents the Merlot grape from becoming too ripe and turning into a full-bodied wine; instead, it is of medium weight.

Visiting Eden Valley wineries

The Eden Valley is an exciting region to visit. Its altitude and soils means its wines are quite distinct from those grown down on the floor of the Barossa Valley, and the cooler temperatures result in a longer growing season. All these factors result in grapes with different flavours. Refer to Figure 18-1 for the locations of wineries in the Eden Valley.

Henschke Wines

Now run by the fifth generation of winemakers, the Henschke winery is indeed one of Australia's most highly regarded wine labels. The head of the family is now winemaker Stephen Henschke, assisted by his wife Prue, a leading research viticulturist.

For years, the Henschke range has been built around some core red wines, such as the **Henschke Mount Edelstone Shiraz** and the **Cyril Henschke Cabernet Sauvignon**. The Shiraz is made from 90-year-old vines and is densely flavoured with liquorice and black berries balanced by a tannin finish. The Cabernet Sauvignon is made from Eden Valley fruit and it shows in the cassis and tobacco flavours so often seen in cool-climate Cabernet Sauvignon.

Henschke's **Hill of Grace** is the winery's most famous wine with a reputation that rivals Penfolds Grange (see the Barossa section 'Touring some well-known wineries', earlier in this chapter). This Shiraz is made from old vines in the spectacularly beautiful Hill of Grace vineyard. The vines themselves were planted back in the 1800s and in winter their gnarled and twisted leafless forms look stunning. The wine itself is a mixture of anise, blackberries and chocolate, balanced by a soft tannin finish.

Henschke also does a wide range of white wines. The **Henschke Tilly's Vineyard Dry White** is an excellent buy at approximately AUD$13.

Today, the Henschke family obtains its fruit from many sources, making wine from grapes grown at Lenswood in the Adelaide Hills (refer to Chapter 17). One of the wines from the region is the **Henschke Lenswood Littlehampton Innes Vineyard Pinot Gris**, a honey and lychee wine that finishes with a lift of acid.

Messing around for Mesh

A joint venture between Clare Valley winemaker Jeffrey Grosset and Robert Hill Smith of Yalumba in the Barossa saw them picking three different vineyards of Riesling in Eden Valley. Each winemaker took the grapes from alternate rows of vines and then made the wine separately at his own winery. The two men had already agreed on the style they were aiming for — a citrus-dominant wine with mineral-like flavours. The wines were tasted and ultimately blended to ensure this was the style that developed. Although **Mesh Eden Valley Riesling** can be enjoyed young, it develops softness and texture after five years in the bottle.

Irvine

An impressive straight Merlot wine is made by James Irvine, and is known as **Irvine Grand Merlot**. This wine was one of the first 100 per cent Merlot wines to be made in Australia and is savoury rather than fruity, with potential to age well.

Mountadam Vineyards

David Wynn chose the site for this vineyard in order to grow Chardonnay. The High Eden Ridge area, a sub-region of the Eden Valley, is perfect for this variety. The vineyard is at an altitude of 550 metres above sea level, so summers are cool. Typically, the **Mountadam Chardonnay** is bottle aged at the winery for a number of years before release and the wine is well weighted in flavour and alcohol, giving the wine a rich texture.

Another wine that is successfully made here is the **Mountadam Pinot Noir/ Chardonnay** sparkling wine, which is aged in the bottle for five years before leaving the cellars. This wine has soft bubbles and complex nutty and savoury tones.

Tin Shed Wines

Recently coming to the attention of wine lovers are the wines from Tin Shed Wines. Yes, the wines were originally made in a tin shed down on the valley floor of the Barossa, but now the two partners in the project have found a naturally insulated eighteenth century stone building in the cool Eden Valley, which is much more suitable for winemaking. Each partner owns a vineyard, one in the Barossa and the other in the Eden Valley, so the wines are often a blend of the two regions. The range from this winery is fairly limited. The wines are made without much intervention and are fermented using wild yeasts (see the sidebar 'Wild about yeast'). Worth trying is the **Tin Shed 3 Vines MSG**, a blend of Mourvèdre, Shiraz and Grenache that is loaded with spices and liquorice, with a touch of tar.

Wild about yeast

Wild yeast is a term that refers to the fermentation of wine using the yeasts that are found in the vineyards, on the skin of the berries and on winery equipment and walls (it is also known as *indigenous yeast*). Instead of selecting a *non-wild yeast* with which to ferment the wine, the winemaker just lets the grapes ferment with whatever yeasts are present. (A non-wild yeast is a yeast culture that has been bred up by the winemaker using commercially available yeast.)

In using the wild yeast method of fermenting wine, the winemaker is taking a calculated risk with the quality of the wine. For example, the winemaker doesn't know whether the acting yeasts are yeasts that can cause the wines to develop nasty flavours during the fermentation process. Aromas and flavours redolent of a barnyard or reminiscent of vinegar do not make a good wine.

The advantage to using wild yeast is that the wine that results may have enhanced mouth feel or other characteristics that the winemaker believes make a better wine. Most wineries in Australia and New Zealand use commercially available yeast for fermentation rather than wild yeasts.

Classy Clare Valley

The Clare (the name by which the Clare Valley is most often known in the region) is the most northern winegrowing region in South Australia, and some believe it to be the prettiest.

At the time of writing, the Clare is awaiting determination by the Geographical Indications (GIs) Committee to approve a number of sub-regions (refer to Chapter 3 for more information about GIs). Never a smooth process, the process has involved a fair degree of local political wrangling over boundaries and definitions, and which vineyards can or can't be included. If they all get approved, the sub-regions will one day be Auburn, Clare, Polish Hill River, Watervale and Sevenhill.

Cooling down in Clare

Because the Clare wine region is the most northern vineyard area in South Australia, you might think it's also the hottest. Yet while the days can get quite warm in the summer, the nights become cool.

From cork to screw cap — a sensible change

More than once in the Clare, the people in the wine industry have taken a stand to protect their reputation — the most recent example being their determination to rid their Riesling (and other wines) of the dreaded cork taint issues.

Corks are known to carry the risk of contamination by the naturally found chemical compound called trichloroanisole, or TCA. In a wine that is delicate and fragrant like Riesling, the slightest bit of taint from a cork ruins the wine. The winemakers became frustrated by the number of bottles that they opened and found to be *corked* (spoilt by the musty, dank flavour of cork taint). As a result, you find that most bottles of Clare Riesling are sealed with the technically sound screw cap seal. You can understand the winemakers' decision — if your next glass of Riesling smelt mouldy and dank, you wouldn't be too pleased.

These days, the screw cap closure method has been adopted for nearly all the Clare wines, both red and white, and has also been taken up by a huge number of wine producers in Australia and New Zealand.

The cool afternoon breezes that blow in during the summer from the Spencer Gulf to the west of the Clare and the region's elevation, which averages 450 metres above sea level, have the effect of producing wines with cool-climate characteristics. This sort of climate allows the fruit to achieve full ripeness and allows the natural acidity to be maintained along with the varietal characters of the fruit.

Experiencing the Clare's best grapes

The Clare Valley is very proud, and rightly so, of the wines it produces. The name Clare Valley sits prominently on the labels of wines that can make the claim that they're made from grapes 85 per cent of which are grown in the Clare Valley. The Clare is most renowned for its Riesling and Shiraz.

Riesling

Riesling is without doubt the star of the Clare. Although third in terms of the plantings in the region (behind Shiraz and Cabernet Sauvignon), its recent leap up the fashion stakes has seen Riesling enjoying the limelight.

Riesling particularly loves *diurnal* temperature changes, that is, warmth during the day and coolness at night. Certain areas in the region have become famous for their style of Riesling — the Watervale area makes wines that are approachable when young and are still delicious after ten to twelve years.

Shiraz

Shiraz is the most planted variety across the Clare, and is mainly found on the lower slopes, which leaves the higher slopes for Riesling that likes it cool. Although the Clare has pockets that are quite hilly and difficult to plant on, large tracts of land exist that allow for reasonably big vineyards. Because of the mild climate, Shiraz from the Clare takes on a more savoury, elegant and refined style in contrast to its big fruity cousins in the Barossa. However, Clare Shiraz still offers plenty of fruit-driven flavours.

Much of the Clare has *friable* red soil, which allows the roots of the vines to delve deep into the ground to absorb any moisture that is available during the growing season. Such a soil can be quite fertile and encourage the vines to grow lavish quantities of shoots and leaves. However, in the Clare, this doesn't pose a problem. As the growing season is quite dry, excessive vine growth isn't possible. (Like all plants, vines need water to grow a lot of foliage.)

Cabernet Sauvignon

While the climate of the Clare Valley allows the fruit for Cabernet Sauvignon to ripen satisfactorily each year, the wine doesn't enjoy the kind of reputation that Shiraz has made for itself.

However, if you're a fan of Cabernet, you won't be disappointed here. The Cabernet made in the Clare is good, with briary tones and the blackberry fruit flavours that are so often associated with the variety. Some years the days get a little too warm and the fruit loses a little of its classic character, but you still find some good offerings from the region. Among the best are those from Grosset Wines and, for some well-made and less-expensive wines, Taylors Wines.

Finding the crown jewels of Clare

The Clare is full of small- to medium-sized wineries (see Figure 18-2). The region has an old-world feeling about it, accentuated by the truly beautiful old buildings that dot the landscape and adorn the towns. The vineyards trail up the hills and over onto the plains and look like they've always been a part of the landscape. Clare, as you can see, is a bit of a favourite of mine. I start this section by describing some of the larger wineries of the Clare and the wines they make.

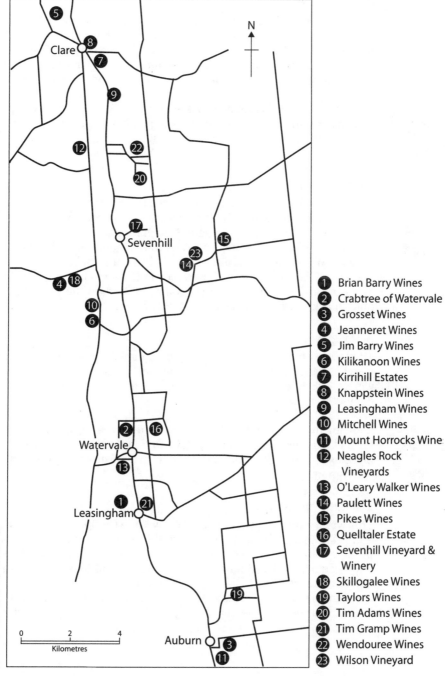

Figure 18-2: Historical beauty among the wineries of the Clare Valley, South Australia.

1. Brian Barry Wines
2. Crabtree of Watervale
3. Grosset Wines
4. Jeanneret Wines
5. Jim Barry Wines
6. Kilikanoon Wines
7. Kirrihill Estates
8. Knappstein Wines
9. Leasingham Wines
10. Mitchell Wines
11. Mount Horrocks Wine
12. Neagles Rock Vineyards
13. O'Leary Walker Wines
14. Paulett Wines
15. Pikes Wines
16. Quelltaler Estate
17. Sevenhill Vineyard & Winery
18. Skillogalee Wines
19. Taylors Wines
20. Tim Adams Wines
21. Tim Gramp Wines
22. Wendouree Wines
23. Wilson Vineyard

Annie's Lane

Annie's Lane is a large production label to come from the Clare, and is owned by Beringer Blass Wine Estates. Two levels of label are available: the standard **Annie's Lane** label and the **Annie's Lane Copper Trail**. Wines bearing the standard label are commercial and medium-priced wines that, while varying a little from year to year in quality, are usually good honest drops.

The **Annie's Lane Copper Trail Riesling** and **Annie's Lane Copper Trail Shiraz** are both fine wines. The Riesling shows the citrus and musk flavours so typically Clare, while the Shiraz resists the temptation to be too dense and ripe and is instead a refined, albeit full-bodied, Clare Shiraz.

Grosset Wines

One of the wineries at the top of my list is Grosset Wines. Riesling with the **Grosset** label was one of the Rieslings that prompted wine lovers to end their love affairs with Chardonnay and Sauvignon Blanc. Certainly, the **Grosset Polish Hill Riesling** is one of the absolute leaders in Australia, and the **Grosset Watervale Riesling** isn't far behind in popularity — both are stunning wines. Still in the Clare Valley is **Grosset Gaia Cabernet Sauvignon.** The wine comes from a small vineyard perched on the side of a hill and is quite blackberry and herbal with a soft finish.

Knappstein Wines

The Lion Nathan wine and brewing company today owns Knappstein Wines, which is fitting since the winery is housed partly in an old brewery. At this winery, you find honest, well-made wines that deliver on fruit flavour at a competitive price.

Look for the fruity and herbal **Knappstein Semillon/Sauvignon Blanc**, the lychee and musk-loaded **Knappstein Dry Style Gewürztraminer,** and the more expensive nutty and cassis **Knappstein Enterprise Cabernet Sauvignon.**

Leasingham Wines

This winery is now owned by the Hardy Wine Company (formerly BRL Hardy) and is another medium-sized label within a large company portfolio. As part of their commitment to showing you just how good aged Riesling from the Clare can be, the **Leasingham Classic Clare Riesling** isn't released until it has been aged in the bottle for four to five years. This is just as well, as most consumers would never have the strength of will to leave a bottle to age that long in their cellar. When eventually sold, the wine is full of nuttiness and soft acidity.

For an inexpensive and good-quality Riesling, you can buy the **Leasingham Bin 7 Riesling** and age it yourself. The wine has citrus and mineral tones when young that continue to develop softly with age. The other steals from this winery are the **Leasingham Bin 61 Shiraz,** a full-flavoured blackberry-fruited wine, and the densely textured cassis and chocolate **Leasingham Bin 56 Cabernet Malbec**.

The **Leasingham Classic Clare Sparkling Shiraz** is a fine example of that quirky Australian sparkling red style of wine — big and juicy ripe fruits with some pepper and spice topped off with fizz.

Taylors Wines

The vineyards of the largest vineyard owner in the region, Taylors Wines, fill the contours of the land perfectly. In the last few years, the quality of the wine from this winery has improved enormously. The three wines in their premium range are **Taylors St Andrews Cabernet Sauvignon**, **Taylors St Andrews Shiraz** and **Taylors St Andrews Riesling**, which are all particularly well made and very much show the characteristics of the Clare — plenty of flavour but without overripeness or a viscous texture.

Taylors Promised Land Cabernet Merlot and **Taylors Promised Land Shiraz Cabernet** in particular are inexpensive wines from this label that are well worth searching out. The wines are multi-regional blends and show good balance of medium body and flavour.

Meeting the smaller jewels in the crown

The labels described in the previous section wrap up the larger players in the Clare. In this section, I list the homes of some of the smaller, harder-to-find wines.

- **Kilikanoon Wines:** While not a large winery, Kilikanon Wines is attracting attention and high praise in wine circles. Quite a wide range is available, at very reasonable prices. The very good **Kilikanoon Morts Block Riesling** shows lemon and lime freshness.

  Top of my list here is the **Kilikanoon Oracle Shiraz,** which, while ripe, allows for the spiciness and pepper of Shiraz to shine through.

- **Mitchell Wines:** This respected winery is tucked away in a little valley near the town of Penwortham. Some of my favourites from this winery are the citrus and floral **Mitchell Watervale Riesling**, the black peppery and spicy **Mitchell Peppertree Vineyard Shiraz,** and the juicy-fruited and raspberry **Mitchell The Growers Grenache**.

- **Mount Horrocks Wines:** You can find this winery at Auburn, the town in the south of the Clare Valley. Alongside the excellent barrel-aged and hence toasty **Mount Horrocks Semillon** and the refined and spicy **Mount Horrocks Shiraz** is the **Mount Horrocks Cordon Cut Riesling**. This wine is made by cutting the cordon, or the cane of the vine, as soon as the grapes are ripe. The grapes are then left to shrivel, or *raisin,* on the cordon, which results in an intensification of the fruit flavours. These shrivelled grapes are then fermented to make a delicious dessert wine that avoids the thickness of texture that is a characteristic of many botrytised wines (refer to Chapter 8 for information on botrytised wines).

- **Neagles Rock Vineyards:** This winery is a newcomer to the Clare yet, already, its wines are coming to the notice of wine lovers for value and quality. Among the best are the black-cherry flavoured and plummy **Neagles Rock Sangiovese**, a deliciously spicy **Neagles Rock Grenache Shiraz** that has a hint of ripe black berries, and the lime-dominant **Neagles Rock Riesling,** which is definitely worth ageing.

- **O'Leary Walker Wines:** This winery is a newly constructed, well-designed ultra-modern facility. Both David O'Leary and Nick Walker were formerly winemakers with big Australian wineries and have acquired a great deal of technical know-how. Among the best from this winery are the **O'Leary Walker Watervale Riesling**, a herbal and musk like wine and the lime and tropical **O'Leary Walker Polish Hill Riesling**.

Highly recommended is the **O'Leary Walker Clare Valley McLaren Vale Shiraz**, which takes the elegance of the grapes grown in the Clare and blends it with the blockbuster personality of McLaren Vale grapes to make a wine that is somewhere in between. (I discuss the wines from McLaren Vale in Chapter 16.)

- **Pikes Wines:** Most of this winery's vineyards are located in the Polish Hill River area, which is at a higher altitude than most of the Clare and has poor, slatey soil. The altitude and soil type mean that the grapes get the chance to ripen slowly — harvest is about two weeks' later than in most other parts of the region — which allows the fruit to build in flavour without becoming overripe.

The **Pikes Riesling** is consistently very good, as is the **Sauvignon Blanc/Semillon**, which is fresh and fruity with a backbone of herbaceous character. Pikes has begun to make the **Pikes Premio Sangiovese,** which is a very appealing fruity wine. If Pikes is the first Sangiovese that passes your lips, you're going to be hooked on it.

The **Pikes Luccio White** and **Pikes Luccio Red** are both blends of a number of white and red grape varieties respectively. The wines are inexpensive, fresh-fruited and soft — perfect for relaxed lunches on the verandah.

- ✔ **Sevenhill Vineyard & Winery:** This winery is operated by Jesuit priests and is unique in Australia. The buildings were established in the 1860s and are still used today; the historical cellar is a must visit for anyone who visits the Clare. Every year, the wines from Sevenhill deliver quality. Among the best are the quite earthy **Sevenhill Shiraz** and the citrus-dominated **Sevenhill Riesling**.

- ✔ **Tim Adams Wines:** This winery consistently makes well-crafted wines. Top of my list are the well made, lemon and orange blossom **Tim Adams Riesling** and the full-flavoured spicy and liquorice **Tim Adams Aberfeldy Shiraz**.

- ✔ **Wendouree Wines:** The wines at this winery, made from grapes grown on very old vines, age beautifully in the bottle. The wines are nearly impossible to obtain, such is the demand. However, unlike other superb and hard-to-get Australian wines, these have remained at a reasonable price. If you can find the wine, look for the **Wendouree Shiraz**, an intensely flavoured blackberry and earthy type of wine.

Noting some other Clare Valley bounty

Some other noteworthy wines from wineries in the region:

- ✔ Brian Barry Wines has been making wine in the region for many years with his best wine being the **Brian Barry Jud's Hill Handpicked Riesling**, a floral and spicy fresh wine.

- ✔ Crabtree of Watervale continues the trend for the Clare Valley's wonderful Riesling wines. Typical of the Watervale region is the **Crabtree of Watervale Riesling** that has rich fruit flavours of citrus and pineapple, and it finishes with a long acid sensation.

- ✔ Jeanneret Wines is a small family producer making the fruity and spicy **Jeanneret Sparkling Shiraz**, along with top class Riesling — the **Jeanneret Riesling**.

- ✔ Jim Barry Wines is situated at the top end of the Clare Valley, a little winery all on its own. The top wine from here is the **Jim Barry The Armagh**, a rich, dense and earthy wine that should probably be stashed in your cellar until it is at least eight years of age.

- ✔ Kirrihill Estates has burst onto the Clare Valley wine scene with a big, brand new winery and large vineyard plantings. The quality of the wine is first class with the **Kirrihill Estates Clare Valley Shiraz** offering a rich palate of dark plums and blackberries. The Kirrihill Estates Clare Valley Riesling just reinforces the height to which this grape variety can reach with a long citrus palate.

- ✔ Paulett Wines produces a lime and mineral-like **Paulett Polish Hill Riesling** that is easy to drink when young but ages well also. The other wine from here that I particularly enjoy is the mellow and soft fruited **Paulett Cabernet Merlot**.

- Skillogalee Wines is a quaint winery in the hills that surround the Clare Valley. The most consistent performer from here is the **Skillogalee Riesling**, a floral wine with quite a rich, textured palate.

- The Wilson Vineyard is a small family business whose **Wilson Vineyard DJW** is a terrific lime-dominated and soft textured wine.

- Tim Gramp wines adds a name to the long list of fine Riesling producers with the citrus and pineapple like **Tim Gramp Watervale Riesling**.

Trailing after Riesling

You can meander through the Clare Valley on foot or on two wheels when you travel the Riesling Trail, a pathway established on a railway line dismantled long ago. The trail runs from Auburn in the south to the township of Clare in the north of the Clare Valley. In total, the trail is 27 kilometres long, and you can start and finish just where you like. Along the pathway are signs directing you to wineries and restaurants, and historical landmarks are also pointed out. Since vines are planted right to the edge of the trail and also cover the slopes of the surrounding hills, following the trail allows you to enjoy some very picturesque and tranquil scenery. Just imagine how good that first sip of Riesling will be after a day's ride . . . and the feeling that you have well and truly earnt it.

Chapter 19

Along the Limestone Coast

. . . .

In This Chapter

▶ Discovering the famed *terra rossa* soil

▶ Meeting the Coonawarra's star performer, Cabernet Sauvignon

▶ Finding out why Padthaway's Chardonnay is in such high demand

▶ Viewing the vistas of vines at Wrattonbully

▶ Enjoying the wines of scenic Mount Benson

. . . .

*T*he Limestone Coast, a Geographical Indications zone (refer to Chapter 3), lies roughly halfway between the cities of Melbourne in Victoria and Adelaide in South Australia. However, to visit the zone and its wine regions, you need to detour south from the highway that links the two cities.

Even if you've never heard of the Limestone Coast, you've likely heard of the Coonawarra wine region. The Coonawarra is the most well known of the wine regions of the Limestone Coast, although the Padthaway, Wrattonbully and Mount Benson regions are far from insignificant.

In this chapter, I introduce you to the famous *terra rossa* soil of the Limestone Coast, the soil that contributes so much to the zone's outstanding wines. After noting the climate and the wine varieties, I take you on a tour of the wineries and describe some of their excellent wines.

Finding the Answer in the Soil

The Coonawarra region produces the most exceptional wines due in no small part to its exceptional *terra rossa* soil. Other types of soil also occur in the region and produce wines with quite a different flavour. The star of the Coonawarra is Cabernet Sauvignon, though the region produces other great red wines.

The terra rossa soil of the Coonawarra is a red loamy soil overlaying porous calcium carbonate (see the sidebar 'Rock of ages'). The vineyards of the region enjoy excellent drainage during the winter rains, and the limestone that lies below, which is about two metres thick, acts as a natural water reservoir.

What all this means for the vines is that the free-draining soil takes the water away from the roots. The vine roots then have to struggle down into the layer of limestone to find water. Because the vine is constantly struggling to find water, it has to work extra hard to produce shoots and leaves and, in turn, grapes. This naturally limits the vine's vigour, with the result that the vine canopy is not overly vigorous, the amount of fruit produced is relatively low and the berries are small. Small berries give a high skin-to-pulp ratio and, since the flavour and the colour of the wine lies in the skin, the flavour of the wine is intensified.

A gently undulating landscape with a generous quantity of terra rossa, Padthaway is dominated by white varieties, especially Chardonnay — so much so that the region is often referred to as 'Chardonnay country', although the region also produces red wine varieties.

Wrattonbully also enjoys the famed terra rossa soil, which encourages the grape growers to plant red wine grapes, notably Shiraz and Cabernet Sauvignon. The vineyards stretch far into the distance, the vines in long straight rows. So far, the big wine companies are the companies that have invested in this region, planting large vineyards in order to grow grapes cost effectively.

Although Mount Benson is the newest kid on the Limestone block, the fact that the region has numerous outcrops of terra rossa points to a promising future; the region is already proving to be a quality producer.

Rock of ages

If you drive from Robe to Coonawarra, you pass over a series of 16 coastlines left behind as, through the ice ages, the ocean withdrew to its present level. Each of these coastlines was limestone, formed by tiny marine animals. Over the millennia, the limestone has broken down and other matter, including minerals, has been deposited on top.

The famous terra rossa soil that is found throughout the Limestone Coast zone — though nowhere in such concentration as in the Coonawarra — is russet-coloured topsoil over a thin layer of *calcrete* (calcium carbonate) that lies above a base of white limestone.

What's in the Coonawarra name?

Of all the Geographical Indication regions that have been defined across Australia, Coonawarra is probably the one that was the most drawn out and expensive to finalise. The problem was exactly how to define Coonawarra.

Many producers wanted the definition to include only vineyards actually situated on the famed terra rossa soil, but that became impractical because the distribution of terra rossa is inconsistent; other types of soil besides terra rossa can be found in a single vineyard.

The other problem was that many of the growers who are very much part of Coonawarra's history own vineyards that wouldn't qualify, because their vineyards are not 100 per cent terra rossa.

Some winemakers suggested that some producers should be allowed to qualify because of

the length of time they had been established in the region. However, this idea was not accepted, and it was off to court. The eight-year battle over the boundaries went as far as the High Court. The final determination resulted in one of the longest definitions ever produced (you can find it on the Australian Wine and Brandy Corporation Web site in Chapter 26). Such is the demand to be part of this region that vineyards planted on the terra rossa soil are on the most expensive vineyard land in Australia, with the land sometimes fetching over AUD$90,000 per hectare.

The easiest method to figure out if you have a genuine Coonawarra wine is to trust the label! If the label says 'Coonawarra', trust that the grapes came from that region. After such a protracted legal battle over region of origin, the Coonawarra label is probably the most regulated in Australia.

Enjoying a Mediterranean Climate

Except for Mount Benson, the climate of the Limestone Coast can be described as *Mediterranean* with *maritime* influences. That is, the climate is warm to hot during the day and is cooled off at night by the sea breezes that come in off the Southern Ocean. (Refer to Chapter 13 for a detailed description of a maritime climate.)

During the growing season, daytime temperatures can be high but drop considerably after night falls. Even at harvest time (late March to early May), the temperature during the day can be as high as 41 degrees Celsius and then drop to 10 degrees Celsius at night. The wide variation between day- and night-time temperatures contributes to the success of the grape-growing regions of the Limestone Coast. The grapes are exposed to full sun during the day and have the night to recover, so the natural acidity of the grapes is retained.

Over at Mount Benson, where the vineyards surround the coastal towns of Robe and Kingston, the climate is pure maritime. Winds, though, can often be very strong; coastal winds in spring can rip the young shoots off the vines and disrupt flowering. The result is a low number of berries and reduced numbers of bunches, though highly flavoured ones.

Rainfall is low, averaging 600 millimetres a year and falling mainly during the winter. The soil structure allows water to drain away from the vine's roots, which prevents waterlogging. This factor is especially important. Since Coonawarra is such a flat region, vineyards can't be planted on slopes, which would allow for the rainfall to drain away from the roots of the vines. Summer time is very dry; sometimes as little as 70 millimetres falls from January to April. Therefore irrigation is used to supplement the vines' water supply during the important ripening period.

Picking the Best Grape Varieties

Of the 23,000 tonnes of grapes this region produced in 2003, 20,000 were red grapes of which nearly 12,000 tonnes were Cabernet Sauvignon and 5,600 Shiraz. Other quality reds produced in the region include Merlot, Pinot Noir, Malbec and Cabernet Franc. White grape varieties include Chardonnay, Riesling, Sauvignon Blanc and Semillon.

Cabernet Sauvignon

Coonawarra is Cabernet country. The grape variety most often linked with Coonawarra and the Limestone Coast, Cabernet grapes thrive in the *terroir* — the soil conditions, climate and aspect. The cooling influence from the afternoon sea breezes tempers the warm days and the grapes ripen quite slowly, gradually building up in intensity of flavour. Because Cabernet is a late-ripening variety, the best years for it are those that have a prolonged autumn, which ensures the grapes fully ripen.

In the occasional year when the autumn weather turns cold too soon, the Cabernet from some vineyards may retain a green herbaceous tone.

Shiraz

Shiraz is having some success in the Mount Benson region, where the French winemaking company, M. Chapoutier, grows grapes. Although Shiraz from Coonawarra is consistently good, the wine hasn't yet built up the reputation of the Shiraz from McLaren Vale and the Barossa. Shiraz from Coonawarra tends to be a good, solid red wine without the big, ripe characteristics of Shiraz from other South Australian regions.

Merlot

Merlot is the third most-grown red variety in the Limestone Coast zone. In the Coonawarra region, Merlot is used mainly for blending, but in the Wrattonbully and Padthaway regions, Merlot is made into a wine in its own right. Straight Merlot is a sweet-fruited wine of medium intensity.

White wines

Although Sauvignon Blanc, Riesling and Chardonnay play second fiddle to red grapes on the Limestone Coast, they're all grown across the zone. Riesling tends to do well in Coonawarra, where the cool night-time temperatures maintain the fresh, fruity style of the grapes.

The wines differ from the Riesling produced in the Eden or Clare Valleys (refer to Chapter 18); the fruit flavours are bigger and the acids, albeit balanced, are less. These are Rieslings that you can enjoy early in their lives.

Chardonnay and Sauvignon Blanc do particularly well in Padthaway. The warm days ripen the fruit fully and the acid is softened. The region rarely experiences damaging amounts of rainfall during the ripening months. Like the Rieslings of Coonawarra, Chardonnay and Sauvignon Blanc from the Limestone Coast are best while still young.

Getting Acquainted with Winning Wines

Coonawarra is really the only wine region of the Limestone Coast zone that caters for the wine tourist. As you drive along the Riddoch Highway (whether you come from the South Australian or Victorian side), signs start to appear announcing the various cellar doors that are open to visitors. Before long, you find yourself surrounded by vineyards. In contrast to this, in each of the regions of Padthaway, Wrattonbully and Mount Benson, you find fewer than three cellar doors (refer to Chapter 2 for information about visiting cellar doors).

Travelling the 'Coonawarra Highway'

The Coonawarra region lies just over the Victorian border, about 400 kilometres south east of Adelaide, and is defined by a strip barely 20 kilometres long, principally between the towns of Penola in the south and Coonawarra in the north.

Many lovers of Coonawarra wines have been disappointed when they arrive there. The utterly flat and unromantic Coonawarra landscape is hardly picturesque. However, people quickly forget their disappointment with the landscape as soon as they start sampling what that landscape produces. Some of the wineries that are well worth a visit are shown in Figure 19-1.

1. Balnaves of Coonawarra
2. Bowen Estate
3. Brand's of Coonawarra
4. Hollick Wines
5. Katnook Estate
6. Leconfield Coonawarra
7. Majella
8. Mildara Wines
9. Parker Coonawarra Estate
10. Penley Estate
11. Punters Corner
12. Redman
13. Reschke Wines
14. Rymill Coonawarra
15. S. Kidman Wines
16. Wynns Coonawarra Estate
17. Zema Estate

Figure 19-1:
Wineries of the Coonawarra region, South Australia.

Among those wineries well worth a visit to check out the wines are

✔ **Balnaves of Coonawarra:** This winery is less well known than some of the other wineries. Winemaker Peter Bissell makes high-quality wines. The premium wine here is **Balnaves of Coonawarra 'The Tally' Reserve Cabernet**, which is a particularly good wine that shows Peter's great understanding of the variety. The wine has the usual flavours expected, with Cabernet-like blackcurrant and spices, but then all the components just seem to meld together. However, 'The Tally' is rather expensive (about AUD$80 at time of writing), so you might like to try the blackcurrant and leafy **Balnaves of Coonawarra Cabernet Sauvignon** or the ripe dark plums and berries **Balnaves of Coonawarra Cabernet Merlot**, which are less than half the price.

✔ **Bowen Estate:** A winery that has forged a strong reputation for making honest red wines at a fair price, Bowen Estate is best known for its ripe and black-pepper spicy **Bowen Estate Shiraz,** and its medium-bodied leafy **Bowen Estate Cabernet Sauvignon.**

✔ **Brand's of Coonawarra:** Like nearly all the wine regions of Australia, Coonawarra reveals a big company presence. Brand's is owned by McWilliam's Wines, one of Australia's largest and most highly regarded family-owned wine companies. A large range of wines is made under the Brand's label. **Brand's of Coonawarra Chardonnay** with its rounded peachiness and honey-like finish shows that the Coonawarra is far more than just red wine country.

The red wines are soft and ripely flavoured without being jammy. Two rich yet well-balanced wines are the tobacco leaf and briary **Brand's of Coonawarra Cabernet Sauvignon** and the full-flavoured **Brand's of Coonawarra Shiraz** with ripe blackberries and plums.

✔ **Katnook Estate:** Wayne Stehbens, senior winemaker at Katnook Estate, is one of the long-time winemakers in the Coonawarra — celebrating 25 years in the job during 2004. The whites and reds that come from this winery are all first class, exhibiting strong varietal and regional characters. Outstanding wines are the soft and fruity **Katnook Estate Merlot**, the truffle- and briary-flavoured **Katnook Estate Cabernet Sauvignon,** and the rich and full-bodied **Katnook Estate Chardonnay.**

The second label of the Katnook Estate portfolio is **Riddoch**, where you can find excellent wines at reasonable prices. Best value are the **Riddoch Chardonnay**, **Riddoch Cabernet Merlot** and **Riddoch Shiraz**.

✔ **Kopparossa Wines:** Two veterans of the wine industry own this winery as well as vineyards in Coonawarra and Wrattonbully — the latter region is showing great potential. Both the **Kopparossa Wrattonbully Cabernet Sauvignon** and the **Kopparossa Wrattonbully Merlot** are fruit dominated and first-class wines of terrific value. The **Kopparossa Coonawarra Cabernet Merlot** has the region's classic leafy and cigar-box tones.

✔ **Lindemans Wines:** Owned by Southcorp Wines, the three Lindemans wines from the Coonawarra region are the famed **St George Cabernet Sauvignon**, **Pyrus Cabernet Sauvignon**, **Merlot, Cabernet Franc** and the **Limestone Ridge Shiraz Cabernet**. All these wines come from old vines that produce grapes with an intense depth of flavour.

✔ **Majella Wines:** Like many other wineries, Majella started life as a grape-growing business. After many years trading as such, the team is now making wine, and production has risen quickly over the past few years. The quality of the fruit from the established vineyards shines through in the wine, which avoids being either over-ripe or over-oaked. For example, the **2002 Majella Cabernet** is 100 per cent Cabernet Sauvignon and is rich, complex and very structured, with layers of blackberries and black fruits. Wines with the Majella label are terrific value in the medium-price bracket.

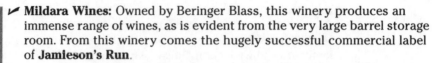

- **Mildara Wines:** Owned by Beringer Blass, this winery produces an immense range of wines, as is evident from the very large barrel storage room. From this winery comes the hugely successful commercial label of **Jamieson's Run**.

  Best value from the label is the slightly minty and leafy **Jamieson's Run Coonawarra Cabernet Sauvignon**. Also made by Mildara Wines is the fruity and full-flavoured **Greg Norman Estates Limestone Coast Cabernet Merlot**, a significant export label for the company.

- **Orlando Wines:** Fruit for the flagship Orlando wines — wines such as the mulberry, leafy and oak-dominant **Orlando St Hugo Cabernet Sauvignon** and the minty and ripe-blackberries-flavoured **Orlando Jacaranda Ridge Cabernet Sauvignon** comes from the Coonawarra.

- **Parker Coonawarra Estate:** The **Parker Coonawarra Estate Terra Rossa First Growth** is a powerful wine full of oak, blackberries, tannin and length. The less expensive **Parker Coonawarra Estate Terra Rossa Cabernet Sauvignon** is a well-balanced wine; although it often shows an oak-dominant aroma, the palate is well rounded and the oak becomes integrated with the fruit.

- **Penley Estate Winery:** This winery is making some terrific wines, especially the **Penley Estate Hyland Shiraz**, a ripe and oak-filled bold wine. For a region not so well known for its Chardonnay, **the Penley Estate Chardonnay** is a rich, barrel-fermented and aged wine with a lovely full body.

  The Penley winery also makes Cabernet-based wines, though some of these can be a touch too herbaceous for my liking.

- **Punters Corner:** At the 2003 barrel auctions (see the sidebar 'Auctioning off the best'), the **Punters Corner Cabernet Sauvignon** shot up the list of wines in demand to become the second-most-expensive wine of the day. (Not surprisingly, the first was Katnook Estate, refer earlier.) The wine is a complex blend of tobacco, cassis and a touch of mint, with a long flavour in the mouth. The interesting thing though is that the Punters Corner Cabernet sold for the equivalent of three times its normal retail price, while the Katnook Estate achieved about current retail value. (In all fairness, I should mention that Parker Estate, Majella, Petaluma and the Hardy Wine Company didn't participate in this particular auction.)

- **Reschke Wines:** A relative newcomer to the scene, Reschke Wines has an excellent **Reschke Vitulus**, a Cabernet Sauvignon wine that is well ripened, allowing it to develop beyond the herbal flavours that can sometimes be a detracting factor in Coonawarra wines.

✔ **Rymill Coonawarra:** This winery has a strong portfolio, including **Rymill Sauvignon Blanc**, which is full of grassy, herbaceous aromas complemented by riper tropical characters. Rymill also produces **Rymill The Bee's Knees**, which is a blend of non-vintage Cabernet Franc, Cabernet Sauvignon and Merlot produced in the traditional *methode champenoise* (and, unfortunately, released only through the cellar door).

The ready-to-drink and well-priced Rymill MC² blends one-third Merlot, one-third Cabernet Sauvignon and one-third Cabernet Franc. These three varieties provide intense fruit aromas with complex flavours. The cellar door is worth a visit (for more information on Rymill Coonawarra, see Chapter 28).

✔ **Wynns Coonawarra Estate:** Established by John Riddoch, Coonawarra's founder, in 1890 and bought by the Wynn family in 1951, Southcorp Wines now owns this winery. The **Wynns Coonawarra Estate Cabernet Shiraz Merlot**, with the distinctive red stripe on the label below the image of the triple-gabled winery, has always been top value. In addition, the wine is an inexpensive one, good to age for five years or so.

The winery's flagship wine is the **Wynns Coonawarra Estate John Riddoch Cabernet Sauvignon**, which is produced only from the top one per cent of the grapes — and only in the years when Cabernet Sauvignon grapes of an exceptional quality are available.

✔ **Zema Estate:** The original vineyard is still hand-pruned and produces high-quality fruit. Traditional and innovative winemaking techniques produce wines that are made for cellaring; they have good structure, plenty of tannin and loads of fruit flavour without over-ripeness.

Look for the **Zema Estate Shiraz**, with pepper and spicy fruit characters, and the **Zema Estate Cluny**, a blend of Cabernet Sauvignon, Merlot, Cabernet Franc and Malbec. The Cluny is a Bordeaux-style wine with rich sweet-fruit flavours and oak overtones.

Other wineries of note are **Leconfield Coonawarra**, **Hollick Wines**, **S. Kidman Wines**, and **Redman**.

Spending time at Padthaway

Padthaway, less than 100 kilometres to the north of Coonawarra, has always been overshadowed by that region's reputation. When the region was first planted in the 1960s, mechanised vineyard practices had already been widely adopted and, as a result, Padthaway has always has a fully mechanised wine industry (see Chapter 20 for information on the use of machinery in viticulture).

The gently rolling landscape of Padthaway resembles that of the Coonawarra, and it shares a similar climate — Mediterranean with coastal influences — and soil, the terra rossa.

As you drive through Padthaway, you see long, neat rows of vines with the trellis posts evenly spaced, rather than small vineyards established in the rather higgledy-piggledy fashion of older wine regions. Padthaway has always produced reliable wines using grapes that, because of the heavy use of machinery, have been grown cost effectively.

In 2003, the total amount of red and white grapes grown was around 27,000 tonnes — a respectable figure, but not enough to satisfy demand. On current projections, the demand in 2008 is likely to be close to 35,000 tonnes. The Padthaway region grows good grapes that ripen fully and have strong fruity flavours; the grape most in demand is Chardonnay, with Shiraz a close second.

A number of wine companies have made substantial investment in vineyards as well as building facilities in the Padthaway region (see Figure 19-2). I discuss several of them in the following sections.

Lindemans

The leading name that you see from Padthaway is the **Lindemans Padthaway** range. The wines from this label remind you again that Lindemans makes good fruity wines at a reasonable price.

Consistently terrific wines for the price are the toasty, citrus-and peach-flavoured **Lindemans Padthaway Reserve Chardonnay** and the soft blackberry-flavoured with hints of chocolate **Lindemans Padthaway Reserve Cabernet Sauvignon**.

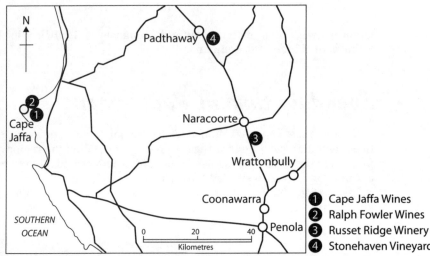

Figure 19-2: The wineries of the Padthaway and Wrattonbully regions, and Mt Benson, South Australia.

Padthaway Estate

This winery is well worth the visit if you get the chance. The old homestead offers luxurious accommodation and fine food — oh, and the wines are good, too. Look for the **Padthaway Estate Eliza Pinot Chardonnay**, a delicately flavoured, well-made sparkling wine.

Stonehaven Vineyards

Under the ownership of the Hardy Wine Company, the vineyards that supply Stonehaven Vineyards are spread across the Padthaway, Coonawarra and Wrattonbully regions. The winery's range extends across three different price levels — Stonehaven Stepping Stone is at the lower end of the market, the Stonehaven Limestone Coast is in the middle price range and the most expensive is the Stonehaven Limited Release.

- ✔ The **2003 Stepping Stone Padthaway Chardonnay** is a highly acclaimed, high-quality wine that is full of regional character, representing excellent value for money.

- ✔ Also in the range is the **Stepping Stone Coonawarra Cabernet Sauvignon**, a medium-bodied wine with ripe blackcurrant and a hint of oak.

Stonehaven sticks to just three grapes per label — Chardonnay, Shiraz and Cabernet Sauvignon — and all are well-made, straightforward wines. Stonehaven is a huge winery with a cellar door.

Yalumba

Yalumba also has a presence on the Limestone Coast with its inexpensive and fruit-driven Padthaway range. In nearby Coonawarra are the vineyards for the often-overripe **Yalumba The Menzies Cabernet Sauvignon**.

Wandering off to Wrattonbully

Like Padthaway, the newly defined wine region of Wrattonbully is known as a grape-growing region rather than a region full of cellar doors and restaurants. Formerly a pastoral area, Wrattonbully lies to the north east of Coonawarra, very close to the Victorian border. Refer to Figure 19-2 for the locations of the wineries in this region. In 1968, the first commercial vineyard was established in this flat landscape.

The big names in the Australian wine industry — the Hardy Wine Company, Cranswick, Mildara Blass, Orlando Wyndham and Yalumba — have vineyards producing fruit in bulk to wineries outside the region.

Two of the best wineries are

✔ **Russet Ridge Winery:** One of the few wineries with a cellar door in Wrattonbully, Russet Ridge is owned by the Orlando Wyndham Group. As a result, you can find the entire Orlando portfolio of wines, with everything from Jacob's Creek to St Hugo available.

The house wines are the **Russet Ridge Cabernet Shiraz Merlot,** a fruit-dominant wine with spice, blackberries and a touch of oak, and the **Russet Ridge Chardonnay,** a peachy and toasty wine from the barrel. Both are well-made commercial wines at reasonable prices.

✔ **Smith and Hooper:** This winery is part of the Yalumba stable, although the label makes no mention of this, perhaps to give the impression that the wine is from a small winery. The wines under this label are typical of the winemaking skills of a technically sound, big wine company. The slick packaging and lack of reference to Yalumba is a clever marketing tool as it would appeal to those drinkers who don't like to be seen partaking in the commercial wine labels (refer to Chapter 3 for more information about labelling). The **Smith and Hooper Limited Edition Merlot** is full of ripe mulberry flavours with a subtle amount of balancing dryness from the oak.

Following the coast to Mount Benson

The scenically stunning region of Mount Benson lies on the South Australian coastline, about 350 kilometres south-east of Adelaide. A relative newcomer on the Australian wine scene, the region is situated between the seaside towns of Robe (famous for its crayfish) and Kingston. The region's climate is cool. Winds from the Southern Ocean can drive in quite strongly, and winters tend to be cold and wet.

Mount Benson is a small but rapidly growing wine region, with many outcrops of terra rossa soil. The first trial vineyard was planted in 1978 by Colin Kidd of Lindemans, and the first commercial vines were planted in 1989. Most expansion took place in the late 1990s. By 2003, the area planted to vines had grown to 430 hectares. Compared with Coonawarra, with 5,336 hectares planted, and Padthaway with 3,618 hectares planted, Mount Benson may look small, but it is by no means insignificant.

Both white and red varieties do well in the region, including Chardonnay and Sauvignon Blanc, and Cabernet Sauvignon and Shiraz. Merlot and Viognier are also being produced successfully.

Four main businesses are involved in producing wine in the region (refer to Figure 19-2). One is a joint venture with the famous M Chapoutier Rhone Valley wine company, and another is owned by the large Belgian shipping company, Kreglinger. Incidentally, Kreglinger also owns Pipers Brook

Vineyard in Tasmania (refer to Chapter 15) and M Chapoutier has vineyards in Victoria's Heathcote region (refer to Chapter 11).

- ✔ **Cape Jaffa Wines:** This winery is located right on the coast, and was the first local winery to begin production. Cape Jaffa is the winery that introduced me to the wines of Mount Benson, and their **Cape Jaffa Sauvignon Blanc** is particularly good, offering ripe yet mineral-like flavours without a sense of herbaceous tones. The **Cape Jaffa Shiraz** is not overripe and shows off the cool climate spiciness you'd expect from this cooler region.

- ✔ **Kreglinger Estate:** A major player in the Mount Benson region is Kreglinger Estate. To date, the vineyards are still being established but they're the largest development in the region, so the label could be one to look out for in the future.

- ✔ **M Chapoutier Australia:** The winemaker at M Chapoutier grows grapes using the biodynamic method, a technique that is suited to the location of Mount Benson. The theory underpinning the biodynamic method is that wines are able to truly reflect the soils and plots on which the grapes are grown because no chemicals have been used that can upset the natural balance of the land. The sea breezes at Mount Benson keep the air flowing through the leaf canopy of the vine so that fungal diseases are reduced — so much so that the vineyard is managed without chemicals. (For more on biodynamic methods, refer to Chapter 6.)

To date, one of the best wines produced by M Chapoutier is the **M Chapoutier Mount Benson Shiraz,** an earthy, mushroomy and liquorice-flavoured wine.

- ✔ **Ralph Fowler Wines:** Another of the four main businesses in the region, this locally owned winery makes the excellent, fresh-fruited **Ralph Fowler Mount Benson Sauvignon Blanc**, as well as a fine, ripe-textured **Ralph Fowler Mount Benson Viognier**.

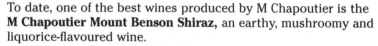

Auctioning off the best

Each year, the wine producers in the Coonawarra and Margaret River regions do something for charity. In Margaret River, the function is the Great Wine Estates of Western Australia Auction, and in the Coonawarra, it's the Coonawarra Barrel Series Auction.

Wineries from the respective regions donate a barrel of their best Cabernet Sauvignon to the auction. For wine investors, the auctions provide a rough barometer of how each wine rates in terms of demand versus supply. In the 2003 auctions, the top-priced Margaret River Cabernet was the Moss Wood Cabernet, and in Coonawarra, Katnook Estate Cabernet took the top price. (Chapter 22 is all about the wine regions of Western Australia, including Margaret River.)

Chapter 20

Riverland: On the Banks of the Mighty Murray

The vineyards of the Riverland region in eastern South Australia produce huge quantities of wine — of all the grapes grown in Australia, 23 per cent come from the Riverland. Yet this region doesn't have the same cachet as other wine regions in South Australia, such as Padthaway and Coonawarra (refer to Chapter 19). Perhaps that's because the region makes good, straightforward, good-value wines with little fanfare.

The region's lack of star quality may also be due to the fact that, in addition to producing the grapes for bottled wine, the Riverland region — along with the vineyards of the Murray–Darling region of Victoria and the Riverina region of New South Wales — makes cask wine.

Although cask wine (also known affectionately as bag-in-the-box wine or Chateau Cardboard) makes wine aficionados cringe, in its early days cask wine introduced many people to wine drinking.

The Riverland region is the only region within the zone known as the Lower Murray, and the main towns are Waikerie, Loxton, Renmark and Berri. In this chapter, I introduce you to the region's vast, flat landscape — a powerhouse of Australian wine production.

Producing Wine on a Grand Scale

When you come across a wine region as large as the Riverland, you tend to compare its vastness with the size of other wine regions in Australia. Here are some interesting statistics from 2003 that may come in handy next time you play Trivial Pursuit:

- ✔ **Number of hectares under vine:** In the Riverland region, 19,551; in the Barossa, 8,720

- ✔ **Tonnes of Shiraz crushed from grapes:** In the Riverland region, 90,572; in the Barossa, 19,426

- ✔ **Tonnes of Chardonnay crushed from grapes:** In the Riverland region, 71,942; in the Padthaway region, 7,724

You can find more information about the Barossa in Chapter 18 and about the Padthaway region in Chapter 19. The Riverland is also home to Australia's largest winery, the Hardy Wine Company Berri Estates, which in 2004 processed 163,000 tonnes of fruit. Well equipped with modern draining, pressing, clarifying and chilling facilities to guarantee the quality of all its products, this winery has the capacity to store over 73 million litres of wine, of which 2 million litres are devoted to wood storage for fortified wine maturation.

The large wine-processing facilities of the Riverland are truly something to see. Hectare after hectare is covered with stainless steel tanks. If you happen to be passing at night during harvest, you witness the lights for the night-shift workers lighting up the sky and shining for miles. From a distance, the wineries look like alien spaceships.

Bag in a box

The term 'cask wine' refers to an inexpensive style of wine. The wine is sold in bulk, that is, in containers that hold 2 or 4 litres. The wine is contained in a strong laminated bag (also called a *bladder*) with a tap built into the bag, and the bag is then packaged in a sturdy cardboard box. On top of the box is a strong handle so that you can easily carry it. After purchase, you access the tap by pulling it through the side of the box near the base and pour yourself a glass of wine.

The thinking behind this form of packaging is based on the realisation that some people want to drink only one glass of wine a day, and don't really want to open a bottle, which would deteriorate after opening. With cask wine, as wine is taken out of the bladder, the bag collapses in on itself, which protects the rest of the wine from exposure to oxygen, which causes deterioration. While the idea is nifty, the wine in fact does slowly deteriorate over a few weeks.

Nonetheless, cask wine has been a huge success in bringing wine at reasonable cost to many Australians. In 2002, cask wine enjoyed sales of 53 per cent of all wine sold in Australia. A couple of the better producers of this style of wine are Yalumba and De Bortoli wines.

Surviving Unrelenting Heat and Aridity

The Riverland has a typically continental climate, which means that during the summer months the days are long, hot and dry, and the nights are cool (due to the region's location inland). Most of the rain falls during the winter months. Low humidity during the growing season means that the risk of fungal disease is low, thus reducing the need for chemical spraying.

The predominant soils in the Riverland are fine, free-draining river soils which don't have very good water-holding ability so, if it wasn't for irrigation during the summer months, vines couldn't survive in the region. The region's vineyards rely on water that gets pumped in from the Murray River. The mighty Murray starts in the Australian Alps in New South Wales, then flows along the border (and, in fact, *is* the border) between New South Wales and Victoria, into South Australia where it enters the sea at Lake Alexandrina.

The fact that the Murray River is such a precious resource has made it the focus of much controversy over the years. The growers of grapes, as well as those who grow other crops and also depend on water from the Murray, have had to work hard to improve their irrigation techniques. Not only is there the risk that the Murray is going to be sucked dry, but the region is also being confronted by increasing levels of salinity as a result of rising water tables, which have, in the main, been caused by too much irrigation and land clearing. This potentially disastrous problem leads to degradation of the soil.

Over recent years, irrigation methods have changed from overhead sprinklers and flood irrigation to drip irrigation, which helps conserve water and is more effective. Techniques such as *partial rootzone drying* (or PRD), have been introduced (refer to Chapter 12).

Making the Most of the Heat

Any grape variety can be grown in a sunny climate so long as the grapes have access to water. However, the flavours of varieties that have delicate fruit aromas suffer in the heat, whereas the flavours of varieties that are more robust are retained in high temperatures, because the more robust a variety's fruit flavours, the better it can tolerate the heat. For example, you'll find no reason why you can't grow Pinot Noir in the Riverland region, and many wineries do; over 3,000 tonnes were processed in 2003. The grape turns into a pleasant, light, red wine that tends to lack the beautiful subtle fragrances of cherries and strawberries that are so essential for a classic Pinot Noir.

As well as producing large quantities of wine, the Riverland region produces a large number of varieties, both red and white. The region also has an excellent climate for the production of fortified wines, using grape varieties such as Muscat Gordo Blanco and Grenache.

The main white varieties produced in the Riverland region are

- **Chardonnay:** By no means should you be surprised that Chardonnay is the main white variety in the Riverland. A versatile grape variety, Chardonnay lends itself to delicate, long-living wines in a cool climate, and full-flavoured fruity and appealing wines in a warm climate.

- **Riesling and Sauvignon Blanc:** To my mind, these two varieties are a little like the white version of Pinot Noir — they're pleasant, albeit non-varietal tasting, white wines.

- **Semillon:** Like Chardonnay, Semillon thrives in the Riverland region. In fact, the demand for Semillon sometimes outstrips supply. The large, tight bunches that are produced by the Semillon vine are able to fully ripen in the Riverland. The dry climate lends itself to the minimal risk that rainfall will cause the diseases to which Semillon is susceptible. Semillon works particularly well as part of a blend with Chardonnay to make a full-bodied fruity wine.

- **Verdelho:** A heat-loving variety, Verdelho is a 100 per cent varietal wine, full bodied and full of flavours such as peaches and herbs. When used in a blend, Verdelho adds backbone and flavour to the less flavour-intense varieties.

In addition to the wines mentioned in the preceding list above, the Riverland produces a mixed bag of white varieties, some of which you may never have heard of before. Varieties such as Sultana (which makes a bland wine that is used for blending with other white wines to bulk them up or increase the quantities), Muscat Gordo Blanco (a fruity wine, used to give flavour to bland wines such as Sultana) and Colombard (used for brandy making and for bulking and blending). Basically, by blending wines here and there and identifying the grape varieties' attributes, plenty of wine can be made in this sunny region.

You're very unlikely to pick up a bottle or cask which states that the wine is made from Sultana or Muscat Gordo Blanco. Although wine producers don't deny that many of their wines are the result of blending, wine producers aren't inclined to proclaim this fact on their labels. You're more likely to find a generic name such as 'Classic White' or 'Vat 6'. If the wine is destined for export, the label may well feature Australian fauna or flora, such as a kangaroo or a bottle brush — even the name of the wine may include words like 'kookaburra' or 'koala' (questionable taste, but if it helps sell the wine...).

The main red varieties produced in the Riverland region are

- **Shiraz:** Like Verdelho, Shiraz loves the heat and can make a well-flavoured wine even when grown at higher crop levels, as is the practice in the Riverland (see the sidebar 'Cropping high, cropping low'). Although Riverland Shiraz doesn't resemble the acclaimed Shiraz from other Australian wine regions, such as the Barossa Valley (refer to Chapter 18) and Heathcote (refer to Chapter 11), Riverland Shiraz is packed with the flavour of blackberry fruits and spicy cloves.

  Shiraz dominates in the Riverland, making up 40 per cent of the varieties planted. Shiraz grapes are used to make a single-variety wine, and are also often blended with Cabernet Sauvignon.

- **Cabernet Sauvignon:** In order to maintain its typical blackcurrant flavour and refined elegant structure, Cabernet Sauvignon needs to ripen slowly in a cool climate. Grown in the warmth of the Riverland, however, the grapes still make some pretty decent red wines. Although the wines may not remind you of the best from Bordeaux, they won't burn a hole in your bank balance either. Mostly the Cabernet shows blackberry and blackcurrant flavours, along with some tannin, but to a lesser degree than found in Cabernet Sauvignons grown in cooler climes.

  Cabernet Sauvignon comprises 27 per cent of the grapes crushed in the Riverland, and is often blended with Shiraz. However, many wineries make a straight Cab Sav.

- **Merlot:** Grape growers and winemakers are very much aware that Merlot has wide appeal as a medium-bodied wine with juicy fruit flavours. As a result, Merlot is the third most-planted variety in the Riverland region, and is either blended or produced as a single-variety wine.

Cropping high, cropping low

The term *high crop levels* is used to refer to a vineyard that produces five or more tonnes of grapes per acre — which means both the grapes and the resulting wine are cheaper to produce. 'Low crop levels' indicates a vineyard where less than one tonne per acre is produced. For those who still think in British Imperial measures, that translates as less than two tonnes of grapes to the acre. (For the purposes of calculation, one acre is equivalent to 0.405 hectares.)

Shiraz in the McLaren Vale and Barossa Valley regions of South Australia and Heathcote in Victoria is grown at low crop levels (refer to Chapter 16 for more on McLaren Vale, Chapter 18 for more on the Barossa, and Chapter 11 for more information on Heathcote). The resulting wines are intensely flavoured, dense in texture and rich in sugar ripeness.

The three grape varieties that are often seen together these days are Shiraz, Grenache and Mourvèdre, in varying proportions. Both Grenache and Mourvèdre are well suited to the warm, dry Riverland region. Grenache just blossoms with the heat, producing incredible sugar ripeness and fruit flavours — so much so, that it often needs the spicy and slightly bitter Mourvèdre to tone it down. Winemakers have come across a winning blend here.

Making Top Drops for a Mass Market

Sometimes, finding a wine from the Riverland region is a little hard to do because the label doesn't always advertise the fact. So you're unlikely to see the name 'Riverland' on the label; instead, you'll see the origin of the wine as 'South Eastern Australia'.

However, a number of wineries are proud of their Riverland connections (refer to Figure 20-1). Of the top 15 winemaking facilities across Australia, six are based in the Riverland. To give you an idea of the size of some of these facilities, the Angove's processing site covers more than four and a half hectares of land. Now that's an awful lot of tanks and barrels and hoses and wine!

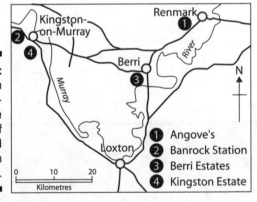

Figure 20-1: Wines from the flat-landscape wineries of the Riverland region, South Australia.

Angove's

One of the proud faces of the Riverland, Angove's, a family-owned business, has been established in Renmark since 1910. The distillation of brandy was carried out right from the beginning of the winery, and **St Agnes Brandy** is still made there. Wine, however, is the main focus at Angove's. The winery makes a wide range of wines, all very well priced, and targeted as everyday wines rather than wines to reserve for special occasions.

Making brandy

Brandy is a spirit that winemakers make from white wine. The grape variety commonly used is Colombard or Chenin Blanc. The grapes are fermented in the same way as for making white wine, then the wine is put through the distillation process.

At Angove's, a family-owned business in the Riverland region of South Australia, distillation is carried out in batches using a *pot still*. A pot distillation is considered to produce a brandy of higher quality and better flavour than the other method of distillation — 'continuous distillation'. In the pot still process, batches of wine are heated up until the vapours and fumes are released from the wine. As these vapours cool,

they condense, forming a colourless liquid, which is now a strong alcohol or spirit.

After distillation, the colourless liquid is aged in oak barrels for many years, during which the brandy develops a rich flavour while the sharpness of the spirit mellows. The shorter the ageing period, the less intense the flavours that develop.

In Australia, brandy can't be sold until it has been aged for two years. A brandy termed 'old' must be at least five years old, and 'very old' refers to a brandy aged more than ten years. Generally, the older the better in terms of softness of taste and depth of flavour. 'Young' brandy is the only type of brandy that should have a mixer added — if you must!

The range includes the Angove's Bear Crossing label, of which the **Angove's Bear Crossing Chardonnay** is amazing for its peachy soft flavours and quality winemaking. The Angove's Butterfly Ridge label offers a fruit-dominated **Angove's Butterfly Ridge Shiraz/Cabernet** and is excellent quality at very reasonable price. Angove's Long Row (the name is a reference to the vine rows in the Nanya Vineyard, which are a staggering five kilometres long) is a range of varietals such as Pinot Noir, Sauvignon Blanc, Chardonnay and Shiraz. The **Angove's Long Row Merlot** is an easy-to-drink wine of mulberry and spice flavours.

Another of Angove's well-priced labels is Stonegate. The **Angove's Stonegate Verdelho** continues to demonstrate that the Riverland is indeed a region that manages this variety well — this wine has loads of fruity tropical flavours and a good balancing acid. You can also find Cabernet Sauvignon/Shiraz, Petit Verdot and Chardonnay in the Stonegate range.

Banrock Station

The Hardy Wine Company owns Banrock Station Wine and Wetland Centre. The vineyard property encompasses 1,700 hectares fronting the Murray River, of which less than a fifth is under vine; the rest is natural bushland (see the sidebar 'Doing it for the environment').

Banrock Station wines are always well made and full of fruity flavours. Look for the slightly more expensive but worthwhile **Reserve** range, which includes the melon- and pineapple-flavoured **Banrock Station Reserve Chardonnay** and the leafy **Banrock Station Reserve Cabernet Sauvignon**. (See Chapter 28 for more information on Banrock Station.)

Berri Estates

The biggest wine-processing facility in Australia, the Hardy Wine Company Berri Estates processed over 163,000 tonnes of fruit in 2004. Busy winemaking by any standards. Most of the wine produced here is for the mass market of cask (or 'bag-in-a-box') wine. The wines are all fruity and pleasant drinks.

Kingston Estate

Another proud Riverland operator and family-owned business, Kingston Estate, produces wine that rates among the most expensive in the region. The philosophy at this winery is to crop lower than usual to maximise the fruit flavour and intensity (see the sidebar 'Cropping high, cropping low').

This winery blends fruit from the Riverland with fruit purchased from other regions, such as the King Valley region of Victoria, and Langhorne Creek and the Adelaide Hills in South Australia (refer to Chapter 12 for more on King Valley, and Chapter 17 for information on Langhorne Creek and the Adelaide Hills).

Blending has the effect of balancing the powerful ripe flavours of the Riverland with the finer fruit components of grapes from the cooler regions. Even though Kingston Estate wines are, overall, more expensive than those from other Riverland wine companies (due to their use of fruit from vineyards in other wine regions where it is more expensive to produce grapes), all of them represent top value for money.

Doing it for the environment

Banrock Station Wine and Wetland Centre not only has a stunning visitors' centre, it also sets the benchmark for industries seeking to protect the environment. Part of the income generated from the sale of each bottle of Banrock Station wine is devoted to the restoration of wetlands. The aim is to re-establish the landscape so as to restore the natural environment of the Murray River after years of excessive irrigation, and the company employs a full-time ranger/ecologist.

As of June 2004, Banrock Station wines had raised AUD$2 million for endangered wetlands across the world. So far, wetlands in Kenya, Sweden, Canada, the Netherlands and Finland, as well as in Australia, have benefited from the money raised in sales.

The **Kingston Estate Tessera Chardonnay Viognier** is a wine quite out of the ordinary, showing loads of honey, peaches and pear flavours and exhibiting quite a dense weight. Also worth buying is the **Kingston Estate Echelon Shiraz.** The fruit for this wine doesn't come from the Riverland; rather it comes from Langhorne Creek and the Clare Valley (a factor which influences cost, so the wine is more expensive at around AUD$20). You can read more about Langhorne Creek in Chapter 17, and the Clare Valley in Chapter 18.

Lindemans

One of Australia's best-selling white wines is made from fruit from the Riverland — **Lindemans Bin 65 Chardonnay**; in terms of quality for a price, this wine is hard to beat. In its annual publication, *The Choice Wine Buying Guide 2004* voted the 2003 Lindemans Bin 65 Chardonnay as its highest scoring budget Chardonnay.

As part of the Bin range made from fruit from the area, I prefer the spicy, generous flavours and easy-drinking style of **Lindemans Bin 50 Shiraz**, and the soft and juicy fruit flavours of **Lindemans Bin 40 Merlot**.

Yalumba

Australia's oldest family-owned vineyard, Yalumba produces another well-known wine. The **Oxford Landing** label was named after a nearby site on the Murray River. Every year, Oxford Landing delivers vibrant and characteristically Australian wines, high on quality and fruit flavours. Costing less than AUD$10 a bottle, this range is inexpensive, and includes the passionfruit and tropical **Yalumba Oxford Landing Sauvignon Blanc** and the mulberry and vanilla-like **Yalumba Oxford Landing Merlot**.

A label from Yalumba that sources some of the fruit from the Riverland to blend with grapes from other South Australian regions is the **Yalumba Y** series. The Yalumba Y series of varietal wines is fresh and fruit-driven, offers consistent quality and represents good value for money. The **Yalumba Y Viognier** is redolent with honey and apricot and is quite a full-bodied white wine. The **Yalumba Y Shiraz** shows pepper and spice and a touch of chocolate.

The role of machinery in making wine

Grape growing and winemaking in the vast quantities that are produced in the Riverland region takes a lot of skill, even though people may believe the wines to be inferior based purely on their low price in the bottle shop.

To make large volumes of technically sound wine and at the same time retain the grape's character isn't as easy as it may sound. First, the grape growing has to be spot on — in this regard, the sheer size of the vineyards is a help. In the flat Riverland region, long rows of vines can easily be established, and these allow for full mechanisation.

In winter, many vineyards first send in a machine to do the bulk of the pruning work. However, for the more prized, older and more fragile vines, teams of hand pruners still do the pruning rather than take the risk of machines damaging the gnarled old vines. On the whole, though, most pruning happens mechanically.

In spring, a leaf-trimming machine is used in the vineyard to remove excess leaves so as to let the sun and the breeze flow through the leaf canopy and onto the berries. At harvest time, a mechanical harvester picks the fruit. All these mechanised operations help keep the cost of the fruit down.

However, other aspects must be taken into account. Anyone can grow lots of grapes on a vine. In the Riverland, the combination of sunshine and irrigation means that the vines can support a large amount of fruit. Yet this isn't necessarily the winemaker's sole strategy. The key is to optimise the amount of fruit per vine without jeopardising fruit flavour, tannin structure and berry skin colour. Basically, the more grapes that grow on a vine, the less these important characteristics become, and a lower-quality wine results.

In order for a vineyard to be viable, it must produce a certain number of tonnes of grapes per hectare, and the quality of the fruit must achieve a certain standard before the winery will purchase it. Grape growers who can maximise both the quality and quantity of their fruit are in high demand.

The machines take care of a lot of the hard work in the vineyard, and the vineyard managers tweak their vine management techniques in order to attain the best yield-versus-quality ratio possible. Then the winemakers get the task of turning the fruit into the best possible product, with clean fermentation, technically sound winemaking and effective packaging.

Chapter 21

Capital Stuff in and around Perth

· ·

In This Chapter

▶ Visiting wineries within easy reach of the city

▶ Seeing vines that thrive in the heat

▶ Enjoying the best of premium wines

· ·

*T*he vast state of Western Australia is separated from the rest of the country by deserts, stretching from the Tanami Desert in the north to the Nullarbor Plain in the south. Until comparatively recently, most Australians in other states were unaware of the quality of the wines being made in the West, such was the high cost of freight across the country.

Nowadays, wines from Western Australia are available all over the country and so highly are they regarded that wine lovers from other states plan their holidays around the winegrowing regions of the West. The wines also enjoy a high profile internationally and sell well overseas.

Although the wineries of Western Australia currently make only 4 per cent of the country's total wine production, the West is far from insignificant. The wine industry in this state is important because of the premium wine the state produces year after year. The West doesn't try to compete with the irrigated, high-volume wineries of the eastern states; instead, the West lets its high-quality wines speak for themselves and reinforce its reputation, a reputation that many in the wine world would find enviable.

Perth is the capital city of Western Australia, and within the Greater Perth zone are three wine regions — the Swan District, which includes the sub-region of the Swan Valley, the Perth Hills and Peel.

In this chapter, I introduce you to each region, with a spot of local history and a note on the development of its vineyards, then I discuss the climate of each region and what impact that has on its wine. Then I describe what each region does best before we meet some of the more interesting regional players.

Getting Orientated around Perth

The wine regions around Perth are among the oldest in the country. You can find many interesting vineyards in the Greater Perth zone, from the Swan District, the state's longest-established wine region, to the Perth Hills and the small region of Peel on the coastal plains south of Perth.

Exploring the Swan District

The Swan District is an extensive area to the north of Perth, and is significant in terms of offering wine lovers a chance to visit vineyards and sample wines only 25 minutes from the centre of the city. The vineyards and wineries are found along the Avon River just north of Midland and on the flat plains of the Swan River around Guildford. The names 'Swan District' and 'Swan Valley' are more or less interchangeable, as the Swan Valley sub-region pretty well makes up the whole of the Swan District.

The history of the Swan District, or Swan Valley, stretches back almost to the establishment of the Swan River Colony in 1829. A significant number of southern Europeans settled in the District after the First World War. The immigrants came mostly from the Dalmatian region of Croatia, where grape growing is very much part of the culture.

Many of the first vines planted in the Swan District were for table grapes, and as you drive through the region, you can still see original vineyards, with the high trellises training the vines up to get maximum exposure to the sun. Gradually, though, as subsequent generations of grape growers take over the vineyards, the eating grapes are being replaced by varieties of grapes destined for winemaking.

The District's proximity to Perth and the alluvial soils of the Swan Valley meant that market gardens were established early on. Vines were planted in the 1800s and by the middle of the century, grape production had grown quite substantially.

Heading for the Perth Hills

The Perth Hills are quite close to Perth, in native bushland east of the city. In the summer, the region offers some respite from the high temperatures. The vineyards are established in the Darling Ranges, with the Chittering Valley to the north and Serpentine in the south. Most of the vineyards and wineries are located around the town of Mundaring.

Until the late 1970s, the region was mostly orchards. Then in the 1980s, the potential for growing grapes was recognised. Vines grow on alluvial soils in the valleys and in less fertile, gravelly soils on the slopes.

Coasting down to Peel

The third wine region in the Greater Perth zone is Peel, only 70 kilometres south of Perth on the coast and a perfect day trip. The town of Williams is on the region's eastern boundary and Peel Inlet lies to its north.

An important agricultural area since the early days of settlement, vineyards were established in the 1930s by immigrants from Italy. However, not until 40 years later was the region developed into a wine region. The soil on the coast tends to be sandy, becoming gravelly further inland.

Enjoying a Sunny Climate

The climate within the Greater Perth zone varies from region to region, although overall each of the three regions enjoys warm to hot summer temperatures.

Blurring the seasons in the Swan District

The vineyards in the Valley are usually the first in Australia to harvest their grapes. One year, I visited the region in mid-January and vintage was already underway. In comparison, the harvest in a cool region like the Mornington Peninsula in Victoria doesn't get going until mid-March. (Chapter 13 covers the Mornington Peninsula.)

The variation between the seasons isn't very distinct in the Swan District. In winter, daytime temperatures don't fall much lower than 20 degrees Celsius. Winter dormancy, which many grape growers believe is one of the keys to growing intensely flavoured fruit, doesn't exist in this region. Also the time between the grapes forming and being picked is relatively short, so again the ability to build powerfully flavoured fruit is reduced. The result is wines with the flavour volume turned down a bit.

The region's climate is considered *Mediterranean*, with cool winters and warm to hot and dry summers. Being close to the coast, the region benefits from the cooling afternoon breezes that blow in from the Indian Ocean. Although the region is generally dry, the harvest can be washed out by February storms.

Cooling breezes in the Perth Hills

Each vineyard in the Perth Hills is quite different to the next, with the elevation of the site the determining factor of the style of wines being made. The altitude in this region ranges from 200 to 400 metres above sea level.

Not surprisingly, this region is wetter than in the Swan Valley, because the rain clouds that travel from the coast often dump their load over the hills. Winters in particular are quite wet and cool. The only danger that the Perth Hills region faces is if the summer–autumn rains come before the vineyards finish harvesting their grapes.

These higher altitude vineyards harvest their fruit later in the season compared to the Swan District vineyards and so are able to take advantage of a slower ripening period. The consistency of the wine from the Perth Hills vineyards rests partly in the lap of the weather gods.

Varying the climate in the Peel region

The climate in the tiny Peel region is similar to that in Perth, albeit a touch cooler. The Mediterranean climate varies the further inland you travel, away from the cooling effects of the ocean breezes.

Making Quality, Not Quantity

If all the wine produced annually in Australia were shown in a pie chart, with the size of each slice reflecting the output of each wine zone, the slice of pie representing Greater Perth would be very slim indeed. Overall, the total of all the grapes crushed in 2003 was 1,900 tonnes of red grapes and 3,780 tonnes of white. To put those figures into perspective, the totals Australia-wide were 787,000 tonnes for red grapes and 568,000 tonnes for white grapes.

In this section, I briefly describe the varieties that the wine regions of Greater Perth concentrate on, and then I take you on a visit of some wineries.

Focusing on the wine varieties grown around Perth

The grapes grown around Perth vary according to the climate — the Swan District is hot and dry while the Peel region enjoys maritime influences.

TECHNICAL STUFF

Breeding up Carnelian

Carnelian is a grape variety that was bred by the University of Davis in California in an attempt to make a variety similar to Cabernet Sauvignon but which was better able to withstand hot climates. Carnelian is double bred, in that they first created a cross between Cabernet Sauvignon and Carignan in the 1930s and, subsequently, in 1972 they crossed that breed with Grenache. The variety of Carignan is planted across much of south-western France where the growers tell you that the climate is really only good for the great quantity of grapes that the vine is able to produce, and the grapes aren't particularly flavoursome.

Moving from fortifieds to table wines in the Swan District

In the beginning, the wine industry in Western Australia focused on fortified wines made from Muscadelle grapes. The European migrants knew how to make wine in a sunny and hot climate, where the grapes quickly ripened. The demand for table wines grew as further migrants arrived, and for decades, the region very much had the feeling of Europe.

However, things have changed. Fortified wines are not being made in much quantity and dry table wines are the main product of the region. The table wine varieties of the Swan District include the following:

- **Chenin Blanc:** The leading grape variety, in terms of amount of grapes crushed per year, is Chenin Blanc. Although this variety isn't known for its high status amongst wine drinkers, the warmth of the West demonstrates that Chenin Blanc can indeed make a fine wine. The sunshine creates a rich well-textured wine that even responds to some bottle age. The famous Houghton White Burgundy is a blend dominated by Chenin Blanc (the other varieties are Muscadelle and Chardonnay).

- **Verdelho:** Second in line in the vineyards of the Swan District is Verdelho. The first Verdelho many Australians would have tried would have come from the West. The Verdelho grape has its home in Portugal so, not surprisingly, it loves the warm, dry climate of the Swan Valley.

- **Shiraz:** The red wine of the Swan District is predominantly Shiraz. The warmth of the region suits Shiraz although the wines never become overly jammy in flavour and texture. The reason for this is that although the region is warm, the ripening period is short. As a result, the fruit doesn't build up the intense flavours so common in South Australian wines. Shiraz from the Swan District is more savoury, with earthy notes and lower levels of tannin.

TIP

Classic or *Chablis* — what's in a name?

For years, Western Australian winemakers have created quite a niche for themselves with a particular blend of white wine. Ordinarily, you find some Chenin Blanc in the mix, with a certain quantity of Semillon and Sauvignon Blanc. For years, the wines were marketed as Chablis.

But Chablis is actually a wine region and town in France, so the term was dropped from the wine label. In its place, the term *classic* is almost universally adopted when referring to wines of this style.

If you select a bottle whose label sports the term *classic*, you know that the wine is fresh and ready-to-drink with a degree of grassy, gooseberry aromatics. And, on occasion, the wine may finish with a touch of sweetness.

Finding diversity in the Perth Hills

Quite a diverse number of grape varieties are grown in the Perth Hills, although the major varieties are the stalwarts of the Australian industry — Shiraz and Cabernet Sauvignon. But you find a bit of Sangiovese, Tempranillo, Grenache, Merlot and, due to a mistake by a vine nursery, a small planting of the little-known Carnelian (see the sidebar 'Breeding up Carnelian'). So far, the Carnelian has been blended with Shiraz at the Western Ranges Winery.

Producing perfectly in the Peel region

Like the Peel region's neighbours, the wineries of the Peel region make a savoury style of Shiraz which, while the flavours of fruits such as blackberry and mulberry also show, exhibits soft savoury flavours with a drying finish. Chardonnay from the region shows generous aromas of peaches and white nectarines with a soft finish.

Touring some winning wineries

Two wineries in the Swan District are quite large — Houghton and Sandalford — whereas the Perth Hills is boutique wine country. (See Figure 21-1 for some winning wines from these regions.) The Peel region also has smaller wineries, albeit with a high profile.

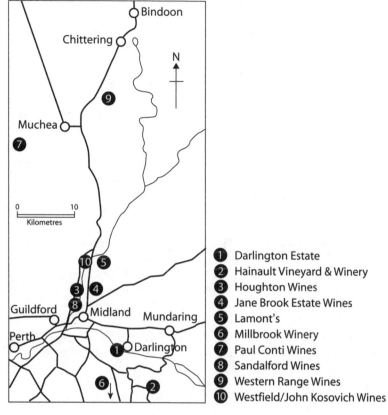

Figure 21-1:
Wineries of
the Swan
Valley and
Perth Hills.

1. Darlington Estate
2. Hainault Vineyard & Winery
3. Houghton Wines
4. Jane Brook Estate Wines
5. Lamont's
6. Millbrook Winery
7. Paul Conti Wines
8. Sandalford Wines
9. Western Range Wines
10. Westfield/John Kosovich Wines

Travelling along the Swan Valley

With the exception of Houghton's and Sandalford, the wineries of the Swan District are quite small family-owned businesses, and most have a cellar door where you can sample a range of usually well-priced wines.

✔ **Houghton Wines:** The biggest and one of the oldest wineries in the Swan Valley is Houghton Wines, established in 1859 and now owned by the Hardy Wine Company. A myriad wines are on offer, from the famous **Houghton White Burgundy** (mentioned earlier in this chapter) to **Houghton Jack Mann**, a stunning red that is predominantly Cabernet Sauvignon and packed with flavours and an abundance of tannins.

✔ The **Houghton White Burgundy**, which for years was Australia's highest-selling white wine, has a dominance of Chenin Blanc in the blend (the other varieties are Muscadelle and Chardonnay). After a few years in the bottle, this White Burgundy is a lovely surprise.

In between the Houghton's White Burgundy and the Houghton Jack Mann, in terms of price, you find the well-priced **Houghton Crofters** range of **Shiraz**, **Cabernet Merlot** and **Semillon Sauvignon Blanc**. You can expect to drink all the Houghton's Crofters wines young and enjoy them for their sheer fruitiness and soft tannins.

Like many of the Swan wineries, Houghton Wines have established grapegrowing operations in other Western Australian regions, so at the cellar door, you also find the excellent mulberry and savoury **Houghton Pemberton Merlot** and the brambly, dry **Houghton Margaret River Cabernet Sauvignon** (Chapter 22 covers Pemberton and Margaret River).

✔ **Jane Brook Estate Wines:** One of the wineries closest to Perth, Jane Brook Estate Wines produces a well-made 100 per cent, fruit-filled Verdelho, the **Jane Brook Estate Verdelho**. The **Jane Brook Estate Shiraz** is an earthy style of Shiraz, and is made from grapes grown in the home vineyard. To add to their winemaking capabilities, Jane Brook now purchases fruit from vineyards in the Pemberton region.

✔ **John Kosovich Wines:** Formerly known as Westfield Wines, this winery changed its name as a tribute to John Kosovich who, in 2002, completed 50 vintages at the winery. John took over the winemaking at the early age of 18, after the sudden death of his father, who founded the winery in 1922.

John's philosophy is that if you pay attention to the little things, the wines attain a high standard. Grapes that are full of flavour are produced in their vineyards in the dry Swan Valley, and also in the cooler climate of Pemberton, where the winery has expanded. The fruit for the **Bronze Wing** label comes from Pemberton.

Favourites from this winery are the elegant **John Kosovich Chardonnay** and the richly textured **John Kosovich Liqueur Muscat.**

✔ **Lamont's:** If you can visit the Swan Valley, don't miss this winery. Not only are the wines first class, especially the tropical **Lamont's Semillon Sauvignon Blanc** and the peppery, intensely flavoured **Lamont's Shiraz**, but also the cellar door, surrounding grounds and restaurant are simply gorgeous.

- **Paul Conti Wines:** This winery is only 30 minutes north of Perth and is worth a visit for their excellent fortified wines, **the Paul Conti Reserve Port** made from old-established Grenache vines with a dash of Shiraz, and the 10-year-old **Paul Conti Reserve Muscat**, which is made from sweet muscat fruit beautifully balanced by a clean dry finish. The Medici Ridge range is excellent, and includes the well-priced (around AUD$16) **Paul Conti Medici Ridge Shiraz** that has a sour-cherry and leathery flavour while the **Paul Conti Medici Ridge Merlot** is a ripe, red-berried wine.

- **Sandalford Wines:** Another of the large companies whose history started in the Swan Valley, Sandalford Wines has operations in both the Swan District and Margaret River. At the easy-drinking end of their portfolio is the **Sandalford Element** range with a blended white and red wine. The **Sandalford Element Merlot** doesn't expect you to sit and discuss the wine too much; rather, it shows a ripe-fruited, soft-tannined flavour that can be drunk young. For an easy-to-drink, everyday wine, this one won't disappoint.

Slightly more expensive are the wines in the Sandalford Premium Range. Particularly good is the peachy and herbal **Sandalford Margaret River Premium Verdelho** and the nutty and complex **Sandalford Margaret River Premium Chardonnay**.

The great, late Jack Mann

Jack Mann made an astonishing 51 consecutive vintages at the Houghton Wines. The winemaker who preceded him was his father, George. Jack's notion of grape growing was that the grapes should be totally ripe — to the point where the grapes fall from the bunches when the vine trunk is kicked — before harvesting. The wines that Jack made were always rich in flavour and texture, and set the Western Australian wine industry on its successful course. Continuing his legacy in the region is his daughter, Corin, who, with her husband Neil, owns and operates the winery at Lamont's in the Swan Valley. In 1989, Jack's grand-daughters, Kate and Fiona, opened a stunning restaurant at the winery.

Finding charm and hospitality in the Perth Hills

The Perth Hills is a relatively new wine region of the Greater Perth zone. Most of the wineries are small-scale, family-owned and family-run affairs that give visitors a warm welcome.

✔ **Millbrook Winery:** A stunning new cellar door facility as well as some quality winemaking has Millbrook Winery set for a rosy future. The **Millbrook Sauvignon Blanc** is full of tropical fruits; the **Millbrook Viognier** is full bodied with an intense flavour, and is a good example of this grape's potential in the warm region.

Millbrook Winery also produces a second, well-priced label (around AUD$17) called Barking Owl range (yes, a local hawk-owl of this name does 'wook-wook' at night!). The **Barking Owl Chardonnay** is a full-bodied style of Chardonnay with fresh fruit flavours; the **Barking Owl Shiraz** has an earthy complexity and is full of dark fruit flavours. (See Chapter 28 for more information on Millbrook Winery.)

✔ **Western Range Wines:** The owners are mostly grape growers who banded together to make wines from their various vineyards and operate a cooperative style of business. Consequently, the range within the portfolio is quite large and also includes a few organic wines.

Shiraz is proving to be one of Western Range's high notes, with the **Western Range Shiraz**, full of juicy black berry flavours, winning friends across the country. Also look for the **Western Range Viognier**, with undertones of dried apricots and peaches, and the **Western Range Shiraz & Grenache**, an inexpensive blend filled with fruit flavours and a spicy and earthy base.

Making a worthwhile stop at Peel

Although only a tiny wine region, Peel is definitely worth a visit if you're on a day trip from Perth or are travelling through on your way south. The place to stop is **Peel Estate Winery,** located at Baldivis. The coastal location adds great regional character to the wine, and the **Peel Estate Shiraz** is consistently well made, showing ripe, sweet fruit characters with chocolate and blackberry flavours.

Chapter 22

South West Australia: Beaches, Forests and Sunshine

• •

• •

*M*anjimup, Yallingup, Willyabrup, Cowaramup, Metricup — if you're Danish, you might think you're back in Denmark. A huge number of the place names in South West Australia end in 'up', the reason being that 'up' means water in one of the local Aboriginal languages. The water in question is the vast Indian Ocean and, of course, the meandering Margaret River.

Margaret River is the main, and perhaps the best-known, region of the South West Australia wine zone. Other regions are Pemberton, Manjimup, Geographe and Blackwood Valley. (The Great Southern region, which is also a part of the South West Australia zone, is covered in Chapter 23.)

Once only attracting surfers in search of the coast's world-famous waves, Margaret River now hosts upwards of 90 wineries, many of which were started in the 1970s by doctors looking for a weekend diversion (as happened in the eastern states). Today, Margaret River is very much a wine destination as well as a magnet for surfers keen to catch big waves.

In this chapter, I take you through the lovely and varied wineries of the Margaret River region, and then I turn inland to the vineyards of Pemberton and Manjimup, two regions that are surrounded by the most spectacularly tall karri trees.

Travelling through the Wine Regions of the South West

If you follow the coast road from Perth to Margaret River, you arrive in the Geographe region. Located between the towns of Bunbury and Busselton, and with Geographe Bay in the west (after which the region is named), Geographe has a few high-profile, quality wineries such as Capel Vale and Hackersley.

After Busselton, the land curves around Geographe Bay and juts out into the ocean. The point beyond Dunsborough in the north-west is Cape Naturaliste and the town of Augusta lies close to the southern extremity of Cape Leeuwin. The town of Margaret River lies more or less halfway between Dunsborough and Augusta, and takes its name from the river that flows into the ocean near Prevelly. As a bit of an aside . . . surfers know that one of the world's most famous surf breaks is at Margaret River; most of the owners of the vineyards and wineries are fairly resigned to the fact that when the surf's up, many of their staff are likely to be hard to find.

As you travel inland from the coast, the scenery changes dramatically from beaches to forests. Head south-east towards Pemberton and Manjimup, and you see some of the tallest trees in the world. The stunning karri trees tower above you and the vineyards of Pemberton and Manjimup, two relatively new wine regions, occupy pockets of cleared land.

If you're travelling between Margaret River and Pemberton, you may pass though the wine region known as Blackwood Valley. Like the Pemberton and Manjimup regions, the land has for many years been home to the soaring jarrah and marri eucalypt trees.

Shooting the Breeze in the Wine Regions

The wine regions on the west coast are inevitably influenced by their proximity to the coast — both in terms of weather and soil fertility. But after you move inland where the giant trees grow, both the fertility of the soil and the higher altitudes change the conditions dramatically.

Cooling winds and varied soils in Margaret River and Geographe

The climate of the Geographe region is influenced by its proximity to the coast. In the summer months, cooling sea breezes flow in, and in winter, the closeness of the sea keeps the temperatures mild. The ocean also influences the climate of Margaret River. The sea breezes that flow in from the Indian Ocean in the west and the Southern Ocean to the south are responsible for its cool-to-warm maritime climate.

The temperature range in both the Margaret River and Geographe regions is very small — over an entire year, the daily mean temperature varies only about 7.6 degrees Celsius. The consistent temperatures mean grapes have a predictable climate in which to ripen, rather than a climate where heat rapidly follows cold and vice versa.

Rainfall in the Margaret River and Geographe regions is relatively high and nearly all of the annual 1,160 millimetres fall over the winter months. For that reason, you often see cereal crops planted in between the rows of vines. This is a strategy to absorb some of the excess water and prevent the soil — and the roots of the vines — from becoming waterlogged. In spring, the cereal crops are slashed and become mulch for the vines, to retain moisture through the very dry growing season. In the growing season, rainfall is only about 200 millimetres.

Soils in the Geographe and Margaret River regions vary a little. Right on the coast, the soils are poor and lack nutrients, becoming more fertile inland around the Ferguson River valley. Vineyards are planted across both soil types. Vines planted in the less fertile soils have to struggle a little but ultimately make good, full-flavoured wines. Vines planted in the more fertile soils need to be well managed so that their vigour (or leaf and shoot growth) doesn't jeopardise their ability to ripen the grapes.

Growing vigorously in the Blackwood Valley

Being inland and away from the coast, the Blackwood Valley region isn't dominated by a coastal climate. During the ripening season, the days are warm, in the high 20s, but often in the late afternoon, sea breezes do find their way through to the valley. Summer nights are often quite cool, around 13 degrees Celsius. This temperature balance allows the vines to recover overnight from the day's warmth and helps to slow down ripening. This means the flavours of the grapes become more intense than they would have been had the nights also remained warm.

The soils in the Blackwood are fertile. As a result, careful vineyard management is required to prevent the vines from becoming excessively vigorous (see the sidebar 'Concentrating the minds of vigorous vines').

Cooling altitudes and rich soils in Pemberton and Manjimup

Both Pemberton and Manjimup enjoy a similar climate. Being inland and less influenced by breezes from the ocean, these two regions escape the summer heat because of their altitude. Vineyards around Pemberton are planted at 100 to 200 metres above sea level, while Manjimup is a little higher in elevation than Pemberton, with vineyards established around 250 to 310 metres above sea level. Manjimup has more sunshine than Pemberton, is warmer and less humid.

What both Pemberton and Manjimup also have are extremely old soils that support the magnificent red gums and karri gums that grow in both regions. The *karri loam* of the Pemberton region is a deep red, fertile soil — almost too fertile, really, as it leads to excessive *vigour* in the vines (that is, the amount of leaves and shoots that the vines produce). Manjimup's *marri* soil is less fertile, and has more sand and gravel than the karri loam. Before vines were planted, the main agricultural pursuit was market gardening with an emphasis on potatoes, which thrive in the soils.

Rainfall in these two regions occurs mainly in winter and spring, although during the ripening season a storm or two often bring varying quantities of rain. Depending on the stage of growth the grapes have reached, this rain may or may not be a problem — a lot of the grapes may be spoiled or the rain may merely provide a gentle drink for the vines.

TECHNICAL STUFF

Concentrating the minds of vigorous vines

In viticulture, the term *high vigour* means that loads of foliage are produced in spring and continue to be produced throughout the ripening season. For a vine to be in balance, viticulturally speaking, as soon as the grapes begin to ripen, leaf growth should stop. The vine is then able to concentrate all its efforts on ripening the fruit, rather than being distracted by growing more leaves.

If a vine is still producing leaves when it should be concentrating on ripening its grapes, two things are happening:

✔ The fruit isn't getting the vine's full attention and isn't getting the opportunity to develop intense fruit flavours

✔ The new leaves are shading the grapes from the sun and the berries aren't getting the opportunity to ripen fully

After some time and experience, vineyard managers had to rethink their early vineyard practices. Some vineyards that had been irrigating during the ripening period either stopped doing so or carefully monitored the irrigation to ensure that excessive leaf growth did not become a problem.

Meeting the Grapes That Margaret and Her Neighbours Do Best

The grapes that have made Margaret River's fame are Chardonnay and Cabernet Sauvignon, two varieties that enjoy the slow ripening that the cool-to-warm maritime climate offers. Also significant in the region is Merlot (usually as a blending partner to Cabernet Sauvignon), Shiraz, Semillon and Sauvignon Blanc.

Interestingly, when I think of cool-to-warm climates, I immediately think of Chardonnay and, in particular, Pinot Noir. Although Chardonnay does spectacularly well in the South West, Pinot Noir does less well. A few producers have tried Pinot Noir, some still make it, but largely, despite the mild climate, Pinot Noir doesn't thrive. The reason probably lies in the *terroir* (a French term for the soil, climate, aspect and the surrounding environment), which is vital to the overall development and suitability of the grapes. Perhaps Pinot Noir doesn't like the intense red soil or the towering karri trees. Maybe the combination of the two produces a microclimate that just doesn't suit Pinot Noir. Who knows? Having said that, you can always find exceptions to the rule and a few producers, notably Picardy and Salitage in Pemberton, do the variety well.

Those of us who live on the eastern seaboard of Australia tend to imagine that Western Australia is always warm. But like anywhere, the local climate can be quite different when you take into account such factors as sea breezes and altitude. The elevation of the vineyards of Pemberton and Manjimup has an effect on the amount of time the grapes take to ripen. The rough rule of measurement is that for every 100 metres you rise above sea level, you drop a degree in temperature. What this means is that, on average, the winemakers of Manjimup, at an elevation between 250 and 310 metres above sea level, harvest their fruit about three weeks later than the winemakers of the Margaret River region on the flat coastline.

Although Manjimup's elevation makes the region cool, being at a higher elevation also makes for a lot of sunshine. With careful site selection and by planting vines on the northern slopes to maximise their exposure to the sun, the winemakers of the region have no difficulties in ripening their fruit. The most successful fruit so far grown in the Manjimup region are Chardonnay and Merlot.

Pemberton is cooler and wetter than Manjimup, and gets less sunshine too. However, the climate is far from miserable. Days during the ripening season are in the mid- to high-twenties degrees Celsius. Pemberton also excels with Chardonnay, and both Shiraz and Sauvignon Blanc are proving successful.

Hens, chickens and clones

The grape of the Gin Gin clone, along with many clones of Chardonnay, often forms bunches that are slightly different to usual Chardonnay grapes. This bunch formation is what is called 'hen and chicken' or, in more technical terms, *millerandage*. Millerandage refers to uneven berry size, that is, both big and small berries grow on the same bunch. The small berries are considered abnormal because they're seedless.

Millerandage occurs during flowering and subsequent fruit set, and is the likely result in some Chardonnay clones if the weather is cold and windy. Some grape growers regard millerandage as a negative trait in Chardonnay because yield is reduced. However, others regard millerandage as a positive, improving the overall flavour, because these little 'chicken' berries become very intense and ripe in flavour and add another dimension to the overall taste of the juice. The flowering conditions in the Margaret River region, as well as the use of particular clones, have meant that millerandage is a fact of life — and a not unwelcome one.

As a winemaking region, Blackwood Valley is still in its early days. Most vineyards have been planted since 1990 and often on quite small plots, generally less than five hectares. So far, the mild climate has allowed for Chardonnay to again shine, along with Shiraz and Merlot.

✔ **Chardonnay:** The darling of the Margaret River, some of Australia's finest Chardonnays hail from that region; the cool-to-warm maritime climate allows the fruit to ripen slowly. Another factor contributing to the success of this variety is a particular clone of the Chardonnay grape that seems to have the edge over other Chardonnay clones in the region (see the sidebar 'Hens, chickens and clones'). The Gin Gin clone has often been referred to as the star quality behind the world famous Leeuwin Estate Chardonnay. (I describe Leeuwin Estate in the section 'Inland and south from Margaret River to the Blackwood Valley', later in the chapter.)

✔ **Semillon and Sauvignon Blanc:** These two varieties feature significantly in the Western Australian white wine portfolio, and are frequently blended. The wines are always incredibly fruity, with loads of tropical flavours and an herbaceous hint. Some of that herbaceousness comes naturally from the Sauvignon Blanc grapes, but it is also seen unusually in the Semillon grapes.

In blind wine tastings, Semillon from the South West Australia zone is often confused with Sauvignon Blanc — in the west, this similarity to Sauvignon Blanc's flavour profile is how Semillon expresses its fruit flavours. Semillon from this zone is quite different from the citrusy mineral tones of the Hunter Valley Semillon (refer to Chapter 5) or the rich honeyed character of Semillon from the Barossa Valley (refer to Chapter 18).

✔ **Cabernet Sauvignon:** Just as Chardonnay is the queen of the whites, Cabernet Sauvignon is the king of the reds in these regions. The long hours of sunshine in the South West ensure that the grapes can ripen fully, in spite of cooling factors such as sea breezes and altitude. The even temperatures during the ripening period also help: You don't get a period where one day reaches 23 degrees Celsius, then the next day shoots up to 35 degrees Celsius, and then the next day back down to the mid-twenties again. Instead, during the ripening period, the daily temperatures consistently remain in the mid- to high 20s. As a result, the wines are refined and elegant, and not at all over-ripe, under-ripe or grassy.

✔ **Merlot:** This variety is mainly used to blend with Cabernet Sauvignon. The fruitiness of the variety adds to the savoury elegance of the Cabernet and helps to fill out the flavours in the mid-palate. Often Cabernet is described as a 'doughnut wine', that is, a wine with a hole in the middle of its flavour profile. Merlot's job, when blended with Cabernet, is to fill this hole.

✔ **Shiraz:** The Shiraz produced in the west appeals to lovers of a more refined style of the grape. If you're an aficionado of McLaren Vale and Barossa Valley Shiraz, a Shiraz from the west may not be for you. The grapes ripen slowly and are picked at a level of ripeness below that of the super-ripe grapes of South Australia. Due to the different climate and soils, the wines tend to be more savoury, offering earthy and plum-dominated flavours in wines of medium body.

Sampling the Regional Wines

The wine regions of the South West Australia wine zone cover a large amount of territory (see Figure 22-1). They essentially follow the coastline and the hinterland areas from Geographe Bay in the north to the town of Karridale in the south, a distance of around 100 kilometres, and then turn inland to Pemberton and Manjimup tucked away in a corner to the south-east.

1. Alexander Bridge
2. Amberley Estate
3. Batista Estate
4. Brookland Valley Vineyard
5. Cape Mentelle
6. Capel Vale
7. Chestnut Grove
8. Cullen Wines
9. Devil's Lair
10. Evans & Tate
11. Fermoy Estate
12. Hackersley
13. Hay Shed Hill
14. Leeuwin Estate
15. Moss Wood
16. Palandri
17. Picardy
18. Pierro Vineyard
19. Ribbon Vale Estate
20. Salitage
21. Sandalford Wines
22. Smithbrook
23. Vasse Felix
24. Voyager Estate
25. Westfield Bronze Wing
26. Wise Vineyards
27. Xanadu Wines
28. Yanmah Ridge

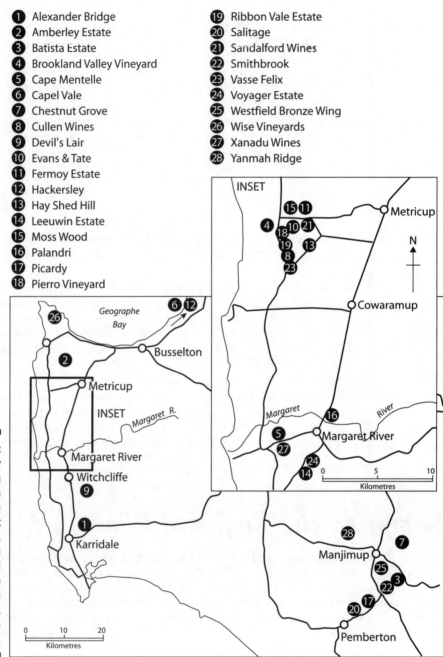

Figure 22-1:
Quality
wines from
the wineries
of the
Margaret
River,
Pemberton
and
Manjimup
wine
regions,
Western
Australia.

The vineyards of the Margaret River region are found in a belt roughly 30 kilometres from east to west, and the wineries are basically clustered around two main areas. A large number of wineries are in the unofficial sub-region of Wilyabrup near the coastline; you find them between Caves Road, the main road that runs all the way through the region from north to south, and the Bussell Highway. Metricup Road runs east to west through the vineyards.

Heading south, you come across just a few wineries before you get to the other cluster of wineries that lie close to the Margaret River itself. If you're visiting the region in springtime, you can also enjoy the sight of all the famous West Australian wild flowers coming out.

Moving south-east to karri country and the beautiful wine regions of Pemberton and Manjimup, most of Pemberton's vineyards lie between the Donnelly River in the north and the Warren River that runs through the region's centre; the vineyards of Manjimup also benefit from these two rivers.

Across all the five regions of the South West Australia zone today, you find over 120 wine producers and many more vineyards. Margaret River is the biggest region in terms of wine producers, with around 80 listed. The Blackwood Valley supports ten wine producers, many of which are of course tiny family-run businesses. Overall, a significant number of people are involved in the wine industry in the south-west of Western Australia.

Wineries north of the Margaret River

A large region north of Busselton, Geographe has relatively few wineries. However, once you swing around to the southern coastline of Geographe Bay, you know you're in serious wine country. The further south you go, the more you see vineyards and wineries on both sides of the road.

Geographe

The Geographe wine region, inland from Geographe Bay, boasts only a handful of wineries. However, these few wineries certainly represent quality.

- **Capel Vale:** This winery is undoubtedly the stand-out one of the region. Having expanded considerably over the years, Capel Vale now offers several ranges. The least expensive range is the **CV Wines** label — uncomplicated wines that are easy to drink. Perhaps the best in the range is the **CV Cabernet Merlot**, a soft fruity wine.

  Other wines I can recommend are in Capel Vale's **Black Label Wines** range: the **Capel Vale 'Whispering' Hill Riesling** is a minerally and lemony wine, and the **Capel Vale 'Kinnaird' Shiraz** is a dark cherry and liquorice spicy wine that cellars well. Capel Vale also makes an excellent Chardonnay, the **Capel Vale Chardonnay**, a peachy and melon-dominant wine.

✔ **Hackersley:** The vineyard at Hackersley mostly grows fruit for other wineries, but it also makes some excellent wines under its own label. Notable for its quality is the **Hackersley Semillon,** which shows lemon and lime flavours with a fresh acidity.

From Cape Naturaliste to Margaret River

The stretch of land from Cape Naturaliste to Margaret River is just laden with wineries. By the time you reach Metricup Road, all you can see is vineyards in a gently rolling and very attractive landscape.

✔ **Amberley Estate:** This winery made its reputation on a fairly grassy Semillon Sauvignon Blanc blend in the days when an extreme grassiness in a wine was acceptable. I must say that I never quite liked this style, but the **Amberley Estate Semillon Sauvignon Blanc** made today is riper with more of the tropical juicy fruit that appeals in this blend.

✔ **Brookland Valley Vineyard:** This winery is now owned by the Hardy Wine Company. The winery and estate vineyard are set on a gorgeous site where the vines are planted down the slopes to the valley so as to maximise the sunny amphitheatre around which the vineyard is planted. Two ranges of wine are made here, Brookland Valley Estate and Brookland Valley Verse 1, which include

 • **Brookland Valley Estate Cabernet Sauvignon Merlot** shows elegance, along with a savoury and fine tannins.

 • **Brookland Valley Verse 1 Semillon Sauvignon Blanc** is a mixture of passionfruit and mango tropical tones with a brisk balancing acidity.

 • **Brookland Valley Verse 1 Chardonnay** is ripe rock melon along with a nice burst of lemony acidity to finish.

✔ **Cullen Wines:** The vineyard at Cullen Wines was one of the first to be planted in the region. Kevin Cullen and his wife Di started planting the vines at their property in Margaret River in 1971 (see the sidebar 'Di Cullen, winemaker'). The winery specialises in quality wines from single vineyard sites. All the wines are quite outstanding.

Cullen Cabernet Sauvignon Merlot is one of my favourite wines and is arguably Australia's finest wine of this style. The wine has incredible concentration of fruit along with a drying tannin and savoury cedar flavour. Certainly this wine is one that can be enjoyed young and can also age for 10–15 years in the cellar.

Another favourite is **Cullen Sauvignon Blanc Semillon**. This wine has all the tropical, fresh fruit flavours that you expect from this blend. However, because the wine is made by using oak barrels (a twist on the usual stainless-steel method of winemaking for these varieties), it possesses far more than just fruitiness and is quite a complex mix of oak, delicacy and fruitiness.

Di Cullen, winemaker

Apart from the odd surfing safari, little was happening around Margaret River at the time Kevin and Di Cullen planted their first vines. As an agricultural region, the economy and future prospects were pretty grim. As the Cullens developed their vineyard, their name gradually became synonymous with very good wine and more and more vineyards were established. In effect, the Cullens pioneered winemaking in the region. Today, the Margaret River is unrecognisable from how the region was in the 1970s.

Very few women were involved in the Australian wine industry in those days, let alone women who physically made the wines themselves. Before long, Di Cullen was winning awards for her wines, and placing the region very much at the forefront of the West Australian wine industry. Di Cullen passed away in 2003, but her daughter Vanya, who has been the winemaker for many years now, continues the excellence of the winery.

✔ **Evans & Tate:** Starting their life as Swan Valley producers, Evans and Tate established themselves in the Margaret River, no doubt partly because of the region's high profile as a wine and tourist region, and also because as winemakers Evans and Tate believed that they could make better wines from the region's fruit. You certainly can't argue with that.

Evans & Tate is now the region's largest winery, and is a reliable and consistent maker of quality wine at reasonable prices. Wines that deserve special mention include

- **Evans & Tate Margaret River Shiraz** is a wine with considerable weight and style offering the Shiraz spectrum of liquorice and dark cherries.

- **Evans & Tate Margaret River Merlot** is a stand-alone wine that doesn't need to be blended with Cabernet Sauvignon to be a top wine. The flavours are typical of those in the region with blackcurrant and cassis along with fine grainy tannins.

- **Evans & Tate Margaret River Semillon** is a wine that is oak-aged to reduce some of the pungent flavours that Semillon can acquire in this region. So expect lots of ripe fruit flavours and a touch of toasty oak.

✔ **Fermoy Estate:** This winery makes a Semillon that is typical of the region's expression of this grape. In the **Fermoy Estate Semillon**, the fruit is ripe yet there is a certain grassiness about the wine, not dissimilar to Sauvignon Blanc. The acid is fresh — if you enjoy New Zealand Sauvignon Blanc, this wine is for you (see Chapter 25 for a description of the wines of the Marlborough region of New Zealand).

✔ **Flying Fish Cove Winery** is one of the region's contract wine-making facilities. A small amount of wine has been made under the label Flying Fish Cove, namely the very well-priced **Flying Fish Cove Cabernet Sauvignon Merlot**, reminiscent of a blackberry jube. The **Flying Fish Cove Semillon Sauvignon Blanc** is a wine with loads of tropical fruits and a touch of sweetness to finish.

The **Suckfizzle** and **Stella Bella** labels, owned by two of the region's most well-known local winemakers, Janice McDonald and Stuart Pym, are made using the Flying Fish Cove facility. Both wines are made using local Margaret River fruit.

One of the top wines from Suckfizzle is the **Suckfizzle Sauvignon Blanc Semillon**, a complex wine that has the tropical fruits and a touch of grassiness but without any the bitterness that is often the downfall of this blend of grapes. The **Stella Bella Sangiovese Cabernet Sauvignon** shows how well a touch of Cabernet structure can work with the fruitiness of Sangiovese.

✔ **Hay Shed Hill:** This cellar door and winery is gorgeous. The winery's range includes the **Hay Shed Hill Semillon Sauvignon Blanc,** the region's famous white blend style; **Hay Shed Hill Chardonnay;** and **Hay Shed Hill Cabernet Sauvignon**. Probably the most renowned comes from the strikingly named Pitchfork label, the **Hay Shed Hill Pitchfork Shiraz Cabernet Rose**. The colour of rosé always seems so summery and this wine is no different — full of spicy and herbal flavours ready to refresh on a warm day.

✔ **Moss Wood:** A winery that easily qualifies as a maker of top Cabernet — it's just a matter of personal preference when you reach quality like this — Moss Wood now has five labels under its control. The labels are Moss Wood Vineyard, Moss Wood Ribbon Vale Vineyard, Moss Wood Amy's Vineyard and Moss Wood Green Valley Vineyard — vineyards that are all in various parts of the Margaret River region — as well as Moss Wood Lefroy Brook Vineyard in Pemberton.

Favourites of mine from Moss Wood include

- **Moss Wood Chardonnay** has an intense toastiness, a meltingly soft and generous texture and a nice lift of acidity on the finish.

- **Moss Wood Cabernet Sauvignon** is dark, brooding and intense in berries and coffee flavours. The finish is soft with ripe, grainy tannins.

- **Moss Wood Ribbon Vale Vineyard Cabernet Sauvignon Merlot** comes from a vineyard acquired by Moss Wood in 2002. The wines are considerably less expensive than the Moss Wood Vineyard range but offer the quality stamp that is typical of all its wines. This wine is fruitier and more ready to drink young than the Moss Wood Vineyard wines.

- **Moss Wood Ribbon Vale Vineyard Semillon Sauvignon Blanc** is a great expression of these two varieties that thrive when blended together. This wine is tropical and fresh with a medium weight, unlike the rather thin wine you sometimes encounter.

- **Moss Wood Lefroy Brook Vineyard Chardonnay** is from the Pemberton arm of the Moss Wood stable. The Moss Wood family doesn't own the vineyard, but they've a long-term agreement to buy the fruit. The wine has loads of fresh Chardonnay fruit flavours, peaches and melon, with a rounded texture.

✔ **Palandri:** The winery sources the fruit for its wines from across Western Australia. Palandri is the biggest vineyard owner in Western Australia, and its biggest vineyard plantings are in the Frankland River in the Great Southern region (see Chapter 23). The winery and cellar door, along with some acreage of vineyards, are in the Margaret River region. By Margaret River standards, the winery is simply enormous; the wines are technically sound albeit without much individuality.

Palandri has a number of labels. The best from the Palandri range are **Palandri Sauvignon Blanc,** which has loads of passionfruit and a touch of fresh grass, and the **Palandri Cabernet Merlot,** which is made from premium parcels of Margaret River fruit, and has soft appealing berry fruits as well as a hint of mocha-like oak.

✔ **Pierro Vineyard:** The showcase wine at this winery is the **Pierro Chardonnay**, which is definitely one of the country's top ten Chardonnays. The wine is ripe and luscious in texture with plenty of everything — nuts, peaches, tinges of complex flavours from the malolactic fermentation and a soft, rounded palate (see Chapter 24 for information on *malolactic fermentation*).

✔ **Sandalford Wines:** This Margaret River winery, with both vineyards and a cellar door facility, was founded in the Swan Valley in 1840 (refer to Chapter 21). Among the best wines here are two in its **Premium Range**: The **Sandalford Margaret River Chardonnay** has loads of citrus fruit and a rounded mouth feel, and the **Sandalford Margaret River Verdelho** has a tropical fruit aroma that almost jumps out of the glass at you.

✔ **Vasse Felix:** The oldest commercial vineyard in the region, the wines from Vasse Felix have always been consistently good, but of late I think they've reached a higher level. Among the wines that are worthy of mention are

- **Vasse Felix Heytesbury Chardonnay** shows full barrel fermentation toastiness, loads of complex Chardonnay flavour and a long lingering finish.

- **Vasse Felix Heytesbury** is a Cabernet blend of Cabernet Sauvignon, Merlot and Cabernet Franc and, although the wine is quite expensive, it offers plenty to please. Cabernet leafiness on the palate is filled out with a cedar-like, blackcurrant flavour. One to stash in the cellar.

✔ **Wise Vineyards:** All alone, right up north at Eagle Bay near Cape Naturaliste, is Wise Vineyards. The vineyards were established in the early 1980s and the quality of the wines has attracted attention among wine drinkers.

In a recent tasting, I found a delightful discovery in the Chardonnay and Semillon Sauvignon Blanc The **Wise Donnybrook Valley Chardonnay** shows rich, intense flavours of nuts and peaches with a soft but balanced mouth feel. The **Wise Eagle Bay Semillon Sauvignon Blanc** topped its price bracket offering loads of tropical fruit, some grassiness and a soft and balanced acid finish.

✔ **Howard Park Wines:** Although all the Howard Park wines are made at its Denmark winery, the fruit is grown in its vineyards in the Margaret River as well as in vineyards across the Great Southern region (see Chapter 23). The **Howard Park Leston Shiraz** is made from fruit grown in the Margaret River and is a lovely, medium-weight savoury wine — a mixture of ripe plums along with truffle-like savouriness — that needs time in the cellar.

Also made from fruit grown in the Margaret River region is the **Howard Park Leston Cabernet Sauvignon**, a wine typical of the region with blackcurrant flavours and a herbal finish, and with plenty of tannin to justify the wine spending some time in your cellar ageing.

Inland and south: Margaret River to the Blackwood Valley

The wine region in the southern part of Margaret River region is top heavy with well-known and super high-quality wine labels. The climate is more moderate here than the more northern vineyard areas. Wineries in this unofficial sub-region are mostly to the east of Prevelly.

Due to their proximity to Cape Leeuwin, where the Indian and Southern Oceans converge, slightly different weather patterns mean the vineyards frequently experience cloud cover. Consequently, the cloud cover moderates the temperature, resulting in milder summer days and less extreme variations between daytime and night-time temperatures in the winter.

✔ **Alexandra Bridge Winery:** Located at the southern tip of the Margaret River wine region, Alexandra Bridge is a newish venture. The winery has two labels, Alexandra Bridge and a Reserve label, Alexandra Bridge 101. The 101 range tends to be big and the texture is sometimes little overwhelming as a result.

My preference is for the Alexandra Bridge label: the **Alexandra Bridge Shiraz** show peppery, plummy and full-bodied flavours without being too overpowering. Also worth looking for is the **Alexandra Bridge Sauvignon Blanc,** which shows good tropical fruits and a lively punch of acidity to finish.

✔ **Cape Mentelle:** Cape Mentelle was first planted in 1970 and was one of the first vineyards established in the Margaret River region. The winery was established by David and Mark David Hohnen and is now owned by Moët Hennessy Wine Estates, the huge French champagne house.

One of the reasons that Margaret River enjoys such high status in the world of wine is because Cape Mentelle consistently produces wines that are first class. The whites wine are particularly outstanding, and include

- **Cape Mentelle Semillon Sauvignon Blanc** shows all the attributes of this blend but above all finishes with acidity, not bitterness, a failing common to this blend.

- **Cape Mentelle Chardonnay** is a lovely easy wine to sip. Enjoy the flavours of nuts, complex fruits and a long finish.

Out of the reds, the one that always stands out for its terrific quality is the **Cape Mentelle Zinfandel.** As a variety, Zinfandel isn't seen much in Australia. The coolish climate of Cape Mentelle allows the fruit to develop spicy, liquorice flavours with sturdy tannins.

✔ **Devil's Lair:** Only two wines are made under the Devil's Lair label, the **Devil's Lair Margaret River Cabernet** and the **Devil's Lair Margaret River Chardonnay**. Both are excellent, with the Cabernet showing cool-climate characteristics of blackcurrant, tobacco leaf and a hint of violets, and the Chardonnay a rich textured mixture of fruits as well as nuts and honey.

To fill out the Devil's Lair wine portfolio and to offer great wine at a good price, the winery also makes a second, less-expensive label called Fifth Leg, which consists of a white blend, a red blend and a rosé.

- **Fifth Leg White** blends together Semillon, Sauvignon Blanc and Chardonnay to make a fresh and fruity white wine.

- **Fifth Leg Red** is usually a blend of Cabernet, Merlot and Shiraz and is a juicy, ripe but elegant wine.

- **Fifth Leg Rosé** is a blend of Merlot and Cabernet Sauvignon.

✔ **Leeuwin Estate:** Leeuwin Estate is one of Australia's most famous vineyards. The **Leeuwin Estate 'Art Series' Chardonnay** has for many years been regarded as one of the top Chardonnays in the country. From the very first vintage, once bottled, the wine was aged for a year or so before being sold. The luxury of being able to hold onto wine and pay the taxes on inventory as well as warehouse space has meant that the wine arrives on the market in peak condition.

After bottling, many wines go though what is unscientifically called 'bottle sickness'. What this means is the wine has gone from ageing quietly in a barrel to being pumped and jostled into the bottle. Often this procedure dulls the fruit and makes the wine's flavours seem disjointed. After six months or so, the wine reverts to its previous condition and the flavours of toastiness and the softening of the acidity (both of which come with age in the bottle) can begin. So the Leeuwin Chardonnay is really being released when it is drinking very well.

✔ **Voyager Estate:** A short distance from Leeuwin Estate, Voyager Estate is confirmation of the fact that this part of Margaret River and Chardonnay have a very strong affinity. The **Voyager Estate Chardonnay** offers stone fruit and cashews on the palate with a background and subtle balancing of acidity — a wine of great class. Equally successful is the **Voyager Estate Shiraz**, a soft-fruited wine with coffee and chocolate nuances and a fine, grainy tannin.

✔ **Xanadu Wines:** Formerly known as Chateau Xanadu, this winery has developed from a small family concern to a stock exchange-listed company, Xanadu Normans. However, the wines from the Xanadu stable haven't lost focus during the transition and the original winemaker is still at the helm.

Particularly good is the **Xanadu Merlot,** a wine that shows the berry rich fruit of this variety with a backbone of savoury character. One of Xanadu's Reserve labels, the most expensive, is the **Xanadu Lagan Estate Reserve Cabernet**. This wine needs time in the cellar to age because, when young, the tannins are quite tough. The background fruits of blackcurrant, some cigar box and a savoury texture point to a good future for the wine.

Under the less-expensive Xanadu Secession label, which focuses on a fresh fruit-driven style of wine, two are worth mentioning. They are

- **Xanadu Secession Chardonnay,** which shows peaches and grapefruit.

- **Xanadu Secession Semillon Sauvignon Blanc**, which is a blend typical of the region with grassy flavours and tangy acid.

Tall timber and wine: Pemberton and Manjimup

Although the two wine regions of Pemberton and Manjimup may not have the pull of the ocean in terms of attracting tourists, the forests of jarrah and karri trees attract a large number of visitors. Visitors soon became aware of the burgeoning wine industry in the area so, if you ever get the chance to visit, you must. The forests are breathtakingly beautiful and a stroll among them is just the thing before or after wine tasting.

Sampling wine in karri country

A good number of white and red varieties are grown in the Pemberton region. Some of the wineries where you can sample some of the best wines are

- **Fonty's Pool Vineyards:** This winery started as a diversification of a market gardening business. The property is and was a significant supplier of vegetables and fruits. In the late 1980s, vines were added to the mix. Look for the **Fonty's Pool Chardonnay**, a fresh, lively, value-for-money wine.

- **Merum:** This winery specialises in quality. Although the vineyard is fairly new, the wines are first class with the spicy and plummy **Merum Shiraz** being the stand-out. As the vines age, I imagine that even better things will come from this winery.

- **Picardy:** An enterprise started by the Pannell family, who were the original owners of Moss Wood winery in the Margaret River, the wines from this label are sophisticated wines with European influences. None of the wines is super fruity; instead they rely on the more tertiary flavours — the way in which the grape's simple fruit characters develop due to winemaking techniques. The **Picardy Chardonnay** has some citrus-like flavours and is also nutty and buttery, rather than just simply fruit driven. The **Picardy Shiraz** has flavours of truffles, an earthy texture and is of medium weight.

- **Salitage:** One of the early commercial wineries to establish itself in the region, the early wines from Salitage were a bit inconsistent, but as time has passed and the region has become better understood, the wines have become better and better. Look for the **Salitage Pinot Noir**, one of the better versions of this variety from the region. Like the Picardy wines, the wine is savoury and reminiscent of the forest floor with an earthy aroma. The second-tier label is Salitage Treehouse, and the **Salitage Treehouse Shiraz** is an example of the excellent savoury Shiraz of the region.

✔ **Smithbrook:** Along with Salitage, Smithbrook was a pioneer in the region. I remember first visiting the vineyard in the early 1990s and being amazed at the immense vigour that the vines had produced. Since then, much work has been done to understand the region and monitor the vigour that the red soils produce. The wines have benefited immensely from this research, as the fruit is more exposed to the sun, allowing even ripening. Among the best from Smithbrook are the **Smithbrook Chardonnay** showing nectarines and citrus fruits, along with a zingy acidity, and the **Smithbrook Sauvignon Blanc**, which is a lively, herbal-dominant wine.

Enjoying what Manjimup does best

The Manjimup region produces a range of wine styles, and some of the best places to enjoy them include

✔ **Batista:** This is a small winery with a leaning towards Pinot Noir. In the Manjimup region, Pinot Noir isn't fruity. The **Batista Pinot Noir** is a savoury wine with mushroom-like flavours and a solid supporting structure of ripe tannin.

✔ **Chestnut Grove:** A huge chestnut tree stands in the centre of the vineyards here and has become the focal point. The winery produces wine under two labels, Chestnut Grove and Tall Timber. The most planted white variety is Verdelho, and the **Chestnut Grove Verdelho** offers loads of tropical fruit with a touch of honey. The **Chestnut Grove Cabernet Merlot** has savoury aniseed flavours with fine tannins and is a wine that is easily approachable when young. The **Tall Timber Sauvignon Blanc Semillon** has plenty of passionfruit with a touch of spiciness to balance.

✔ **Yanmah Ridge:** The vineyards of this winery are among the coolest in the region, standing at an altitude of 250 to 315 metres above sea level. To focus on reducing the level of vigour in the vineyard, the winegrower has planted more vines per hectare than is usual. This strategy creates competition between the vines for water and nutrients and decreases the amount of growth per vine. The outstanding wine is the **Yanmah Ridge Chardonnay**, which exhibits integrated toasty oak flavours and melon nuances.

Chapter 23

Fulfilling Its Promise: The Great Southern Land

*T*he Great Southern wine region of the South West Australia zone is a fairly isolated part of Australia. The town of Mount Barker, a drive of about three and a half hours south-east of Perth, is considered the centre of the region; Mount Barker is also the name of a sub-region. If you want to continue your journey to the four other sub-regions — Albany, Denmark, Frankland River and Porongurup — you've at least another half-hour on the road.

Even by Australian standards (Aussies think nothing of a two-hour drive to see friends at the weekend), this is a region fairly well out on its own. As a whole, the region covers a large tract of land spanning 150 kilometres from north to south and 100 kilometres from east to west.

The Frankland River sub-region is west of Mount Barker, Porongurup is to the east and the sub-regions of Albany and Denmark are right on the coast to the south. All have some of the most stunning landscapes. The towering granite outcrops of the Porongurup Mountain Range surround the Porongurup region, and the coastline around Denmark and Albany is one of the most pristine and spectacular in Australia. Oh, and the wines are worth talking about, too!

In this chapter, I take you through the small, though high-quality, wine-making sub-regions that make up the Great Southern wine region.

Establishing a Fine Wine Region

Not much was happening in the Great Southern part of Western Australia 30 years ago. Sheep farming and beef farming were the two biggest farm activities. In 1965, the Western Australian Department of Agriculture planted some vineyards as a trial at what is now the Forest Hill winery in Mount Barker. Then in 1968, Plantagenet Wines established itself as a small operation. The first real wave of expansion in the area began with Goundrey Wines in the late 1970s.

Vineyards were also established purely to grow grapes for the larger wine companies, selling their fruit to wineries such as the Swan Valley-based Houghton Wines. Little by little, more small operations started, and then expanded. Howard Park and Ferngrove Estate are two wineries with high profiles in terms of the quality of their wines and size of their operations.

Mount Barker and Frankland River have the most land planted to vineyards in the region; companies such as Goundrey and Plantagenet have operations in Mount Barker, and Ferngrove Estate and Frankland Estate are established in Frankland River.

Today, the early plantings are considered to be mature vines, and you can find vines that are 30–40 years old in some vineyards. The quality of the wine from these well-established vines confirms what many of the early grape growers knew — that the Great Southern region had tremendous potential for viticulture. With the confidence born of success, the region now boasts about 40 wineries, many of which are tiny operations, some less than two hectares in size. But size doesn't seem to matter in a region that has built a strong reputation for quality.

Intensifying the Flavour in a Perfect Climate

Both Denmark and Albany are strongly influenced by their close proximity to the Southern Ocean. The breeze tempers the warm summer days and keeps the *diurnal* temperature difference (the difference between day and night temperatures) to a minimum. The coastal aspect also means that the sub-regions sometimes have a fog or mist swirling around until late morning, which adds to the coolness of the vineyards.

The rate at which the grapes ripen in these two sub-regions is slow but even, allowing early-ripening grape varieties such as Pinot Noir, Chardonnay and Merlot, in particular, to flourish, because a drawn-out ripening period allows for a build-up in flavour intensity.

Moving away from the coast and to the north-west, Frankland River is considered to have a continental climate with some Mediterranean influences. Cooling breezes from the Southern Ocean can reach the sub-region, 100 kilometres away. Frankland River is also far enough inland to have cool-to-cold summer and autumn nights with warm-to-hot days and plenty of sunshine. Riesling and Cabernet Sauvignon thrive in this climate, which allows slow ripening.

Mount Barker is around 50 kilometres from the coast, so the sea breezes are able to temper the afternoon summer heat by a few degrees. The sub-region's altitude also helps cool the vines — many vineyards are 300 metres above sea level. (Refer to Chapter 22 for an explanation of higher altitude vineyards.)

Mount Barker enjoys plenty of sunshine during the ripening months, which allows the grapes to ripen fully. The cool nights, often below 10 degrees Celsius, slow the ripening process and allow the grapes to maintain their natural acidity. Consequently, the wines tend to age well. The best varieties so far from Mount Barker have proved to be Riesling, Chardonnay, Cabernet Sauvignon and Shiraz.

The Porongurup sub-region stands out as the coolest within the Great Southern region, due to its elevation of 350 metres above sea level. Site selection is important, and vineyards are planted on the north-east face of the ranges to best optimise the sunshine. Riesling is this sub-region's strong point.

Rainfall across the Great Southern region tends to occur mainly in the winter months; summer and the months when the grapes are ripening remain fairly dry across the whole region.

Grapes That Excel in the Great Southern

The Great Southern certainly lives up to its early promise as an outstanding viticultural area. Significant among the varieties of grape grown in the region are the following:

- **Cabernet Sauvignon:** This grape does exceptionally well in the region. The slow, constant ripening allows this late-maturing grape to really fill out its flavour profile with loads of blackberry, blackcurrant and fine elegant weight.

- **Chardonnay:** A climatically adaptable grape variety, Chardonnay can make a very good wine in the region. The extra warmth that the Frankland River and Mount Barker sub-regions offer particularly suits Chardonnay.

- **Riesling:** The Rieslings from the Great Southern region are gradually finding their way into wine drinkers' hearts. For some years, overshadowed by the wonderful Clare and Eden Valley Rieslings (refer to Chapter 18), Great Southern Riesling has had a hard time making a name for itself. Now the citrus yet flinty wines from the region are definitely standing up to be counted.

- **Shiraz:** A grape that loves the cool-to-warm climate of this vast region, Shiraz is able to slowly ripen and intensify its black plum and dark cherries flavour. The wines don't tend to be overripe and I think they fit into the medium- to full-bodied weight of a wine, rather than the blockbuster Shiraz from the warm Barossa Valley (refer to Chapter 18) and McLaren Vale (refer to Chapter 16).

Growing Notoriety: The Pick of the Best

Such a large region as the Great Southern experiences certain variations in climate, and of course these variations influence the varieties of grape that can be grown successfully. In this section, I take you on a tour of the sub-regions and describe some of the wineries that produce fine examples of the varieties that thrive in the Great Southern wine region. Figure 23-1 shows the locations of these wineries.

The significance of the region

Much of Western Australia's top wines come from the Great Southern, and the region is firmly established as an important one for the state. In 2003, of all the Shiraz grown in the state, 32 per cent came from the Great Southern region; for Cabernet Sauvignon, the figure is 24 per cent.

Turning to white wines, a staggering 84 per cent of all the Riesling grown in Western Australia came from the Great Southern region — evidence of the grape variety's success and suitability here. The region also produced 1,900 tonnes of Chardonnay, a variety that seems to thrive wherever you plant it — which translates into 22 per cent of all the Chardonnay harvested in Western Australia.

In terms of whites versus reds in the Great Southern region, reds make up 60 per cent of all grapes grown there. However, in Western Australia as a whole, the ratio of white wines to red is a fairly even 50:50.

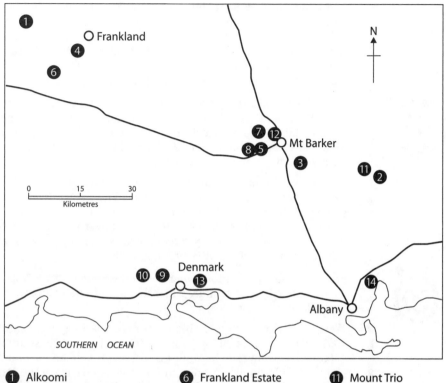

Figure 23-1: Wineries of the Great Southern wine region, Western Australia.

1. Alkoomi
2. Castle Rock Estate
3. Chatsfield
4. Ferngrove Vineyards Estate
5. Forest Hill Vineyard
6. Frankland Estate
7. Galafrey Wines
8. Goundrey Wines
9. Howard Park Wines
10. Karriview Wines
11. Mount Trio
12. Plantagenet Wines
13. West Cape Howe Wines
14. Wignalls Wines

Cool-climate Albany and Denmark

The cool-climate grapes of Pinot Noir and Chardonnay do well in the maritime-influenced Mediterranean climate, where the Southern Ocean cools the day's warmth with sea breezes and cloud cover. The following wineries in Albany and Denmark are typical of the producers of high-quality wines in these sub-regions

✔ **Howard Park Wines:** Although the winery and cellar door are in Denmark, Howard Park has vineyards across the Great Southern region, in Frankland River, Mount Barker and Porongurup. (Howard Park also has a cellar door and vineyards in Margaret River; refer to Chapter 22.) Two outstanding wines from this winery are the **Howard Park Riesling** and **Howard Park Scotsdale Cabernet Sauvignon**. The Riesling consistently ranks among the best produced in the country, and is a complex mix of lime blossom, orange zest and a blast of acid; give the wine some time to mature in the bottle and it softens beautifully. The Cabernet Sauvignon is a sophisticated and elegant wine with plenty of fruit weight to allow the wine to age gracefully.

As a bargain in terms of quality for what you pay, look for the **Howard Park MadFish** label. Two generic white and red blends come under the Madfish label, and are fresh fruity and ready to drink, as well as **the MadFish Chardonnay**, a stone fruit and lemony wine, and the **MadFish Shiraz,** a spicy and savoury wine.

✔ **Karriview Wines:** Typical of the local small winery scene, this winery is set on a two-hectare block in Denmark. The owners were looking for some way to intensively farm their land but knew little about grapes. The then winemaker and co-founder of Howard Park, John Wade, helped them get underway. Excellent winemaking by Wade at Howard Park resulted in wines of very high quality.

Karriview has quite a following for its **Karriview Pinot Noir,** which is a savoury, earthy and truffley wine, that should be drunk before it's been in the bottle for five years.

✔ **West Cape Howe Wines:** This venture is relatively new, established in 1997 as a contract-making facility. Most of the fruit is sourced from established vineyards in Mount Barker with a small vineyard on the property in Denmark. Among the best wines here are the **West Cape Howe Riesling**, a lime and lemon wine with a zing of acid to finish; the **West Cape Howe Shiraz**, which is medium in weight with soft tannins and rounded fruit flavours; and the **West Cape Howe Chardonnay**. Although it has some dominant oak characters when young, the fruit-driven style of this Chardonnay develops well over three to five years.

✔ **Wignalls Wines:** Located in Albany, this winery has been flying the flag for Pinot Noir in the West for many a year. I've not generally been a fan of Western Australian Pinots — somehow the variety doesn't seem to do well in that state. Wignalls is one of the exceptions. **Wignalls Pinot Noir** is consistently an elegant wine with aromas of mushrooms and truffles. This wine isn't fruit driven as, say, a Mornington Peninsula Pinot Noir would be (refer to Chapter 13); rather, this wine is earthy and savoury.

Enjoy the Wignalls Pinot Noir when young; it tends to lose its intensity of flavour after more than five years in the bottle.

Another Wignalls wine that I commend is the **Wignalls Chardonnay**, which has gone from strength to strength and has a flint-like flavour.

Flavoursome Frankland River wines

At around 100 kilometres from the coast, Frankland River offers a stable climate for grapegrowing. The wines are generous in flavour and texture without being too big. Among the wineries are

✔ **Alkoomi Wines:** Established in 1971, Alkoomi produces wines that are among the region's best. The **Alkoomi Frankland River Shiraz** is a well-priced wine showing spicy, dark plums. The excellent **Alkoomi Blackbutt** from the Super-Premium range is a blend of the very best Cabernet Sauvignon, Cabernet Franc, Malbec and Merlot produced in each vintage.

From Alkoomi's range of white wines, look for the **Alkoomi Frankland River Riesling** in the Premium range; this is a minerally long-living wine with lime and citrus flavours.

✔ **Ferngrove Vineyards Estate:** The owners of this winery are quite new to the wine scene, having been beef and dairy farmers for generations and turning to grapegrowing in 1997. Already the winery has secured a big reputation after winning wine award after wine award for its **Ferngrove Estate Cossack Riesling** in the Premium Orchid range. The vines have to struggle in poor soil and intense flavours develop; this wine can be cellared for up to eight years, such is its potential.

Another top wine from this winery is the medium-bodied **Ferngrove Vineyards Estate Shiraz,** which is typically spicy with a touch of earthiness.

✔ **Frankland Estate:** Another vineyard and winery set up on a sheep farm (where sheep still run) is Frankland Estate. In my view, the outstanding wine here is the **Frankland Estate Isolation Ridge Riesling** which, like the Ferngrove Estate Cossack Riesling, is going to age gracefully in the bottle for many a year. Also worth looking for is the **Frankland Estate Olmo's Reward**, a Cabernet Franc and Merlot blend which is soft-fruited and has fine tannins.

At the hub in Mount Barker

Mount Barker is home to some of the largest wineries in the Great Southern region. The sub-region has seen widespread expansion over the past five years and has forged a reputation as a quality producer within Western Australia.

Among the excellent wineries are the following:

- ✔ **Chatsfield:** Located In the westerly shadow of the Porongurup Ranges, this winery gets the cool air that pools down from the ranges, as well as good winter rain. The cool nights slow the rate at which the grapes ripen and allow them to maintain their natural acidity. The two wines that stand out are the **Chatsfield Riesling**, packed with lime and lemon flavours, and the **Chatsfield Shiraz**, a peppery spicy example of this variety.

- ✔ **Forest Hill Vineyard:** The oldest vineyard in the sub-region of Mount Barker, Forest Hill has had a number of owners since it was established in 1965. Until recently, it was owned by the Margaret River Vasse Felix winery and much of the fruit grown here went into the excellent Vasse Felix Heytesbury label. The new owners are currently revamping the winery and business. A brand new winery was completed in 2003 just in time for the vintage, and since then a cellar door facility has opened. Look for the **Forest Hill Riesling**, a citrus-dominated wine with a soft mouth feel.

- ✔ **Galafrey Wines:** A small, family-run and quality producer, Galafrey was one of the first to recognise the potential of Mount Barker.

The **Galafrey Mount Barker Riesling** develops good nutty and toasty characters with age.

- ✔ **Goundrey Wines:** A blockbuster-sized winery in quiet rural Australia, Goundrey Wines has grown from small beginnings to a winery with enormous tracts of land devoted to vines and a very up-market cellar door. Goundrey makes good commercial wines, while the Reserve end of the range is of a very high order.

The best wines here are the **Goundrey Reserve Chardonnay**, a buttery, peachy wine with good balance, and the **Goundrey Offspring Shiraz**, a wine redolent of ripe red berries and full of liquorice spiciness.

- ✔ **Plantagenet Wines:** One of the pioneering winemakers of the region and a winery that hasn't fallen by the wayside as others have arrived, Plantagenet Wines is named after the local shire. The first vines were planted in 1968, with 1974 seeing the inaugural vintage. Since establishment, the company has continued to grow each year, and the high quality hasn't faltered. In the Plantagenet Reserve range is the savoury, cedary and rich-fruited **Plantagenet Cabernet Sauvignon** and the nutty and grapefruit-like **Plantagenet Chardonnay**.

The Plantagenet Omrah range is excellent value for money and includes the fruity **Plantagenet Omrah Chardonnay**, the spicy **Plantagenet Omrah Shiraz** and a soft **Plantagenet Omrah Merlot Cabernet**.

Porongurup: Sweeping views and sensational wines

The coolest sub-region within the Great Southern, picturesque Porongurup takes its name from the spectacular range of ancient granite outcrops known as the Porongurup Mountain Range. Not surprisingly, most of the vineyards are at an altitude of around 350 metres above sea level.

The soil is quite poor, which means that the crop levels per hectare are also poor. However, low-quantity production means high-quality fruit. Among the producers to take advantage of the growing conditions of the high country are

✔ **Castle Rock Estate:** Probably the country's most spectacular cellar door can be found at Castle Rock Estate — the views over the Porongurup Ranges are breathtaking. The vineyards were established on the north-east face of the slopes in order to maximise the amount of sun the vines receive.

One of Castle Rock's top wines is the **Castle Rock Estate Riesling**, which packs a powerful punch of citrusy flavours along with bold acidity. This wine has excellent ageing potential, so stash it in your cellar for up to ten years.

✔ **Mount Trio:** Another winery in the region is Mount Trio, named after one of the mountains in the Stirling Ranges north of the region. The venture is relatively small but the wines are very good indeed. Best from Mount Trio's range is the **Mount Trio Pinot Noir**, which has clearly enjoyed the cool-climate ripening and has plum and sour-cherry flavours.

The **Mount Trio Chardonnay** is a leaner style of wine with good ageing potential, and is well worth the effort of tracking it down.

Part V
New Zealand Wines

www.moir.com.au   *Alan Moir*

In this part . . .

This part includes a diverse group of New Zealand's vineyards that stretch from the tip of the north to the bottom of the south islands. The vineyards off the coast of Auckland on Waiheke Island produce some pretty smart Cabernet wines. And the famous Martinborough (Wairarapa) region put New Zealand Pinot Noir on the world wine map. Add to these the beautiful wines of Hawke's Bay, one of the few regions in New Zealand that can make top wines from the Merlot grape.

Not to mention the third largest producer of New Zealand wine, the Gisborne region, and the smaller, quieter in reputation Bay of Plenty and Waikato region. And the famous and delicious Chardonnay that hails from the Kumeu part of Auckland. And all of that bounty is just on the North Island.

Down south is the region that causes a few people to dive for an atlas. Just where did this amazing glass of Sauvignon Blanc hail from? And just when the atlas is put away, the Central Otago Pinot Noir bursts onto the scene. This southern-most vine-growing region in the world has sent the wine world a little crazy, such is the quality of the liquid booty from here. So there isn't a thing to stop you now. Grab that atlas and discover the wines of New Zealand.

Chapter 24

Liquid Gold from New Zealand's North Island

*M*any similarities exist between the wines and the regions of Australia and New Zealand, for all the intense competition between the winemakers of both countries. After all, having rivalries with your closest neighbour is almost compulsory — Australia and New Zealand's started with rugby union.

The beginnings of the wine industry in both countries are closely linked. James Busby, the man closely involved in the birth of the Australian wine industry, was also influential in New Zealand, planting a vineyard on the North Island in 1836. As the years passed, other pioneers began to plant vineyards, too.

As was the case in many other countries at the time, prohibition laws made selling wine increasingly difficult. So although the wine industry in New Zealand was burgeoning in the middle of the nineteenth century, the wine industry wasn't able to develop into what is today a very significant industry for the country until after the Second World War. European migrants, mostly from Croatia, were significant players in the establishment of the wine industry in New Zealand. (See the sidebar 'Creating a wine industry: the Croatians'.)

In this chapter, I describe the six wine regions of the North Island and their individual sub-regions. The regions are Northland, Auckland, Bay of Plenty, Gisborne, Hawke's Bay and Wairarapa (see Figure 24-1). By the way, you often find that wine people refer to the Wairarapa region as 'Martinborough'.

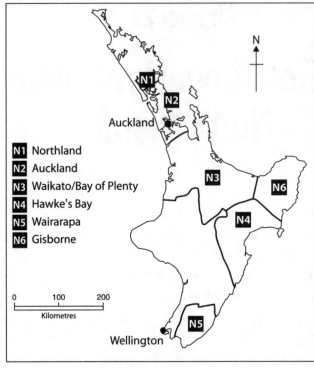

Figure 24-1:
The wine
regions of
the North
Island of
New
Zealand.

N1 Northland
N2 Auckland
N3 Waikato/Bay of Plenty
N4 Hawke's Bay
N5 Wairarapa
N6 Gisborne

In and Around Auckland

Auckland is situated in the northern part of New Zealand's North Island. In fact, Auckland's southern latitude isn't dissimilar to that of Sydney in neighbouring Australia: Sydney is 34 degrees south and Auckland is a little further to the south at about 37 degrees latitude.

Auckland (New Zealand's capital city) was once the centre of the wine industry in New Zealand. Most of the country's large winemaking firms have wine-processing facilities in the region; much of the wine coming out of Auckland-based wineries is actually made from fruit grown as far away as the South Island's Marlborough region. Today the Auckland region only makes up 3 per cent of the total vineyard area in the country.

The sub-regions of Auckland are Matakana/Mahurangi, Kumeu/Huapai, Henderson, Waiheke Island and South Auckland. The tiny region of Northland, which produces less than one-half a per cent of the country's total wine production, is to the north of Auckland.

Working in a damp climate

Not surprisingly, given their latitude and proximity to the coast, most of the vineyards in the Auckland region have to cope with high rainfall as well as high humidity — not unlike the Hunter Valley region of Australia (refer to Chapter 5). Northland has a rather unfavourable climate and is unlikely to expand to any significant degree in the future.

The most westerly sub-region of Auckland is that of Kumeu/Huapai, which is a little drier than other mainland Auckland vineyards. The wine that is vinified in the local wineries is done so mostly from grapes brought into the region. Only Kumeu River Wines and Harrier Rise Vineyard (see the section 'Picking the best of the Auckland bunch', later in the chapter) make wines solely from grapes grown in the Kumeu/Huapai area, and both producers are making top-class wines.

Auckland has a high rainfall during the growing season (spring into summer), which means that shoot and leaf growth is vigorous, potentially resulting in disease problems. Consequently, only those vineyard managers who are very careful with their viticulture succeed in growing high-quality fruit. Added to the risk of fungal disease (which can result from dense leaf coverage creating canopies) are the associated problems that occur when the fruit is unevenly exposed to the sun (see the sidebar 'The challenges of a high-rainfall region').

No really striking differences in climate or topography can be identified in the sub-regions of Auckland. The land is fairly uniformly flat or undulating, and the altitude is low — almost everywhere is less than 40 metres above sea level. Apart from Waiheke Island, which is further east and hence a little drier, all sub-regions have relatively high rainfall.

The challenges of a high-rainfall region

In a region of high rainfall where dense foliage grows easily, grapes are at risk of being shaded by the leaf canopy. Shading of fruit causes uneven ripening and produces wines that taste unbalanced since they're made from a combination of ripe grapes and unripe grapes. Even so, vineyard operators who manage their vines expertly can meet the challenge and make high-quality wine, except in the odd year when the rain upsets fruit ripening at the harvest time.

As is well recognised in the industry, the better vineyard sites are those that are sloping with well-drained soils, or those that have had the soil structure modified. Growing a strip of grass in the soil between the rows of vines is a way of modifying the soil structure: The grass absorbs some of the rainfall, thus reducing the amount of water available to the vines. Less water to the roots of the vines results in a less dense canopy of vine leaves.

Growing the grapes that suit the Auckland region

The most planted varieties in the Auckland region are Chardonnay and Merlot, which are almost equal in the number of planted hectares, with 23 and 21 per cent of the total respectively. Behind Merlot comes Cabernet Sauvignon. However, due to the difficulty of getting the grapes for Cabernet Sauvignon to fully ripen, this variety is gradually being replaced with Merlot and, increasingly, Cabernet Franc.

Chardonnay

Chardonnay from the Auckland region is typically fruit-driven, showing aromas of peaches, cashews and stone fruits. Compared to Chardonnay grown in other parts of New Zealand, these wines are rich with soft acidity. One of the truly outstanding wines comes from the Kumeu River. In most cases, the regions in which the fruit is grown are listed on the label; exceptions are generic blends of the less expensive wines. See Chapter 3 for more information about labelling requirements.

TECHNICAL STUFF

Kumeu River revelation

In the Auckland region, and more particularly in the Kumeu sub-region, Chardonnay and Kumeu River wines are hard to separate. One of the first New Zealand wines I ever tasted was a Kumeu River Chardonnay from the late 1980s.

The wine's individuality has stuck in my memory ever since — this wine was a big, generous ripe style of wine with such dense texture that I thought I was having a meal in a glass. A stunning wine! As it turns out, early Kumeu River Chardonnays turned many a head, but mainly in disgust. Why? Read on.

At the time, the winemakers were among the first to dabble in the more Burgundian style of winemaking. The *Burgundian* style was to ferment wine in oak barrels rather than in stainless steel. The result was a loss of the fresh fruitiness of the wine and a gain of a subtle oak character.

Also, because the wine was fermented in the barrel, after fermentation of the grape sugars to alcohol was complete, the yeast cells died and settled on the bottom of the barrel.

Yeast cells can offer interesting biscuity and nutty flavours as well as a rounded texture. A technique from Burgundy, therefore, is to regularly stir the wine in the barrel to redisperse the yeast through the wine so as to achieve some of these flavour and texture attributes.

Today, wines from the Kumeu River are much revered. Wine lovers are now used to ripe fruit that has undergone a *malolactic fermentation* (the conversion of the harsh tasting malic acid to the softer in texture lactic acid) to give a rich texture and to transform simple, tropical fruit flavours into nutty, intensely flavoured and interesting wines.

Other white wines

Of late, some very impressive Pinot Gris wines have been making a name for themselves. Typically, these exhibit the nutty and pear-like characters of Pinot Gris in a more rich, full style than in the austere Pinot Grigio style (see Chapter 2 for more information on this variety).

Wineries with bases in the Auckland region also produce some excellent Sauvignon Blanc, though the fruit mostly comes from the Gisborne region or from the Marlborough region of the South Island of New Zealand (see Chapter 25).

Merlot

So far, this grape variety has shown itself to be the best of the reds produced in the Auckland region. As the climate dictates, high vine vigour is a characteristic of vineyards in this region. *High vine vigour* means that the vine produces a lot of shoots and leaves per vine. The dense canopy of leaves on the vine means the grapes get less exposure to the sun, which in turn means the grapes take longer to ripen than would grapes growing on a vine with a sparser leaf canopy (see the sidebar 'The challenges of a high-rainfall region'). Since Merlot ripens a little earlier in the season than does Cabernet Sauvignon, this variety ripens before the autumn weather cools and begins to turn wintry.

Integral to the ripening of the grapes is the development of skin colour and flavour, as well as the ripening of the tannins. Ripe tannins are vitally important, both in the skin and in the seeds of the fruit. If you taste unripe tannin in a wine, your mouth tends to pucker up as the tannin strips the moisture from your mouth. If the leaf canopy shades the grapes from the sun, green herbaceous flavours develop, the tannins are difficult to ripen and the acid level remains high — none of which are attractive characters in red wine. Selecting the right site for the vineyard is therefore of paramount importance, as is efficient vineyard management, after the vines are planted, to ensure that the fruit gets enough sun exposure.

Much of the Merlot grown in the Auckland region goes into a blend, almost always as part of a classic Bordeaux blend of Cabernet Sauvignon, Merlot and Cabernet Franc.

Cabernet Sauvignon

The question of whether Cabernet Sauvignon can be successfully produced in a country with such a cool climate is yet to be resolved. As a late-ripening variety, Cabernet needs a vineyard site that receives enough autumn sunshine to ripen away any of the green capsicum aromas and harsh flavours that are so unpleasant in a not-quite-ripe Cabernet. Cabernet is particularly prone to these characters if the vine leaf canopy is dense and not properly managed.

Some of the Cabernet Sauvignons that are getting a good reputation, however, come from Waiheke Island where the days are warmer and the summers a little drier than around Auckland.

Picking the best of the Auckland bunch

In spite of high rainfall and high humidity, some of the best-performing wines come from the coastal area in the northern part of the Auckland region. A number of wineries have managed to overcome the climatic obstacles and are producing wines of note (see Figure 24-2).

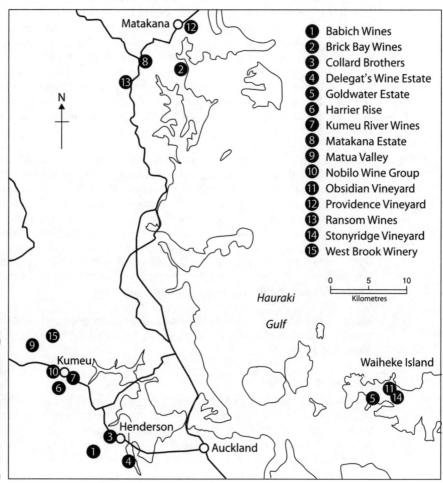

Figure 24-2: Coastal wines from the wineries of the Auckland region, North Island.

1. Babich Wines
2. Brick Bay Wines
3. Collard Brothers
4. Delegat's Wine Estate
5. Goldwater Estate
6. Harrier Rise
7. Kumeu River Wines
8. Matakana Estate
9. Matua Valley
10. Nobilo Wine Group
11. Obsidian Vineyard
12. Providence Vineyard
13. Ransom Wines
14. Stonyridge Vineyard
15. West Brook Winery

Babich Wines

Founded by Josif Babich in 1910, the winery is still owned by the Babich family. Like many of its neighbours in the region, Babich has expanded its vineyard holdings, mainly into areas to the south such as Hawke's Bay and Marlborough. Among the best the winery produces are the **Irongate Chardonnay,** a citrus-dominated wine that will age well for upwards of five years, and **Irongate Cabernet Merlot,** a wine also capable of aging well with the cassis flavours developing into complex tobacco-like characters over time. The grapes are grown in the gravelly soils of Gimblett Road in the Hawke's Bay region. (See the sidebar 'Gimblett Gravels'.)

Goldwater Estate

One of the top producers from the sub-region of Waiheke Island region is Goldwater Estate. This winery produces an excellent briary **Goldwater Estate Cabernet Sauvignon Merlot** that shows soft tannin characters.

Harrier Rise

This winery produces only red wine, with Merlot and Cabernet Franc dominating. The wines are quite distinct, being fermented on skins for longer than most wines. Unlike most red wines that are pressed off skins around the second week, the Harrier Rise reds — such as the **Harrier Rise Uppercase Merlot**, a chocolate- and briary-flavoured wine, and the **Harrier Rise Monza Cabernet**, a coffee and tobacco wine — are left on their skins for six to seven weeks after fermentation. While the resultant wines lose their fruit-driven characters, they instead become savoury food-friendly wines.

Kumeu River Wines

Chardonnay is at the top of the list at this winery, and three labels at different price levels are available. At the top of the Chardonnays is the **Kumeu River Mate's Vineyard Chardonnay**, named after the founder of the vineyard, Mate Brajkovich, which is a powerful fruit- and oak-flavoured wine made from the best grapes of the vintage. Perhaps the best-known Chardonnay from this winery is the mid-priced **Kumeu River Chardonnay**. The wine is intensely flavoured with rounded texture on the palate.

A good buy (and also the least expensive) is **Kumeu River Brajkovich Chardonnay**, a blend of barrel-aged wine and wine from a stainless steel fermentation. This process makes the wine lighter in body than would have been the case if full barrel fermentation had been used.

An apricot and lychee-like **Kumeu River Pinot Gris** has been added to the wine list, along with a savoury, briary **Kumeu River Brajkovich Merlot**.

An early German variety

Müller Thurgau is a crossbreed of a grape that was developed in the 1880s in the German town of Thurgau by a man called Hermann Müller. The variety is thought to be a cross between Riesling and Sylvaner, although many people believe the variety is actually a cross between two clones of Riesling. Müller Thurgau was mostly planted in the early days of the New Zealand wine industry, to be made into a sweetish, fruity white wine. For many years it was the backbone of New Zealand's white wine market. Today, less and less is under vine as local wine tastes embrace varieties such as Chardonnay, Sauvignon Blanc and, more recently, Pinot Gris.

Matakana Estate

Some of the highest-quality wines come from Matakana Estate. Not only is the **Matakana Estate Merlot/Cabernet** blend a ripe blackberry and cedar-like savoury wine, but the vineyard has also planted some Syrah (or Shiraz, as it's also known). The **Matakana Estate Syrah** shows full ripeness without the jammy character so often present with this wine — instead, it is spicy and chocolatey.

Matua Valley

Matua Valley is now owned by the giant Beringer Blass wine group. Within Matua's portfolio of wines are the top-value Shingle Peak wines, of which the zesty and herbal **Shingle Peak Sauvignon Blanc** and the raspberry and cherry **Shingle Peak Pinot Noir** are both worth a try. Both, incidentally, are made from grapes grown in the Marlborough region (see Chapter 25).

A wine made from the North Island region of Gisborne, the **Matua Valley Ararimu Chardonnay** is a densely flavoured wine full of nutty flavours. And from a vineyard in Hawke's Bay comes the **Matua Valley Ararimu Merlot, Syrah, Cabernet Sauvignon**. This wine shows briary and cassis flavours, and is only made when the season ripens the grapes fully.

Nobilo Wine Group

This winery was started by a Dalmatian migrant. Since the winery's early days as a family-owned estate, Nobilo has seen quite a metamorphosis. First, Nobilo Wines purchased its highly successful neighbour, Selaks Wines, then the Hardy Wine Company, the large Australian wine business, bought Nobilo Wines.

Throughout the change in ownership, Nobilo has been making well-priced, fruit-driven wines, of which its **Nobilo Drylands Marlborough Sauvignon Blanc** is an excellent example, full of zesty passionfruit along with a touch of herbal flavours. The Nobilo Wine Group has retained the Selaks brand name; the **Selaks Premium Selection Marlborough Chardonnay** is a rich and toasty wine.

Obsidian Vineyard

One of the top-quality vineyards on the island of Waiheke, Obsidian Vineyard is the producer of a classic Cabernet blend of Cabernet Sauvignon, Merlot, Cabernet Franc and Malbec, a wine that shows the blackcurrant fruit so often seen in these blends. **Obsidian** is the vineyard's flagship wine.

Ransom Wines

The most inland vineyard in the region, the Ransom Wines vineyard is relatively small, with only six hectares under vine. The **Ransom Clos de Valerie Pinot Gris** is juicy fruited with a good weight of pear and citrus flavour. The **Ransom Barrique Fermented Chardonnay** is as its name says — a barrel-fermented wine with a lovely rich texture with some oatmeal biscuit flavours.

Stonyridge Vineyard

Not far from Obsidian Vineyards on the island of Waiheke is Stonyridge Vineyard, another of the island's top producers. This winery is run by the charismatic Stephen White, a man who is never short of a word for the praise of the island and its wines. His **Stonyridge Larose Red Blend** is a Bordeaux-style blend of Cabernet Sauvignon, Merlot, Cabernet Franc, Malbec and Petit Verdot, and is one of New Zealand's finest reds, with long dry tannins and savoury dry flavours. (The wine is named Larose in recognition of 'La Rose', an intensely aromatic and beautiful flower.)

Other wineries that must be mentioned

Other vineyards worthy of note are **Collard Brothers,** especially for its **Collards Rothesay Chardonnay**; and **Delegat's Wine Estate** for its great-value **Delegat's Reserve Chardonnay** and **Delegat's Reserve Merlot.** Look out for its Oyster Bay label, too. **West Brook Winery** produces a ripe, well-made **West Brook Barrique Fermented Chardonnay** along with an intensely tropical **West Brook Marlborough Sauvignon Blanc.**

Proof that vineyards in the inclement coastal areas in the north of the region can produce outstanding wines can be found in the **Brick Bay Wines** Pinot Gris and the **Providence Vineyard** Merlot/Cabernet Franc/Malbec blend. Both these wines wave a very powerful flag for the vineyards near the coast and for the region. Today, the wine known as **Providence** from Providence Vineyard is New Zealand's most expensive wine, which of course may or may not mean that it's the best!

Scattered Around the Bay of Plenty

The vineyards of the Bay of Plenty and Waikato region only constitute a very small percentage of the total of planted vines in New Zealand. Today, 12 wineries have established themselves here, and a number of very good wines are being produced.

Winemaking in a wet climate

The climate is very similar to that of the Auckland region, that is, the summers are quite warm though often rainy, with high rainfall continuing into autumn. The vineyards are often deluged with rain coming in from the Pacific Ocean. The high rainfall results in high relative humidity during the growing and ripening seasons, thus there is always the looming risk of diseases that could damage the grapes, such as mildews and bunch rot. Mildew and rots love wet and humid conditions, and readily grow on the leaves of the vines and the bunches of grapes, causing damage and possible total crop loss. So, over time, a region that once boasted over 5 per cent of the total vineyard plantings in New Zealand has slipped in importance.

Growing locally and bringing grapes in

The most-planted in the Bay of Plenty and Waikato region is Chardonnay, with Cabernet Sauvignon a close second. Like other New Zealand labels, the wineries of this region rely on fruit grown in other regions to supplement their production. So while the wineries might be based in the Bay of Plenty or Waikato region, don't assume that the wines are made from local fruit. The vast majority of fruit used by the local wineries is from vineyards in Hawke's Bay and Marlborough. In the case of the Firstland Vineyards, only 10 per cent of its vineyards are located within the region.

Chardonnay
The most successful wine from the region's vineyards is the Chardonnay, which is grown on very free-draining river silt soil (see the sidebar 'Rooting for infertile, free-draining soil') and is typically full flavoured due to the abundance of sunshine and warmth.

Cabernet Sauvignon
Few Cabernet Sauvignon wines are made in the region; the bulk of the fruit is blended with grapes grown in other regions. This grape variety can do well in favourable years, when rainfall isn't too high and autumn temperatures remain warm enough to ripen the grapes fully. Apart from a group of small wineries that make wines that are estate-grown, the three main wineries supplement their businesses with grapes from elsewhere.

Finding some excellent wines from the Bay

The best-quality wines in the Bay of Plenty and Waikato region come from **Firstland Vineyards, Mills Reef Winery** and **Morton Estate**. Although most of the fruit comes from elsewhere, the wineries are headquartered in the Bay of Plenty region.

Firstland Vineyards Ltd

Like its neighbours, Firstland Vineyards uses very little fruit from its own region, preferring the quality of the fruit available from its vineyards in the Marlborough and Hawke's Bay regions. The best value-for money wines from here are the **Firstland Marlborough Sauvignon Blanc** and the **Firstland Reserve Cabernet Sauvignon/Shiraz**.

Mills Reef Winery

The fruit for the **Mills Reef Elspeth Syrah**, a wine worth looking for, is grown in Hawke's Bay. The wine has the lovely savoury and spice character so attractive in Shiraz without an overwhelming fruitiness.

Morton Estate

Morton Estate is a medium-sized winery, producing about 200,000 cases of wine a year. The most well-known wine in its range, the **Morton Estate Hawkes Bay Chardonnay**, is made from fruit grown in Hawke's Bay and is typically full of peaches and apricots flavours with good balancing acidity.

Names with a story to tell

One of the first things you notice when looking at New Zealand wines is the often impossible-to-pronounce name on the label — names such as Te Kairanga and Ngatarawa. Well, as usual, a story is attached.

The Maoris, the indigenous people of New Zealand, played a big part in naming places and towns in the country. More recently, wine labels have adopted the names of the localities.

Learning how to pronounce the names of these wines can take some time.

Like the languages and dialects of Aborigines in Australia, Maori languages tell a story in which the name of something is usually closely related to things to do with the land and the climate. So Te Kairanga means 'the land where the soil is rich and the food plentiful' and Ngatarawa means the 'land between the ridges'.

Glorious Gisborne

Gisborne is the most eastern vineyard region on the North Island, flanked by the Pacific Ocean. Although no vineyards are located right on the coast, the region does have cooling sea breezes. Like the Auckland region, Gisborne is fairly flat and vineyards are planted at low altitudes, to 20 metres above sea level or less. Unlike many wine regions in Australia, such as the Whitlands in Victoria (refer to Chapter 12) and the Adelaide Hills in South Australia (refer to Chapter 17), the cooling effect of a high altitude plays no part in adjusting the temperatures.

Today, the Gisborne region produces about 25 per cent of the grapes grown across New Zealand. In spite of this, only 16 wine companies are established and fewer than 10 wineries are operating in the region, because the grapes are mostly shipped off to be processed at wineries in other regions. Much of the fruit grown in the region finds its way into reasonably priced commercial labels; for example, New Zealand's largest wine company, Montana, has extensive vineyards here, but the wine itself is made at the company's Auckland or Hawke's Bay wineries.

Making wet- and warm-weather wine

Climate-wise, the most significant things about the Gisborne region are the warmth and the high rainfall it experiences. While the high rainfall limits the region's suitability for grapegrowing, the warmth of the summer months extends into early autumn and, in most years, makes grapegrowing a viable proposition. In bad years, though, heavy rain can come too early and vineyards can be devastated by *bunch rot* and split berries. Bunch rot occurs in wet years where the skin of the grape gradually becomes more and more swollen due to the vine taking up the water from the rainfall. As a result, the skin of the berries becomes fragile and susceptible to attack by bunch moulds. The grapes then lose their quality and take on a mould-like tang. Which isn't exactly the taste the winemaker is looking for!

The grape varieties that ripen early, such as Chardonnay (the region's dominant variety in terms of hectares planted), soak up the sun, becoming ripe before being ruined by the heavy rains. On average, the region receives over 500 millimetres of rain during the growing season, October to April; often much of this rain falls in the critical months of February to April when the grapes are most susceptible to damage. The earlier the grapes ripen, therefore, the more likely it is that the harvest will be successful.

The other thing that high rainfall brings is high vine vigour. Unfortunately, that can bring its own problems in the form of mildew, bunch rot and the shading of the fruit by the vine canopy. Like the viticulturists in other high-vigour regions, such as Auckland, the winemakers pay careful attention to the density of the vine canopy. Thinning out excessive shoots and canopy has greatly improved the quality of the grapes being grown and, of course, the wines being made.

Monopolising the Gisborne grapes: Chardonnay

Chardonnay dominates the Gisborne region with almost 60 per cent of the vines planted to this grape. Gisborne is also home to some of the less well-known white varieties, the grapes that are behind the generic white blends of wines, such as Chenin Blanc, Müller Thurgau and Muscat, which together make up around 16 per cent of the grapes planted in Gisborne. You won't necessarily find bottles with labels on them stating that the wine is made from any of these varieties; more often than not the grapes are used to make inexpensive sparkling wine, are blended together and sold under the name of 'classic white', or are made into a wine that is given a specially devised name. For example, at Pouparae Park Winery, its blend of Müller Thurgau and Muscat is simply known as Pouparae Park Solstice Blanc.

Grapes produced in the Gisborne region for making red wine aren't of a particularly high quality and, in fact, only make up around 8 per cent of the total Gisborne plantings. Pinot Noir and Merlot are planted about equally. Both varieties ripen too late for this region and so are susceptible to the mid-season rains.

Chardonnay

The appeal of a Gisborne Chardonnay lies in its early ripening — grape growers can ripen the fruit and then harvest it before damaging rains arrive. Chardonnay responds well to abundant sunshine and heat, resulting in full-flavoured wines that have instant appeal to the consumer. The Chardonnay from the Gisborne area is bursting with peaches, honey and ripe citrus flavours. Usually the wines are drink-now styles.

Gewürztraminer

While Gewürztraminer only makes up around 3 per cent of the vines planted, the wines made from this variety are becoming well known. The grape's delicious spicy and lychee character develops in the warmth of the region's sunshine. The only problem with this variety, though, is that in the wet years, the tight-berried bunches are likely to suffer from *Botrytis cinerea*, or bunch rot (refer to Chapter 8 for more information on this fungus), which ruins the delicate fruit flavours.

Enjoying the best from Gisborne

Selecting the best is never easy, but here are four wineries that set the standard for the Gisborne region (see Figure 24-3).

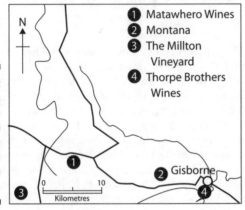

Figure 24-3: Wineries (with reputation) of the Gisborne region, North Island.

① Matawhero Wines
② Montana
③ The Millton Vineyard
④ Thorpe Brothers Wines

Matawhero Wines

One of the pioneers of the region and the winery that put Gewürztraminer on the map in New Zealand is Matawhero Wines. This winery also focuses on fruit from the Gisborne region, unlike many of the other wineries on the North Island. Although Gewürztraminer is a delicious wine, it isn't nearly as popular as Chardonnay or Sauvignon Blanc.

Such is the reputation of the Matawhero Gewürztraminer that the winery has two price levels — the less expensive **Matawhero Estate Gewürztraminer** and the top-priced **Matawhero Reserve Gewürztraminer**. Both wines are typical of the variety, showing loads of honey and lychee and musk. The Matawhero Reserve Gewürztraminer is full of fruitiness, and has an extra level of refinement that permeates the wine.

Millton Vineyard

Another excellent winery is the Millton Vineyard. The varieties planted at this vineyard are Chardonnay, Riesling, Chenin Blanc and Viognier, the latter a variety little known so far in New Zealand.

One of the best wines produced at the Millton Vineyard is the **Millton Te Arai Vineyard Chenin Blanc**. Depending on the season, the Chenin Blanc is more or less honeyed in character — a wetter season results in a greater honeyed character because of the influence of *Botrytis cinerea*, whereas a drier season means more acidity and vibrancy to the wine, allowing it to age well. Either way, the winemaker here knows how to produce the best, whatever the season brings.

Creating a wine industry: the Croatians

As you look down a list of the surnames of the wine pioneers in New Zealand, you see a lot of names ending in 'ich'. Which makes you wonder whether the people who are involved in the industry originally came from Eastern Europe — and you would be right.

Croatian migrants are largely to be thanked for starting New Zealand's hugely successful industry. Labels such as Kumeu River, which was started by Mate Brajkovich; Babich was started by Josif Babich; Delegat's was started by Nikola Delegat; West Brook by Mick Ivicevich and his son Tony, and Tony's son Anthony is now at the helm. Nobilo was begun by Nikola Nobilo. And so the list goes on.

Montana

The country's largest winery, Montana has its origins in Croatia (see the sidebar 'Creating a wine industry: the Croatians'). Founded by Ivan Yukich in 1944 and then developed by Ivan and his sons Mate and Frank, Montana is a wine company that has grown to represent 50 per cent of New Zealand's wine production. Since the family sold the last of its interest in the company in 1973, Montana has had various owners (the company was acquired in 2001 by the multinational Allied Domecq).

The **Montana Ormond Estate Gisborne Chardonnay** is a good-value wine, harvested from the very ripest fruit from the Ormond Estate in Gisborne.

Thorpe Brothers Wines

Thorpe Brothers Wines is located right on the coast at Poverty Bay. The winery produces a richly flavoured **Thorpe Brothers Longbush Chardonnay** as well as a musky and spicy **Thorpe Brothers Longbush Gewürztraminer.**

Hawke's Bay, East of the Ranges

Hawke's Bay is one of the of the best-known and recognised wine regions in New Zealand. In terms of vineyard area planted, the region is the second biggest after Marlborough in the South Island. The main centres in the region are Napier on the coast and Hastings, a little inland. Most of the vineyards are located on the flat plains known as the Heretaunga Plains around Hastings, with the odd vineyard closer to the coast.

The Hawke's Bay region has many unofficial sub-regions. The Esk Valley region is to the north of Napier on the coast; inland and west of Hastings is the Mangatahi sub-region, which is, unusually for the North Island, at some altitude. At around 100 metres above sea level, vineyards in this area are making some very good Chardonnay and Pinot Noir wines. However, the most famous sub-region is that known as the Gimblett Gravels (see the sidebar 'Gimblett Gravels').

Experiencing less rainfall

While the climate of the Hawke's Bay region is by no means a hot one, sunny days are commonplace. The main indicator as to whether or not the season is going to be a good one is the amount of rain and just when it falls. Hawke's Bay is, though, less prone to disastrous autumn rains than Gisborne, to the north.

Being located on the eastern side of the Ruahine and Kaweka Ranges, the Hawke's Bay vineyards experience less rainfall than other places on the east coast. As rain clouds move east over the mountains, the rain falls onto the mountains before the clouds arrive over the flat plains of the east coast. However, the region can hardly be called dry — Hawke's Bay receives an average of 370 millimetres during the October to April growing period. Even so, compared with Gisborne that averages 520 millimetres and Auckland that averages 650 millimetres, you can see that Hawke's Bay is certainly drier than the neighbours.

In the summer months, the Hawke's Bay vineyards close to the coast are several degrees cooler than those further inland because of the sea breezes that arrive in the early afternoon to cool things off. As a result, these vineyards are less able to ripen the late-maturing varieties such as Cabernet Sauvignon. A little further inland, around Havelock North, just south of Hastings, and on the Heretaunga Plains, the temperature is warmer, thus the ability to grow Cabernet Sauvignon and Cabernet Franc and Shiraz is enhanced.

Grape growers everywhere like to think their vineyards have the edge over others, and the grape growers of the Hawke's Bay region are no different. Grape growers from the Gimblett Gravels area (see the sidebar 'Gimblett Gravels') believe that the cooler years favour their vineyards. The other contender for the title of top-quality red grape-growing area is the Ngatarawa Triangle (also known as the Redmetal Triangle). Grapes here typically ripen up to a week later than those grown elsewhere and the area is favoured in the warmer years.

Gimblett Gravels

The Gimblett Gravels area is a very infertile, shingle-soiled and dry region that is undoubtedly making some of New Zealand's best wines. The little area takes its name from Gimblett Road that runs through its gravelly terrain. In contrast with the other wine-producing regions of the country, the vines of Gimblett Gravels are very low vigour and thus yield low crops. The grapes also ripen a little earlier, because the area experiences days where temperatures are around 3 degrees Celsius higher than those of the surrounding areas. The stony soil absorbs the warmth from the sunshine thus creating a warm microclimate in the vineyard.

Due to this slightly warmer environment, the vines flower a little earlier in the spring and the grapes ripen a little earlier, allowing Cabernet Sauvignon, in particular, to develop fully before the season cools down.

The grape growers in this area claim that it forms a distinct sub-region, the Gimblett Gravels Wine-growing District. If this branding is used on the wine label, at least 95 per cent of the wine must be made from grapes grown in the district. Some of the top wine labels from the Gimblett Gravels area are C J Pask Gimblett Road, Mills Reef Elspeth, Trinity Hill Gimblett Road and Stonecroft.

The Ngatarawa Triangle is a sort of triangular-shaped parcel of land adjacent to the Gimblett Gravels. The soils are fairly infertile and have a red-metal gravel base, hence its alternative name of 'the Redmetal Triangle'. The grapes grown on this soil ripen up to a week later than the grapes grown at nearby Gimblett Gravels. In the warmer years, the grapes in both areas ripen fully, whereas in cooler years, probably only the fruit of the warmer, earlier-harvesting Gimblett Gravels vineyards achieve absolute, optimum ripeness.

Enjoying some excellent Hawke's Bay varieties

Going along with the trend across New Zealand, Chardonnay is the most planted variety in Hawke's Bay, making up around 27 per cent of the total. The local wineries proudly make their wines from locally grown grapes, while also supplying grapes to many of the wineries in Auckland and the Bay of Plenty so they can supplement their range of wines (see the previous sections 'In and Around Auckland' and 'Scattered Around the Bay of Plenty').

Hawke's Bay is increasingly forging a reputation as being the best region in New Zealand to make high-quality Bordeaux-style wines from Cabernet Sauvignon, Merlot and Cabernet Franc. The sunshine that extends from summer into autumn gives these varieties a chance to fully ripen, with the only possible hitch being rainfall during or before ripening. Site selection is crucial, too, to avoid too much influence from cool afternoon sea breezes. These three varieties of red wine also do well in poor soil, as long as the soil is well drained (see the sidebar 'Rooting for infertile, free-draining soil').

TECHNICAL STUFF

Rooting for infertile, free-draining soil

Growing vines in free-draining soil has great advantages in regions that experience high rainfall. For vineyards that are low-lying, free-draining soil is important — when rain falls, it quickly drains away, thus preventing the roots of the vines from getting waterlogged, something that vines detest. Also, the more free-draining the soil, the less likely the vineyard is to be plagued by mildew and other diseases caused by too much moisture.

Free-draining structure and relatively infertile soil are great advantages in growing the three red grape varieties of Cabernet Sauvignon, Merlot and Cabernet Franc, because they keep the vine and thus the leaf vigour to a minimum. The poor quality of the soil also tends to restrict the amount of fruit a vine can produce, so, if a vine is racing against the seasonal clock to ripen its fruit, the less fruit the vine has to ripen, the better. Don't be surprised when you hear grape growers expounding the virtues of poor soil.

Chardonnay

TIP

Chardonnay from this region is among New Zealand's best. The fruit flavours are at times more restrained compared to the full flavours of, say, wines produced in the Gisborne region. The grapes also retain more natural acidity during the ripening period and so are very often wines that can be aged well for more than five years.

Sauvignon Blanc

The other important white variety in Hawke's Bay is Sauvignon Blanc. While the wine might suffer in reputation compared to the famous Marlborough Sauvignon Blanc, some fine wines are indeed being made from this variety.

Cabernet Sauvignon and Merlot

Of the red varieties grown in this region, the most successful reds are straight Cabernet Sauvignon styles and straight Merlot, which are among the best in the country. However, when these wines are blended together, along with a touch of Cabernet Franc, some outstanding wines are also produced.

Having the best of Hawke's Bay

The top wineries in the Hawke's Bay region produce some memorable Merlots and Chardonnays, among other excellent drops (refer to Figure 24-4).

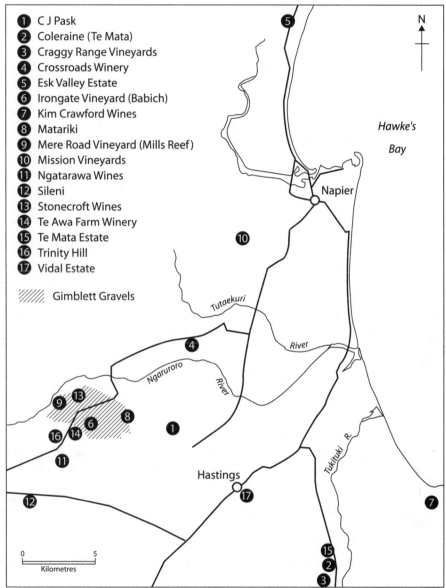

1. C J Pask
2. Coleraine (Te Mata)
3. Craggy Range Vineyards
4. Crossroads Winery
5. Esk Valley Estate
6. Irongate Vineyard (Babich)
7. Kim Crawford Wines
8. Matariki
9. Mere Road Vineyard (Mills Reef)
10. Mission Vineyards
11. Ngatarawa Wines
12. Sileni
13. Stonecroft Wines
14. Te Awa Farm Winery
15. Te Mata Estate
16. Trinity Hill
17. Vidal Estate

Gimblett Gravels

Figure 24-4: Memorable wines from the wineries of the Hawke's Bay region, North Island.

Some of the best wine producers are discussed in the following sections.

C J Pask

Among the first to put his confidence into the Gimblett Gravels area was Chris Pask of C J Pask (see the sidebar 'Gimblett Gravels'). Back in the early 1980s, people thought he was mad planting vines on this almost arid country.

At that time most vineyards in New Zealand were planted on quite fertile to very fertile soils and the vines always looked healthy with a mass of leafy growth.

As time went on, grape growers realised that this 'healthy' foliage was not all that desirable, and a shift to soils that produced low-vigour vines began. Pask was there already, and finding some success in the Gimblett Gravels. Today, the wines produced vindicate his decision to plant. The excellent range includes the **C J Pask Gimblett Road Merlot, C J Pask Gimblett Road Chardonnay** and **C J Pask Gimblett Road Cabernet Sauvignon.**

Craggy Range Vineyards

This vineyard is fairly new to the scene in Hawke's Bay. The main thrust of this winery is to make wines from the grapes of single vineyards. An outstanding wine is made from the home vineyard — the berry-filled *soft-tannined* **Craggy Range Seven Poplars Vineyard Merlot** (see the sidebar 'Tannin tastes and long livers'). Also from this vineyard comes the cashew and biscuity **Craggy Range Seven Poplars Vineyard Chardonnay**.

Ngatarawa Wines

You can find wines in several price brackets at Ngatawara. One of the best-priced wines is the **Ngatarawa Glazebrook Merlot**. Every vintage that I've tasted of this wine shows ripe yet savoury fruit flavours with no green-tasting tinges often associated with New Zealand reds. Also worth the search is the **Ngatarawa Alwyn Reserve Chardonnay** that, when young, shows dominant citrus character, and with age, has soft rounded fruit and nut tones. This vineyard also makes an excellent Sauvignon Blanc.

Stonecroft Wines

Another vineyard in the Gimblett Gravels area, this winery produces an outstanding **Stonecroft Syrah** with shows restrained spicy fruit.

Worth looking for here is the inexpensive red, **Stonecroft Ruhanui**, a blend of Cabernet Sauvignon, Syrah and Merlot.

Te Mata Estate

While the vineyards that grow the grapes for all the Te Mata wines are dotted across the Hawke's Bay region, much of the best fruit comes from the Ngatawara region and the hills around Havelock North. The vineyards here face the sun and are protected from the cooler breezes so, perhaps not surprisingly, the fruit ripens well almost every year.

The Te Mata wines are often referred to as being quite Bordeaux-like in structure, with flavours that can be described as savoury, fine tannined and long livers (see the sidebar 'Tannin tastes and long livers').

Tannin tastes and long livers

You frequently come across terms including the word *tannin* in descriptions of wine. *Soft-tannined* refers to a wine that has a soft finish rather than a astringent 'grippy' sensation as the wine leaves your mouth. *Fine tannin* refers to a wine that has an almost grainy texture rather than a grippy and bitey sensation. The tannins sort of melt slowly in your mouth.

For a wine to be age worthy, or a long liver, it needs to have good fruit intensity when young and a good dose of tannin — but fine tannins in order to age into a balanced wine. If the tannins are very aggressive and feel like sandpaper in your mouth when the wine is young, they may well soften with time. However, they will always outbalance the fruit flavours in the wine.

Along with many other Australians, I was once sceptical that New Zealand could make decent Cabernet Sauvignon blends of wines. However, I'm very impressed by the **Te Mata Estate Coleraine Cabernet/Merlot**, and have also enjoyed the notably excellent **Te Mata Estate Elston Chardonnay**.

The Te Mata range also includes the **Te Mata Estate Awatea Cabernet/Merlot**. Both the **Te Mata Coleraine** and the **Te Mata Awatea** reds are quite expensive wines, so to try a wine that comes from one of the best wineries in the country but at a lower cost, try the **Te Mata Estate Cabernet/Merlot**.

To add to Te Mata's already well-recognised success in the Chardonnay and Cabernet/Merlot fields, the estate's recent vintages of **Te Mata Estate Bullnose Syrah** round off a very impressive range of wines.

You find excellent value in wines made under the Vidal Estate label, part of the Villa Maria empire (see Chapter 25 for more on Villa Maria). Not all the fruit for Villa Maria wines come from the Hawke's Bay region. The high-quality **Vidal Estate Chardonnay** has fresh fruity appeal. The **Vidal Estate Reserve Hawke's Bay Cabernet Sauvignon Merlot** is produced only in years where the fruit is fully ripened, and the wine that results is dominant in cassis and savoury spices.

Also in the Vidal Estate Reserve range is the lush and concentrated **Vidal Estate Reserve Hawke's Bay Noble Semillon** dessert wine.

Other wineries that must be mentioned

Other top Chardonnay producers are the **Crossroads Winery, Kim Crawford Wines, Misson Vineyards** and **Trinity Hill.**

Other Gimblett Road producers of note, especially for their reds and Chardonnay, are **Babich Wines** at its Irongate Vineyard (refer to the section 'Picking the best of the Auckland bunch', earlier in this chapter), **Te Awa Farm Winery,** and the Mills Reef **Mere Road Vineyard** (the Mills Reef Winery is based in the Bay of Plenty region; see the earlier section 'Finding some excellent wines from the Bay') and **Matariki**.

The Rugged Wairarapa Region

Most people don't associate the name Wairarapa with any wine region in New Zealand. The place name most often heard in connection with the wine of this region is Martinborough, the best known of the winegrowing districts in the Wairarapa region, and the focus of this section.

Martinborough certainly takes the limelight in terms of its now-famous wines. Further north of the town of Martinborough is Masterton, where substantial investments have been made in vineyard plantings.

The Wairarapa region is flanked to the west by the rugged Rimutaka and Tararua mountain ranges, and to the south-east are the Aorangi Mountains. Below these ranges lies a flat plain where the vineyards are located.

Although the wines of the Wairarapa region enjoy world recognition, the region itself is small at less than 5 per cent of the country's vineyard hectares. The wineries and vineyards are also mostly small enterprises, free of domination by the big wine companies.

Finding a drier climate

Naturally, the surrounding mountain ranges have a great influence on the climate of the Wairarapa region. The presence of the mountain ranges to the west of the vineyards means that rainfall is reduced. As the rain-bearing clouds travel from west to east over the ranges, much of the rain falls on the mountains, with the result that the air over the vineyard plains remains relatively dry.

In a country that often struggles with excessive rain on its crops, the influence that the mountains have is obviously of great benefit. At Martinborough, rainfall in the growing season averages around 380 millimetres, compared to the wetter region of Auckland that averages over 650 millimetres in the same season. In fact, most years, the vineyards in the region struggle to manage with the amount of rainfall they receive in summer, and irrigation is necessary.

Overall, the climate isn't hot — the average temperature of the warmest month is around 18.5 degrees Celsius.

The rain and wind that come up from the south pose the greatest threat to the vineyards. While the storm fronts can be quite severe, if they aren't too wild, they can be beneficial: During *fruit set* (the time in spring when the flowering vines create the berries for the coming season), the wind can have quite an impact. Strong winds blowing through the vineyards can negatively affect the transition from the flower stage to the berry stage. Where fewer berries have been formed, each vine naturally reduces the amount of fruit it can produce. While on the one hand the grape growers obtain less fruit, on the other hand, the quality of that fruit is believed to be higher. Vines that yield lower crops are linked to the production of higher-quality, more intensely flavoured fruit.

The Wairarapa region is only 30–40 kilometres away from the coast, and nights in Martinborough are cooled by the evening sea breeze. This nightly drop in temperature is highly desirable for the region's flagship variety, Pinot Noir.

Thriving Pinot Noir

Pinot Noir, Pinot Noir and Pinot Noir. Some pretty smart Chardonnays come from the region, too, as well as the odd Syrah, but Pinot Noir put Martinborough on the wine lovers' map — and not just in quality — Pinot Noir accounts for over 40 per cent of the region's land under vines.

Usually, where Pinot Noir does well, so does Chardonnay, as Chardonnay also enjoys the same climatic conditions. Most lovers of Pinot Noir vote a good, complex Chardonnay as their favourite white variety.

Pinot Noir

The reason why Pinot Noir is so successful is the equable climate — not too hot and not too wet. These conditions allow the grapes to struggle a bit and intensify in flavour, and the cool night air allows the vines the all-important *overnight rest period*. Vines that get the chance to rest overnight in cooler temperatures produce grapes of more intense flavour. In climates where the overnight temperature isn't much less than the daytime temperature, the vines keep working through the night — poor things. As a result, the fruit on the vines ripens quickly without really having had any time at all in which to intensify in flavour.

The cool night air produces Pinot Noir grapes that make wines of a deep colour, firm tannin and full of flavour and ageing potential.

Sauvignon Blanc

Sauvignon Blanc is the second most-planted grape, a smidgen more popular than Chardonnay — 19 per cent versus 16 per cent. Coming from vines that typically produce low crops, the Sauvignon Blanc wines are intensely flavoured and tropical, and with great acid zing. Compared to the Sauvignon Blanc produced in the Marlborough region (see Chapter 25), these wines are riper and a little less herbal.

Meeting Martinborough's finest

A number of outstanding wineries from the Wairarapa region, clustered around Martinborough, enjoy a good reputation internationally. Because most are quite small producers, their wines, unfortunately, can be hard to find (see Figure 24-5).

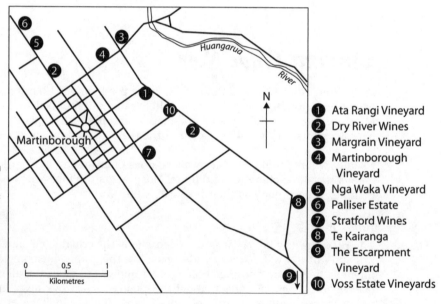

Figure 24-5: Wineries of Wairarapa's Martinborough region, North Island.

❶ Ata Rangi Vineyard
❷ Dry River Wines
❸ Margrain Vineyard
❹ Martinborough Vineyard
❺ Nga Waka Vineyard
❻ Palliser Estate
❼ Stratford Wines
❽ Te Kairanga
❾ The Escarpment Vineyard
❿ Voss Estate Vineyards

Dry River Wines

Dry River is a highly regarded vineyard, where all the wines are mid- to full-bodied and display a definite depth of flavour. The **Dry River Gewürztraminer** is very seductive, showing musk and spice with a touch of sweetness, and the **Dry River Pinot Gris** has excellent varietal pear and stone fruit flavours. The **Dry River Pinot Noir** is big in all things — flavour, texture, tannin and longevity — as is the **Dry River Syrah**, which is one of the best in the country.

The Escarpment Vineyard

The Escarpment Vineyard is a new venture by the man who made Martinborough famous, Larry McKenna. A part-owner in the Escarpment, McKenna has planted a vineyard that is 70 per cent Pinot Noir, although the winery also produces the **Escarpment Chardonnay**, the **Escarpment Pinot Gris** and the **Escarpment Riesling**.

To date, I've only tried the **Escarpment Pinot Noir** which, without a doubt, is worth looking for. This wine is savoury and quite dominant in tannins — although not the 'sandpaper' style of tannin. You experience the dominance of the dryness from the tannin on the finish of the wine (see the sidebar 'Tannin tastes and long livers' for more information on tannins). I have no doubt these tannins will integrate with the wine's fruit flavours with time.

Martinborough Vineyard

This vineyard was the first to produce the flagship wine of the Martinborough district. The **Martinborough Vineyard Pinot Noir** is a sturdy wine, needing some time in the bottle before it is ready for drinking. Like other Martinborough district Pinot Noirs, this is a full-bodied style rather than delicate and fragrant.

Of equal quality to the Pinot Noir is the **Martinborough Vineyard Chardonnay**, full bodied yet with a balanced acidity.

Palliser Estate

From a beautifully appointed winery and cellar door come the Palliser Estate wines. The **Palliser Estate Pinot Noir** is the top wine from the Estate and is loaded with dark cherries, ripe plums and a backbone of oak-derived mocha flavours. **Palliser Estate Sauvignon Blanc** is definitely one of the North Island's best, with good ripeness and a balanced lift of acidity.

Pencarrow is the second label from Palliser Estate and a less expensive option. When it comes to value for money, the **Pencarrow Pinot Noir**, a ripe raspberry and fruit-dominant wine, and the **Pencarrow Sauvignon Blanc** are unbeatable. For more information on Palliser Estate's cellar door, see Chapter 28.

Other wineries that must be mentioned

Ata Rangi produces a relatively expensive and highly sought-after Pinot Noir; the wines from this vineyard tend to be dense in fruit flavour with a good dose of French oak. Nearby at **Voss Estate Vineyards**, the Pinot Noir is also very good, though different — the wine is more perfumed, if you like, more 'feminine' than its neighbour, with soft tannins and medium weight.

To the south of Palliser Estate lies the **Nga Waka Vineyard**, a winery that confirms this region's ability, with the excellent **Nga Waka Chardonnay** and the **Nga Waka Sauvignon Blanc**.

Other Chardonnay and Pinot Noir wines worth checking out are

- **Stratford Wines of Marlborough Chardonnay:** Shows a terrific nutty and mineral tone.
- **Stratford Wines of Marlborough Pinot Noir:** Has rich truffle and cherry wine flavours.
- **Margrain Vineyard Pinot Noir:** Made by the same winemaker as the Stratford wines, this Pinot Noir is a plum and black cherry flavoured well-oaked wine.
- **Te Kairanga Reserve Chardonnay:** Is a butter and nut flavoured white with a dense texture.
- **Te Kairanga Reserve Pinot Noir:** Is quite fruit dominant with subtle, well-integrated tannins.

Chapter 25

Liquid Distinction from New Zealand's Cool South Island

· ·

In This Chapter

▶ Revelling in the outstanding wines of Marlborough

▶ Finding excellent white wines in and around Nelson

▶ Sampling Pinot Noir and Chardonnay in Canterbury

▶ Enjoying the mountain views and heady wines of Otago

· ·

*I*f you haven't been there lately — or at all — you may believe that the South Island of New Zealand is the sleepier of the two islands. For years, the South Island made its name as the sheep-farming capital of the world (as there are many more sheep per square kilometre than there are people) and, apart from tourism, its economy rested on the backs of the woolly critters.

However, the economists stopped joking long ago about the backward nature of New Zealand's southern isle. The boom in wine exports from this beautiful part of the world has very much helped the local economy. In 2002, New Zealand winemakers exported over 66 per cent of their wine, up from a mere 9 per cent in 1990. Much of this growth has been due to the huge reputation that the wines of Marlborough have carved for themselves, particularly the Marlborough Sauvignon Blancs.

In this chapter, I take you through the prominent wine regions of the South Island — Marlborough, the small Nelson region, and the Central Otago region, the expanding Canterbury region, which is ever-increasing in profile (see the map in Figure 25-1).

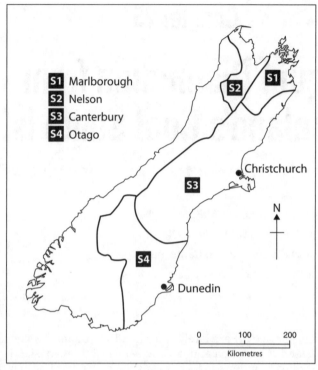

Figure 25-1:
The wine regions of the South Island of New Zealand.

Finding Much to Admire in Marlborough

Marlborough arguably is the most famous wine region in New Zealand. Certainly the Marlborough region is the most heavily planted: Nearly 7,000 hectares are under vine, or 43 per cent of New Zealand's total. Compare that to the next most-planted region of Hawke's Bay on the North Island, where almost 4,000 hectares, or 24 per cent, are under vine.

The Marlborough region is incredibly beautiful. The large flat Wairau Plains stretch for miles and are filled with vineyards as far as the eye can see. I have been lucky enough to fly over the region and watch how the landscape changes, from the rugged coastline to the inland plains, to areas of row upon row of vines. This scene is ever-changing, from bareness in winter to lush green leaves through spring and summer, and finishing off with the lovely autumn colours.

Many of the vineyards take their names from nearby geographical features, such as Cloudy Bay, the bay into which the Wairau River feeds, and Wither

Hills, the hilly area surrounding the Wairau Plains. The Wairau Plains lie between the towns of Blenheim and Renwick and are within the Wairau Valley. So we have the Wairau River, Wairau Plains and Wairau Valley — making the name Wairau pretty famous in Marlborough. Most of the vineyards are on the Wairau Plains, inland from the town of Blenheim.

To the south of the region beyond the dry ranges of the Wither Hills is the Awatere Valley, where vineyards border the Awatere River.

Finding success in a varied climate

The location of the Marlborough region is without doubt one of the main reasons for its success. The region's topographical advantages include the Marlborough Sounds to the north of Blenheim, which protect the vineyards from the strong north-westerly winds. To the south are the Kaikoura Ranges that stop the cold southerly winds coming up from the Antarctic. And the location of the Richmond Range to the west means that the region has less rainfall that land further west, as the rain falls on the mountains before the clouds reach the Marlborough region.

Marlborough is similar to Hawke's Bay and Martinborough in the North Island (refer to Chapter 24) in terms of the amount of rainfall it receives in the critical growing season of October to April. In fact, drought isn't unusual in summer. The autumns are generally stable, though — only occasionally is it wet at vintage time. I describe the temperatures of the Marlborough region in the section on Sauvignon Blanc a bit further on in this chapter.

The biggest climatic problem the Marlborough region faces is frost. Cool air settles on the wide flat Wairau Plains in the very early mornings. Devastating spring frosts aren't uncommon — the young shoots are literally frozen on the vine and, of course, subsequently die. Frost doesn't affect the quality of the grapes, just the quantity. In some years, you may find it just a bit harder to get your hands on a bottle of your favourite Sauvignon Blanc.

Whenever the danger of frost is likely, the local helicopter pilot is kept busy at night, hovering over the vineyards in an attempt to keep the air moving and to bring down the layer of warmer air that is sitting above. If the grape grower can't contract a helicopter, other techniques are used, such as running wind machines and building small fires throughout the vineyard.

With the nearby ranges and the coast exerting influences on the climate, not surprisingly, each individual vineyard has its own microclimate. Some vineyards are more affected than others by the way in which proximity to the coast and the rivers influences the temperature. Some vineyards are more protected than others by the Richmond Range and have less rainfall and cooling air. And some vineyards are at greater risk of frost than others.

Starring grape varieties

Many grape varieties are grown across Marlborough, but Sauvignon Blanc is the 'star', with the 'Rising Star' medal going to Pinot Noir. All other varieties have a place, but they sit in the shadow of the famous Marlborough Sauvignon Blanc. The favourable climate and soils of the Wairau Plains contribute to this variety's success.

One of the striking things about the Wairau Plains is that, although they're only 10 kilometres wide from the Richmond Range to the Wither Hills, great changes in soil type occur. To the north of the Wairau River, the soils are very stony and gravelly, but on the southern side of the river, silt and clay are found.

Vineyards on gravel produce lower-vigour vines, while those on clay (which has a far greater capacity to retain water than gravel does) produce more vigorous vines. (The term *vigour* refers to a vine's ability to produce leaves and shoots.)

Sauvignon Blanc

Marlborough is the home of New Zealand's world-famous Sauvignon Blanc, which makes up over 50 per cent the plantings. The grapes from vineyards on the north bank of the Wairau River, a lower-vigour area where every berry on the vine ripens, produce a Sauvignon Blanc in which tropical fruit is dominant. In contrast, vines growing in the silt and clay of the south bank produce a Sauvignon Blanc that is less fruity, and more herbaceous and grassy.

In Marlborough, summer daytime temperatures are warm, around 23–25 degrees Celsius, rarely reaching above 30 degree Celsius. However, summer nights around Blenheim are cold, dropping to 10–12 degrees Celsius. These temperature variations give the grape growers a great advantage in growing an acid-loving variety such as Sauvignon Blanc.

During the day, sunshine allows the fruit to develop its trademark tropical, herbaceous flavours, while at night, the drop in temperature — usually a drop of over 10 degrees Celsius — means that the vines shut down their activity overnight and the grapes don't continue to ripen. This rest period allows the grapes to maintain their acidity, a key to making top-class Sauvignon Blanc. Leading makers are those who are able to capture the gorgeous tropical fruit flavours along with a hint of herbal variety.

Riesling

The Marlborough climate also contributes to the success of the Riesling grape. The mild, warm summer days that stay around the mid-20s degrees

Celsius allow the grapes to soak up some warmth. At night, the ripening process is brought to a halt as the temperature drops at least 10 degrees Celsius. Like Sauvignon Blanc, this halt in the ripening process allows the Riesling grapes to maintain their acid levels — an important factor in maintaining the freshness of flavour in a white wine.

Like the other grape varieties grown in Marlborough, Riesling has had to take a back seat to Sauvignon Blanc. Even so, you can find some top-class Rieslings with flavours of lime and lemon being made.

Chardonnay

Another white variety that manages to do well in this region is Chardonnay. The mild days allow the grapes to fully develop their fruit flavours and the cold nights give the grapes the chill they need to maintain their acidity. The resulting high-acid level means that *malolactic fermentation* plays quite a part in the wine's development, giving the Marlborough Chardonnays a weighty mid-palate and a soft acid finish (see the sidebar 'Malolactic fermentation' for further information).

Pinot Noir

Of the reds, Pinot Noir has forged the biggest reputation of the reds, making up 15 per cent of the vines planted, while the second most-planted red, Merlot, has just 2 per cent of plantings.

Pinot Noir is a variety on the ascent in Marlborough. Pinot Noir vines like the region's varied soil conditions, so most wineries source fruit from vineyards located on the stony soils and vineyards located on the silt and clay soils. The stony soils allow the fruit to get some depth in colour and body. Pinot Noir vines growing on the water-retaining soils comprising clay and silt continue to ripen their fruit throughout the warmer months without becoming stressed by lack of rain, and the berries acquire the fruity flavours that fill out the wine's structure.

TECHNICAL STUFF

Malolactic fermentation

Malolactic fermentation is the term used when *malic acid*, a harsh acid, is converted by bacteria to softer acid, *lactic acid*. Malic acid occurs naturally in fruits — most people encounter it when they bite into a green apple. Lactic acid is the most predominant acid found in milk.

Basically, the winemaker is swapping the hard acid for a softer acid, and in doing so reduces the total amount of acid in the wine. The result is a softer, rounder wine. All red wines go through a *malo* (the colloquial term), and many non-aromatic varieties do, too, especially Chardonnay.

The Pinot Noir grapes also do well as a result of the low-vigour vines grown in many of the vineyards and the low temperatures at night, which allow this delicate grape to shut down and rest for the night.

In my view, Pinot Noir is likely to become an increasingly important variety in the region, especially given the success to date of some of the wineries.

Meeting Marlborough's finest

The reputation of the large wine-producing region of Marlborough is being maintained by a large number of notable wineries (see Figure 25-2). Of these, the following deserve special mention.

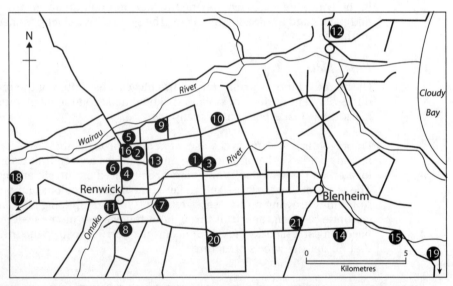

Figure 25-2: Wineries of the Marlborough region.

1. Allan Scott Wines
2. Clifford Bay Estate
3. Cloudy Bay
4. Forrest Estate
5. Foxes Island Wines
6. Framingham Wine Co.
7. Fromm Winery
8. Highfield Estate
9. Huia
10. Hunter's Wines
11. Isabel Estate
12. Johanneshof Cellars
13. Lake Chalice Wines
14. Lawson's Dry Hills
15. Montana Brancott Winery
16. Nautilus Estate
17. Oyster Bay
18. Seresin Estate
19. Vavasour Wines
20. Villa Maria Estate
21. Wither Hills

Cloudy Bay

Cloudy Bay must surely be the most renowned winery in New Zealand. The **1985 Cloudy Bay Sauvignon Blanc** put New Zealand and its talent with this grape on the world wine map; New Zealand and Sauvignon Blanc have been talked about ever since its debut. However, in addition to its great Sauvignon Blanc, Cloudy Bay produces some other very impressive wines. Among them are the following:

- ✔ **Pelorus Vintage-dated:** An excellent rich, creamy and complex wine, Pelorus is Cloudy Bay's sparkling wine label.

- ✔ **Cloudy Bay Chardonnay:** Cloudy Bay makes its Chardonnay in the traditional French method, that is, through malolactic fermentation, in order to give the wine a softness in texture (the winery also ferments the juice in barrels). Malolactic fermentation modifies the wine so that instead of being just fruity, toasty and biscuity flavours are added to the wine. The resulting wine is soft and full in texture with peaches and citrus flavours along with toasty oak.

- ✔ **Cloudy Bay Gewürztraminer:** This Gewürztraminer is so startling when you first smell it and then taste it, because of its intensity. The wine has loads of lychee, spicy musk and a long, honeyed flavour.

- ✔ **Cloudy Bay Pinot Noir:** Toasty oak plays a part in this wine, but it doesn't dominate the savoury and spicy cherry flavours of the wine.

Forrest Estate

Over at Forrest Estate, the wine that stands out is the **Forrest Estate Riesling** which has a lime zest aroma and palate finishing with just a tiny bit of sweetness. The **Forrest Estate Dry Riesling** is just that — bone dry and with a lovely minerally character that allows it to age well over five years or so.

Fromm Winery

Another high-profile winery, although relatively small in size, is **Fromm Winery**, which specialises in Pinot Noir. The vines are grown on the slightly more fertile south bank of the Wairau River, near the town of Renwick, which could result in over-cropping of the grapes (see the sidebar 'To thin or not too thin' for more information on grape crops and crop thinning).

Over-cropping isn't a problem at Fromm Winery, however, where the vineyards are carefully managed to prevent this happening. The vines are planted close together to reduce vigour and, in summer, crop thinning is common. In addition, a lot of thought has gone into the careful selection of low-vigour clones and rootstocks (see the sidebar 'Cloning and rootstocking in the wine industry').

To thin or not to thin

Grape vines produce as many grapes as their environment allows them to. An excessive crop of grapes can result in a number of adverse outcomes, including

✔ Non-uniform ripening of the berries, which gives a green tinge to the wine.

✔ Wine that is low in quality and flavour.

To avoid these outcomes, vineyard managers practise *crop thinning*, which is when whole bunches are removed from the vine. The amount of the crop to be left on the vine is calculated easily — by the 'gut feel' of the grape grower. The grape grower may be slightly more scientific and do a bunch count of a few vines. With this information, the crop across the whole vineyard plot can be calculated (the average number of bunches per vine is multiplied by the number of vines). Then, using past vintage crop levels as a guide, the grape grower can determine the optimum number of bunches. Anything in excess of that number is removed.

No hard and fast rule applies to crop thinning, as each vineyard site has its own characters and the winemaker's goal is simply to make the best wine with the particular grape variety. For example, the usual gauge when making a top-quality Pinot Noir is somewhere around four to five tonnes per hectare. Of course, the accountant's view on such matters need to be borne in mind. However, the formula for successful winemaking can't be reduced to the simplistic model of more grapes = more wine = more profit.

Most winemakers regard quality of wine as the greatest determinant — and hope that quantity is following closely behind. And quality is a paramount reason for thinning the bunches of grapes on a vine. By reducing the number of berries on a vine, the vine puts energy into ripening and the remaining berries have a more-concentrated flavour, skin colour and tannins.

The high quality of the wines from Fromm Winery are testament to the wine maker's attention to detail.

The **Fromm La Strada Pinot Noir** is highly regarded for its intense fruit flavours of dark plums and an Asian-spices spiciness. Less well known is **Fromm La Strada Reserve Syrah,** which is gaining a reputation as a high-quality, deeply coloured black peppery wine. (*Syrah* is the French word for Shiraz.)

Hunter's Wines

Hunter's is one of the pioneering wineries of the region. That this winery has long experience in producing excellent wines shows in its zesty, tropical **Hunter's Winemaker's Selection Sauvignon Blanc** and the slightly herbaceous **Hunter's Sauvignon Blanc**. Also well priced and filled with fruit are the **Hunter's Pinot Noir** and the **Hunter's Chardonnay**, a biscuity and citrus-infused wine.

Isabel Estate

The winery at Isabel Estate has forged a strong reputation for itself. One of its outstanding wines is **Isabel Estate Sauvignon Blanc**, which is a tropical-flavoured wine but which, with some barrel-ageing, has lost any herbal flavour; this wine is quite rich in body as well. Another excellent wine from Isabel Estate is the **Isabel Estate Pinot Noir**, a powerful, dark, cherried wine.

Johanneshof Cellars

From another winery called Johanneshof Cellars is something a little different. Here the winery makes a wine called **Johanneshof Noble Late Harvest,** which well and truly tricked me (and many others) in a 'blind tasting'. Unusually, this wine is made from Chardonnay grapes (late-harvest wines are usually Semillon or Riesling) and a touch of Sauvignon Blanc. The wine is an amazingly dense in texture with loads of apricot and candied orange peel flavours.

Lawson's Dry Hills

The winery of Lawson's Dry Hills is at the base of the Wither Hills, which are to the south of the Waimea Plains. The name of the hills says it all; when the summer rains are over, the grasslands of the hills wither and die. Lawson's Dry Hills derives most of its fame from its spicy, fruity and powerful **Lawson's Dry Hills Gewürztraminer**, and the **Lawson's Dry Hills Sauvignon Blanc**, a gooseberry-like wine with a dash of acid to finish.

Montana Brancott Winery

Montana is easily the largest vineyard owner in Marlborough and continues to raise its profile as a top-class winemaker, even though the company is big c (the two are not always compatible). Montana's success in making many different wines across a range of brand names has helped raise its profile. Montana's Marlborough vineyards, of which it owns 2,500 hectares, or 16 per cent of the region's total, are where most of the fruit for its Sauvignon Blanc is produced.

Among the best of Montana's wines are the following:

✔ **Montana Reserve Sauvignon Blanc** and the **Stoneleigh Sauvignon Blanc:** These two wines are Montana's stand-out Sauvignon Blanc labels. Both are made from grapes grown on vineyards close to the Wairau River in the north of the Wairau Plains. The soil here is very pebbly and infertile, so the vigour is reduced. The site is also warmer, allowing the wine to develop more of the ripe, tropical fruit flavours. The Stoneleigh Sauvignon Blanc is a hugely successful wine for Montana; there can be few Australian Sauvignon Blanc lovers who haven't bought a bottle.

Cloning and rootstocking in the wine industry

Cloning left the realms of science fiction years ago, and is alive and well in the wine industry. A grape *clone* is like a variety within a variety — a sub-variety. For example, Pinot Noir is the variety and the prefixes of 114, 115, MV6 represent the clones. So you hear people talking of Pinot Noir clone 114, Pinot Noir clone 115, Pinot Noir MV6 and so on. Each clone results in a slightly different characteristic to the vine, whether it be in the way the vine grows, the time in which its grapes ripen, the amount of tannin its grapes produce and so on.

Added to this point of difference among the vines are the various rootstocks available for use. Just as fruit trees or rose bushes are grafted onto rootstocks, so are many vines. The rootstock is simply the base of the plant whose roots sit in the soil. The plant material to be grafted on — whether it be grape vine, peach or rose in origin — is grafted on to the rootstock, approximately halfway up its trunk. The fruit or flowers that subsequently result are the product of the grafted-on material, not the rootstock.

What the rootstock does is modify the growing conditions. For example, in an area that has a high salt table, the rootstock used would be one that can tolerate high levels of salt in the soil. In high-vigour wine regions, such as those in many parts of New Zealand, rootstock that is only moderately vigorous is preferable. The result is a drop in vigour for those grafted vines. Rootstock selection is a way of modifying and controlling vines and their grapes.

✔ **Montana Sauvignon Blanc:** Another excellent label from Montana, much of the fruit for this wine comes from the southern side of the Wairau Valley, a cool and fertile position that produces conditions in which the gooseberry and herbaceous flavours of Sauvignon Blanc can develop.

✔ **Deutz Marlborough Cuveé:** Also in the Marlborough region, Montana produces Pinot Noir and Chardonnay grapes for its sparkling wines. The premium brand is the **Deutz Marlborough Cuveé**, a wine made in partnership with the Champagne House of Deutz.

✔ **Lindauer Brut:** The second tier of sparkling wines from Montana is the Lindauer range. Like all top sparkling wines, this wine is a blend of varieties from different regions. The grapes for the Lindauer Brut are Pinot Noir, Chardonnay and Chenin Blanc and are mostly grown in the Marlborough region, with some additional fruit from Hawke's Bay and Gisborne. The range of Lindauer sparkling wines is well priced and offers vanilla and slight strawberry flavour and a good soft bubble.

✔ **Montana Reserve Pinot Noir:** This Pinot Noir has the reputation of a good wine at a reasonable price. The wine exemplifies Montana's aim to be represented in all wine categories and it was one of the first big wine companies to tackle Pinot Noir, and to do it well.

Nautilus Estate

One of the medium- to large-sized wine operations in Marlborough is Nautilus Estate. Again, the Sauvignon Blanc grape stands out, with the **Nautilus Estate Marlborough Sauvignon Blanc** showing plenty of mango, passionfruit and lime zest. The **Nautilus Estate Marlborough Pinot Noir** is consistently praiseworthy with complex and spicy fruit.

Villa Maria Estate

This winery has connections with other wine regions. Much of this winery's prestige comes from the wines it produces from grapes grown throughout the Marlborough region. Outstanding examples are

- ✔ **Villa Maria Reserve Marlborough Pinot Noir**, a sturdy, richly concentrated wine.
- ✔ **Villa Maria Reserve Marlborough Noble Riesling**, a luscious, delicious dessert wine.
- ✔ **Villa Maria Cellar Selection Marlborough Sauvignon Blanc**, a herbal and green olive-like wine.
- ✔ **Villa Maria Cellar Selection Marlborough Chardonnay**, a barrel-fermented, toasty wine.

Wither Hills

Wither Hills has recently been sold to the giant Lion Nathan beer and wine company, yet it was started very much as a family affair. Brent Marris has been the driving force behind the huge growth of the label, but it was his father, John Marris, who started it all. Back in the early 1970s, John was involved in selling land to Montana and later became a contract grape grower for them. Today, Wither Hills makes three well-priced wines:

- ✔ **Wither Hills Chardonnay**, a rounded, soft textured wine with biscuity barrel fermentation flavours
- ✔ **Wither Hills Sauvignon Blanc**, a touch herbal with loads of zesty acid and a softness on the finish
- ✔ **Wither Hills Pinot Noir**, a feminine Pinot Noir with a background of spicy cherries

Brent Marris makes no reserve wines at Wither Hills because he believes that by making a reserve wine he is taking something special from his main blend, thus reducing the quality of his standard label.

Other wineries that must be mentioned

Top wine producers in the Marlborough region also include

- ✔ **Allan Scott Wines:** This winery makes the excellent **Allan Scott Sauvignon Blanc**, a herbal-dominant expression of this variety, and the lemon and lime **Allan Scott Riesling.**

- ✔ **Foxes Island Wines:** You can't go past the elegant and subtle **Foxes Island Pinot Noir** and the **Foxes Island Chardonnay**, which is a richly textured wine.

- ✔ **Framingham Wine Co.:** This winery has assumed the role of Riesling promoter in the region, such is the quality of the mineral and lime **Framingham Classic Riesling**. Also good is the **Framingham Gewürztraminer,** which shows those lovely honeyed and musk aromas so often seen in this variety.

- ✔ **Highfield Estate:** Bucking the trend of having its top wine an aromatic white wine is **Highfield Estate** with its **Highfeld Estate Pinot Noir**. The wine is full bodied — as full bodied as Pinot Noir gets — and delivers a rich mouthful of black cherries and plums.

- ✔ **Huia:** Also making top-quality Gewürztraminer is Huia. The **Huia Gewürztraminer** is rich in texture while the **Huia Riesling** is an acid-dominant wine crying out to be cellared for five years or so.

- ✔ **Seresin Estate:** This winery is notable for its rich and toasty **Seresin Estate Chardonnay** and its **Seresin Estate Sauvignon Blanc**, a ripe tropical wine.

Travelling to the Awatere Valley wineries

The Awatere Valley is south of Marlborough, beyond the Wither Hills, where vineyards border the Awatere River. The soils in the Valley aren't particularly fertile and the close proximity to the coast means that the climate is cool. Typically, the wines have more acid and are less-fruit dominant than the Marlborough wines. Harvest time in the Awatere Valley is generally a little later than in the Marlborough vineyards. Two wineries are stand-outs:

- ✔ **Clifford Bay Estate:** This Awatere Valley winery produces the **Clifford Bay Estate Sauvignon Blanc**, a fresh and zesty wine with long, lingering flavours.

- ✔ **Vavasour Wines:** This winery was the first to plant vines on the southeast side of the Wither Hills in the Awatere Valley. The **Vavasour Marlborough Sauvignon Blanc** is typical of the cooler-climate expression of Sauvignon Blanc, showing grassy and gooseberry flavours with a decent dose of refreshing acid.

Doubling in Size: The Nelson Region

Compared to Marlborough, Nelson is a small region with only 454 hectares of vines, or less than 3 per cent of New Zealand's plantings. However, this figure is double the size it was as recently as 2002. The increase is partly due to a surge in land prices in the Marlborough region.

The region of Nelson lies to the west of Marlborough. Vineyards are established around the city of Nelson, on the Waimea Plains, and a smaller group of vineyards is located to the north-west of Nelson in a hilly area called Upper Moutere.

The soils of Upper Moutere are clay based and are therefore heavier than the silt and gravel soils of the Waimea Plains. Clay soils retain water well, which helps the vines survive the dry summer months.

The ability of the soil to retain water is particularly good for Pinot Noir, because Pinot Noir needs water to keep the fruit from shrivelling in the summer months. A shrivelled grape makes the wine taste more like jam than Pinot Noir — a taste sensation not held in high esteem by winemakers or by wine drinkers. Because it is an early-ripening variety, Pinot Noir berries are quite developed in summertime and are thus susceptible to dehydration caused by overexposure to the sun. Soil with the ability to retain water from springtime rainfall is an added advantage.

Most of the vineyards in Nelson are small. However, due to the diminishing income derived from the apple orchards, once the main agricultural pursuit, vineyard planting is booming.

Finding protection from the weather

The Tasman Bay lies to the north of the Nelson region, which is protected from cold southerlies and the often-wild westerlies by mountain ranges. In comparison with the neighbouring wine regions, Nelson experiences about the same warmth as Marlborough but is warmer than Canterbury (see 'Cooling Off in Canterbury', later in this chapter). In summer, temperatures may reach 25 degrees Celsius though the temperatures drop dramatically at night, like Marlborough.

From the perspective of the grape growers, the amount and timing of rainfall is critical. Every year, the grape growers race seasonal changes and hope to get their fruit in before the autumn rains begin, typically in late April.

Focusing on white wines

The main focus of the Nelson region is on white wines, particularly aromatic whites such as Riesling, Gewürztraminer and Sauvignon Blanc. The warm days followed by cool nights serve to capture the aromatic flavours of these varieties, while at the same time preserving the acidity.

Chardonnay too shows distinction with full ripe flavours and enough acidity to balance the fruitiness. Of the reds, Pinot Noir is being planted and, with the kind of clay soil that suits it, some promising wines are being made.

Exploring the wines of Nelson

A number of vineyards in the Nelson region deserve special mention for their excellent white wines and Pinot Noir (see Figure 25-3). Among them are the ones discussed in the following sections.

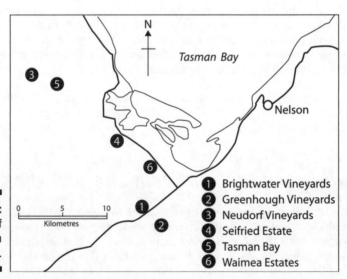

Figure 25-3: Wineries of the Nelson region.

1 Brightwater Vineyards
2 Greenhough Vineyards
3 Neudorf Vineyards
4 Seifried Estate
5 Tasman Bay
6 Waimea Estates

Neudorf Vineyards

One of the smallest yet best vineyards in the Nelson region is Neudorf Vineyards in the Upper Moutere area. Here the soils are heavier than on the plains, consisting more of clay and gravel, giving the wines some good depth of flavour. The **Neudorf Moutere Chardonnay** is highly acclaimed, whilst the **Neudorf Riesling** and **Neudorf Sauvignon Blanc** are simply awash with fruits and fresh acidity.

The **Neudorf Vineyards Moutere Pinot Noir** has made locals realise the potential of this grape in the Nelson region. While most grape growers realise that the region has still a lot to learn in growing and making Pinot Noir, at Neudorf Vineyards the future seems rosy.

Seifried Estate

Close to the coast and on the Waimea Plains is the local pioneer, Seifried Estate. The Seifrieds first planted vines in 1973 in the face of strident criticism from the local orchardists. But many years later, and with many more hectares planted, the vineyard's bold move has been vindicated. Seifried Estate is the region's largest vineyard and is making some outstanding wines, such as the dense and richly textured **Seifried Estate Winemaker's Collection Chardonnay** and the rich and lively **Seifried Estate Winemaker's Collection Barrel Fermented Riesling**.

Other wineries that must be mentioned

Other wineries of note include

- ✔ **Brightwater Vineyards:** The stand-out wine here is the **Brightwater Vineyards Sauvignon Blanc** with lemon and lime flavours.
- ✔ **Greenhough Vineyards:** This winery produces the richly textured and buttery **Greenhough Nelson Chardonnay** and the dense and quite spicy **Greenhough Hope Vineyard Pinot Noir**.
- ✔ **Tasman Bay:** A notable wine here is the excellent **Tasman Bay Marlborough Chardonnay**, a wine with a rich and melon-like flavour.
- ✔ **Waimea Estates:** For a herbal and crisp Sauvignon Blanc, you can't go past the **Waimea Estates Sauvignon Blanc**.

Cooling Off in Canterbury

Although the Canterbury wine region is the fifth largest in New Zealand, in size it is a long way behind its northern neighbour, Marlborough: Canterbury has only 614 hectares of vineyards compared to Marlborough's 6,823 hectares. Nevertheless, Canterbury on the east coast is a burgeoning region that focuses on quality Pinot Noir and Chardonnay.

The Canterbury region can be divided into two distinct sub-regions — the most planted is the Waipara area, a fairly hilly region north of Christchurch, the main city in the region, and the other around Christchurch, namely, the Canterbury Plains.

Warming weather on the east coast

Both the Waipara area and the Canterbury Plains have low rainfall during the growing season and are also affected by hot drying winds that come in from the north-west. Like so many other parts of New Zealand, the surrounding mountain ranges get most of the rainfall with the result that the climate in the vineyard areas is relatively dry. Waimea is about as warm in summer as Marlborough is, with daytime summer temperatures around 25 degrees Celsius. Because the Waipara region is situated close to the coast, it receives cool night breezes. These breezes reduce the nightly temperatures dramatically with the result that the grapes get the chance to rest overnight.

In terms of the effect the sun has on grape ripening, the vineyards of the Waipara area are about two weeks' warmer than the vineyards on the Canterbury Plains. The Canterbury Plains area is cooler due to the cold easterlies that come straight off the ocean into the vineyards.

The vineyards on the Canterbury Plains are certainly affected by the relative lateness of the ripening season; the risk that the grapes aren't going to reach full ripeness is all too regular. Site selection is therefore of paramount importance. Finding a warm sheltered spot in which to plant has certainly proved successful for vineyards such as Kaituna Valley.

Humidity in the Canterbury region is relatively low, which is turn means that the risk of the vines suffering from fungal diseases is low, a distinct advantage to grape growers.

Starring with Pinot Noir

Pinot Noir makes up 30 per cent of the plantings in the Canterbury region, with Chardonnay comprising 24 per cent. Current predictions are that these two varieties, particularly Pinot Noir, will increasingly dominate the vineyards.

Both Pinot Noir and Chardonnay are early ripening varieties, ideal in an area where the risk that the grapes aren't going to fulfil their ripeness potential is always present. The other successful grape in this region is Riesling, an aromatic grape that thrives in conditions where it can ripen slowly, thus giving the grape the chance to retain its zingy acidity.

Quaffing wines in Canterbury

Naturally, Pinot Noir features prominently in the repertoire of the wineries of the Canterbury region. Figure 25-4 shows the wineries of the Canterbury region. The outstanding wineries are discussed in this section.

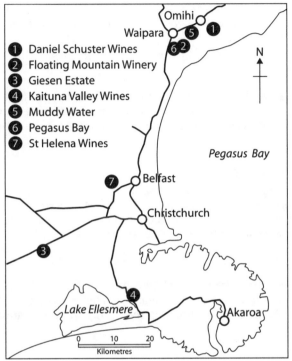

Figure 25-4:
Wineries of
the
Canterbury
region.

Daniel Schuster Wines

Many of the stand-out labels are produced by the wineries of the Waipara area, and Daniel Schuster Wines is one such winery. Daniel Schuster is a consultant viticulturist to Stag's Leap in California and to Antinori in Italy, and has also written about winemaking and viticulture. Naturally, you therefore expect the man himself to make some pretty smart wines — and he does. The **Daniel Schuster Omihi Hills Vineyard Selection Pinot Noir** is full, ripe and weighty.

Floating Mountain Winery

Mark Rattray owns Floating Mountain Winery and is a winemaker with a particular passion for Pinot Noir and Chardonnay. His devotion to these wines shows in his excellent **Floating Mountain Waipara Pinot Noir**, which exudes weight and dense fruit flavours. The other wine of note is the **Floating Mountain Waipara Chardonnay**, a rich and dense wine that is barrel fermented, a process that gives it a full-bodied texture (refer to Chapter 24 for an explanation of barrel fermentation).

Giesen Estate

In the south of the region, one of the best wineries on the Canterbury Plains is Giesen Estate. Owned by three German brothers, it is the Riesling that shines with its citrus flavours and a dry, tart acidity — not surprisingly, given the Giesen family's German heritage. Of late, the family has established vineyards in the Marlborough region, where the climate is rather reliable and the grapes are more often able to reach the full ripeness that the Giesen brothers are striving for.

The standard **Giesen Pinot Noir** is a delightful, fruit-driven Pinot Noir at a reasonable price, while the **Giesen Reserve Barrel Selection Canterbury Pinot Noir** is a more serious wine with plenty of weight and savoury, almost Bonox-like flavours.

Kaituna Valley Wines

The vineyards at Kaituna Valley are in a warm, sheltered belt of land that makes it possible for the grapes to fully ripen nearly every year. To date, it is the **Kaituna Valley Vineyard Canterbury Pinot Noir** and its dense, elegant, savoury structure that has the attention of wine lovers.

Muddy Water

While Muddy Water may be less well known, the wines from here are beginning to create quite a stir. Particularly worthy is the minerally and intense **Muddy Water Dry Riesling** and the earthy, complex **Muddy Water Pinot Noir**.

Pegasus Bay

At Pegasus Bay, you find the richly textured **Pegasus Bay Riesling** that also has a zing of acidity, as well as the complex, full-bodied **Pegasus Bay Chardonnay**.

St Helena Wines

The oldest winery in the area is St Helena Wines where, as early as 1978, the grape growers saw fit to plant Pinot Noir (at the time, most grape growers thought red wine meant just Cabernet Sauvignon).

The **St Helena Pinot Noir** is a fragrant, strawberry style of wine, while the pear-flavoured and spicy **St Helena Pinot Gris** shows much promise — this one is definitely a wine to look out for.

Heading South to Otago

Central Otago, or Otago as the wine region is often simply referred to, is breathtakingly beautiful. The chance of finding a more beautiful vineyard area in the world is slim. Many of the vineyards lie beneath snow-capped mountains — stunning backdrops for the wine-loving photographer.

Several distinct sub-regions lie within the Otago region. Queenstown lies at the centre of the region, and to its north is the Wanaka area, where just two vineyards are established to date. To the east of Queenstown are the Cromwell Basin and Alexandra sub-regions: Cromwell comprises over 60 per cent of Otago's vineyards. West from Cromwell on the way to Queenstown is the Gibbston sub-region, second only to the Cromwell Basin in terms of hectares planted.

Variations in soil type affect the wines of the region. Nearly all of the vineyards in the Gibbston area are situated along the Kawaru River and are typically planted on silty, free-draining soils. The wines are less full-bodied than those from the Cromwell Basin, but nevertheless have a fine flavour.

Otago is New Zealand's fourth biggest wine region and is second only to Marlborough in terms of its reputation within the wine world. When people think of Otago, they think of good-quality wine — and often rather expensive prices.

Growing vines in the cold, dry south

The Otago region is the most southerly winegrowing area in the world, so immediately you would think that the region must be cold and wet. Well, actually, it isn't. First of all, this land is seriously dry: During the critical growing season, the average rainfall in Otago is less than 270 millimetres — in fact, I remember seeing a sign near the Felton Road Vineyard that told passersby that they were in a desert region and to use water wisely.

The reason for Otago's dry climate is that the region is situated so far inland. As we have seen with other wine regions in New Zealand, rain-bearing clouds pass over mountain ranges where most of the rain falls before arriving over vineyards. In the case of Otago, as the clouds travels from west to east, the rain falls on the mountains; in the winter, the rain turns to snow.

Otago is a land of extremes. Ski resorts sit above vineyards, yet summer temperatures can be some of the highest in the country, often exceeding 30 degrees Celsius. When the grapes are ripening in autumn, temperatures are warm to cool by day and cold at night.

Conditions can vary even when relatively short distances are involved. In the Gibbston sub-region, the climate is cooler than in the Cromwell Basin, and the harvesting time of the same grape variety can vary by up to one month.

With such extreme variations in temperature, having the ability to select a good site for a vineyard is critical for a grape grower: The vines need to grow in a warm pocket to enable the grapes to reach full ripeness. What this climate means, though, is that the ripening period is stretched out, which allows the grapes to accumulate layer upon layer of flavour. The result is wines of incredible intensity.

Savouring Otago's Pinot Noir

Pinot Noir reigns supreme in Otago, comprising 63 per cent of the vines in the region. Chardonnay is next in importance, with 15 per cent, and the other plantings are shared fairly equally between Pinot Gris, Riesling and Sauvignon Blanc. A word on some of these varieties:

- **Pinot Noir:** The Wanaka area is the coolest of the Otago sub-regions, and it is the least reliable in terms of its grapes achieving absolute ripeness. In colder years, Pinot Noir from Wanaka can assume a herbal tone, whereas in the warmer years, it can be fragrant and perfumed with a decent dose of acidity. The Pinot Noirs of the warm Cromwell Basin are amazingly full bodied with dense, ultra-ripe flavours. The Alexandra and Gibbston sub-regions produce a Pinot Noir with juicy fruit flavours and a supple texture.

- **Chardonnay:** Otago produces a Chardonnay that tends to be on the lean and tight side, with citrus flavours and good acidity. These wines also tend to age well.

- **Pinot Gris:** A variety that has had much success in the Otago region, Pinot Gris is often made in a style common in the Burgundy region of France, that is, with barrel fermentation (refer to Chapter 24) and lees stirring. (see the sidebar 'Stirring up a storm in a pot'.

Stirring up a storm in a pot

Lees stirring is a technique that makes use of the dead yeast cells that lie on the bottom of the barrel. What happens during fermentation is that all the grape sugars are converted to alcohol by the mirco-organisms, yeasts. After all the sugar has been depleted, the yeasts have no food and they die. Over a period of time, a few weeks, the yeasts gradually settle to the bottom of the fermentation vessel.

However, yeasts can add valuable flavour to the wine as well as texture, so regular stirring of the barrel occurs to re-suspend these yeast cells within the wine. Stirring usually takes place once a week or every two weeks. The sorts of flavours that result are along the lines of vanilla and honeycomb. The textural changes that take place in the wine are a softening and a rich and complex middle palate.

Taking the best of Otago

As with the Marlborough region, identifying the best wines and wineries is difficult because so many of them are of a very high standard (see Figure 25-5). However, the following names can lead you to some of the best wines in Otago.

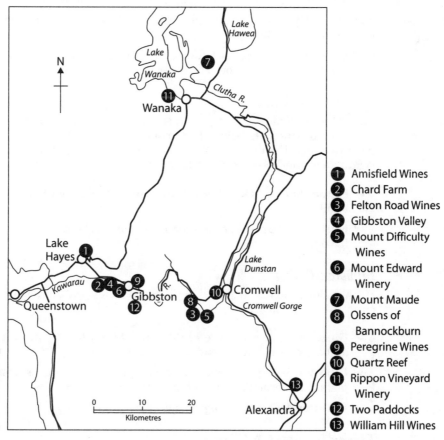

Figure 25-5: Wineries of the Otago region.

1. Amisfield Wines
2. Chard Farm
3. Felton Road Wines
4. Gibbston Valley
5. Mount Difficulty Wines
6. Mount Edward Winery
7. Mount Maude
8. Olssens of Bannockburn
9. Peregrine Wines
10. Quartz Reef
11. Rippon Vineyard Winery
12. Two Paddocks
13. William Hill Wines

Chard Farm

This vineyard lies in the Gibbston sub-region of Central Otago, and boasts a range of four Pinot Noirs as well as an excellent Chardonnay. (For more information on this vineyard, turn to Chapter 28.)

These wines are

- ✔ **Chard Farm Lowburn Pinot Noir:** A weighty wine grown in the Cromwell Basin.
- ✔ **Chard Farm Blacksmith's Pinot Noir:** The grapes used in this wine are grown on the home property in Gibbston.
- ✔ **Chard Farm Finla Mor Pinot Noir:** A wine with enormous depth and intensity; the grapes are grown in the Cromwell Basin.
- ✔ **Chard Farm River Run Pinot Noir:** A well-made, fragrant wine at a reasonable price.
- ✔ **Chard Farm Judge and Jury Chardonnay:** This wine shows richness and nuttiness from the influences of barrel fermentation.

Felton Road Wines

One of the best-known vineyards in the Cromwell Basin, the vineyard at Felton Road Wines sits below the Carrick Range that shelters it from the rain-bearing winds. The early autumn days are warm and this shows through in Felton Road wines, the best of which are

- ✔ **Felton Road Block 3 Pinot Noir:** Super intense, mouth-filling and quite tannic.
- ✔ **Felton Road Barrel Fermented Chardonnay:** Fantastic texture and fruit flavours.

Gibbston Valley

Further along the Karawu River is Gibbston Valley, whose range is all top class. Among them are

- ✔ **Gibbston Valley Reserve Pinot Noir:** Chunky in weight, with a savoury and dark plum flavour and fine tannins.
- ✔ **Gibbston Valley Reserve Chardonnay:** Rich butteriness from malolactic fermentation and barrel ageing.
- ✔ **Gibbston Valley Riesling:** Zingy, citrus acidity.

Rippon Vineyard & Winery

This stunning vineyard is planted on the edge of Lake Wanaka and the high mountains that surround it are snow-capped for much of the year. Rippon Vineyard & Winery enjoys one of the warmest spots in this marginal region. Extra warmth is reflected off the waters of the lake and the soil, which is primarily river silt over schist gravels, means that any warmth from the sun is absorbed and retained. The warmth radiating from the soils makes the air around the vines just that little bit warmer, giving the grapes an extra helping hand in ripening.

Not every season allows the grapes grown in this vineyard to achieve full ripening, but in a good year, the best wines are

- **Rippon Vineyard Pinot Noir:** Spicy with an occasional tinge of beetroot, especially in the cooler years.
- **Rippon Vineyard Gewürztraminer:** Zesty and with an aroma of limes.
- **Rippon Vineyard Riesling:** Mineral flavours that demand cellaring for at least three years.

Two Paddocks

I'm not listing this vineyard because the New Zealand-born actor Sam Neill owns it . . . but because it produces some very worthwhile wines. Admittedly, the owner's identity does mean that this vineyard has a certain number of wine-loving movie fans among its regular consumers. Such is Neill's passion for Pinot Noir, this is the only variety he produces.

The **Two Paddocks Neill Pinot Noir** is a complex wine with cherries and black plum fragrances.

Other wineries that must be mentioned

The top wine producers in the Otago region also include

- **Amisfield Wines:** One of the top wines from this winery is the austere **Arcadia Non Vintage** sparkling wine.
- **Mount Difficulty Wines:** Set in the Cromwell Basin, this winery makes top-quality, intensely textured and earthy **Mount Difficulty Pinot Noir.**
- **Mount Edward Winery:** Not far from Sam Neill's Two Paddocks, this winery has its **Mount Edward Pinot Noir** as its centrepiece. The wine shows the great softness of this variety, along with grainy tannins.
- **Mount Maude:** This winery in the Wanaka area produces a richly textured **Mount Maude Pinot Noir.**
- **Olssens of Bannockburn:** You find an excellent Pinot Noir at this winery; **Olssens of Bannockburn Slapjack Creek Reserve Pinot Noir** is definitely worth cellaring.
- **Peregrine Wines:** Peregine is worth a visit for its ripe full-bodied **Peregrine Gewürztraminer** and the warm-fruited **Peregrine Pinot Noir.**
- **Quartz Reef:** A mixture of influences can be detected at this winery. One of the owners is Clotilde Chauvet, who spends half her time making wine at the family-owned Champagne House of Marc Chauvet in France, and half her time in Otago. At Quartz Reef, she, along with the other owner, Rudi Bauer, make a racy and fine sparkling wine, known as **Quartz Reef Chauvet**, as well as a savoury and textured **Quartz Reef Pinot Noir.**
- **William Hill Wines:** In the south-east corner of the Central Otago region is the Alexandra sub-region, where the William Hill Wines makes soft-textured, fruit-dominant **William Hill Alexandra Pinot Noir.**

Part VI
The Part of Tens

www.moir.com.au

Alan Moir

In this part . . .

Here is a bit of an indulgence — my chance to put a few of my favourites from Australia and New Zealand into the mix. In this part, I cover the best Web sites in Chapter 26; the Internet really is a medium that changes on an almost-daily basis. Some of the wineries that own Web sites are a fantastic browse as well, and often lead you on to other links of interest.

In Chapter 27, I present my best Australian and New Zealand wines. My choices reflect many different reasons, which I explain in the chapter. While the list could go on to cover 100 of the best, I choose to limit my choices to just ten.

And in Chapter 28, I introduce you to a few of the most stunning, relaxing and professional cellar doors. Plan a weekend and enjoy the huge offering of wine and food waiting for you now.

Chapter 26

Ten Best Web Sites for Wine Buffs

. . . .

In This Chapter

▶ Immersing yourself in information about wine

▶ Researching Australian and New Zealand wines at Web sites based overseas

▶ Deciding what food to have with your wine

▶ Finding out what your wine cellar is worth

▶ Tracking down your favourite wine at the best price

▶ Investigating the local wine industries with the top wine directories

. . . .

*P*eople the world over are increasingly turning to the Internet to find information on all sorts of things, and the wine industry has not been slow to make the most of this trend. Most wineries have Web sites that promote their products. In addition, each wine region has a tourist information centre that encourages tourists to visit the wineries to sample not only wine but also other attractions such as restaurants and accommodation.

This chapter is the launching pad for your online research into wine in Australia and New Zealand. The Web sites listed here can provide you with a huge range of information on the wine industry in both countries — some of the sites present hard, cold facts and statistics; some provide interesting articles and opinions; and some tempt you to buy online. Many of the sites also provide links that take you to yet more wine sites. Surfing wine Web sites (with a favourite red to sip) on a cold winter's afternoon is a very rewarding way to keep warm!

Australian Wine & Brandy Corporation

www.awbc.com.au

You find a wealth of information on everything to do with the Australian wine industry at this Web site. The site provides state-by-state statistics, the latest happenings on the wine scene, and information on the wine regions and their boundaries, and how to contact the various regional associations. You can read about the regulations that govern the wine industry — such as what must be written on the label of a wine bottle — and follow links to sites that provide even more technical information.

Although this Web site is aimed more at those working within the wine industry, the site provides a fascinating overview of the elements that play a part in the production of a bottle of Australian wine.

Australian Wine Bureau London

www.australianwinebureau.com

Based in the United Kingdom, the Australian Wine Bureau site provides information on Australian wines and promotes them in the United Kingdom. You can find reports on vintages, news from the vineyards, information about wine tours, and details on the new and interesting wine varieties being grown in Australia. Overall, this is a fabulous site for checking up on Australian wines.

Berry Bros. & Rudd

www.bbr.com

Another site that is based in the United Kingdom, Berry Bros. & Rudd, also has retail outlets there. This Web site includes a search facility that can help you find a good bottle or two, whether you want the wine for quaffing, cellaring or just enjoying with friends who are knowledgeable about their wines. The Web site also provides the latest news and articles on wine worldwide.

You can also check out their FAQs page (Frequently Asked Questions) and find the answers to all manner of things to do with wine. Even if you're not interested in buying wine from here, the site is a good place to browse and pick up interesting information on wine.

Bob Campbell Co NZ

> www.bobcampbell.co.nz

A great site to find out what's going on in the world of wine in New Zealand, Bob Campbell's site also provides information on the world of wine beyond the shores of his country. You can find articles and recommendations on wine, as well as links to other interesting sites. This site is a good all-round resource that gives you a good feel for New Zealand wine.

Cuisine

> www.cuisine.co.nz

When you open the home page of the Web site of the magazine *Cuisine*, you are left in no doubt that the site is devoted to 'food, wine and good living'. Even though you don't have access to the current issue of the magazine, you've plenty to read. You can browse through the archives for information from past issues, and read all about food and, more to the point, how wine can enhance your dining experience.

Langtons, Wine Auctions & Exchange

> www.langtons.com.au

Langtons Web site is linked to its auction house. While you need to become a member of Langtons before you can trade, a wealth of information is available on wines that you may want to sell.

You can type in the name of any wine in your cellar and, if that wine has been sold through Langtons at any stage, you're able to get a rough idea of its current value. The site also lists wines that are likely to give you a good investment return if you buy now and sell later — without, of course, pulling the cork and enjoying them first! Langtons also produce a magazine that carries articles on prominent wineries and their latest exploits.

New Zealand Wine and Grape Industry

> www.nzwine.com

The official site of the New Zealand Wine and Grape Industry provides loads of information. You can look up statistics on grape production, pore over maps of the various wine regions, find directories of wineries in each region, research the history of winemaking in New Zealand, and so on. A great starting point as you explore the wines of New Zealand, this site also answers some of the more technical questions about wine in this country.

On Wine

> www.onwine.com.au

To get the maximum benefit from this site, you need to be a subscriber — well worthwile. The site is run by Jeremy Oliver, an independent wine writer who keeps the site stocked with just about everything you could want to know about the world of wine, albeit with the main focus on Australia and New Zealand.

You can get Jeremy's latest tasting notes on new releases, find out how the wine companies listed on the stock exchange are faring, and read about various topics that involve wine — ranging from tax reform to personal profiles of winemakers.

WineRobot

www.winerobot.com

WineRobot is an Australian-based site that tracks down a wine you've been looking for, at the best possible price. You simply type in the name of the wine you want, and WineRobot goes off to search the top online stores that stock the wine, and lets you compare the prices. You can either buy your wine online or go to the store with the best price and buy it there.

Winetitles

www.winetitles.com.au

The information available on this Web site might be a little too in-depth for some. However, the site is an excellent guide to publications on the more technical side of winemaking, viticulture and wine appreciation.

Winetitles is Australia's specialist multimedia publisher to the international grape and wine industry. The site directs you to a range of publications, including the wine industry 'bible', the *Australian and New Zealand Wine Industry Directory*, which covers nearly everyone and everything involved in wine production in these two countries.

Chapter 27

Ten (Plus a Few) Best Wines in Australia and New Zealand

....

In This Chapter

▶ Finding a great Chardonnay in New Zealand

▶ Getting fortified with Tokay and Muscat

▶ Excelling at Pinot Noir on both sides of the Tasman

▶ Enjoying a Cabernet Sauvignon Merlot

▶ Choosing two excellent Rieslings

▶ Fizzing over bubbly

▶ Investigating some great wines at reasonable prices

▶ Laying it down for later: Good wines to cellar

....

*N*ow this is a pretty big call! Deciding on the best wines that Australia and New Zealand have to offer is more than difficult, it's practically impossible — so many criteria come into play, not least of which is personal preference. However, in selecting my 'Top Ten', I've ranged across price and across varieties to draw up a list of wines that are representative of the best that the wine regions of Australia and New Zealand have to offer.

Some of the wines I recommend in this chapter are easier to find than others. You may have to hound your local wine retailer, or maybe even contact the winery itself for some of them. The Internet is always a good place to start your search (refer to Chapter 26 for some useful Web sites).

This list of wines is by no means the definitive one; no list ever could be. However, what the list does give you is an insight into which wines are consistently good, either from the perspective of value for money or sheer outstanding quality — or these and more factors all rolled into one. I haven't given a particular vintage year for these wines; each wine has such a reputation that you likely to be well satisfied with whatever vintage you find.

Checking Out the Chardonnays

My choice is split here; I can't really make up my mind between two excellent Chardonnays from the North Island of New Zealand. They are the **Kumeu River Chardonnay** and the **Kumeu River Mate's Vineyard Chardonnay**. Neither of these first-class wines can be found at bargain-basement prices, but their quality is remarkable.

The North Island produces wines of an outstanding quality. Both of these wines are rich, concentrated and soft-textured, showing the great attention to detail that goes into every bottle from this fine producer.

Blending the Perfect Fortified

Choosing the best fortified wine is almost impossible, as we have a small but stunning pack of producers in this part of the world — but choose I must. My choice has to come from the home of fortified wines in Australia, Rutherglen in Victoria, and my favourites are Campbells Tokay and Muscat.

Campbells make stunning fortified wines. At the top of its range are **Campbells Isabella Rare Rutherglen Tokay** and **Campbells Merchant Prince Rare Rutherglen Muscat**. Both these wines have been made blending old, intensely flavoured and textured wines with newer, younger wines. Campbells' blending techniques are borrowed from the method used to make the great Port wines from Portugal. The result is wines of allure and inviting aromas, finished off with all manner of delicious fruitcake-like flavours. If you can't find these two wines, another excellent one is **Campbells Classic Rutherglen Tokay**.

Picking a Top Pinot Noir from Australia

Pinot Noir seems to have made itself very much at home in Tasmania; the island to the south of the Australian mainland produces many a fine Pinot.

One of the finest Pinot Noirs around, and one that's hard to go past, is the richly flavoured and soft-textured **Freycinet Pinot Noir**. Year after year, despite being grown in a climate that can be difficult in cooler years, the Pinot Noir from Freycinet Vineyards is consistently terrific.

Picking a Top Pinot Noir from New Zealand

Well, since Pinot Noir is a bit of a favourite of mine, I make no apologies about choosing another one! Like all the other selections I make in this chapter, choosing my favourite variety was a tough decision. Should it be a Pinot Noir from Central Otago, or a Sauvignon Blanc from Marlborough, or one of the many other varieties from New Zealand?

The quality of wine coming from the south island of New Zealand is extremely high. In the end, my choice is a Pinot Noir from Felton Road Wines in the Otago region, the **Felton Road Block 3 Pinot Noir**. The wine is incredibly intense in flavour and texture, making it almost full-bodied in style.

Getting into the Red

One wine that I'm happy to drink any time is the **Cullen Cabernet Sauvignon Merlot** from Cullen Wines in Margaret River, Western Australia. Unlike many versions of this style of wine being made in Australia, this wine doesn't rely on super-ripe fruit to make an impact. Instead, it has a savoury, refined palate of dusty tannins, ripe black fruits and a dry finish.

This wine also proves to be a terrific wine to cellar for ten or more years.

Rhapsodising over Riesling

Finding one good Riesling is terrific. Finding two good Rieslings is fantastic! So I'm going to name two Rieslings that are so closely related, coming from the same producer and from vineyards not really that far apart, they both deserve top billing. My choices are the **Grosset Polish Hill Riesling and Grosset Watervale Riesling** — you just can't help but love them.

These Rieslings come from Grosset Wines in the Clare Valley region of South Australia. The Grosset Polish Hill shows all the trademarks of cool-climate Riesling, that is, outstanding ability to age for many a year. The grapes are grown on slate-like soil that may, coincidentally or not, give the wine a real mineral character.

The quality of the Grosset Watervale is in keeping with its warmer vineyard site. The wine is so full of flavour and bursting with juicy oranges and lemons, that it's pretty hard to stop yourself from twisting the screw cap on the bottles. (Jeffrey Grosset was one of the first winemakers to bottle his wines using screw caps, as a reaction to the high incidence of faulty corks.)

If you can resist opening these wines, the Polish Hill will still excite after ten years and the Watervale can easily age for six to eight years.

Bubbling over a Top Sparkling Wine

Despite my time as a winemaker with this company prior to 1996, I have no qualms about nominating the sparkling wines produced by Domaine Chandon as the best of the lot.

Certainly, you can find some pretty hot contenders in the sparkling wine category. The Arras made by the Hardy Wine Company is extremely good but, to my mind, can't beat the quality and range of Domaine Chandon wines. While the winery itself is situated in the Yarra Valley in Victoria, the grapes used to make the wines come from Victoria, South Australia and Tasmania.

The range includes the **Domaine Chandon Vintage Brut**; the simply delicious **Domaine Chandon Rosé**; a **Chandon Greenpoint Cuvée**, which is a late-disgorged wine that has spent over five years ageing on lees, thus giving it superb complexity; and a quirky wine known as **Chandon Cuvée Riche**, a luscious sweet dessert or aperitif-style bubbly. This producer also makes the **Chandon Vintage Blanc de Blancs**, a 100 per cent Chardonnay wine that has the elegant aromas and flavour of traditional sparkling wines.

Getting Value #1: Peter Lehmann Wines

Year after year, the least expensive labels from Peter Lehmann's range are top drinking wines. The wines produced at this South Australian winery possess an amazing quality for the prices at which they're sold, especially the **Peter Lehmann Semillon** and the **Peter Lehmann Riesling**. Both these wines are full of flavour and fruitiness, with a nice zing of acid to balance the wine.

Considering the very reasonable amount you pay per bottle (around AUD$12 at the time of writing), this winery is hard to beat. The **Peter Lehmann Clancy's Red** is a blend of Shiraz, Cabernet Sauvignon, Merlot and Cabernet Franc that is all too easy to enjoy, given its rich fruit and spice flavours.

Getting Value #2: Zilzie Wines

You can find truly amazing value at this Murray Valley vineyard situated in the north-west irrigation area of Victoria. For years, the Zilzie family have been selling fruit to the bigger wine companies, and only recently did they decide to have a go at producing their own label.

The wines produced by Zilzie Wines have taken the bargain-yet-value wine end of the market by storm. The **Zilzie Buloke Reserve Shiraz** is good value, while the **Zilzie Show Reserve Chardonnay** shows how versatile this variety can be in warm or cool climates. (At the time of writing, the Shiraz costs about AUD$10 and the Chardonnay about AUD$18. Let's hope they don't get too successful and the bubble bursts!)

Ageing Gracefully: The Best White Wine to Cellar

Australia has quite a reputation for its aged Hunter Valley Semillons, and McWilliam's and Tyrrell's wines are leaders in Semillon in the region. A good Hunter Valley Semillon will age beautifully.

Look for the **McWilliam's Mount Pleasant Lovedale Semillon** and **Tyrrell's Vat 1 Semillon**. When you find your bottles of treasure, give them ten or more years in the bottle. When you eventually crack the bottles, you're going to find the young plain wine transformed into a stunning honeyed and toasty-flavoured top drop.

Ageing Gracefully: The Best Red Wine to Cellar

If you're looking for an outstanding red wine to cellar, I find it hard to go past the **Cullen Cabernet Sauvignon Merlot**. From the West Australian wine region of Margaret River, this Cabernet Merlot is consistently of a very high quality and has plenty of character to develop well over the years. You can cellar this red for 10–20 years. The fruit flavours gradually develop into more savoury and dry characters, making the wine just delightful to sip slowly.

Chapter 28

Ten (Plus One) of the Best Winery Cellar Doors

●　●

In This Chapter

▶ Saving the Murray as part of a wine-tasting experience

▶ Finding the wineries with the best view

▶ Taking your wine tasting seriously: Forget the view

▶ Mixing architecture with wine appreciation

▶ Sampling good food as well as good wine

●　●

*W*hat is called 'the best' is really often a matter of what someone personally prefers. Some people like the stylish architecturally designed tasting rooms of some of the newer wineries. Others prefer the smaller, often older and more traditional tasting rooms because of their ambience.

Some wineries have a restaurant adjoining the tasting room and serve casual lunchtime meals. Other wineries focus on their wines and nothing but the wines. Occasionally, you may find that tours of the winery are available; if you visit during harvest, don't miss the opportunity, as a winery operating at harvest time is a great thing to observe. Many cellar doors offer spectacular views that almost make tasting the wines of secondary importance — well, I did say 'almost'.

This chapter tells you about a selection of Australian and New Zealand wineries that offer different architectural styles, different landscapes and, of course, different wines. All of them are well worth a visit.

Banrock Station, South Australia

Situated in South Australia's Riverland, the Banrock Station visitor's centre is about more than just wine. The property has been set up as a wetland rejuvenation project with a focus on restoring the health of Australia's greatest river, the Murray River. For decades this river has been used to support the types of agriculture that use a lot of water, and this includes vineyards. Due to high levels of irrigation, the river basin of the Murray has been affected not only by reduction in flow but also by the rising salt table.

The Banrock Station visitor's centre showcases the work that has been done to improve the Murray River and attracts wine tourists as well as those interested in the environment. On arrival at Banrock Station, you may like to take one of the two walks through the beautiful wetland areas following a well-thought-out map that describes the various plants and wild life.

Afterwards, you can take a walk into the cellar door where you're rewarded with a wine tasting and perhaps a light lunch. Among the excellent wines on offer, those in the Banrock Station 'The Reserve' range set a benchmark for Riverland wine. The Banrock Station The Reserve Chardonnay is particularly good with loads of pineapple and citrus flavours. Also worth trying is the spicy Banrock Station The Reserve Shiraz and the fruity Banrock Station The Reserve Petit Verdot. A visit to Banrock Station is highly recommended (refer to Chapter 20 for details of the unique Banrock Station Wine and Wetland Centre).

Brown Brothers, Milawa, Victoria

Some people may well think of Brown Brothers Milawa cellar door as being old fashioned. That may be, as it doesn't offer the views and glitz that is becoming common to cellar doors across Australia.

However, Brown Brothers more than make up for this by offering an astonishing variety of different wines to the wine taster. I bet that this cellar door was the first place at which many people tried the less mainstream varieties that are sweeping wine lists across the country — wine varieties such as Barbera, Sangiovese and Tempranillo.

The tasting area at Brown Brothers is set up in the traditional way of a stand-up bar where a trained staff member takes you through the wines from whites to reds and then dessert wines. A veritable smorgasbord of choice is available and you can sample most of the company's 40-plus wines.

Chard Farm, New Zealand

Chard Farm is in Central Otago, a wine region of the South Island of New Zealand. The vineyard's tasting area is perched overlooking a river gorge — I mean right on it, the road winds around clinging to a hillside.

The quality of all the wines is first class, particularly the range of Chard Farm Pinot Noirs all of which show terrific ripe fruit with a savoury finish. Also a speciality here is the citrus and nutty Chard Farm Judge and Jury Chardonnay.

If you're driving, watch how much tasting you do at this cellar door. When you finish concentrating on the excellent range of wines here, you need to turn your concentration onto the road going out!

Coriole Vineyards, South Australia

Coriole Vineyards in the McLaren Vale, south-eastern South Australia, is definitely one of my favourite smaller cellar doors. The old building has been restored, but not so much so as to lose its character. The small outdoor seating area is sheltered from the cool sea breeze that can whip up from the nearby Gulf St Vincent, so that even on a winter's day you can enjoy the warm sun.

The little tasting room offers well-made and well-priced wines. Coriole Shiraz is the vineyard's flagship red, and is a stalwart favourite of mine, being spicy and restrained in flavour and body. Another wine worth trying is the Coriole Semillon Sauvignon Blanc, a well-made fresh and fruity wine. In addition to the wines, you find a range of olive oils and handcrafted cheeses that are some of Australia's best.

Millbrook Winery, Western Australia

Millbrook Winery offers a wine and food experience that you might think was only available in the higher profile Margaret River region.

Nestled in the beautiful Perth Hills only one hour from Perth, this winery is set in lovely landscape and is well worth a visit. The cellar door at Millbrook is newly finished and is very modern and sophisticated. Excellent wines are available and you can also indulge in a lovely lunch at Millbrook. Millbrook offers two ranges of wine. The less-expensive range is the Barking Owl label of which the Cabernet Sauvignon Merlot and the Barking Owl Chardonnay are well worth sampling. Under the Millbrook label is a ripe and full-bodied Millbrook Viognier as well as a spicy and blackberry Millbrook Shiraz.

Montana, New Zealand

The Montana winery at Brancott in the Marlborough region of New Zealand looms up from the flat valley floor. If the building itself seems a little overpowering in the landscape, the interior is welcoming. Here you can try the range of Montana's wine at a tasting bench served by a well-informed staff member. The tasting area is spacious, so even on the busiest days you don't feel crowded as you taste the wines.

You can enjoy a fine lunch in the restaurant before being taken on a tour of the extensive winery, home to the famous Montana Sauvignon Blanc, New Zealand's biggest wine export. In addition, the winery is the headquarters for the Deutz sparkling wine arm of the business, a joint venture with the French Champagne house of the same name.

Palliser Estate, New Zealand

Palliser Estate is located in Martinborough in the southern part of the north island of New Zealand. The cellar door here is set among glorious grounds, so you feel the touch of 'something special' the moment you arrive.

The small cellar door has a tasting bench where knowledgeable staff serve you. The lovely thing about Palliser Estate is that the cellar door area is understated. Rather than relying on extraordinary architectural feats to lure you to the winery, Palliser Estate lets its outstanding wines do the talking. Among the best from the winery are the Pinot Noirs — the Palliser Estate Pinot Noir and the second-tier Pencarrow Pinot Noir — and the herbal and fresh Palliser Estate Sauvignon Blanc.

Rosevears Estate, Tasmania

Views, winery cellar doors and restaurants seem to go hand in hand. Here at Rosevears Estate in northern Tasmania, the recently completed restaurant, winery and accommodation have taken full advantage of nature with the building nestled into the hillside overlooking the stunning Tamar River. You can sip the wines and take in the view from the tasting area.

Everything, especially the wines, is top class. The two cool-climate varieties of Pinot Noir and Chardonnay do particularly well here in Tasmania. The Rosevears Pinot Noir shows a spiciness and raspberry-leaf flavours while the Rosevears Estate Chardonnay is full of citrus and peach flavours. If you're in the north of Tasmania, making a detour to Rosevears Estate is definitely worth doing.

Rymill Coonawarra, South Australia

In a region where the cellar doors tend to be rather dark and old fashioned, Rymill Coonawarra stands out. The modern, newly finished winery of Rymill Coonawarra is in the noted winegrowing area of Coonawarra in south-eastern South Australia. The cellar door is part of the winery building and large glass windows allow you to watch the activity in the winery from above. If you time your visit well, you can take a tour of the winery with staff that certainly know what they're talking about.

The Coonawarra region is renowned for Cabernet Sauvignon, and the Rymill Coonawarra Cabernet Sauvignon is worthy of this reputation for quality. Also good from here is the fruity Rymill MC^2, a blend of Merlot, Cabernet Sauvignon and Cabernet Franc.

Shaw and Smith, South Australia

The Shaw and Smith winery is located in the Adelaide Hills, less than one hour from the centre of Adelaide. The cellar door was recently completed and you can now enjoy quite a unique wine experience.

For around $10, you can buy a 'wine flight' — a selection of all Shaw and Smith wines that come with a tasting mat. This mat explains the various winemaking techniques that go into making the wines, and also tells you about the wine itself, such as the aromas and flavours. Alternatively, you can buy wine by the glass. The outstanding wine is the Shaw and Smith Sauvignon Blanc, a zesty and fruit-packed wine. However, do try the Shaw and Smith M3 Vineyard Chardonnay, a complex, fruity and all-round delicious wine.

Yering Station, Victoria

Yering Station in the Yarra Valley of Victoria is a winery that falls into the 'architecturally stunning' bag. The locals quote all sorts of figures when telling you how much the building actually cost — suffice to say that it was an awful lot.

The views of the smoky blue coloured hills in the distance are partly what makes the cellar door so beautiful. The wines on offer are also pretty good, and don't forget to make time to enjoy lunch in the restaurant, which is well worth a visit.

Yering Station offers a range of cellar-door-only releases, as well as the wines in the winery's range that are more widely available. Outstanding from this winery is the Yering Station Reserve Pinot Noir, the Yering Station Shiraz Viognier and the Yering Station Chardonnay. As staunch supporters of rosé, the Yering Station winemakers have produced a very good soft and fruity Yering Station Pinot Noir Rosé ED (the 'ED' stands for Extra Dry). The winery is also home to the delicately flavoured Yarrabank Cuvée sparkling wine, a blend of Chardonnay and Pinot Noir grapes.

Appendix

Publications to Keep You Right Up to Date

• •

*T*housands of words are written on the subject of wine every year, and the publications I mention in this appendix barely scratch the surface of the huge body of work that is wine literature. But this appendix is a start. First a word of advice: You nearly always find wine reviews at the back of a magazine on food or lifestyle — I don't know why we wine writers get relegated to the end, but that seems to be our wine lot in life!

Reading All about It: The Newspapers

The major newspapers in Australia and New Zealand have their own wine writers, who usually write very informative and often very entertaining columns on food and wine. Among the best known are the following:

✔ *The Adelaide Advertiser*: This South Australian newspaper runs its wine reviews on Wednesdays. Naturally, the wine pages focus on the vineyards of South Australia, but the rest of Australia is also covered. This edition of *The Advertiser* also reviews restaurants.

✔ *The Age*: The Melbourne (Victoria) newspaper, *The Age*, has a Tuesday supplement entitled 'Epicure', which is full of the latest happenings and new wine releases, and also includes reviews of a few wines. The supplement also reviews restaurants across a range of prices.

✔ *The Courier-Mail*: This Brisbane (Queensland) newspaper features articles on wine and food in a supplement every Tuesday.

✔ *The Daily News*: This major New Zealand newspaper regularly features articles on wine and food. These articles cover most aspects of the wine industry, including company merges and acquisitions, new wine releases and the general industry news.

- ✔ *The Australian Financial Review*: Every Friday, *The Australian Financial Review* runs a wine column discussing the wine industry as a whole, especially the financial side, and also makes wine recommendations. Once a month, a glossy supplement also has features on wine.

- ✔ *The Sydney Morning Herald*: This Sydney (New South Wales) newspaper has a Tuesday supplement called 'Good Living', which is similar to 'Epicure' in *The Age*. You can find reviews of wines and Sydney restaurants and other wine news.

- ✔ *The West Australian*: The wine and food pages appear on Thursdays to keep you up to date with wine and culinary happenings in Western Australia. The wine and food columns of this publication are written in a chatty style and you can find some good recommendations about the latest releases.

Checking Out the Magazines

Many magazines have the occasional article on wine, food and lifestyle. The magazines I list here are devoted to these topics, discussing them from all angles and often in great depth. You can find information on the wine industry internationally, as well as in Australia and New Zealand.

- ✔ *Cuisine*: This magazine is the food and wine bible in New Zealand, and some months, it's as thick as the Bible, too. Loaded with reviews of wines from both New Zealand and Australia, and with recommendations for tastings, you can find plenty to interest you. Local wineries also feature heavily.

- ✔ *Divine*: You can find this magazine in some newsagents as well as in speciality wine and food stores. The articles are written in a sassy fashion, focusing on the latest and greatest events for the epicure and wine lover. Most issues look at one wine region or wine style in depth, with just a few other articles on other aspects of food and wine, and focus on what's happening in Australia and New Zealand. The photography is usually very appealing and is in a class of its own.

- ✔ **The Wine Magazine from the** *Australian Gourmet Traveller*: You get a glossy look at the wine world beyond the shores of Australia and New Zealand. Although this magazine focuses mainly on Australian wine regions, it also covers New Zealand and, to a lesser degree, other wine areas of the world.

- ✔ *Winestate*: If you want lots of information on tastings, regional wines and reviews of wine releases in Australia and New Zealand, this magazine is for you. From time to time, *Winestate* covers current issues in the wine industry story.

Paying Attention to the Wine Guides

In this section, I recommend wine guides for those who are seriously interested in wine and want to research the subject. These guides are all updated annually, so you can be sure that the information in them is as current as possible. You can easily recognise the authors of these guides — they're the ones in the tasting room whose teeth are stained black.

- ✔ ***Don't Buy Wine Without Me***: This book by Stuart Gregor is an amusing guide to Australian wines that are readily available. No serious pontificating here.

- ✔ ***James Halliday's Australian Wine Companion***: This guide contains extensive wine reviews on wines from over 1,500 Australian wineries. Each listing offers some background on the winery, a list of all the various labels produced by the winery and often a review of some of them. The author suggests the year in which the wine should be drunk and also makes suggestions for the right kind of food.

- ✔ ***Michael Cooper's Buyer's Guide to New Zealand Wines***: This book is a comprehensive guide comprising tasting notes on New Zealand wines. Michael Cooper's guide is a bit of a New Zealand institution.

- ✔ ***Quaff***: Written by Max Allen and Peter Forrestal, this guide is all about wines that are 'quaffers'; that is, mainly Australian wines under AUD$15.

- ✔ ***The OnWine Australian Wine Annual***: Written by Jeremy Oliver, this guide includes more than 1,700 wine reviews of Australian wineries. Each entry has a current review and lists past vintages, how Jeremy rates them, when to drink them and how long they should be cellared in order to enjoy them at their peak.

Index

・・

• *T* •

• U •

• V •

FOR DUMMIES®

A world of Australian resources to help you grow

Australian Editions

Business

Small Business FOR DUMMIES

1-74031-109-4
$39.95

Superannuation FOR DUMMIES

1-74031-061-6
$39.95

GST and BAS FOR DUMMIES

1-74031-033-0
$39.95

Quickbooks FOR DUMMIES

1-74031-002-0
$39.95

Personal Finance

Personal Finance FOR DUMMIES

1-74031-004-7
$39.95

Investing FOR DUMMIES

1-74031-041-1
$39.95

Share Investing FOR DUMMIES

1-74031-034-9
$39.95

Australian Wills and Estates FOR DUMMIES

1-74031-067-5
$39.95

Technology

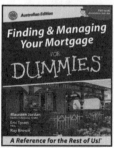

Finding & Managing Your Mortgage FOR DUMMIES

1-74031-052-7
$39.95

PCs FOR DUMMIES

1-74031-086-1
$39.95

The Internet FOR DUMMIES

1-74031-056-X
$39.95

MYOB Software FOR DUMMIES

1-74031-095-0
$39.95

For Dummies, the Dummies Man logo, A Reference for the Rest of Us! and related trade dress are trademarks or registered trademarks of Wiley. All other trademarks are the property of their respective owners.

Australian Editions

FOR DUMMIES

Plain-English solutions for everyday challenges

Culinary and Hospitality

Reference

1-74031-010-1
$39.95

Gourmet Cooking FOR DUMMIES

1-74031-040-3
$39.95

1-74031-071-3
$39.95

Health and Home

1-74031-007-1
$39.95

1-74031-038-1
$39.95

1-74031-042-X
$39.95

1-74031-028-4
$39.95

1-74031-094-2
$39.95

1-74031-054-3
$39.95

For Dummies, the Dummies Man logo, A Reference for the Rest of Us! and related trade dress are trademarks or registered trademarks of Wiley. All other trademarks are the property of their respective owners.

FOR DUMMIES®

The easy way to get more done and have more fun

Sport and Leisure

Australian Editions

1-74031-009-8
$39.95

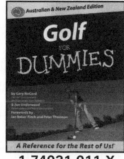

1-74031-011-X
$39.95

1-74031-044-6
$39.95

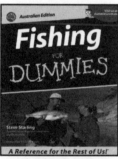

1-74031-006-3
$39.95

1-74031-059-4
$39.95

1-74031-035-7
$39.95

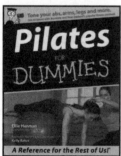

1-74031-074-8
$39.95

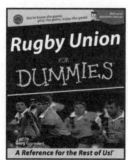

1-74031-073-X
$39.95

Also available in the *For Dummies*® range

Video RRP $29.95
DVD RRP $34.95

For Dummies, the Dummies Man logo, A Reference for the Rest of Us! and related trade dress are trademarks or registered trademarks of Wiley. All other trademarks are the property of their respective owners.